FALL OF THE ROMAN REPUBLIC

PLUTARCH (*c.* 50–*c.* 120 AD) was a writer and thinker born into a wealthy, established family of Chaeronea in central Greece. He received the best possible education in rhetoric and philosophy, and travelled to Asia Minor and Egypt. Later, a series of visits to Rome and Italy contributed to his fame, and it was said that he had received official recognition by the emperors Trajan and Hadrian. Plutarch rendered conscientious service to his province and city (where he continued to live), as well as holding a priesthood at nearby Delphi. His voluminous surviving writings are broadly divided into the 'moral' works and the *Lives* of outstanding Greek and Roman leaders. The former (*Moralia*) are a mixture of rhetorical and antiquarian pieces, together with technical and moral philosophy (sometimes in dialogue form). The *Lives* have been influential from the Renaissance onwards.

REX WARNER was a Professor of the University of Connecticut from 1964 until his retirement in 1974. He was born in 1905 and went to Wadham College, Oxford, where he gained a 'first' in Classical Moderations, and took a degree in English Literature. He taught in Egypt and England, and was Director of the British Institute, Athens, from 1945 to 1947. He wrote poems, novels and critical essays, worked on films and broadcasting, and translated many works, of which Xenophon's *History of my Times* and *The Persian Expedition*, Thucydides' *History of the Peloponnesian War*, and Plutarch's *Lives* (under the title *Fall of the Roman Republic*) and *Moral Essays* have been published in Penguin Classics. Rex Warner died in 1986.

ROBIN SEAGER is Honorary Senior Fellow in Classics and Ancient History at the University of L⸺ ⸺pey: *A Political Biography* (

CHRISTOPHER PELLING ⸺ ford University. He publishe⸺ ⸺e of *Antony* in 1988 (Cambri⸺ ⸺version of his 1997 Italian ⸺ ⸺ves of Philopoemen and Flamininus (Rizzoli) is to be published by the Classical Press of Wales. Most of his articles on Plutarch were collected in his *Plutarch and History* (Classical Press of Wales and Duckworth, 2002).

PLUTARCH

Fall of the Roman Republic

Revised Edition

Translated with Introduction and Notes by
REX WARNER
Revised with translations of Comparisons and a Preface by
ROBIN SEAGER
With Series Preface by
CHRISTOPHER PELLING

PENGUIN BOOKS

PENGUIN CLASSICS

Published by the Penguin Group
Penguin Books Ltd, 80 Strand, London WC2R ORL, England
Penguin Group (USA) Inc., 375 Hudson Street, New York, New York 10014, USA
Penguin Group (Canada), 10 Alcorn Avenue, Toronto, Ontario, Canada M4V 3B2
(a division of Pearson Penguin Canada Inc.)
Penguin Ireland, 25 St Stephen's Green, Dublin 2, Ireland
(a division of Penguin Books Ltd)
Penguin Group (Australia), 250 Camberwell Road, Camberwell, Victoria 3124, Australia
(a division of Pearson Australia Group Pty Ltd)
Penguin Books India Pvt Ltd, 11 Community Centre, Panchsheel Park, New Delhi – 110 017, India
Penguin Group (NZ), cnr Airborne and Rosedale Roads, Albany, Auckland 1310, New Zealand
(a division of Pearson New Zealand Ltd)
Penguin Books (South Africa) (Pty) Ltd, 24 Sturdee Avenue, Rosebank 2196, South Africa

Penguin Books Ltd, Registered Offices: 80 Strand, London WC2R ORL, England

www.penguin.com

This translation first published 1958
Revised edition 1972
Revised and expanded edition 2005

3

Copyright © Rex Warner, 1958
Notes copyright © Robin Seager, 1972
Corrections to text, Preface and Comparisons copyright © Robin Seager, 2005
Penguin Plutarch copyright © Christopher Pelling, 2005
All rights reserved

The moral right of the editor has been asserted

Set in 10.25/12.25 pt PostScript Adobe Sabon
Typeset by Rowland Phototypesetting Ltd, Bury St Edmunds, Suffolk
Printed in England by Clays Ltd, St Ives plc

ISBN-13: 978–0–140–44934–1

Contents

Penguin Plutarch

The first Penguin translation of Plutarch appeared in 1958, with Rex Warner's version of six Roman Lives appearing as *Fall of the Roman Republic*. Other volumes followed steadily, three of them by Ian Scott-Kilvert (*Rise and Fall of Athens* in 1960, *Makers of Rome* in 1965 and *The Age of Alexander* in 1973), and then Richard Talbert's *Plutarch on Sparta* in 1988. Several of the moral essays were also translated by Robin Waterfield in 1992. Now only fourteen of the forty-eight Lives remain. It is planned to include these remaining Lives in a new edition, along with revised versions of those already published.

This is also an opportunity to divide up the Lives in a different way, although it is not straightforward to decide what that different way should be. Nearly all Plutarch's surviving biographies were written in pairs as *Parallel Lives*: thus a 'book' for Plutarch was not just *Theseus* or *Caesar* but *Theseus and Romulus* or *Alexander and Caesar*. Most, but not all, of those pairs have a brief epilogue at the end of the second Life comparing the two heroes, just as many have a prologue before the first Life giving some initial grounds for the comparison. Not much attention was paid to this comparative technique at the time when the Penguin series started to appear, and it seemed natural then to separate each Life from its pair and organize the volumes by period and city. The comparative epilogues were not included in the translations at all.

That now looks very unsatisfactory. The comparative technique has come to be seen as basic to Plutarch's strategy, underlying not only those brief epilogues but also the entire pairings. (It is true, though, that in the last few years scholars have become increasingly alert to the way that *all* the Lives, not just the pairs, are crafted to complement one another.) It is very tempting to keep the pairings in this new series in a way that would respect Plutarch's own authorial intentions.

After some agonizing, we have decided nevertheless to keep to something like the original strategy of the series, though with some refinement. The reason is a practical one. Many, perhaps most, readers of Plutarch will be reading him to see what he has to say about a particular period, and will wish to compare his treatment of the major players to see how the different parts of his historical jigsaw fit together. If one kept the pairings, that would inevitably mean buying several different volumes of the series; and if, say, one organized those volumes by the Greek partner (so that, for instance, *Pericles–Fabius, Nicias–Crassus* and *Coriolanus–Alcibiades* made one volume), anyone primarily interested in the Roman Lives of the late Republic would probably need to buy the whole set. That is no way to guarantee these finely crafted works of art the wide reading that they deserve. Keeping the organization by period also allows some other works of Plutarch to be included along with the Lives themselves, for instance the fascinating essay *On the Malice of Herodotus* along with the Lives of Themistocles and Aristides and (as before) several Spartan essays along with the Spartan Lives.

Of course the comparative epilogues must now be included, and they will now be translated and printed along with the second Life of each pair, just as the prologues are conventionally printed before the first Life. Each volume will now also usually include more extended introductions to each Life, which will draw attention to the importance of the comparison as well as other features of Plutarch's technique. This is a compromise, and an uncomfortable one; but it still seems the better way.

The volumes will, however, sort the Lives into more logical groups. The early Roman figures will now be grouped together in a single volume entitled *The Rise of Rome*; the Life of Agesilaus will migrate from the *The Age of Alexander* to join the rest of the Spartan Lives, and the Life of Artaxerxes will join the *The Age of Alexander* collection; the rest of the new translations of Roman Lives will join those of the Gracchi, Brutus and Antony in a new *Rome in Crisis* volume. The introductions and notes will be revised where necessary. In due course we hope to include the *Moral Essays* in the project as well.

In a recent bibliometric study (*Ancient Society*, 28 (1997), 265–89) Walter Scheidel observed that the proportion of scholarly articles devoted to most classical authors had remained more or less constant since the 1920s. The one author to stand out for an exceptional rise was Plutarch. That professional pattern has been matched by a similar surge in the interest in Plutarch shown by the general reading public. The Penguin translations have played a large part in fostering that interest, and this new, more comprehensive project will surely play a similar role in the future.

Christopher Pelling

2004

Preface to Revised Edition (2005)

In preparing this new edition I have made the following revisions and additions.

I have completely revised Rex Warner's translations of the six lives which make up the volume. More specifically I have corrected his very occasional errors and omissions, re-phrased passages where it seemed to me possible to get closer to Plutarch's exact meaning and, for the benefit of students of Roman history, rendered more precisely certain Roman social, political and military terms. I have not, however, made any attempt to alter the somewhat free and strikingly individual manner in which Warner handled Plutarch's syntactical and grammatical structures, except in those rare cases where I judged it to have misrepresented or obscured Plutarch's meaning.

I have revised my own introductions and notes to the individual lives, and updated and enlarged the Further Reading section to provide a selection of general works on the late Republic, biographies of the subjects of the lives and studies of Plutarch as a biographer.

I have also added translations of the four surviving Comparisons (Lysander and Sulla, Nicias and Crassus, Agesilaus and Pompey, Demosthenes and Cicero). In so doing I have made no attempt to imitate Rex Warner's style. My model has been rather the versions by Bernadotte Perrin in the relevant volumes of the Loeb Classical Library (1914–26). These combine in remarkable degree intelligible and fluent English and close fidelity to Plutarch's own syntax, an example which I have done my best to follow.

It is perhaps appropriate to comment briefly on the nature and value of the Comparisons. From the historian's viewpoint they unfortunately add very little of value to the material contained in the Lives proper. Very occasionally Plutarch refers to events he has not treated in the relevant life, but such allusions are mostly too vague and oracular to be of much use. On the literary side Plutarch more often than not has to make desperate efforts to discover or invent points of contact between his two subjects. Sometimes there is at least one basic such point. Nicias and Crassus were both at least partially responsible for major military disasters; Agesilaus and Pompey were men of great ability who nevertheless in the end give an impression of failure; Demosthenes and Cicero were the greatest orators of their ages and cities. But at any deeper or more detailed level Plutarch spends most of his time glumly explaining (with perfect truth) that in fact his Greeks and Romans had very little else in common.

For good advice on various problems in the text and its translation I am very grateful to my colleague Alexei Zadorozhnyy.

Robin Seager
2003

Translator's Introduction

Plutarch was one of the last of the classical Greek historians; indeed one may almost say that he was one of the last of the classical Greeks. In his thought he went back to Plato; in his local patriotism he remained affected by the tradition of the city-state which, however antiquated politically, is always spiritually valuable; he retained the old pieties which were soon to be swept away; he was a learned man, a sympathetic man and a most brilliant popularizer, by means of biographies, of great events, great characters and ideals of conduct which have, through Shakespeare and many others, influenced us all.

He was born about AD 46 and died some time after AD 120. Thus he saw some of the worst and some of the best aspects of the early Roman Empire. Most of his life seems to have been spent in his native town of Chaeronea in Boeotia in central Greece. This was never a particularly important place, but important battles were fought near it and it is not far from the great religious centre of Delphi, where Plutarch, from middle age onward, held a priesthood. He makes the most of it whenever Chaeronea or Delphi appears in his narrative (e.g. in the *Life of Sulla*). Clearly he was proud of his local attachments and enjoyed performing his civic and religious duties. But Chaeronea, though the centre, was by no means the end of his world. When the Emperor Nero, in AD 66, visited Greece, Plutarch was studying at Athens. He became a philosopher, that is to say a man capable of discussing and lecturing upon physics, rhetoric, literature, natural science, metaphysics and morals. There is an imposing catalogue of his works in all these subjects. He also travelled, not only in Greece but to Egypt,

and went at least once on official business to Rome, where
he had many friends in cultivated circles. He received a
high government appointment in Greece from the Emperor
Hadrian.

Like Tacitus, whom he may have known, he wrote his historical works rather late in life, during the period of the reigns of
Trajan and Hadrian – a time when, after a long lapse, something
in the nature of free speech (providing that the imperial idea
was respected) was encouraged. Yet Plutarch, not being a
Roman, has none of the intensely personal fervour of Tacitus
when he writes of Roman history. Nor is he 'engaged', as
Thucydides was. He is already writing 'ancient history'. He is
not so much concerned with the causes of revolutions or of the
rise or fall of great powers. These are events he takes for
granted. What really interests him is character, the effects of
birth or education, the drama of an individual's success or
failure, and the various moral reflections which can be made
on these subjects. It is natural that his history should take the
form of a series of biographies of great men. Since he was a
Greek living under the Roman Empire, it was natural too that
he should, as a moralist looking back over the two great western
civilizations, write about both the Greeks and the Romans.
Here, however, his precise method seems to have been rather
artificial. Most of his biographies are composed in pairs. First
there is the life of a famous Greek, then a life of a famous
Roman, and then a comparison between the two. Thus, for
example, Alexander the Great is compared with Julius Caesar,
and Nicias with Crassus. There are twenty-three pairs of lives
and four lives that have been left unpaired.

This method no doubt appealed to Plutarch's moralizing
tendencies, but the bases for the comparisons are often very
inadequate. There seems, for instance, to have been nothing in
common between Nicias and Crassus except that both men
were rich and both suffered a great military defeat at the ends
of their lives. The modern reader, I think, will only be confused
if he has to jump backwards and forwards between Greeks and
Romans. I have therefore grouped together some of the lives
which belong to one critical period of Roman history, in the

hope both of pleasing the reader and of doing honour to Plutarch.

This period, or rather the great men of this period of the collapse and fall of the Roman Republic, evidently interested Plutarch particularly. In addition to the six Lives included in this volume there are five more (Lucullus, Sertorius, Brutus, Cato, Antony) which deal with the same theme. Each throws light on each, and one must admire Plutarch's narrative skill in repeating himself so seldom even when he is dealing in two or more Lives with precisely the same events.

The period is one of continual war and revolution. There are the great campaigns abroad of Marius, Sulla, Lucullus, Pompey and Caesar. There are the civil wars between Marius and Sulla and between Pompey and Caesar; and there is the perpetual struggle for power or for survival in the confused, corrupt and squalid world of Roman politics. It is an appalling period and very suited to one who, like Plutarch, is fond both of dramatic incidents and of moral reflections. Indeed it seems almost incredible that Rome should have survived at all from these terrible years.

It is interesting to recall that Rome not only survived but, at the expense of what was known as 'liberty', became stronger and more efficient than before. It is also to be noted that in these years there appeared (in the works of Cicero, Catullus, Lucretius and Caesar) for the first time in Roman history a literature which could bear comparison with the literature of Greece. How could such notable achievement and so much of promise exist in circumstances so savage, so corrupt, so apparently hopeless?

Plutarch makes no attempt to answer this question. He is a moralist and (as Shakespeare was to recognize) a dramatic artist. He accepts rather uncritically the Roman aristocratic tradition and applauds the ineffectual and indeed disastrous moralizing of Cato or of Brutus. Yet in his presentation of the characters themselves he goes some way towards amending some of his more facile judgements. He is a fair man and cannot help showing, for instance, that Sulla was even more of a monster than Marius, that Cato was a bit of a prig, that

Caesar, though disreputable in some ways, was, alone of the dynasts of his time, merciful to his enemies.

One may say indeed that, though it is as a dramatic artist that Plutarch excels, this ability of his is by no means a disadvantage to a historian. He gets a few dates wrong; he is almost unaware of the necessity for that revolution which was carried out by Caesar; he has not the extraordinary intellectual power and passion of Thucydides; he lacks the all-embracing curiosity and zest of Herodotus, and the experience of Xenophon; yet he too is a Greek and a historian with his own peculiar importance and with his particular charm. I have called him the last of the Greek classical historians. It should be added that he is the first of modern biographers. He has not only a keen eye for a dramatic situation but shows a very modern interest in individual psychology.

His style is, on the whole, a simple one, though from time to time he will indulge himself in a complicated or a purple passage. No one who remembers the use which Shakespeare made of one of these passages in *Antony and Cleopatra* will regret this occasional self-indulgence.

Rex Warner

Introduction

THE MAN AND HIS WORKS

Plutarch (*c.* AD 45–*c.*120)* was born at Chaeronea in Boeotia.
In his day Greece had been under Roman rule for some two
hundred years, although many Greek cities had retained a
measure of local administrative autonomy. The period of
Roman domination had spanned the transition, by way of the
dictatorship of Julius Caesar and the triumvirate of Antony,
Octavian and Lepidus, from the aristocratic oligarchy of the
republic to the increasingly more thinly veiled autocracy of the
empire. For provincials, as for the Romans themselves, the most
positive aspect of the empire had been the establishment of
peace after the traumatic upheavals that had marked the end
of the republic and the triumviral period. That peace had,
however, been disturbed by civil strife after the fall of the
Julio-Claudian dynasty in AD 68, which, in Greece as elsewhere,
had revived old tensions between the provincial upper classes
and their Roman masters. As a writer, teacher and philosopher,
but also as a priest, ambassador and conscientious participant
in local civic duties, Plutarch worked to ease those tensions and
foster a renewed harmony between Greeks and Romans and
their respective cultures and made a major contribution to the
Greek cultural renaissance.

Virtually all that we know of him comes from his own works.
He mentions his father and two brothers. By his wife Timoxena,
he had a daughter, also called Timoxena, who died young, and

* All dates are BC unless otherwise stated.

not less than four sons, at least two of whom survived to manhood. For his philosophical and rhetorical training he went to Athens, where he later received a grant of honorary citizenship. In his maturity he travelled widely, visiting Rome on at least two occasions and gaining Roman citizenship thanks to the good offices of the Emperor Vespasian's friend L. Mestrius Florus. Several other Roman administrators whose duties brought them to Greece were numbered among his friends; one of the most distinguished was Q. Sosius Senecio, to whom Plutarch dedicated the *Parallel Lives* and the *Tabletalk*[1].

But most of Plutarch's life was spent at home in Chaeronea, where he appears to have been the leader of an informal intellectual circle. He held the archonship[2] and other minor offices and probably a priesthood. He was certainly a priest at Delphi, where he would have worked to revive the influence of the oracle under the emperors Trajan and Hadrian. It is likely that his services were rewarded by Trajan with a grant of the consular ornaments,[3] which probably implies that he had already received the honour of equestrian rank.[4]

Plutarch was well aware that he, like all Greeks of his time, was a subject of the Roman empire. In this he found little to complain of. His studies had confirmed what every educated man knew, that the last age of the republic had been marked by ever escalating moral and political decline. From Sulla's seizure of Rome in 88 the brutality, greed and ambition of individuals (above all Sulla himself, Pompey, Crassus and Caesar, then Octavian and Antony) had led to anarchy in the late fifties and civil war, first between Pompey and Caesar (49–48), then between Octavian and Antony (31–30), from which the monarchy founded by Octavian/Augustus in 28 offered the only conceivable escape.

Plutarch valued the Roman peace, Rome's concern for ordered government (the merits of which would have been freshly brought home to him by the disturbances that troubled the East after the fall of Nero) and her consistent support of the pro-Roman upper classes (in other words, people like himself) in the cities of Greece and elsewhere, although he had misgivings about the Roman obsessions with wealth, luxury, imperial expansion and the pursuit of military glory. Much also depended on the nature of the emperor himself. Under Domitian (AD 81–96) the profession of Stoic philosophy had been associated with political dissent; prominent Romans who shared Plutarch's philosophical interests had been subject to persecution, and the pursuit of literature may have seemed unrewarding if not actually hazardous. But in Plutarch's world Roman supremacy was a fundamental fact. This fact he accepted, and his political beliefs and the political advice he gave were framed in the light of it.

The principal objective of the upper classes in the Greek cities should, Plutarch held, be internal concord, a goal which was not only desirable in itself but also minimized the risk of attracting the unwelcome attention and perhaps intervention of the imperial power. Rome valued stability and knew that it was best assured by the collaboration of the Greek ruling class. The best way for Greeks to benefit Greece was therefore to cooperate with Rome. But to do this effectively they had to shoulder the administrative and liturgical burdens of Greek civic affairs. Plutarch speaks as if he did not approve of those Greeks who disdained these local, parochial tasks in favour of a career in the imperial civil service (organized and run from Rome, and to some extent dependent on imperial patronage). He may eventually have accepted the procuratorship[5] of Achaea from Hadrian in AD 119, but if so it will surely have been a sinecure. He also criticized those (both Epicureans and Stoics) who used the tenets of philosophy as an excuse for opting out of public life. He himself continued to be active in the public sphere to the very end of his days, no doubt with imperial encouragement since Hadrian shared his predilection for the shrine at Delphi. Perhaps he found a measure of consolation in keeping busy, for several close friends had died towards the end of Trajan's reign.

Plutarch was a most prolific author, particularly in his latter years after the death of Domitian (AD 96), no doubt inspired by the broad sense of social, political and intellectual renewal that came under Nerva, Trajan and Hadrian. His major works are the *Moralia* and the *Parallel Lives*. The essays, dialogues and pamphlets loosely grouped as *Moralia* cover an immense variety of fields: morals, philosophical technicalities, antiquarianism, literature, rhetoric and science. It is important to remember that the Lives were not conceived as history, but as expositions of the character of their subjects for the purpose of moral instruction and edification. But they need not be seen as a bridge-building operation on Plutarch's part between the educated classes of Greece and Rome. In his time no such bridges were needed, though of course some tensions still existed. The Lives rather serve to advertise and commemorate the integration of Greek and Roman culture.

Plutarch's deployment of ethical, political and military material and the degree to which he indulges in relatively straightforward 'historical' narrative vary enormously from Life to Life, according to the immediate point he is trying to make, the amount and type of information available to him, and his personal preferences. But he is always more concerned with men and character than with actions, and often pays more attention to historically trivial incidents when these, in his estimation, are more revealing of some essential aspect of his subject's nature. This leads him to be highly selective in his coverage, and he is always inclined to give short shrift to the political background and historical context of the events he chooses to highlight, at times presenting instead a sequence of isolated cameos or epiphanies.

His use of sources has at times been criticized more harshly than it deserves. He did read sources of all kinds: histories, biographies, memoirs, letters, plays and poetry. How good his Latin was is debated, but he may have had Latin sources translated for him. He was aware of the value of works contemporary with the events they described and of the possibility of positive or negative bias. He was as far removed from avowed historians of his own time as he is from those modern scholars and students who, often with a measure of largely unjustified irritation, attempt to use him in his turn as a source. Greek and Roman historians alike emphasized the role of the gifted and ambitious individual in shaping the course of history and often declared a didactic purpose that was not merely practical but moral: the commemoration for the betterment of posterity of conspicuous examples of virtue and vice.

THE LATE REPUBLICAN *LIVES*: SUBJECTS, NATURE AND USEFULNESS

It is unfair, as remarked above, to criticize Plutarch for not writing like a historian of his own time, and far more so to complain because he did not set great store by at least some of the qualities that for a modern historian of the ancient world make a Greek or Roman author a useful and reliable source. Nevertheless it is likely that many of the users of this book will be students and teachers involved in courses with titles like 'Roman History 133–44 BC' or indeed 'The Fall of the Roman Republic', whose primary interest in Plutarch and his Lives will be precisely in their value as a source. It may therefore be helpful to give some information on the men about whom Plutarch wrote and to call attention to some of the ways in which his principles and preoccupations affect his handling of the material at his disposal and his presentation of those events he sees fit to include.

Something must also be said about the question of the order of composition, on which very little can be asserted with confidence. Of the six Lives presented here, the *Cicero* is certainly the earliest. The *Marius* and the *Sulla* may come next; of them, the *Sulla* may have been written first. The other three seem to have been written as part of a larger project which also included the *Brutus*, *Cato Minor* and *Antony*. But given the lack of any clear chronological framework it is futile to look for systematic cross-referencing. Where a common theme may be discerned in more than one Life – for instance, the deleterious effect on the commonwealth of rivalries between individuals – there is no attempt at a conscious development from Life to Life.

Gaius Marius

C. Marius was born in 157 into a leading family of the local
aristocracy of Arpinum. As a 'new man', the first of his family
to attempt a career in Roman politics, he needed patronage,
which he received from the Caecilii Metelli, though his relationship with them was chequered. He reached the tribunate in 119
and the praetorship in 115.

In 109 the consul Q. Metellus took Marius with him to
Numidia, where war had broken out against King Jugurtha two
years before. Marius asked leave to return to Rome to stand
for the consulship of 107, but was contemptuously refused. By
promising to bring the war to a rapid conclusion he gained the
backing of businessmen and demagogues critical of aristocratic
corruption and incompetence, and was duly elected.

As consul he took the novel step of recruiting men who
owned no land and instituted other military reforms. These had
the unintended effect of making armies potentially more loyal
to their generals than to the state. Thanks to good luck and
the diplomatic skills of his quaestor Sulla, Marius captured
Jugurtha and ended the war, though the question of who really
deserved the credit was to be the source of bitter hostility
between him and Sulla. Rome now faced another military threat
in Gaul from two migratory Germanic tribes, the Cimbri and
Teutones. A disastrous defeat at Arausio in 105, caused in part
by aristocratic obstinacy, worked to Marius' advantage, and
he secured a remarkable series of five successive consulships,
104–100. He brought the Cimbric War to a successful conclusion, but to maintain his position was forced into an uneasy alliance with the violent reformers L. Saturninus, tribune
in 103 and 100, and C. Glaucia, praetor in 100. He broke
with them late in 100 and both were killed in the resulting
disturbances.

Marius then suffered a decade in eclipse and served without
distinction in the Social War in 90. Nevertheless he hoped for
a new command against the aggressively expanding kingdom
of Pontus, ruled by Mithridates VI. But his rival Sulla, who
had done well in the Social War, secured both a consulship for

88 and the Mithridatic command. Marius allied himself with
another tribune, P. Sulpicius, and drove Sulla from Rome.
Sulpicius then transferred the command to Marius. But Sulla
marched on Rome and Marius was forced to withdraw, eventually finding refuge in Africa. When Sulla departed to fight
Mithridates, Marius returned to join forces with the rebellious
consul of 87, L. Cinna. They in their turn seized Rome, and the
old and embittered Marius carried out a ruthless purge of his
opponents. He secured the seventh consulship that soothsayers
had promised him, but died in January 86, less than a month
after taking office.

One of the principal characteristics that Plutarch discerned in
Marius was his self-confidence and consequent readiness to
provoke and give offence to the nobility. This marks his behaviour during his tribunate, which might have been deemed
inappropriate in one of his inexperience and modest background, while a little later Plutarch again remarks on his self-
confidence, despite Marius' lack of the standard props of wealth
and eloquence.

Marius' provocative attitude showed itself again in his un-
willingness to kowtow to his superior Metellus in the war
against Jugurtha. It thus serves to introduce the first of the
personal conflicts which Plutarch uses to shape his narrative.
The quarrel with Metellus leads to Marius' first consulship,
when he again shows himself ready if not positively eager to
offend the nobility. But the Jugurthine War also sowed the
seeds of the much more dangerous enmity between Marius and
Sulla, the development of which was for a time delayed by the
renewal of the Cimbric War in 107.

Plutarch clearly felt at home with the narration of wars, and
often devoted inordinate amounts of space to a more or less
straightforward narrative of a military campaign. (The reason
for this will be considered below.) His treatment of the Cimbric
War here is an obvious case in point. But he is always on the
look-out for the personal angle. Another rivalry occupies the
foreground, that between Marius and his fellow-commander
Catulus, particularly at the battle of Vercellae (101). But Sulla's

autobiography is cited as a source for these events, and so the more important relationship between himself and Marius is kept in the forefront of the reader's mind.

Marius' feud with Metellus then plays a vital role in the account of his dealings with Glaucia and Saturninus. Plutarch was never happy with the detail of republican political struggles. He plainly found them difficult to understand – nothing similar existed in his own day. What is more, he surely disapproved since, for him, these selfish rivalries were a symptom of the self-destructive tendencies that had brought the republic down. When he could not avoid talking about politics, as here, he often chose to fix on a personal motive to the exclusion of all else. So for him the sole purpose of the alliance was to enable Marius to avenge the insult that Metellus had offered him by implying that he could never hope to reach the consulship.

One of Plutarch's most deeply rooted prejudices is also apparent here. He could not always approve wholeheartedly of those who claimed to be acting in the name of law and order, for he knew that their methods were often brutal and their aim was self-aggrandizement. But to those whom he perceived as the conscious agents of disorder and anarchy – in the *Marius*, first Saturninus and Glaucia and then Sulpicius – he is merciless in his contempt and makes no attempt to understand what lay behind their actions.

The dedication by King Bocchus of Mauretania of the statues portraying his surrender of Jugurtha to Sulla brings back the major theme of the hatred between Marius and Sulla, but again the reader is kept in suspense, this time by the outbreak of the Social War in 91. That war was one of the most important events in the story of the late republic, since it eventually led to the concession of Roman citizenship to all Rome's Italian allies. But for Plutarch its only function is to delay the confrontation between Marius and Sulla; all that interests him is their respective performances in the field.

The theme of their enmity reaches its climax in the contest for the Mithridatic command and the subsequent vicissitudes of the years 88 to 86. Marius' adventures during his escape from Italy in 88 show Plutarch at his best. Here he finds a vivid and gripping tale that is rich in entertainment and moral instruction, and he does it full justice. But even in Sulla's absence from the story Plutarch still contrives to use Marius' hatred of him as a motivating force for his actions. Marius' collaboration with Cinna is determined at least in part by Sulla's dislike of Cinna, which made Marius correspondingly well-disposed towards him. So too Marius' eagerness to secure his fated seventh consulship is presented as inspired by an alleged (and very premature) report that Sulla had defeated Mithridates and was on his way home in quest of vengeance on his enemies at Rome. Even after Marius' death the theme of the mutual hatred between him and Sulla is sounded yet again in the epilogue on the fate of his son at Sulla's hands.

Sulla

L. Cornelius Sulla was born in 138. His family was noble and patrician, but impoverished. Sulla first achieved distinction as quaestor to Marius in the Jugurthine War, where he persuaded Bocchus of Mauretania, with whom Jugurtha had taken refuge, to hand the Numidian over to the Romans. This incident was the germ of his later rivalry with Marius. Sulla then served with some distinction in the Cimbric War and at some time in the nineties (the exact dates are debated) was governor of Cappadocia. When the Social War broke out in 91 he was one of the two most successful Roman commanders. (The other was Pompey's father, Cn. Pompeius Strabo.)

His performance in the Social War was rewarded with a consulship for 88 and command in the imminent war against Mithridates. As consul Sulla attempted reforms, including legislation to reaffirm the supremacy of the senate in the government of Rome. But his quarrel with the tribune Sulpicius, who was supported by Marius, led to violence in which he was driven from the city. He persuaded the army he had assembled outside Nola to march on Rome. Marius and Sulpicius fled and Sulla was reinstated as consul. He soon departed to fight Mithridates, and his successor in the consulship, L. Cornelius Cinna, undid his reforms and declared him a public enemy. When fresh

violence broke out in the city Cinna was briefly expelled but
recaptured the city with the aid of Marius. After Marius' death
in 86 Cinna, with his associate Cn. Carbo, controlled the city
till his own assassination in 84.

In 85 Sulla brought the Mithridatic War to a premature
conclusion with the Peace of Dardanus, the terms of which
were so lenient to the king as to verge on treason. This left Sulla
free to seek vengeance on those at home who had driven him
out and who refused to acknowledge his achievements. He
invaded Italy in 83. Among those who supported him were
Pompey, Crassus and Metellus Pius, son of Marius' enemy
Metellus Numidicus. Resistance was soon crushed and Sulla's
capture of Rome in 82 was followed by violence and bloodshed on an unprecedented scale. The massacre of his enemies
was at first carried out indiscriminately, then formalized in the
so-called proscriptions: the lives and property of senators and
members of the equestrian order became forfeit and their
descendants deprived of civil rights.

Sulla then allowed himself to be appointed dictator, with the
remit of setting the state in order. No time limit was laid down,
but it was understood by all, including Sulla, that he would
abdicate as soon as his mission had been successfully completed.
The thrust of all his measures was to ensure that the senate,
the size of which he doubled from 300 to 600, would in future
be able to govern unchallenged by demagogic tribunes or con-
tumacious army commanders. Whether he realized that any
future commander bent on seizing power would, if he felt strong
enough, ignore his legislation and follow his example of seizing
Rome by force, we cannot know. But in 81, satisfied that he
had done all he could to give the senate its chance, he laid down
the dictatorship. In 80 he held a second consulship, but by the
time of his death in 78 his reforms were already under attack.

The *Sulla* inevitably covers much of the same ground as the
Marius and its construction displays similar devices and characteristics. The Jugurthine War serves, as in the *Marius*, to introduce the rift between the two men. In Plutarch's account of
Sulla's distinguished service in the Cimbric War Sulla's status

as a source for the ill feeling between Marius and Catulus keeps his relationship with Marius in the reader's mind.

His governorship of Cappadocia is a brief interlude before the quarrel with Marius breaks out again thanks to Bocchus' dedication. As in the *Marius* a confrontation is postponed by the Social War, which is treated in exactly the same fashion in both Lives. Sulla's successes against the Italians led to his election to his first consulship, but here too Plutarch concentrates exclusively on the struggle for the command against Mithridates; again he seizes the opportunity to excoriate Sulpicius. The narrative of the march on Rome highlights the personal relationship between Sulla the attacker and Marius the defender.

The Mithridatic War is then recounted at a length not entirely justified by the prominent part played by Plutarch's hometown of Chaeronea, while the civil war that took Sulla to the dictatorship also receives substantial treatment. Even at this point, several years after Marius' death in 86, Plutarch manages to allude to their enmity in his story of the prophetic dream that promised Sulla victory before the battle of Signia in 82.

The dictatorship is introduced by a brief comparison of the characters of Marius and Sulla, prompted by Sulla's chilling remark on the slaughter of the Samnite prisoners taken at the battle of the Colline Gate (1 November 82). The horrors of the violence and above all of the proscriptions naturally engage the moralist's attention. Plutarch's desire to blacken those whom he sees as truly wicked reveals itself again in his mention of Catiline, whose conduct during these events was notorious.

But in Sulla the politician and constitutional theorist Plutarch has no interest. Hence he has not a word to say of the far-reaching measures by which Sulla tried in vain to crush the various threats to senatorial supremacy that had emerged in the course of the preceding fifty years and restore the senate's corporate authority. Instead he offers a series of anecdotes that for him tell us something about Sulla the man: most of them serve to illustrate his arrogance and autocratic manner.

Crassus

M. Licinius Crassus was born *c*. 112. During Cinna's supremacy at Rome (86–84) he took refuge in Spain, returning when Sulla invaded Italy in 83. He performed valuable service; in particular he deserved most of the credit for the victory in the last battle of the civil war, against the Samnites at the Colline Gate on 1 November 82. But Sulla paid more attention to the young Pompey; despite his tolerance of his supporters' excesses he disapproved of the ruthlessness with which Crassus enriched himself during the proscriptions. The roots of the rivalry between Crassus and Pompey are to be found in Sulla's treatment of them.

The slave revolt led by Spartacus began in 73. After Spartacus had defeated several Roman commanders, Crassus was appointed to command against him in 72. His success earned him an ovation, the highest honour[6] possible in the circumstances. But Pompey, returning in 71 from the war against Sertorius in Spain, wiped out a small band of fugitives from Spartacus' army and on that account claimed the credit for ending the war. Despite his resentment, Crassus collaborated with Pompey to secure their first joint consulship for 70. Their only joint action while in office was to restore the tribunes' right to legislate, which had been abolished by Sulla.

In the sixties Crassus held the censorship in 65, but accomplished nothing. Like Pompey, he took an interest in the young Caesar, and when Caesar returned in 60 from his governorship in Spain he persuaded Crassus and Pompey first to support his campaign for the consulship of 59, then to work together despite their mutual dislike to secure their political goals in the coalition sometimes called the 'First Triumvirate'. Relations between Crassus and Pompey remained uneasy, but in spring 56 the coalition was patched up after meetings between Caesar and Crassus at Ravenna and Caesar and Pompey at Luca.

It was agreed that Pompey and Crassus should advertise their reconciliation with a second joint consulship in 55. They extended Caesar's term of command in Gaul and secured provinces for themselves: Spain for Pompey and Syria for Crassus.

Jealous of Pompey's military glory, which was now being matched by Caesar's victories in Gaul, Crassus was determined to start a war against Parthia, victory in which would raise him to the same level of renown. But the campaign ended in disaster at the battle of Carrhae (53), where the defeated Crassus fell victim to Parthian treachery and was put to death.

If rivalry between the protagonists links the *Marius* and the *Sulla*, it is a theme that comes even more into its own in the Lives of Crassus, Pompey and Caesar. Sulla's treatment of them made Pompey and Crassus enemies, and from that point on in Plutarch's narrative their rivalry becomes the main motif. That rivalry informs the account of the rising of Spartacus and is more or less the only thing that Plutarch finds of moment in their shared consulship in 70. The treatment of the sixties is very brief, touching on Crassus' censorship and his putative involvement in the machinations of Catiline in 63. Then his relationship with Pompey again takes pride of place when Plutarch comes to the agreement between the three dynasts negotiated by Caesar.

Because of the ill feeling between Crassus and Pompey the coalition was always precarious, and nothing else about it really interested Plutarch. So his narrative leaps from 59 to 56, when dissension between Pompey and Crassus reached such a pitch that a breach seemed inevitable, until Caesar managed to prevent it at his meeting with Pompey at Luca in 56.

The second joint consulship of Pompey and Crassus in 55 gave rise to Crassus' Syrian command, which began amid a multitude of unfavourable omens. Plutarch had already devoted much space to the Spartacus campaign, but his treatment of Crassus' Parthian adventure with its disastrous conclusion at Carrhae and all too literally tragic aftermath, when the Parthians used Crassus' head as a prop in a production of Euripides' *Bacchae*, is by far the most extreme example of his tendency to write overlong accounts of wars and battles.

Pompey

Cn. Pompeius, later surnamed Magnus, was born in 106. His
father was consul in 89, but was so universally hated that
Pompey had to make his own way in politics almost as if he
were a 'new man'. His first successes were in support of Sulla,
first in Italy (83–2), then in Sicily (82) and North Africa (81).
Sulla treated him with exaggerated respect (thus offending
Crassus), and eventually allowed him to celebrate a triumph on
12 March 81. But then Sulla quarrelled with him over his
support of M. Lepidus for the consulship of 78, and cut Pompey
out of his will.

When Lepidus rebelled in 78 Pompey helped to suppress the
rising, then in 77 he managed to secure a command in Spain
against the renegade Sertorius, who had gone there in 83 when
resistance to Sulla in Italy proved hopeless and had succeeded
in gaining control of most of the country. In rank Pompey was
the equal of his fellow-commander Metellus Pius (consul with
Sulla in 80), even though he had held no magistracy at all. His
record in Spain was not distinguished; only after Sertorius had
been murdered in 73 did he and Metellus stamp out the
rebellion.

Both generals were awarded triumphs. Returning to Italy in
71 Pompey destroyed a few survivors from Crassus' suppres-
sion of Spartacus' slave revolt and tried to deprive his rival of
the glory Crassus deserved. But the two held the consulship
together in 70, even though Pompey was legally too young
and had held none of the junior magistracies. After his consulship Pompey disdained a normal governorship, preferring
to wait for another extraordinary command. In 67 he was
appointed to deal with piracy in the Mediterranean, which had
increased to an intolerable degree. His brilliant success against
the pirates served as springboard for another command, against
Mithridates (66). The Mithridatic War had broken out again
in 74, since when L. Lucullus had commanded with varying
fortunes. Pompey brought the war to a conclusion in 63, but
only after Mithridates had been assassinated. Before returning
to Rome he reorganized the provinces and client kingdoms of

Asia Minor with such efficiency that his arrangements survived
with little change for more than fifty years.

On his return to Rome in 62 Pompey wanted two things:
ratification by the senate of his Eastern arrangements and land
for his veteran troops. Both were blocked by his opponents in
the senate, led by Cato, and Pompey was eventually driven into
supporting Caesar for the consulship of 59 and accepting the
reconciliation with Crassus that Caesar negotiated. In 59 he
married Caesar's daughter Julia, and Caesar's legislation gave
him what he wanted. But he was subject to constant attacks by
Clodius and others, especially in 58, when Clodius was tribune.

Pompey was forced to accede when Clodius drove Cicero
into exile. But in 57 he secured Cicero's return, using another
gangleader, Milo, to combat Clodius on the streets. Cicero
repaid him by proposing a law to give Pompey control of the
corn supply for five years. Cicero hoped to win Pompey away
from Caesar, but at Luca in 56 Caesar once more reconciled
Pompey and Crassus. The pair held a second joint consulship
in 55, and Pompey received Spain as his province, which he
governed in absentia, preferring to remain in the vicinity of
Rome. In 54 the chief bond between Pompey and Caesar was
broken when Julia died in childbirth, then in 53 the death of
Crassus at Carrhae made an eventual confrontation between
the two survivors seem likely.

Politics at Rome was marked by increasing anarchy, which
Pompey may have fostered in the hope of being offered a dictatorship to deal with the crisis. Violence came to a head in
52 when Milo murdered Clodius. The senate responded by
granting Pompey not the dictatorship but the consulship
without a colleague. Pompey acted decisively, putting Milo
(who for Pompey had made himself redundant by actually
killing Clodius) on trial and ensuring his condemnation despite
Cicero's appearance for the defence.

For the next three years Pompey tried to make himself the
sole arbiter of events by playing off Caesar in Gaul against
those at Rome who wished to recall him. But he could not
endure Caesar's claim to be treated as his equal, and in 50
Caesar's enemies forced him to commit himself to defend the

republic against Caesar. When Caesar invaded Italy in 49 Pompey was unprepared. He was also hampered by the fact that he had not been granted supreme command and so could only make requests, not give orders to other republican commanders. It was they who finally pressed him against his better judgement into risking a pitched battle at Pharsalus in 48.

During the battle Pompey clearly panicked. After it he still had good prospects for a war of attrition, but decided for the moment to withdraw to Egypt. There he was murdered and his head was presented to Caesar when he arrived, for the Egyptians had decided for the moment to support the winning side.

In the *Pompey* Plutarch operates in more or less identical fashion to the *Crassus*. He understands that Pompey always wanted preferential treatment from senate and people, to be the special case in whose favour all constitutional rules must be bent if not actually broken. But the narrative proceeds as before by way of a series of confrontations between individuals. Pompey's first steps are viewed in the light of his relationship with Sulla, culminating in Sulla's withdrawal of his opposition to Pompey's first triumph and their quarrel over Pompey's support of Lepidus. The accounts of the campaigns against Sertorius and Spartacus are of modest length, but the second enables Plutarch to focus yet again on the rivalry between Pompey and Crassus. As to Pompey's role in their shared consulship of 70, only two things catch Plutarch's attention: the censorial review of Rome's cavalry, which makes a good story and illustrates to perfection Pompey's vanity and desire for special treatment, and the elaborately staged reconciliation with Crassus that took place at the end of the year.

Plutarch's treatments of the wars against the pirates and Mithridates differ markedly. The former is relatively brief, the latter long and largely devoted to a sequence of anecdotes. Plutarch seizes the chance to highlight the quarrel between Pompey and his predecessor Lucullus, but says nothing about the way in which Pompey's settlement transformed the shape of the Roman East.

The account of the period from Pompey's return from the East in December 62 to the patching up of the coalition at Luca in 56 is particularly confused and disjointed. Plutarch clearly finds it difficult to discern any linking thread of a kind that would appeal to him. The best he can come up with is the relationship between Pompey and the demagogue Clodius, whom he demonizes as a negative, disruptive force in much the same way as he does Saturninus and Sulpicius. From 55 onwards Plutarch's theme is the growth of anarchy at Rome, but key stages are again marked by events of a personal nature that concern individuals: the deaths first of Julia, then of Crassus at Carrhae. The culmination of this phase is Pompey's sole consulship of 52, but despite his interest in Clodius earlier in this work and in the *Cicero* Plutarch makes no mention of Clodius' murder, though it had led to Pompey's appointment. Instead he prefers to draw attention to Pompey's new marriage to Cornelia, thus preparing the ground for the significant role she was to play in his account of Pompey's death.

Two highly personal incidents dominate Plutarch's version of the preliminaries to the civil war: first the popular reaction to Pompey's illness and recovery, then the episode of Marcellus and the sword. The narrative of Caesar's invasion and the war itself show Plutarch close to his best. Factors that he can comprehend and likes to write about, such as the constant personal and psychological problems that Pompey encountered in his dealings with the other republican commanders, are of genuine importance here, and he displays a considerable understanding of Pompey's difficulties and also deals well with Pompey's panic at Pharsalus. After Pharsalus Cornelia, as already noted, is prominent, while the epilogue on the fate of Pompey's murderers and Caesar's reaction to the news of his death goes at least some way towards setting the end of the story in its historical context.

Caesar

C. Julius Caesar was born in 100 to a patrician family that claimed descent from Venus but had long been out of the limelight. His early career was essentially normal, though marked by signs of daring and ambition eagerly seized on, at the time and later, by those who wished to believe that Caesar was born to be king.

In the sixties he attached himself to both Crassus and Pompey. He was aedile in 65, then in 63 achieved the remarkable coup of election as *pontifex maximus*, Rome's chief priest, an honour usually reserved for senior ex-consuls. In the same year, despite accusations of complicity in the conspiracy of Catiline, he gained the praetorship for 62. In that year the women's festival of the Bona Dea, held in Caesar's house, was profaned by P. Clodius, disguised as a woman. Caesar divorced his wife but took no further action.

Caesar then governed Further Spain in 61, where he famously remarked that he would rather be the first man in an Alpine village than the second man in Rome, and earned a triumph for suppressing a rebellion he had provoked. On his return he asked the senate for permission to stand in absentia for the consulship of 59, since if he entered the city in time to hand in his nomination he would have to give up his triumph. The senate refused, expecting him to choose the triumph, but Caesar preferred the consulship. He secured the support of Pompey and Crassus, both of whom had their own grudges against the senate, and was duly elected. He then persuaded them to work together, pointing out that if they did so they could jointly control Rome.

As consul Caesar passed the measures that Pompey and Crassus wanted, and provided for his own future with a five-year command in Gaul and Illyricum. But the three met with widespread opposition and obloquy, and violence was needed to force their measures through. For much of the year the senate was largely ignored and its ability to govern gravely undermined. From 58 Caesar was occupied with the conquest of Gaul and the invasions of Britain, but he kept an eye on politics at Rome, where relations between Pompey and Crassus were always strained. But thanks to Caesar's efforts at Luca the coalition survived, and as consuls in 55 Pompey and Crassus extended his command in Gaul for a further five years.

The deaths of Julia, Caesar's daughter and Pompey's wife, in 54 and Crassus in 53 brought the possibility of a confrontation between Caesar and Pompey closer. But as the campaign in Rome to recall Caesar gathered momentum, Pompey seemed ready to protect him as long as Caesar was prepared to acknowledge Pompey's superiority. This Caesar was increasingly reluctant to do, and despite the efforts of Cicero and others war broke out in January 49. Caesar's lightning invasion of Italy took Pompey by surprise and forced him to abandon Rome and withdraw to Greece. After gaining control of Spain Caesar pursued him and was victorious at Pharsalus in 48. Subsequent campaigns against pockets of opposition took him to Egypt (where he met Cleopatra), Asia Minor (47), North Africa (46) and Spain (45).

He then celebrated a magnificent but unpopular triumph. In 46 he had been appointed dictator for ten years. In 44 he became dictator in perpetuity. It is clear that he intended to retain sole power, though he may not have decided how best to formulate it. His proposed expedition against Parthia, to avenge the defeat of Crassus, may have been a way of postponing a decision. Whether or not he wanted the title of king does not really matter: Caesar was killed for what he was, not for anything he might become. His autocracy meant that political life as it was understood by the ruling class, namely competition for power and prestige under the aegis of senatorial government, had ceased to exist, and his spectacular lack of tact towards the senate as a body and prominent individuals merely rubbed salt into the wounds.

Republicans, spared by his much vaunted clemency, were outraged. His own supporters were also unhappy. They had hoped that he would act like Sulla: kill the competition, sort out the crisis, then retire and leave them to reap the benefits. His retention of power meant that for his followers the rewards of victory had lost their lustre. Hence the conspirators who assassinated him on the Ides of March 44 comprised former enemies and former friends in roughly equal numbers. They seem to have believed that with Caesar dead the republic would somehow be revived as if by magic. But his henchman Mark Antony was eager to take his place, his veterans and the common people were angered by his murder and the republicans were weak and indecisive. Soon another aspirant to power appeared on the scene, Caesar's posthumously adopted great-nephew, the young Octavian, whose final victory over Antony at last put an end to the protracted death throes of the republic.

In the early chapters of the *Caesar* (the beginning of which is presumed lost) Plutarch is on the alert for presages of future greatness. He also highlights the links, positive and negative, between Caesar and the great men of the previous generation, Marius and Sulla. The link with Marius is prominent in the account of Caesar's aedileship, which also introduces another important theme, Caesar's popularity. Another negative relationship, the feud between Caesar and Catulus, links Caesar's election as *pontifex maximus* and his role in the Catilinarian disturbances.

But Caesar's praetorship of 62 is barely mentioned. Plutarch jumps instead to the Bona Dea affair, with a lengthy narrative of Clodius' sacrilege. Events then move rapidly: the governorship in Spain (as peg for the famous anecdote), the refusal of the triumph and the formation of the coalition with Pompey and Crassus. Caesar's first consulship was a momentous year in the tale of the republic's decline, but Plutarch uses it only as a springboard for another attack on Clodius, whose election to the tribunate for 58 is accorded ample space.

There follows a very long narrative of the Gallic War, punctuated by references to the meeting with Pompey at Luca and the death of Julia. Plutarch notes Caesar's popularity with his men and there are anecdotes of his performance as a general, mostly illustrative of his daring and lack of caution. Then comes the last and greatest in the series of conflicts between powerful men that tore the republic apart; the confrontation between Caesar and Pompey. Pompey's vanity and capacity for self-delusion contributed much to the outcome. But to Plutarch it seemed that the end result, whoever won, must be monarchy. He had the benefit of hindsight, but even at the time many had felt that Crassus' death must lead sooner or later to a contest for sole supremacy between the two surviving dynasts.

The keynotes for the story of Caesar's invasion of Italy, the war and to some extent the dictatorship itself are his daring and swiftness of action. Plutarch draws a sharp contrast between Caesar, dynamically active and in sole control, and Pompey, indecisive and under constant pressure from others. He shows some grasp of strategic considerations, for example the consequences of Caesar's lack of ships, and again points up the risks Caesar took in crossing the Adriatic. His account of the fateful battle of Pharsalus is long, but concentrates more on the circumstances that led to its being fought than on the actual fighting. The Alexandrian campaign serves to introduce, with some admiration, the Egyptian queen Cleopatra, who was to figure much more prominently in the *Antony*; it also continues the theme of Caesar's readiness to take risks. Speed and danger feature yet again in the African and Spanish wars.

Caesar's dictatorship interweaves a number of themes. His reluctance to take precautions for his own security is carried over from his conduct in the field. The exaggerated honours heaped upon him and his arrogant treatment of the senate offset any good impression caused by his clemency, and even that could arouse more resentment than gratitude. Plutarch sees clearly the significance of the perpetual dictatorship, which made him king in all but name. For those who found Caesar's rule intolerable there was now no constitutional remedy: assassination was the only solution.

It is interesting to contrast the accounts of the conspiracy and the actual murder in the *Caesar* and the *Brutus*. The theme of divine vengeance is prominent in both. But in the *Caesar* the role of Marcus Brutus is minimized, except at one crucial point where it is said that Caesar stopped fighting back when he saw that even Brutus was attacking him – though Plutarch seems to doubt the authenticity of this story. In contrast the contribution of Decimus Brutus is stressed, whereas in his own Life Marcus

quite naturally occupies centre stage throughout and Decimus
virtually disappears. Here it is only in the immediate aftermath
of the murder that Marcus comes into his own, only to be
quickly upstaged by the reading of Caesar's will and the popular
reaction to Antony's display of the corpse (though in this
account Plutarch does not mention Antony's name).

As in the *Pompey* Plutarch rounds off the story with a comment on the subsequent fortunes of the killers, the tone of which
makes it clear that the gods were not pleased at what had
happened, despite the earlier suggestion of an element of divine
vengeance for the death of Pompey. The hint of moral uncertainty here may reflect Plutarch's own doubts concerning the
deserts of the individuals concerned, or the attitude of the gods
might stem from their displeasure at the assassins' interference
with Rome's destined progression from republic to monarchy.

Cicero

M. Tullius Cicero was born in 106. Like Marius, he belonged
to one of the leading families of Arpinum, and like Marius he
was the first of his family to essay a career in Roman politics.
But Cicero's sphere of excellence was oratory, not war. After
military service in the Social War (91–89) he first made a name
for himself with his defence of Roscius of Ameria (80). In
75 he was quaestor at Lilybaeum in Sicily, where his honesty
impressed the Sicilians. So, seeking an advocate in 70 to prosecute the outrageously extortionate governor C. Verres, they
turned to Cicero. Cicero won a famous victory in the case,
which established him as Rome's leading orator.

Throughout the sixties Cicero was in the difficult position of
needing the support of both Pompey and Pompey's enemies,
which sometimes led him into inconsistencies. As praetor in 66
he spoke in favour of Manilius' bill giving Pompey the command against Mithridates, but when Manilius was prosecuted
at the end of the year Cicero, as president of the court, first
tried to rush through a condemnation, then in response to the
public outcry promised to defend Manilius in the following
year.

When Cicero stood for the consulship of 63 there were various manifestations of social unrest, all of which he chose to blame on his fellow-candidate Catiline. It was expected that Pompey would return from Asia Minor in 63. It was therefore desirable that the consuls of the year should do their best to deter him from using his army to seize power. Cicero was perceived as a champion of law and order and the sanctity of private property and seemed to be on good terms with Pompey. Catiline and his running-mate C. Antonius had both been associated with Sulla; both were burdened with debt, and Catiline had a reputation for violence. If elected they might well egg Pompey on to imitate Sulla's worst excesses. This is why Cicero romped home at the head of the poll.

As consul Cicero was concerned to force all malcontents out into the open and deal with them himself before Pompey came home, so that Pompey could not use the need to restore order as an excuse for not disbanding his army. He hounded Catiline into open revolt and succeeded in arresting his alleged confederates in Rome, led by Lentulus Sura. Lentulus and company were put to death without trial, an action that was to have drastic consequences for Cicero later. His boasting about his achievements led to a coolness between him and the equally conceited Pompey, and in 61 he earned the undying enmity of Clodius by destroying his alibi at the Bona Dea trial.

It is a tribute to Cicero's talent that Caesar urged him to join the coalition of himself, Pompey and Crassus in 59, but Cicero refused on principle. When Clodius secured the tribunate for 58, Pompey and Caesar made half-hearted efforts to protect Cicero, but Clodius outmanoeuvred them. Faced with condemnation for putting Lentulus and his fellow-conspirators to death without trial in 63, Cicero withdrew into exile. Once Clodius was out of office in 57 Pompey worked for Cicero's return, and Cicero repaid him by proposing the law that put Pompey in charge of Rome's corn supply. Cicero hoped to drive a wedge between Pompey and Caesar, but the renewal of the coalition at Luca in 56 dashed his hopes and severely curbed his freedom of action. He was forced to support the dynasts in the senate and defend their friends in court. It required some courage for him to defend Milo after the murder of Clodius in 52, in obvious defiance of Pompey's wishes, even though his nerve failed on the day and he broke down.

In 51 Cicero was compelled much against his will to govern the province of Cilicia. His tenure was exemplary. He clearly had unusually high standards where provincial administration was concerned, though unfortunately this rarely deterred him from defending in court men whose conduct fell far short of his ideal. When he returned to Rome in 50 the civil war between Pompey and Caesar was imminent. Cicero did his best to mediate, but in vain. For some time he agonized over which side to join: he liked Pompey better (though in his darker moments he thought one was as bad as the other), but he owed Caesar money. In the end he went to Pompey's camp, where his sarcastic remarks made him unpopular. After Pharsalus he was offered the command (as the senior ex-consul present), but refused, for he thought it pointless to fight on.

After making his peace with Caesar he devoted himself largely to scholarship, since under Caesar's autocracy neither the senate nor the courts offered him a meaningful forum. He did, however, press Caesar to pardon all his former opponents and even tried to persuade him to retire, as Sulla had done, once the immediate crisis was past. After Caesar's murder, which he greeted with unseemly exultation, Cicero devised the scheme of using the young Octavian to get rid of Antony, whom he attacked in a series of speeches that he called the *Philippics*, after Demosthenes' diatribes against Philip of Macedon, with the intention of then getting rid of Octavian once he had served his purpose. But Octavian outsmarted Cicero at every turn. In 43 he and Antony were reconciled, and with another former Caesarian, M. Lepidus, formed the triumvirate.[7]

One of the triumvirs' first actions was to institute proscriptions on the Sullan model. Octavian was allegedly reluctant to see Cicero's name put on the list, but Antony was implacable. Cicero was duly hunted down and killed.

In speaking of Cicero's education Plutarch alludes not only to his early promise but also to the resentment it aroused in men of less talent but greater social standing. This resentment, and the ways in which Cicero's temperament led him to aggravate it, remain an important theme in his Life. During his rhetorical studies in Greece Cicero at times displayed an inability to control the sharpness of his tongue.

Cicero's return from his quaestorship of 75 establishes two other key themes: his fondness for praise and his excessive concern for the good opinion of others. Convinced that everyone would be talking about his achievements in the province, he was much aggrieved to find that the only man who knew he had been in Sicily did not know which of the two Sicilian quaestorships he had held. Unfortunately Plutarch presents a very feeble version of the story told by Cicero himself in the *Pro Plancio*.[8]

Sicily provides a bridge to the trial of Verres in 70. Plutarch's account is confused as to the facts and is little more than a peg for a catalogue of Ciceronian witticisms. This anecdotal vein continues to pervade the treatment of Cicero's praetorship, in which the version of events at the trial of Manilius is particularly confused, though Plutarch can hardly be blamed since Cicero was doing his considerable best to be confusing.

Cicero's consulship on the other hand is one of the most satisfactory sections. Plutarch is aware of the background of social and economic unrest. He also understands Cicero's need for support from both Pompey and Pompey's most distinguished opponents and that what chiefly recommended Cicero to the latter was the fact that he was not Catiline. Only when he comes to the conspirator Lentulus does he once more become anecdotal. The final act, the punishment of the conspirators, is brought under the rubric of Cicero's concern for his reputation. Two other features merit comment. Plutarch's eagerness to show the interaction of major figures leads him to highlight Caesar's contribution to the debate on the appropriate penalty for Lentulus and his confederates and to events at the end of Cicero's consulship, while his predilection for the personal element in public events shows itself in the attention he pays (not for the last time) to the role and character of Cicero's wife Terentia. There follows a much less coherent passage on the theme of how, thanks to his gift for making himself obnoxious, Cicero destroyed the position of strength he had gained. Plutarch offers no more than a string of examples, pertinent enough, but in no sort of order and completely devoid of any historical context.

Only with the Bona Dea trial in 61 does Plutarch once more find a thread to follow: the feud between Cicero and Clodius, which shapes his whole account of the years 61 to 52. Much space is again allotted to Terentia in the account of the scandal and the trial. Clodius' campaign for revenge dominates 59 and 58, though Pompey's betrayal of Cicero is duly censured. Then the conflict between Clodius and Pompey occupies the foreground. When Pompey gained the upper hand in 57 Cicero could return from exile in triumph, but Clodius' measures of 58 still had a damaging effect on relations between Cicero and another leading figure, Cato, who could not urge the repeal of Clodius' legislation without invalidating his own annexation of Cyprus, since his mission had been created by another of the tribune's laws.

Plutarch then makes another great leap, to Milo's murder of Clodius in 52 and Cicero's defence of Milo, to which the attitude of Pompey was again of the greatest importance. On Cicero's governorship of Cilicia in 51 Plutarch's judgement is largely sound; the performance of Roman governors abroad was a subject of direct interest to him. On his return to Rome Cicero found himself torn between conflicting obligations to Pompey and Caesar. This is the kind of situation that fascinates Plutarch and he makes good use of it. But once Cicero had committed himself to Pompey, Plutarch falls back on the familiar theme of Cicero's unbridled tongue, as evidenced in the malicious epigrams he gave vent to in Pompey's camp. Nor does he have much to say on Cicero's relationship with Caesar after the civil war, concentrating instead on the orator's domestic problems, his divorce and the death of his daughter Tullia.

The focal points of Plutarch's version of the last phase of Cicero's career are Cicero's consuming hatred of Antony and, yet again, his desire for distinction. But Cicero tends to vacillate between the dominant figure so familiar from his own account in the *Philippics*, who schemes and sets events in motion, and something not much more than a puppet manipulated by others, in particular Octavian. His failure leads swiftly to his own death, in which a part was played by that lack of resolution he had already shown during his exile.

The epilogue is striking. Plutarch saw no need to expatiate on the fall of Antony; that could wait until he came to write Antony's own Life. Instead we are given the gruesomely cautionary fate of Philologus, the treacherous freedman of Cicero's brother Quintus, who had betrayed Cicero to his pursuers (though Plutarch is careful not to vouch for the tale's veracity). But then come two highly significant items: the belated tribute paid by Augustus not only to Cicero's learning but to his patriotism, and the consulship he vouchsafed to Cicero's son in 30, the very year that saw the senate pass various decrees in condemnation of Antony's memory. So Cicero, the republic's most eloquent voice, gained some memorial at least from the creator of the nascent empire.

SUMMARY

Two elements perhaps stand out above all others in Plutarch's late republican Lives. The first is the unbridled pursuit of personal power. Every Life in this selection displays the incessantly disruptive and ultimately ruinous effects of competition and ephemeral collaboration for purely selfish ends between a handful of prominent individuals, none of whom was quite powerful enough to achieve sole supremacy until Caesar put an end to the dominance of the oligarchy that had spawned him in the last stage of its decline.

The second is the amount of coverage that Plutarch sees fit to give to wars both foreign and civil. To a certain extent this need occasion no surprise. In the eyes of the Roman ruling class military glory was the highest form of distinction to which its members might aspire. The biographer of leading Romans could hardly avoid writing about war, and a man's conduct in the field might well provide illuminating insights into those recesses of his character that Plutarch sought to penetrate. Yet much of his military narrative seems, as observed earlier, to be there for its own sake, regardless of any light it might shed on the protagonists' moral or psychological make-up.

The reason for both these features of Plutarch's work lies in the standard perception of the republic and its fall that quickly developed under the empire. Everyone knew that the republican ruling class, by its dedication to the quest for wealth and personal power, had destroyed itself and the system of government it claimed to cherish. That Plutarch should share this perception is not remarkable. Explanation would be needed only if he did not.

But the republic had also been a time of almost constant warfare. The link between this fact and the unbridled pursuit of personal ambition is obvious, and was obvious to Romans of the early empire. Success in war was the surest way for an individual to increase his wealth and standing, and so the ruling class had a vested interest in ensuring that opportunities for such increase did not dry up.

It is worth noting in this regard that two imperial writers of the mid-2nd century AD, Florus and Appian, whose histories cover much of the same ground as Plutarch's Lives, chose to cast their work in the form of loosely linked accounts of a series of wars. Appian in particular takes a far greater interest than Plutarch in the minutiae of politics and devotes much more space to such matters, but he calls this history *The Civil Wars*. In conceding such importance to wars and battles, Plutarch demonstrates, within the limits imposed by the biographical genre, that he too is aware of this crucial aspect of the republic's rise and fall.

In hindsight, the late republic's dominant feature can be seen as meaningful aristocratic competition for power, often finding its expression in wars of expansion and in the end of self-destruction. But the new order put an end to all that. That was the price that had to be paid for restored stability: '*pax et princeps*', as Tacitus put it, writing at about the same time as Plutarch. Tacitus' romantic republicanism moved him to bitter lamentation for the passing of the glorious age of conquest and querulous apology for the meagre matter that the present age offered the ambitious historian. But both self-interest and self-preservation (or let us call it simply realism and common sense) led those with their feet on the ground, not least among them Plutarch, to stifle any nagging regrets they may have felt – though many truly felt none – and take a more positive view of the transition from oligarchy to autocracy, from republic to empire.

R.S.

NOTES

1. Nine books of discussions of various questions that might be not too seriously debated by intelligent and educated men over dinner.
2. The nine archons chosen annually at Athens performed various administrative, judicial and religious duties. The senior or eponymous archon gave his name to the year in which he held office.
3. Under the empire the insignia of the consulship were sometimes granted as a form of decoration to men whose distinction, like Plutarch's, lay in other fields than Roman political life.
4. The equestrian order comprised those of the upper classes who were not members of the senate. Under the republic they had at times supplied jurors in the criminal courts and had been prominent in business and finance, especially tax-farming, though they also owned land. Augustus was concerned to give them a place in the new order and so created career opportunities for them in the army, provincial administration and the embryonic imperial civil service. Membership of the order could be granted, as here, to deserving persons of distinction.
5. Procurators of equestrian rank might govern minor provinces or serve as assistants to the governor in larger ones. In the latter case their function was in part to keep an eye on the governor in the emperor's behalf. But for such a man as Plutarch the appointment would have been purely honorific; he would not have been expected to carry out the usual duties associated with the post.
6. An ovation was an honour less exalted than a triumph, granted

for campaigns which did not qualify for the higher award. Only a war against a foreign enemy could legitimately earn a triumph; civil wars and slave revolts could not. Crassus' resentment will have been exacerbated by the fact that the war against Sertorius, for which Pompey gained his second triumph, had been questionably adjudged to be not a civil war but a war against a foreign enemy (i.e. Sertorius' Spanish forces).

7. The triumvirate of 43 was a formal office of five years' duration in the first instance, with the remit of setting the state in order. It was thus quite unlike the purely private arrangement made by Caesar, Pompey and Crassus in 60/59, which is therefore better not called the 'first triumvirate'.

8. Delivered by Cicero in 54 on behalf of Cn. Plancius on a charge of bribery at the elections for the aedileship of that year. Though almost certainly guilty, Plancius was acquitted.

Further Reading

THE PERIOD

Cambridge Ancient History IX^2 (ed. Crook, Lintott, Rawson), Cambridge 1994 (= *CAH*).

R. Syme, *The Roman Revolution*, Oxford 1939 (= Syme, *RR*).

THE SUBJECTS OF THE LIVES

Marius

T. F. Carney, *A Biography of C. Marius*, Assen 1961 (= Carney).

R. J. Evans, *Gaius Marius, a Political Biography*, Pretoria 1994 (= Evans).

Sulla

A. Keaveney, *Sulla, the Last Republican*, London/Canberra 1982.

Crassus

A. Ward, *Marcus Crassus and the Late Roman Republic*, Columbia MO 1977.

Pompey

R. Seager, *Pompey the Great*^{2}, Oxford 2002.

Caesar

M. Gelzer (trans. P. Needham), *Caesar, Politician and States-man*, Oxford 1968 (= Gelzer, *Caesar*).
C. Meier (trans. D. McLintock), *Caesar*, London 1996.

Cicero

D. Stockton, *Cicero, a Political Biography*, Oxford 1971.
  N.B. (a) I have not included references to most of these works
  in the notes to the translation except on certain specific points
  that might otherwise go unnoticed. In general the reader
  can locate any information required easily enough from the
  relevant tables of contents and indices. (b) The reader should
  remember that the careers of several of these men were inti-
  mately linked. Useful information on one is therefore often
  to be found in books whose nominal subject is one of the
  others.

PLUTARCH AND THE LIVES

T. Duff, *Plutarch's Lives: Exploring Virtue and Vice*, Oxford
  1999.
C. P. Jones, *Plutarch and Rome*, Oxford 1971.
R. Lamberton, *Plutarch*, New Haven/London 2001.
C. Pelling, *Plutarch and History*, London 2002.
D. A. Russell, *Plutarch*, Bristol 2001.
B. Scardigli, *Essays on Plutarch's Lives*, Oxford 1995.

The following editions of individual lives have valuable intro-
  ductions:
J. R. Hamilton, *Plutarch, Alexander*, Oxford 1969.
J. L. Moles, *Plutarch, The Life of Cicero*, Warminster 1988.
C. B. R. Pelling, *Plutarch, Life of Antony*, Cambridge 1988.

FALL OF THE
ROMAN REPUBLIC

I

GAIUS MARIUS

[157–86 BC]

The biography of Marius is one of the least satisfactory of
Plutarch's Roman lives from the historian's point of view.
Marius and his political importance disappear almost completely behind a smoke-screen of moralizing. The poverty of
Marius' family and his lack of education are considerably exaggerated, and Marius' relationship with the Metelli – a paradigm
case of that characteristic Roman phenomenon, the young
man rich in talent but poor in connections taken up by a distinguished and powerful family – is obscured, as is the real
significance of his marriage into an aristocratic house in temporary decline. Plutarch shows no appreciation of the political
skill with which Marius fostered and exploited equestrian and
popular discontent in order to oust Metellus from the Numidian
command. Even when due allowance is made for subsequent
rhetorical schematization, there can be no doubt that Marius
successfully presented himself as the symbol of the claims of
personal merit against the inherited supremacy of a corrupt
and incompetent ruling clique. From the moment that Marius
secures the command against Jugurtha, Plutarch is chiefly concerned with the narrative of his military achievements and of
course with the dramatic vicissitudes of his escape from Sulla
in 88. He makes no attempt to analyse the formation or the
collapse of the uneasy alliance between Marius and the violent
popular tribune Saturninus, who had seen in the Marian veterans a possible source of that protection which any would-
be revolutionary or reformer had to secure, since the death of
C. Gracchus had made it clear that legal safeguards were inadequate to deter the forces of law and order from murder.

Indeed, perhaps the gravest criticism that can be made of Plutarch is that he failed to highlight the consequences of Marius' enrolment of the *capite censi*. This measure created the armies of the last century of the republic, dependent on their generals for rewards when their service was done and ready to follow them if need be against Rome itself. Marius never used the weapon he had forged against the state, but it was he who made possible the last precipitous stage in the fall of the republic that began with Sulla's march on Rome in 88.

1. We do not know of any third name for Gaius Marius, just as we do not know of a third name for Quintus Sertorius,[1] who occupied Spain, or for Lucius Mummius, who took and sacked Corinth.[2] Mummius was given the surname 'Achaicus' because of his achievements, as Scipio was called 'Africanus' and Metellus 'Macedonicus'. This is the chief argument used by Posidonius when he imagines that he is disproving the view that among the Romans the third is the proper name (e.g. Camillus, Marcellus, Cato). If this were so, he maintains, those with only two names would have had no proper name at all. But he fails to observe that, if he follows this line of argument, he must deprive all women of their proper names, since women never have the first name, which Posidonius imagines was the proper name among the Romans. Of the other two names one was the family name (e.g. the Pompeii, the Manlii, or the Cornelii – just as, among us Greeks, the Heracleidae or the Pelopidae) and the other a kind of title or epithet referring to a person's nature or deeds or some purely physical characteristic or defect – Macrinus, for instance, or Torquatus or Sulla (like the Greek names Mnemon, Grypus or Callinicus). However, because of the irregularity of custom there is plenty of room for controversy on this subject.

2. As for what Marius looked like, there is a stone statue of him at Ravenna in Gaul which I have seen myself. It agrees well with the rough, bitter character which is supposed to have been his. He was by nature a very virile type, a person devoted to war, whose whole training had been in the army rather than in

civilian life;[3] and when he had power he was incapable of controlling his passions. It is said that he never studied Greek literature and never used the Greek language on any occasion that mattered. It was ridiculous, he thought, to study a literature the teachers of which were subject to others. So after his second triumph[4] when at the consecration of a temple he presented some Greek theatrical performances, he just came into the theatre and sat down and then went off again immediately. Plato used often to say to the philosopher Xenocrates, who had the reputation of being rather too harsh in his disposition, 'My dear Xenocrates, sacrifice to the Graces.' So in the case of Marius, if only someone had persuaded him to sacrifice to the Muses and Graces of the Greeks, he would not have brought his career, so splendid both in war and peace, to so ugly a conclusion, and would not have been cast up upon the shores of a bloodthirsty and savage old age, shipwrecked by his passions, his ill-timed ambition and his insatiable greed. All this, however, will shortly appear from the facts.

3. His parents (Marius and Fulcinia) were entirely undistinguished. They were poor people who lived by the labour of their own hands.[5] For a long time he never saw Rome or got any taste of city life. During this period he lived in the village of Cirrhaeaton, near Arpinum, in a style rough and unrefined, if compared with the polished ways of cities, but temperate and in accordance with the ancient Roman standards of education.

His first military service was against the Celtiberians at the time when Scipio Africanus was besieging Numantia.[6] He attracted the general's attention by showing a bravery which was outstanding among the rest of the recruits and by the cheerful way in which he accepted the changed regime which Scipio was imposing on an army corrupted by luxury and extravagance. He is also said to have fought single-handed with one of the enemy and to have struck him down in the sight of the general. As a result Scipio conferred many marks of distinction on him. There was one occasion when during a conversation after dinner the talk turned on generals, and one of those present, either because he really wanted to know or merely out of flattery, said to Scipio, 'What commander and what leader can the Roman people possibly find to be a worthy successor to you?' Scipio then gently tapped Marius on the shoulder, as he reclined next to him, and said: 'Perhaps this is the man.' So each revealed great natural gifts – Marius by showing himself to be great when he was still only a youth, Scipio by being able to see from the beginning what the end would be.

4. We are told that it was largely because of this remark of Scipio's, which he regarded as prophetic and inspired, that Marius' hopes were raised to embark on a political career. He stood for and obtained the office of tribune of the people with the backing of Caecilius Metellus,[7] of whose house he had been from the first a hereditary client.

While tribune he proposed a law in connection with the method of voting and it was considered that this law would weaken the power of the nobles in the courts of justice.[8] The consul Cotta opposed him and persuaded the senate to declare against the law and to summon Marius to appear and explain his conduct. This resolution was carried and Marius appeared before the senate. However, far from behaving like a young man who had only just begun his career in politics and had no distinguished record behind him, he put on all the assurance warranted by those great actions of his which were still in the future and threatened to drag Cotta off to prison unless he had his decree rescinded. Cotta then turned to Metellus and asked him for his opinion, and Metellus stood up and declared that he was in agreement with the consul. Marius called in the officer from outside and ordered him to lead Metellus himself off to prison. Metellus appealed for help to the other tribunes, but none of them supported him and so the senate gave in and rescinded its previous vote. Marius left the meeting in triumph, appeared before the people and had his law ratified. He had won the reputation of a man of dauntless courage who could not be turned from his course by conventional feelings of respect, a formidable opponent of the senate in the interests of the common people. However, another action of his immediately caused this opinion of him to be revised. When a law was proposed providing for a distribution of corn to the citizens, he vigorously and successfully opposed it, and so made himself equally respected by both parties as a man who would favour neither at the expense of the general good.

5. After his tribunate he stood for the higher aedileship.[9] (There are two grades of aediles – the 'curule' aediles who take the name from the chairs with curving feet on which the magistrates sit when they are carrying out their duties, and the less important officials called 'plebeian'.) When the chief aediles have been elected, another vote is taken afterwards for the aediles of the lower grade. Marius, seeing that he was obviously losing in the first election, quickly changed over and stood for the inferior office. But people thought him too forward and lacking in modesty, so he was defeated. He was thus in the unprecedented position of having lost two elections in one day; but this had no effect whatever on his own opinion of himself. Soon afterwards he stood for the praetorship and very nearly failed again.[10] He was last on the list of those elected and he was prosecuted for bribery.

The greatest suspicion was aroused by the fact that a servant of Cassius Sabaco, who was a very great friend of Marius, had been seen inside the railings among the voters while they were casting their votes. Sabaco was called to give evidence in court and stated that the heat had made him so thirsty that he had asked for some cold water; that his servant had brought him some in a cup and, as soon as he had drunk it, had gone away at once. Sabaco was, nevertheless, expelled from the senate by the censors of the next year, deservedly, it was thought, either for giving false evidence or for his intemperance. Gaius Herennius was also summoned to appear as a witness against Marius, but claimed that it was not the normal procedure for a patron (the Roman word for what we call 'protector') to give evidence against a client and that the law actually exempted patrons from having to do so. The parents of Marius and originally Marius himself, he said, had been dependants of the Herennii. This plea to avoid giving evidence was accepted by

the court, but Marius himself opposed it and told Herennius
that from the time that he had first been elected to an official
post he had ceased to be a client. (This was not quite true. Not
every office, but only those whose holders are legally entitled
to the curule chair, frees a dependant and his descendants from
the duties owed to a patron.) However, although Marius did
badly in the first days of the trial and found the court hostile to
him, on the final day the votes for and against were exactly
equal and, contrary to expectation, he was acquitted.

6. His praetorship, then, was not particularly distinguished. But
after the praetorship he was allotted the province of Hispania
Ulterior, and he is said to have put down banditry in the area
under his command. This province was still uncivilized and
savage in its ways. The Spaniards in those days still thought
that to be a bandit was a most honourable profession.

When he returned to politics he lacked both wealth and
eloquence,[11] the two chief means used by great men of the time
for influencing the people. However, the very intensity of the
confidence he showed in himself, his unremitting exertions and
his plain way of living combined to make him popular. The
esteem in which he was held brought him nearer to power, so
that he was able to make a brilliant match by marrying Julia,
who came from the aristocratic family of the Caesars. She was
the aunt of that Caesar who later became the greatest man in
Rome. As I have stated in my Life of him, he seems in some
ways, because of this relationship, to have modelled himself on
Marius.[12]

There is evidence to show that Marius was temperate and
had great powers of endurance. An example of his endurance
can be found in his behaviour when under the hands of a
surgeon. It appears that both his legs were badly affected with
varicose veins. He did not like their ugly appearance and
decided to receive medical attention. So, without being tied
down, he thrust out one leg and, without making a movement
or uttering a groan, with a fixed expression and in complete
silence, endured the most extreme pain under the surgeon's
knife. When the surgeon proposed to repeat the operation on

the other leg, Marius declined to have it done. 'I can see,' he said, 'that the improvement does not justify the pain.'

7. When Caecilius Metellus, as consul, was appointed commander-in-chief for the war against Jugurtha, he took Marius with him to Africa as a legate.[13] Here, now that he had got the chance of a share in great actions and glorious battles, Marius, unlike the rest, took no trouble at all to increase the prestige of Metellus or to play up to him. It was not so much Metellus, he considered, who had appointed him an officer; rather it was Fortune who had presented him with a perfect opportunity, a great theatre in which to play an active part himself; and so he displayed every kind of bravery. It was a hard war, but he was not afraid of any undertaking, however great, and was not too proud to accept any task, however small. He surpassed his equals in rank by the advice he gave and his foresight into what was needed, and he won much affection from the soldiers by showing that he could live as frugally as they did and endure as much. Indeed it seems generally to be the case that our labours are eased when someone goes out of his way to share them with us; it has the effect of making the labour not seem forced. And what a Roman soldier likes most to see is his general eating his ration of bread with the rest, or sleeping on an ordinary bed, or joining in the work of digging a trench or raising a palisade. The commanders whom they admire are not so much those who distribute honours and riches as those who take a share in their hardships and their dangers; they have more affection for those who are willing to join in their work than for those who allow them to take it easy.

By these actions and in this way Marius won the hearts of the soldiers. First Africa and then Rome were soon full of his name and of his glory, and the men in the army wrote in their letters home that the war against the barbarian could never be brought to a proper conclusion unless Marius were elected consul.

8. Metellus was, quite obviously, displeased with all this. He was particularly upset by what happened in the case of

Turpillius, a man connected with him by a long-standing tradition of guest-friendship. At this time Turpillius was serving
in his army as chief of engineers. He had been put in command
of the garrison of the large city of Vaga. Here his security
measures consisted in doing no harm to the inhabitants, but in
treating them kindly and considerately. Before he knew what
had happened, he found himself in enemy hands; for the people
let Jugurtha into the city. However, they did no harm to Turpillius who, at their request, was released safe and sound. As a
result he was charged with treachery and Marius, who was one
of those trying the case, spoke so bitterly against him himself
and so incensed most of the others against him that Metellus,
much against his will, was forced to condemn the man to
death.[14] Soon afterwards it became clear that the charge had
been a false one, and everyone except Marius sympathized with
Metellus in his grief. But Marius was exultant; he claimed that
the whole thing had been his doing and was not ashamed to go
about saying that he had let loose on Metellus an avenging
spirit who would punish the guilt of having put a friend to
death.

   After this Marius and Metellus were on terms of open hostility. It is said that on one occasion when Marius was present
Metellus deliberately insulted him by saying, 'So you are going
to abandon us, are you, my dear fellow? You intend to sail
home and stand for the consulship? Will it not be enough for
you to stand at the same time as this boy of mine?' (Metellus'
son was at this time only a very young man.) Nevertheless
Marius still pressed to be allowed to go, and, after many delays,
about twelve days before the date of the consular elections,
Metellus gave him leave. Marius completed the long journey
from the camp to Utica and the sea in two days and one night.
Before he sailed he made a sacrifice, and the soothsayer is said
to have told him that heaven had in store for him good fortune
so great that it was beyond all belief and expectation. Encouraged by this prophecy he set sail, and with a following wind
made the crossing in three days. His appearance was greeted at
once with enthusiasm by the people. He was introduced to the
assembly by one of the tribunes and, after making a number

of damaging attacks on Metellus, he asked for the consulship, promising that he would either kill Jugurtha or capture him alive.

9. He was triumphantly elected and at once began to raise troops.[15] Contrary to law and custom he enrolled in his army many poor men of low standing, a class of people who used not to be accepted by commanders in the past, who gave arms, like other honours, only to those qualified by their property – the idea being that each man's property served as a pledge of loyalty. But Marius made enemies in other ways than this; particularly in the violent speeches, full of contempt and arrogance, by which he offended the aristocracy.[16] He had carried off the consulship, he would proclaim, as spoils of war from the effeminacy of the noble families and of the rich; and, he said, he made an impression on the people by showing the wounds on his own body, not by an exhibition of sepulchral monuments or of other people's portraits. He would often refer by name to those generals who had come to grief in Africa (Bestia, for example, and Albinus),[17] men of famous families, but unfortunate individuals, lacking in military ability, who had been defeated through want of experience; and he would ask his audience if they did not think that the ancestors of these people would have been more pleased to have had descendants like himself, seeing that they themselves had become famous not because of high birth but because of merit and noble deeds. These speeches of his were not mere braggadocio. He was quite deliberately making himself hated by the upper classes, and the people, who were delighted when insulting language was used against the senate and who always measured the greatness of a man's spirit by his capacity to make much of himself in words, kept on encouraging him and urging him, if he wished to give pleasure to the masses, to show no mercy to important personages.

10. When he crossed over to Africa Metellus refused to meet him. He was both jealous of him and made extremely angry by the thought that, while he himself had finished the war, leaving nothing to be done except actually to secure the person of

Jugurtha, Marius, who had grown great because of ingratitude towards himself, was now arriving to take the crown and the triumph. He therefore went away privately, leaving his legate Rutilius[18] to hand over the army to Marius.

In the end some sort of retribution came to him for his behaviour; for Sulla took from him the credit of the final success, just as Marius had taken it from Metellus. I shall explain how this happened briefly, since the details are given more fully in my *Life of Sulla*.

The king of the natives in the interior was Jugurtha's son-in-law, Bocchus. He did not appear to have given Jugurtha much help in the war, and his excuse for this was that Jugurtha was untrustworthy; he was also frightened of his growing power. But Jugurtha was now a fugitive with nowhere to go to. He was forced to seek refuge with his son-in-law, as the only hope left to him. Bocchus, rather because he was ashamed to reject such an appeal than from any more generous motive, received him and kept him under his eye. He then openly wrote to Marius, interceding for Jugurtha and stating, in no uncertain language, that he was not prepared to surrender him. Privately, however, he was planning to betray him and he sent for Lucius Sulla, who was Marius' quaestor and had been of some help to Bocchus in the course of the campaign.[19] Sulla, relying on his word, made the journey up country, but now the native changed his mind and began to regret what he had done. For several days he was weighing up which of two courses to follow – to surrender Jugurtha or to keep Sulla too under arrest. Finally he decided upon his original plan of treachery and delivered Jugurtha over alive to Sulla.

It was this that sowed the first seed of that irreconcilable and bitter hatred between Marius and Sulla which very nearly brought Rome to ruin. There were many who, out of envy of Marius, gave the whole credit for the affair to Sulla, and Sulla himself used to carry a signet ring which he had had made on which was engraved the scene of Jugurtha being surrendered to him by Bocchus. By constantly using this ring he greatly irritated Marius, who had the keenest sense of his own honour, no notion of sharing glory with anyone else, and was quick to take offence. Sulla was egged on by Marius' opponents who, with a view to undermining Marius' prestige and the unique esteem in which he was held by the people, attributed to Metellus the first and greatest achievements of the war and to Sulla the credit for having finally ended it.

11. Soon, however, all envies, hatreds, and calumnies against Marius were done away with and forgotten. Danger threatened Italy from the West. Rome required a great general and sought a helmsman to save her from this tempest of war. At the consular elections no one showed any interest in the candidates from great or rich families, and Marius, in spite of being absent from Rome, was proclaimed consul.[20]

It was only just after the news had arrived of the capture of Jugurtha that reports began to come in about the Teutones and the Cimbri.[21] At first what was reported about the numbers and strength of the invading armies seemed incredible; later it appeared that rumour fell short of the truth. Three hundred thousand armed warriors were on the march, and hordes of women and children in much greater numbers were said to be marching with them, all seeking land to support such vast hosts and cities in which to settle and live, just as, before their time, as they had discovered, the Gauls had seized the best part of Italy from the Etruscans and were still occupying it. Who these people were and from what part of the world they had set out to fall on Gaul and Italy like a thundercloud no one knew; for they had no contact with other peoples and had already travelled a very great way. The likeliest guess seemed to be that they were some of the German tribes, whose territory extends up to the northern ocean. This conjecture was based on their great size, the light blue colour of their eyes, and the fact that the German word for plunderers is 'Cimbri'.

There are some, however, who say that the country of the Celts is so wide and extensive that it stretches from the outer sea and the subarctic as far to the east as Lake Maeotis, where it touches Pontic Scythia, from which point on there is a mixture of the two races, Celts and Scythians. According to this theory it was from here that they had started not all at once or in a

continuous stream, but every spring moving a little further
westward and so in the course of time, fighting all the way,
they had crossed the whole continent. So, though there were
different names for different contingents in the army, the force
as a whole was called 'the Celto-Scythians'.

Others say that the Cimmerians, our first knowledge of
whom comes from the ancient Greeks, did not constitute an
important part of the entire race; they were merely a body of
exiles or some minority which was driven out by the Scythians
and crossed from Lake Maeotis into Asia under the leadership
of Lygdamis; meanwhile the greater and most warlike part of
the race lived at the end of the world by the outer ocean in a
land of shade and forests so thick that the sun is never visible
because of the size and thickness of the trees which extend
inland as far as the Hercynii. Geographically they are situated
under that part of the sky where, because of the declination of
the parallels, the pole has a great elevation and appears to be
not far from the zenith; and the year is divided into two equal
periods, one of night and one of day. (All this Homer found
useful in his account of the visit of Odysseus to the dead.)
According to this theory the native tribes set out against Italy
from this part of the world, being originally called 'Cimmerii'
and then, by a not unnatural change, 'Cimbri'. All this, however, is based rather on conjecture than on definite historical
evidence.

As for the numbers of the invaders, according to many authorities they were not less but greater than the figure which I
have given. Their courage and daring were irresistible; in their
fighting they rushed into battle with the speed of a raging fire;
nothing could stand up to them, and all who came in their way
were carried off as the booty and spoils of war. Even large
Roman armies and their generals, stationed to protect Transalpine Gaul, had been ingloriously destroyed.[22] Indeed, it was
the poor account given of themselves by these Roman armies
which had encouraged the native tribes to sweep on to Rome.
For, having conquered all who opposed them and having won
great quantities of booty, they made up their minds not to settle

down anywhere until they had destroyed Rome and ravaged
the whole of Italy.

12. With news of this kind coming in from all sides, the Romans
summoned Marius to take over the command. He was
appointed consul for the second time, although it was illegal
for a man to be elected consul unless he was actually present in
Rome or to hold a second consulship until a fixed time had
elapsed since his first consulship. However, the people would
tolerate no opposition. This was not the first time, they considered, that the law had given way to the general interest and
there was no less cogent reason for it to do so on the present
occasion than there had been at the time when, contrary to the
law, they had made Scipio consul.[23] Then they had desired the
overthrow of Carthage: now they feared for the destruction of
Rome.

So it was decided and Marius crossed over with his army
from Africa. On 1 January, which is the beginning of the year
with the Romans, he assumed the consulship and held his
triumph. In the procession he afforded the Romans a spectacle
which they had never hoped to see – Jugurtha in chains. For no
one had imagined that the enemy could ever be subdued while
Jugurtha remained alive, so clever was he at adapting himself
to every change in the situation and so remarkably did he
combine great courage with every kind of crooked dealing.
However, he went clean out of his wits, so they say, after he
had been forced to march in the triumphal procession and,
when it was over, had been thrown into prison. Here, while
some stripped the clothes from his body, others, struggling to
tear off his golden earring, pulled off with it the lobe of his
ear. He was then thrust down naked into the dungeon and,
thoroughly disturbed in the head and with a kind of grin on his
face, cried out 'Hercules! What cold baths you have!' For six
days he struggled with the pangs of hunger, clinging up to the
last moment to his will to live, until finally he paid the just
penalty for his crimes.

In the triumphal procession was carried, it is said, 3,007 lb weight of gold, 5,775 of uncoined silver, and 287,000 drachmas in coined money.

After the procession Marius called a meeting of the senate on the Capitol. Whether through absentmindedness or because he was making a vulgar display of his good fortune, he came to the meeting still wearing his triumphal robes. He soon saw, however, what offence he was causing in the senate, and he got up and went out, returning again when he had changed into the normal toga with a purple border.

13. After he had set out for the front he gave his army an intensive course of training while on the route. There was practice in all kinds of running and in long marches; and every man was compelled to carry his own baggage and to prepare his own meals. This was the origin of the expression 'one of Marius' mules', applied later to any soldier who was a glutton for work and obeyed orders cheerfully and without grumbling. Though others derive the expression from a different occasion. They say that Scipio, during the siege of Numantia, decided to inspect not only the arms and the horses, but also the mules and baggage wagons, to see how the men were looking after them and in what condition they were. Marius, at this inspection, produced a horse which he had kept in splendid condition and a mule far healthier, easier to manage and stronger than any of the others. The general was delighted and would constantly mention these animals of Marius in conversation, so that it became a joke in the army to praise any hardworking, patient, industrious soldier by calling him 'one of Marius' mules'.

14. Now Marius seems to have had a great stroke of luck. The oncoming wave of native tribes washed back again, as it were, and streamed first into Spain. This gave Marius time to toughen the bodies of his men and to improve their morale and – most important of all – to make them understand what sort of a man he was himself. That fierce manner of his in command and his inflexibility in imposing punishments seemed to them, once they had got the habit of discipline and obedience, not only right and proper but a positive advantage. His angry temper,

rough voice and that forbidding expression with which they
gradually grew familiar, seemed more terrible to the enemy
than to themselves. What particularly pleased the soldiers was
his uprightness in dispensing justice, an example of which can
be found in the case of Gaius Lusius, a nephew of his, who was
serving under him as an officer and who was not a bad man,
apart from having a weakness for beautiful young men. This
Lusius fell in love with one of the young soldiers under his
command, Trebonius by name, and made frequent unsuccessful
attempts to seduce him. Finally he sent a servant to him by
night to fetch him to his tent. The young man came, since he
could not disobey an order; but when he was brought into the
tent and Lusius attempted to use violence on him, he drew his
sword and killed him. Marius was not with the army when this
happened; but on his return Trebonius was court-martialled.
As many spoke against him and no one was prepared to defend
him, he boldly came forward himself and told the whole story,
producing witnesses to show that Lusius had often made
advances to him, which he had refused, and that, though large
offers had been made to him, he had never prostituted himself
to anyone. Marius admired his behaviour and was delighted
with it. He ordered the crown, which was the traditional decoration for valour, to be brought and with his own hands placed
it on the head of Trebonius, honouring him for having performed a most noble action at a time when such good examples
were particularly needed.

   This story was repeated in Rome and was of considerable
help to Marius in securing his third consulship,[24] though it was
also the fact that the native tribes were expected in the spring
and the Romans were unwilling to risk battle against them
under any other general. However, they did not appear as soon
as had been expected, and once again the period of Marius'
consulship ran out. As the time for the consular elections was
at hand and his colleague in the consulship had died,[25] Marius
came himself to Rome, leaving Manius Aquillius[26] in command
of the army. There were many men of real ability who were
standing for the consulship; but Lucius Saturninus,[27] the tribune
who had most influence with the people, was won over by

Marius and, in all his speeches, called upon the people to elect
Marius consul. Marius on his side pretended reluctance and
said that he did not really want to stand, and Saturninus then
called him a traitor to his country for refusing the command
in such a time of peril. It was quite obvious that Saturninus
was acting, very unconvincingly, a part in which he had been
prompted by Marius. Nevertheless the people, seeing that the
situation required his ability and his luck, voted him consul
for the fourth time. They appointed as his colleague Lutatius
Catulus,[28] a man who was much esteemed by the noble families
and not disliked by the common people.

15. As soon as he heard that the enemy were approaching,
Marius quickly crossed the Alps and constructed a fortified
camp by the Rhône. He brought large quantities of supplies
into this camp, so that he should never, through lack of provisions, be forced to give battle against his better judgement.
He speeded up and improved the transport by sea of supplies
to the army – previously a slow and expensive business. For the
mouths of the Rhône, where they joined the sea, were barred
and almost blocked up with sand and mud and clay brought in
by the sea swell, so that it was difficult, troublesome and slow
for transport ships to enter the river. As the troops had nothing
to do, Marius brought them here and dug a big canal into
which he diverted a great part of the river and brought it round
to a suitable place on the coast where the water was deep
enough for even large ships to lie at anchor and where the entry
into the sea was smooth and calm. The canal bears his name to
this day.

The native army now divided itself into two parts. The task
allotted to the Cimbri was to march inland by way of Noricum
against Catulus and to force a passage there, while the Teutones
and Ambrones were to march along the coast through Liguria
against Marius. The Cimbri were held up by various delays,
but the Teutones and Ambrones set out at once, crossed over the
intervening country, and soon came into sight. Their numbers
appeared to be infinite; they were hideous to look at; their
speech and their shouting were unlike those of other peoples.

Spreading over a large part of the plain, they made their camp and challenged Marius to battle.

16. Marius allowed the challenge to pass unheeded. He kept his soldiers inside the fortifications and spoke sharply to those who wanted to show their daring. 'Traitors to your country' was what he called those whose high confidence made them eager and anxious to rush into battle. This, he said, was no occasion for a man to gratify his personal pride in seeking triumphs and trophies; their task was to dispel so great a cloud and thunderbolt of war and so save Italy. This was what he said in private to his officers and equals. As for the soldiers, he would station them in detachments along the fortifications and tell them to have a good look at the enemy. In this way he got them gradually used to contemplating them without fear and to listening without terror to the quite extraordinary and bestial noises that they made. He encouraged them to study their equipment and movements, so that in course of time what had at first seemed frightening became, as they grew accustomed to the sight, familiar and understandable. His view was that when a thing is strange it will seem more frightening even than it is, but that when one has got used to something, even something really formidable, it will cease to inspire terror.

So in the case of these soldiers of Marius the sight they had of the enemy every day took away something of their astonishment. Not only that, but their anger was roused and their spirits stirred and set on fire by the menacing gestures of the natives and by their intolerable boasting; for the enemy, not content with ravaging all the country round about, actually had the effrontery to make various daring attacks on the fortifications of the camp.

Indignant complaints from the soldiers now began to reach the ears of Marius: 'Does Marius think that we are cowards? Otherwise why is he keeping us out of battle under lock and key, as though we were women? Why don't we behave like free men and ask him straight out whether he's waiting for some other army to fight for Italy and is only going to use us as a labour corps, digging ditches when necessary, clearing up mud and diverting a few rivers? Was this the idea of all the intensive training he gave us? Is this all he'll have to show for his consulship when he gets back to Rome? Or is he frightened of being defeated by the enemy, as Carbo and Caepio were?[29] But they were nothing like Marius either in reputation or in real quality, nor were the troops they led anything like us. Surely it's better to go into action, even if we suffer for it as they did, rather than to sit down here and just watch our friends and allies having all their property destroyed.'

17. Marius was delighted to hear that this was what the soldiers were saying. He calmed them down by telling them that it was not at all true that he lacked confidence in them; what he was doing was to await, as he had been instructed to do by certain oracles, the right time and place for victory. And he did in fact carry round with him in great state a Syrian woman, called Martha, who was supposed to be a prophetess. She was carried in a litter and he made sacrifices in accordance with her directions. She had previously sought an interview with the senate about this war and had volunteered to predict the future; but the senate would have nothing to do with her. She then addressed herself to the women and showed them what she could do. Her most important contact was with Marius' wife, at whose feet she sat during a contest of gladiators and successfully foretold the winners. Marius' wife sent her to her husband and Marius himself was much impressed by her. Usually she was carried along in a litter, but when she attended the sacrifices she used to wear a double purple robe fastened with a buckle and carried a spear with ribbons and garlands on it. The theatrical nature of this performance made many people wonder whether, in making a show of this woman, Marius really believed in her himself or was only playing a part and pretending to do so.

But the story about the vultures, told by Alexander of Myndus, is certainly remarkable. He says that before Marius' victories two vultures were always to be seen flying above his armies and following them on the march. These birds could be recognized by the bronze collars on their necks; for the soldiers had once caught them, fitted on the collars and let them go again. Afterwards, whenever they recognized the birds they used to greet them gladly and the sight of them when they were marching out used to make them confident of victory.

Many other prodigies appeared at this time. Most were of the ordinary type; but it was reported that from the Italian cities of Ameria and Tuder there had been seen in the sky at night flaming spears and shields; at first they were moving in different directions, but then they clashed together in just the formations and with just the movements of men fighting in battle; finally, with one side retreating and the other side in pursuit they all streamed off towards the west. About this time too Bataces, the priest of the Great Mother, came from Pessinus and announced that the goddess had spoken to him from her shrine and had told him that victory in the war would go to the Romans. The senate believed his story and voted that a Victory temple should be built for the goddess; but when Bataces appeared before the assembly of the People and wished to tell them about it, one of the tribunes, Aulus Pompeius by name, refused to allow him and, calling him an impostor, pulled him ignominiously down from the platform.[30] It was an action which did more than anything else to gain credit for Bataces' story. For, after the assembly was dissolved, Aulus scarcely managed to get home before breaking out into such a violent fever that he died within a week; and this was well known and talked about by everyone.

18. The Teutones meanwhile, seeing that Marius continued to make no move, attempted to take his camp by storm. They were met by showers of missiles hurled down on them from the rampart and, after some losses, decided to march forward, hoping to cross the Alps without opposition. So they packed up their belongings and began to march past the Roman camp. There certainly one could see how enormous their numbers were, both from the length of their column and from the time it took them to go past; for they are said to have marched in a steady stream past the fortifications of Marius for six days on end. They marched close by the camp, asking the Romans, with

shouts of laughter, whether they had any messages for their wives, 'For', they said, 'we shall soon be with them.'

Once the natives had passed by and began to move forward Marius also broke camp and followed after them, never losing contact with them and always halting close beside them, but fortifying his camps strongly and keeping difficult ground between himself and the enemy, so as to be able to pass the night in safety. So they went on until they reached a place called Aquae Sextiae.[31] From here a short march would take them into the Alps, and here Marius prepared to give battle.

He chose a place for his camp which was strong enough, but not very well supplied with water. This, they say, he did deliberately so as to encourage his soldiers to fight. Certainly when there were many complaints from people saying that they would be thirsty, Marius pointed to a river running close by the native encampment and said: 'There is some drinking water for you, but you will have to pay for it with blood.' 'Why, then,' they said, 'don't you lead us against them at once, before our blood dries up?' To which he replied in a mild voice: 'First we must fortify the camp.'

19. The soldiers obeyed his orders, though reluctantly. But the great crowd of camp-followers, who had no water either for themselves or their animals, went down to the river in a body with their water-jars, carrying hatchets, axes and even swords and spears, determined to get water even if they had to fight for it. Only a few of the enemy came out against them at first. The majority were enjoying a meal after bathing and some were still bathing. For the place is full of hot springs and by these springs the Romans surprised a considerable number of the natives, who were feasting and enjoying themselves in the novelty of their pleasant surroundings. But more of the natives came running up when they heard the shouting, and Marius found it difficult to restrain his soldiers who were worried about the safety of their servants. Now too the most warlike division of the enemy, the Ambrones, had sprung up from their meal and were hurrying to arms. It was they who had previously defeated

the Roman armies under Manlius and Caepio.[32] There were more than thirty thousand of them.

These Ambrones, though their bodies were gorged with food and their minds disturbed and intoxicated with strong drink, did not come rushing on in any frantic or disorderly manner; nor was there anything inarticulate about their battle cry. They came forward clashing their arms together rhythmically, and all leaping up together in the air, often shouting in unison their name 'Ambrones! Ambrones!', either as an encouragement to themselves or to strike terror into the enemy by making themselves known. The first of the Italians to go down against them were the Ligurians, and when they heard and understood what the enemy were shouting, they too shouted back the same word, as it was a national name of their own and the Ligurians claim to be Ambrones by ancestry. So before they came to close quarters the shouting swung backwards and forwards between the two sides, and the armies on each side took up the cry in turns, each being ambitious to shout down the others, and the effect of all this din was to rouse and infuriate the fighting spirit of the combatants.

The river cut the Ambrones into two divisions. Before they could form up on the other side of it the Ligurians had quickly rushed down on those who had been the first to cross and had engaged them at close quarters. Then the Romans came to the aid of the Ligurians and, charging down on the natives from the higher ground, forced them back and routed them. Most of them, herded and jostled together in the stream, were cut down on the spot and the river was filled with their blood and with the bodies of their dead. The Romans then crossed over and, finding that the enemy would not stand up to them, went on killing them as they fled right up to their camp and their wagons. Here the women came out against them, armed with swords and axes and making the most horrible shrieking, and tried to drive back both the pursuers and the pursued – the former as their enemies, the latter as men who had betrayed them. They threw themselves into the thick of the fighting, tearing at the Romans' shields with their bare hands or clutching at their swords, and, though their bodies were gashed and wounded, they endured it to the end with unbroken spirits. It seems, then, that the battle by the river took place rather by accident than by the design of the general.

20. After killing great numbers of the Ambrones the Romans withdrew and night fell. They had had a great success, but there were no songs of victory in the camp, no drinking in the tents, or cheerful conversation over dinner or – what is the best thing of all after winning a battle – untroubled sleep. Instead they passed a night that was, more than any other, full of fear and confusion. For their camp had no stockade or wall; there were still thousands upon thousands of the barbarians who were undefeated and who had been joined by the survivors of the Ambrones; and from this huge host all through the night there arose and echoed among the mountains and over the river valley a cry of lamentation – not a cry that sounded like the wailing and mourning of human beings, but something which, while expressing imprecations, menaces and complaints, was more like the howling of wild animals. As the awful noise filled the whole plain, so were the Romans filled with terror and Marius himself was afraid as he awaited some disorganized and tumultuous night attack. However, they made no attack that night or on the following day. Instead they spent the time in reorganizing their forces and making ready for battle.

Meanwhile Marius had not been inactive. On the far side of the position occupied by the natives there were some steep wooded glens and valleys where the trees afforded good cover. Here he sent Claudius Marcellus[33] with 3,000 regular infantry and ordered him to lie there in ambush until the fighting began and then to show himself in the enemy's rear. The rest of the soldiers had their supper at the proper time and then a good night's sleep. At dawn Marius led them out and formed them up in front of the camp, sending a cavalry screen down into the plain. At the sight of this the Teutones could not restrain themselves and wait until the Romans should come down and fight with them on equal terms. Instead they hurriedly armed themselves and charged furiously up the hill. Marius sent

officers all along the line ordering the soldiers to stand firm and
keep their ground, to hurl their javelins when the enemy came
into range, and then to draw their swords and force them
backwards with their shields. He pointed out that the enemy
were on difficult ground and that their blows would have
no force, nor would there be any weight behind their locked
shields, since the unevenness of the ground would prevent them
from standing firmly together in a continuous line. He was
visible himself in the front rank, putting into practice the advice
which he had given, for he was in as good training as anyone
and in daring he far surpassed them all.

21. So the Romans awaited the enemy's attack, then joined
with them and checked them as they charged uphill, and then
little by little forced them backwards down into the plain. Here,
just as the natives in the front were beginning to form their line
on level ground, there arose shouting and commotion in the
rear. Marcellus had not missed his opportunity. As soon as the
sounds of battle had come to him over the hills, he had brought
his men up at the double and with great shouting had fallen on
the enemy's rear, cutting down the hindmost. These, being
forced into those in front of them, quickly threw the whole
army into confusion. Exposed to attack from two directions
their resistance soon gave way and they broke line and fled. In
the pursuit the Romans killed or captured more than a hundred
thousand of them, and seized their tents, their wagons and their
property. All of this, apart from what had been looted by
individuals, was given to Marius by a vote of the soldiers. It was
indeed a splendid gift; yet, considering how great the danger had
been, it was generally thought to be less than his generalship
had deserved.

Other authors give different accounts both of the division
of the spoils and of the numbers killed. None the less it is said
that the people of Marseilles fenced their vineyards round with
the bones and that the soil where the dead bodies, soaked in
the rain which fell throughout the winter, had rotted away was
fertilized to a considerable depth by the putrefied matter and
became so rich that it yielded in future years quite extraordinary

harvests, thus justifying the saying of Archilochus that 'in such ways the fields are fattened'.

It is said too that it is a fairly general rule for there to be excessive rainfall after great battles. It may be that some supernatural power hallows and cleanses the earth with pure water from above; or it may be that the blood and rotting flesh send up moist and heavy vapours which cause condensation in the air, which is a most variable element and can undergo the greatest alterations for the slightest reasons.

22. After the battle Marius set aside from the arms and the spoil taken from the barbarians the pieces that were most remarkable and undamaged and capable of making a show in his triumph. The rest he heaped on to a huge pyre and then made a magnificent sacrifice. The army stood all round under arms and with garlands on their heads; Marius himself, wearing the purple-bordered robe that was customary on these occasions, had taken a lighted torch and, after holding it up in both his hands to heaven, was just about to set fire to the pyre with it, when some friends of his were seen coming rapidly towards him on horseback. There was silence all round as everyone waited to see what the news was. And when the horsemen drew near, they leaped to the ground and greeted Marius with the good tidings that he had been elected consul for the fifth time[34] and gave him letters to confirm the news. With this great joy coming on top of their victory celebrations, the soldiers showed their delight by raising a great shout and clashing their arms together. The officers crowned Marius again with a wreath of laurel and he then set fire to the pyre and completed the sacrifice.

23. However, there is something (you may call it Fortune, or Nemesis, or natural necessity) which prevents the enjoyment of any great success from ever being pure and unalloyed, and diversifies human life by blending good and evil together. Thus within a few days Marius received news of his colleague Catulus, which, like a cloud in a clear calm sky, once more enveloped Rome in another tempest of apprehension.

Catulus, who was facing the Cimbri, had decided against making an attempt to hold the Alpine passes, fearing that he would be too much weakened by having to disperse his forces. He had marched down directly into the Italian plain and placed his army behind the River Adige. He had occupied the river crossings, putting up strong fortifications on both banks, and had built a bridge, so that he could come to the help of his men on the further bank if the barbarians should come down through the passes and attack the forts. As for the barbarians they were so full of confidence in themselves and of contempt for their enemies that they went out of the way to give, quite unnecessarily, exhibitions of their strength and daring. They went naked through snowstorms, climbed to the summits of the mountains through the ice and snow drifts, and from there came tobogganing down on their broad shields, sliding over the slippery slopes and the deep crevasses.

When they had made their camp near the river and had examined the crossing place, they began to dam it up, tearing down the hills all round, like the giants in the old stories. They carried down to the river whole trees, roots and all, great fragments of cliff and mounds of earth, blocking up its course. And they floated down the stream against the piles of the bridge heavy masses of material which made the whole bridge quiver under their blows. Finally the greater part of the Roman soldiers lost courage, abandoned their main camp and began to retreat.

It was now that Catulus behaved like a really great commander and showed that he put the reputation of his countrymen above his own. He had failed to induce his soldiers to stand their ground and saw them running off in terror. He then ordered the standard to be taken up and ran forward so as to put himself at the head of the fugitives, wishing that the disgrace should be his and not Rome's, and that the soldiers should appear to be not running away, but retreating under the leadership of their general.

The barbarians then attacked and captured the fort on the other side of the Adige. They so much admired the conduct of the Romans who were defending it and who put up a fine resistance, fighting worthily for their country, that they let them

go on parole, after making them take an oath on their bronze
bull. This bull was subsequently captured after the battle. They
say that it was brought to Catulus' house, as the chief trophy
of the victory. But now the country was without defenders, and
they poured over it and ravaged it.

24. It was to meet this situation that Marius was recalled to
Rome. When he arrived there, everyone expected that he would
celebrate the triumph which had been decreed to him by a most
enthusiastic vote of the senate. However, he refused to do
so, either because he did not wish to deprive his soldiers and
comrades-in-arms of their share in the honour, or with the
intention of increasing public confidence at this crisis by showing that he was, as it were, investing all the glory of his first
victory with the Fortune of Rome, in the hope that, after a
second victory, it would be returned to him with interest. So,
after having said what was required of him by the situation,
he set out to join Catulus and to raise his spirits. Meanwhile he
had sent for his own army from Gaul, and, when it arrived, he
crossed the Po and attempted to keep the barbarians from
advancing into that part of Italy which is south of the river.
They, however, refused a decisive engagement. They claimed
that they were waiting for the Teutones to arrive and were
surprised that they were so long in coming. Perhaps they were
really ignorant of their fate, or perhaps they merely wanted to
give the impression that they did not believe it. Certainly they
gave very rough treatment to anyone who brought them news
of it and they kept on sending messengers to Marius asking him
to give them land both for themselves and for their brethren
together with a sufficient number of cities for them to settle in.
When Marius asked their ambassadors whom they meant by
'their brethren', they replied 'the Teutones'. At this the Romans
began to laugh and Marius sarcastically remarked: 'Never mind
about your brethren. We have given them land enough and it
will be theirs for ever.'

The ambassadors saw what he meant and turned on him in
fury. 'You will be made to pay for this,' they said, 'by the
Cimbri now and by the Teutones when they have arrived.'

'But they are here now,' Marius replied, 'and it would not be at all right for you to go away before greeting your brethren.' And with these words he ordered the Kings of the Teutones to be brought forward in chains. (They had fled into the Alps and had been captured by the Sequani.)

25. When the Cimbri heard of this they again marched against Marius, who stayed behind the fortifications of his camp without making a move.

They say that it was in preparation for this coming battle that Marius first altered the construction of the javelin. Before this time the shaft was fastened into the iron head by two nails of iron; now Marius, leaving one of these nails as it was, removed the other and put in its place a weak wooden pin, the idea being that on impact with the enemy's shield the wooden pin would break and, instead of the javelin sticking straight out, the shaft would twist sideways and trail down, though still held in place by the twist in the point.[35]

Now Boeorix, the King of the Cimbri, rode out with a small body of cavalry to the Roman camp and challenged Marius to fix a day and a place and then to come out and fight for the ownership of the country.

Marius replied that it had never been the Roman way to consult enemies about when and where to fight; however, on this occasion, he was willing to do them a favour. And so they decided that the day should be the third day following and the place should be the plain of Vercellae, which was suitable ground for the Roman cavalry and spacious enough for the Cimbri to deploy their full force of numbers.

So they waited for the appointed time and then drew up their armies for battle. Catulus had 20,300 men under his command and Marius had 32,000. According to the account of Sulla, who fought in this battle, the troops of Marius were divided between the two wings, with those of Catulus in the centre. Sulla goes on to say that Marius had expected the main brunt of the fighting would be on the two wings, since in very long battle lines the centre usually tends to fall back, and that he had arranged the forces in this way so that the whole credit for the victory should go to himself and his soldiers, leaving no share of it to Catulus who would not even be engaged. Catulus too, we are told, in his defence of his conduct in the battle, said much the same thing and accused Marius of having acted towards him in bad faith.

Now the infantry of the Cimbri began to move slowly forward from behind their fortifications. They marched in a square, each side of which was thirty furlongs in extent. Their cavalry, 15,000 in number, were a splendid sight as they came riding out. They wore helmets like the heads and gaping jaws of terrible wild beasts and other strange creatures, and these, heightened with great feather plumes, made them look even taller than they were. They had iron breastplates and shining white shields. Each man carried two javelins for throwing, and for fighting at close quarters they used large heavy swords.[36]

26. Instead of charging the Roman line directly in front, the cavalry moved away to the right, trying to draw the Romans gradually in that direction so as to get them between themselves and their infantry, who were drawn up on their left. The Roman generals saw the purpose of this manoeuvre, but were not in time to hold their soldiers back. As soon as one soldier had shouted out: 'They are running away,' all the rest rushed forward in pursuit. And now the barbarian infantry came sweeping on like a great ocean on the move. Marius then washed his hands and, lifting them up to heaven, vowed to the gods a sacrifice of a hundred beasts. Catulus too raised his hands to heaven and vowed that he would consecrate a temple to the 'Fortune of that day'. They say also that when Marius was sacrificing and had been shown the victims he cried out with a loud voice: 'The victory is mine.'

However, according to the accounts of Sulla and his friends, once the troops had moved into action, Marius underwent an experience which seems to indicate that heaven was displeased with him. As was to be expected, a huge cloud of dust was raised and enveloped the two armies. Marius, when he first led his men into the attack, missed the enemy altogether, passed right by their line and for some time moved about the plain without making contact with them. Meanwhile, as chance would have it, the barbarians all bore down on Catulus, so that he and his soldiers, among whom Sulla says that he himself was stationed, bore the brunt of the fighting. Sulla adds that important factors on the Roman side were the heat and the sun which was shining full into the faces of the Cimbri. They were quite remarkable in their ability to endure cold since, as I have said, they had been brought up in ice-bound countries full of forests. But now they were quite disheartened by the heat; they were covered in sweat and found it hard to breathe and tried to ward off the heat from their faces with their shields. (The battle was fought after the summer solstice which, by Roman reckoning, is three days before the new moon of the month now called August, but then Sextilis.) The dust cloud also, by hiding the enemy, helped to improve morale among the Romans. Instead of seeing the whole great mass from a distance they ran forward and had engaged in battle with those immediately opposed to them before the sight of the enormous host could strike terror into them. And they were so tough and well trained that not a single Roman was seen to be short of breath or sweating, in spite of the stifling heat and of the fact that they had come into action at the double. This, they say, is what Catulus wrote himself in commendation of his soldiers.

27. In this engagement the greater part of the enemy and their best warriors were cut to pieces; for in order to preserve an unbroken line those who were fighting in the front ranks were fastened together by long chains which were passed through their belts. Those who fled were driven back to their fortifications by the Romans, who then were confronted by a most appalling sight. For the women, all dressed in black, stood on the wagons and killed the fugitives – their husbands, their brothers, their fathers; then they strangled their little children with their own hands, hurling them down under the wheels of the wagons or the feet of the animals; and finally they cut their own throats. There was one woman, they say, who hung herself from the end of a wagon pole with a child dangling from each ankle; and the men, for lack of trees, tied themselves by

the neck to the horns or feet of the oxen and then drove the animals forward with goads so that they were either dragged or trampled to death. Yet in spite of this mass suicide more than 60,000 prisoners were taken. Twice as many as this were said to have been killed.

The enemy's personal possessions fell into the hands of Marius' soldiers, but the spoils of battle, the standards and trumpets were brought, they say, to the camp of Catulus – which was the main argument used by Catulus to prove that it was he who deserved the credit for the victory. It was a point which, as was natural, was angrily debated by the soldiers as well, and some representatives of the city of Parma who were present at the time were chosen to act as arbitrators. They were taken by the soldiers of Catulus to inspect the dead bodies of the enemy, who had clearly been pierced by their javelins. These could be recognized through having the name of Catulus cut into the shafts. In spite of this, however, the whole credit for the action went to Marius because of his former victory and his superior rank as consul. And the people in particular gave him the title of the third founder of Rome; he had saved the city, they said, from a danger just as great as had been the invasion of the Gauls; in their own homes, when they celebrated the occasion with their wives and children, they would always make their offerings and libations in honour of 'the gods and Marius'; and they thought that he, and he alone, should celebrate both triumphs. Marius, however, did not do this. He shared his triumph with Catulus, wishing to show that he could behave with moderation even in the midst of such great good fortune. Though it is also probable that he was afraid of the soldiers who were under arms and quite prepared, if Catulus was deprived of his triumph, not to allow Marius to triumph either.

28. He was now coming to the end of the period of his fifth consulship, but he set his heart on a sixth with all or more than the enthusiasm of a man standing for election for the first time. He did everything to win popular support, ingratiating himself with the common people and giving in to them. In so doing he was not only lowering the standard of his high office but doing

violence to his own nature; for he wanted to be a soft and subtle demagogue, whereas by nature he was nothing of the kind. Indeed in any political situation where he was confronted with heckling from the crowd he used to behave quite timidly, so careful was he of his own reputation; and all the steadfastness and firmness which he showed in battle forsook him when he stood in a popular assembly, so that he was put out of countenance by the most ordinary expressions of praise or blame. There was, it is true, an occasion when, after he had granted the rights of citizenship to as many as a thousand men of Camerinum for their gallantry in the war and, his action being considered illegal, he was called to account for it, he is said to have replied that the din of warfare had drowned the voice of the law.[37] All the same he seemed to find the shouting at public meetings more dreadful and terrible than that. In war his great reputation and supreme power came to him because he was needed; in civilian life his supremacy was restricted and so he resorted to attempts to win the goodwill of the mob, not minding so much whether he was the best man so long as he could be the greatest. Of course he came into conflict with all the nobility, but the man whom he feared particularly was Metellus, who had been treated by him with ingratitude and who because of his genuine good qualities was naturally opposed to those who used dishonourable methods in their approach to the masses, and sought to win power by giving pleasure. Marius therefore schemed to have Metellus exiled.[38] With this end in view he allied himself with Glaucia and Saturninus, most dangerous agitators who controlled a great mob of impoverished and unruly characters, and he brought forward a number of laws through their agency. He also stirred up feeling in the army, got the soldiers to join in the public assemblies, and so organized a party to oppose and to overwhelm Metellus. According to the account of Rutilius (a good man with a keen sense of truth, though certainly he had a private quarrel with Marius),[39] this sixth consulship of his, which he obtained, came as the result of distributing large sums among the voters, and bribing people not to elect Metellus but instead to give him as a colleague Valerius Flaccus, who acted more like a servant than as a fellow

consul.[40] However, the people had never before elected one
man to so many consulships. The only exception is Corvinus
Valerius[41] and in his case there were forty-five years between
his first and last tenure of the office, while Marius, once elected
for the first time, ran through five more consulships without a
break.

29. It was in this sixth consulship that he made himself particularly hated because of his share in many of the crimes of
Saturninus and his party. Among these crimes was the murder
of Nonius, assassinated by Saturninus because he stood against
him in the election to the tribuneship.[42] As tribune Saturninus
brought forward his law for the distribution of land, adding to
the law a clause that the senate should publicly swear an oath
to abide by the people's vote and not oppose it in any way.[43] In
the senate Marius professed to be opposed to this section of the
law; he said that he himself would not take the oath and that,
in his view, no sensible man would take it; for even if there
were nothing wrong with the law, it was still an affront to the
senate to have to show its approval under constraint instead of
voluntarily and in response to persuasion. He said this, not
because it was what he thought, but in order to put Metellus
into a position from which there was no way out. He personally
regarded lying as a mark of ability and a sign of cleverness; his
undertakings to the senate meant nothing to him and he had
no intention of abiding by them; but he knew that Metellus was
a man of principle who believed, as Pindar says, that 'all heroic
virtue rests on truth', and so he wanted to get him to commit
himself beforehand by stating in front of the senate that he
would not take the oath and then, when he did refuse to take
it, to bring down upon him the inexorable hatred of the people.
     And this indeed was what happened. After Metellus had
stated that he would not take the oath, the meeting of the senate
ended. Then after a few days Saturninus summoned the senators
to his tribune's platform for them to take the oath under compulsion. There was total silence as Marius came forward and
everyone hung upon his words. As for Marius he went right
back upon those admirable sentiments which he, or rather his

voice, had expressed in the senate. He now said that he had not such a big mouth that he could pronounce an opinion once and for all on this very important subject; for his part he would take the oath and submit to the law – if it really was a law. (This final piece of sophistry was put in to cover the infamy of his behaviour.)

At this there was great applause from the people who were delighted to find him taking the oath; but the nobility were utterly dejected and hated Marius for his change of front. So, through fear of the people, they all took the oath in order until it came to the turn of Metellus. His friends most urgently entreated him to take it and not to put himself in the hopeless position of incurring the penalties proposed by Saturninus for those who refused. But Metellus stuck to his resolution and refused to swear the oath, being true to his principles, and prepared to suffer any evil rather than to act dishonourably. As he left the forum he said to those who were with him: 'It is certainly sordid to do the wrong thing, and anyone can do the right thing when there is no danger attached; what distinguishes the good man from others is that when danger is involved he still does right.'

Saturninus then had it voted that the consuls should proclaim that Metellus was debarred from fire, water and shelter. And the more disreputable elements of the people were quite ready to kill him. However, the better sort of people were on his side and hurried round him to support him. But Metellus would not allow any civil disturbance to break out on his account. With the following sensible reflection he left Rome. 'Either', he said, 'things will get better, the people will change their minds and I shall return at their invitation; or else things will remain as they are; and in that case it is better for me to be away.' In his exile, which he spent at Rhodes in the study of philosophy, he was greatly honoured and esteemed. All this will be more appropriately described in my 'Life' of him.[44]

30. Saturninus, in his reckless thirst for power, now proceeded to go to all lengths and Marius, in return for the service he had done him, was compelled to look on. So, without meaning to

do so, he became the instrument of quite intolerable forces which, by means of civil war and assassination, were leading directly towards dictatorship and the subversion of the constitution. Having a certain respect for the nobility but being at the same time anxious to have the favour of the people, he was led to perform an action that was thoroughly undignified and dishonest. When some of the leading men had come to him by night in an attempt to make him take a stand against Saturninus, without their knowledge he brought Saturninus into the house by another door. Then, pretending to both parties that he was suffering from diarrhoea, he kept running from one end of the house to the other, speaking now to the nobles and now to Saturninus, exacerbating feelings on both sides and making mischief between them.

However, when the senators and the propertied classes joined together to express their indignation at the way things were going, he did bring his troops into the forum, and, after driving the rebels to take refuge on the Capitol Hill, forced them to capitulate for lack of water.[45] They gave up hope once he had cut off their water supply and, calling for Marius in person, they surrendered on the terms known as 'the public faith'.[46] Marius certainly did everything he could to preserve the men's lives, but it was of no use. They were slaughtered as they came down into the forum. As a result he was equally disliked both by the nobility and by the people. When the next election for the censorship came he did not stand for the office as he was expected to do. Instead he allowed other candidates less distinguished than himself to be elected, because he feared that he would be defeated. (Though he tried to put a good face on the affair by saying that he did not want to make himself unpopular with a lot of people by carrying out a strict investigation of their lives and conduct.)

31. When it was officially proposed that Metellus should be recalled from exile, Marius did and said what he could to prevent the proposal being carried.[47] But his efforts were in vain and in the end he had to give them up. The people accepted the proposal with enthusiasm and Marius, not able to bear the

sight of Metellus returning home, set sail for Cappadocia and Galatia.[48] He gave out that he was going to make the sacrifices which he had promised to the Mother of the Gods; but he had another reason for going abroad which was not generally recognized. The fact is that he had no aptitude for peace and civilian life; he had grown great through warfare and believed that now his power and his reputation were gradually fading away while he remained unemployed and inactive; so he was looking for something which might lead to a critical situation.

What he hoped was to make trouble among the kings of Asia, and, in particular, to goad on Mithridates, who was thought to be on the point of making war on Rome; he would then immediately be given the command against him and would be able to delight Rome with the spectacle of more triumphs and to fill his own house with the spoils of Pontus and with the wealth of kings. It was for this reason that, when Mithridates treated him with the greatest politeness and respect, he refused to be mollified in any way, and simply remarked: 'King, either try to be stronger than the Romans, or else keep quiet and do what you are told.' Mithridates was staggered by the words. He had often heard the Roman language before, but had never heard it used with such freedom.

32. When Marius returned to Rome he had a house built for himself near the forum. He chose this position either because, as he said himself, he wished to spare those who came to pay their respects to him the trouble of a long walk, or because he thought that it was merely because of the distance involved that he did not have larger crowds at his doors than anybody else did. This, of course, was not so at all. The real reason was that he lacked the abilities which others had of making themselves pleasant socially and useful politically; so he was left on the side, like military material in peace time.

He disliked all who outshone him, but the particular object of his hatred was Sulla, who had become a person of importance because of the jealousy which the nobility felt towards Marius, and who had made his quarrel with Marius the first principle of his political life. So when Bocchus the Numidian had been

given the title of 'ally of the Romans' and had dedicated on the
Capitol some statues of Victory with trophies and alongside
them gilded figures representing Jugurtha being surrendered by
him to Sulla, Marius nearly went out of his mind with rage
and jealous anger at the idea of Sulla stealing the glory of his
achievements, and he was planning to have the statues forcibly
removed. Sulla on his side was just as angry, and the conflict
between the two of them was on the point of taking the form
of open violence when this was prevented by the sudden outbreak of war between Rome and her Italian allies.[49] In this
war the strongest and most populous races of Italy combined
together against Rome and very nearly put an end to Roman
supremacy. They were well supplied with arms and with men;
their generals were amazingly daring and intelligent and quite
a match for the Romans.

33. The events of this war were complicated and its fortunes
constantly changing, but in the course of it what Sulla gained
Marius lost in power and in reputation. He was thought to be
lacking in initiative, timid and unenterprising, whether because
the energy and fire that he used to have had been quenched by
age (he was now over sixty-five) or, as he said himself, because,
though physically unfit and suffering from a muscular com-
plaint, he still, from a sense of shame, stood up to the hardships
of a campaign that was beyond his strength. Yet in spite of this
he won a great victory in which he destroyed 6,000 of the
enemy. Nor did he ever allow the enemy to get a hold over him.
Even when he was surrounded by their entrenchments he bided
his time, quite unmoved by challenges or by insults. They say
that once Publius Silo,[50] the most powerful of the enemy commanders and the one with the greatest reputation, said to him:
'If you really are a great general, Marius, come down and fight
it out.' To which Marius replied: 'If you are a great general,
make me fight against my will.' And there was another occasion
when the enemy had given him an opportunity to attack but
the Romans had shrunk from going into action and both sides
had withdrawn. Marius then called an assembly of the soldiers
and said: 'I don't know whom I should call the greater cowards,

you or the enemy. You couldn't stand up to the sight of their backs, and they were frightened by the napes of your necks.'

In the end he gave up his command on grounds of ill health.

34. Later, when finally the Italians had given in, there was much rivalry at Rome for obtaining the command in the war against Mithridates.[51] Claims were canvassed by means of the popular leaders, and, to everyone's surprise, the tribune Sulpicius, a most violent character, brought Marius forward and proposed that he should have the command with the rank of pro-consul.[52] The people themselves were divided. Some supported the claim of Marius; others were in favour of Sulla and said that Marius ought to go and take the warm baths at Baiae and look after his health, since, according to his own account, he was worn out with old age and catarrhs. For at Baiae near Cape Misenum Marius had an extremely expensive house, luxuriously furnished, where he used to live in a style that seemed too effeminate for a man who had played an active part in such great wars and campaigns. It is said that this house was bought by Cornelia for 75,000 drachmas. Not long afterwards Lucius Lucullus purchased it for 2,500,000, so rapid was the rise in prices and so greatly did the tendency towards luxury increase. Marius, however, showed himself just as eager for distinction as if he were a young man. He shook off the burden of his age and ill health and went down every day to the Field of Mars, where he engaged in athletic exercises with the young men. Here he showed himself to be still quick and expert in the use of his weapons and a fine horseman, though in old age he was too bulky to look elegant, and had put on excessive weight.

These performances of his gave pleasure to some people, who would go down and watch him competing keenly in athletic contests; but the best people were moved to pity by the sight of his greed and ambition. He had risen from poverty to enormous wealth, from obscurity to greatness; yet he could put no limit to his own good fortune; instead of being content with being admired and quietly enjoying what he had, here he was, after all his triumphs and the fame he had won, acting as though he still had everything to gain and setting out, at his age, for

Cappadocia and the Euxine Sea to fight in battle with Archelaus and Neoptolemus, the satraps of Mithridates. And the excuse which Marius offered for this behaviour was considered quite ridiculous; he said that he wanted to be there himself in order to see that his son got the right military training.

35. Rome had long been suffering from a hidden disease. Now the disease came to a head; for in the violent character of Sulpicius Marius had found just the right instrument for bringing the whole state to ruin. Sulpicius was in most respects an admirer and imitator of Saturninus; except that he blamed him for having been too timid and hesitant in his political actions. He himself, avoiding such defects, went about with a bodyguard of 600 men from the propertied classes outside the senate and called them his 'anti-senate'; he made an armed attack on the consuls when they were holding an assembly, and when one of them fled from the forum, Sulpicius had his son seized and killed.[53] Sulla, the other consul, as he was being chased past the house of Marius, did what no one could have expected and rushed inside, thus escaping his pursuers who ran on past the house; and it is said that he was let out safely from another door by Marius himself and so slipped out of the city and reached his camp. But Sulla himself in his Memoirs denies that he fled to the house of Marius. He says that he just withdrew there in order to discuss with Marius the measures which Sulpicius was trying to compel him to take; that Sulpicius had surrounded him with a circle of drawn swords and was forcing him towards Marius' house; and that finally he went from there to the forum, and, as Sulpicius and his party had demanded, cancelled the decree for the suspension of public business.

Sulpicius was now in control and, by a vote of the people, had the command against Mithridates conferred on Marius. Marius began to make his preparations for setting out and sent two military tribunes to take over the army from Sulla. But Sulla worked on his soldiers' minds (he had at least 35,000 regular infantry) and led them against Rome.[54] First they fell on the tribunes whom Marius had sent and killed them.

Marius also put to death a number of Sulla's friends in Rome and made an offer of freedom to slaves if they would join him. Only three of these, it is said, came forward. He put up a brief resistance as Sulla entered the city, but was soon driven out and took to flight.

As soon as he had left the city his followers scattered in different directions and, as it was dark, he took refuge on one of his country estates called Solonium. He sent his son to get provisions from some farms in the neighbourhood which belonged to his father-in-law Mucius, while he himself went down to the coast at Ostia, where a friend of his, Numerius, had a ship ready for him. Then, without waiting for his son, he took with him his step-son Granius and set sail.

Meanwhile young Marius came to Mucius' farms. It was day before he had finished packing up the supplies and he had not entirely shaken off the enemy, as could be seen when a party of cavalry rode up to the place, evidently suspecting something. But the farm bailiff saw them coming and hid Marius in a cart-load of beans. He then yoked the oxen and drove the cart past the cavalry whom he met on the way to Rome. So Marius reached his wife's house, took from there what he needed, and at night went down to the sea. Here he boarded a ship bound for Africa and made the crossing safely.

36. His father, after having put to sea, was carried along the Italian coast by a following wind. But he was afraid of a man called Geminius, one of the leading people in Terracina, and so told the sailors to keep clear of Terracina. They were willing enough to do as he asked, but the wind veered and began to blow from the open sea, bringing in great waves, so that it looked as though the ship could not weather out the storm; Marius also was suffering badly from seasickness. So they made for land and, with great difficulty, reached the coast near Circeii.

As the storm was increasing and their food was giving out, they left the ship and came to land. Here they wandered about with no aim in view but behaving as people usually do when they are at their wits' end – always trying to escape from the present evil as though it were the greatest and resting their hopes on uncertainties. The land was their enemy and so was the sea; they were frightened of meeting anyone and, because of their lack of food, they were frightened of not meeting anyone. Late in the day, however, they came across a few herdsmen. These men had nothing to give them to satisfy their hunger, but they recognized Marius and told him to go away as quickly as possible, since numbers of cavalry had been seen there only a little time ago ranging over the country in search of him.

Marius was now in the most extreme perplexity and what made matters worse was that his companions were in a state of exhaustion from lack of food. So for the time being he turned off the road and plunged into a deep wood where he passed a night that was disagreeable enough. Next day, pushed on by hunger and wishing to make some use of his strength before it left him altogether, he went forward along the shore, trying to put some heart into his companions and begging them not to give in yet. Let them wait, he said, for his final hope to be fulfilled; it was a hope which kept him going, since he trusted firmly in some predictions that had been made a long time ago. For when he was only a boy and was still living in the country, he had caught in his cloak an eagle's nest, with seven eaglets in it, as it was falling; his parents had been amazed at the sight and had consulted the prophets; and the prophets had declared that he would be the greatest man in the world and was fated seven times to hold the supreme power and authority.

Some say that this really did happen to Marius. Others say that the story is a complete myth, but was reported by those who believed in it when they heard it from Marius on this occasion and at other times during his exile. For, they say, the eagle never lays more than two eggs, and even Musaeus was wrong when, speaking of the eagle, he says:

'Three she lays and two she hatches; only one of these she rears.'

However, it is generally admitted that in the times of extreme danger during his exile Marius used often to say that he would attain a seventh consulship.

37. Now they were already within three or four miles of the Italian city of Minturnae when they saw in the distance a squadron of cavalry bearing down on them. At the same time by chance two merchant ships came in sight sailing along the shore. So, summoning up what strength they had, they ran as fast as they could to the sea, threw themselves into the water and began to swim out to the ships. Granius and his party reached one of them and crossed over to the island opposite, Aenaria. Marius, because of his weight and bulk, had to be supported by two slaves who, with great trouble and difficulty, kept his head above the water and got him aboard the other ship.

By this time the cavalry had reached the shore. They shouted out to the sailors either to bring their ship in or to throw Marius overboard and then sail where they pleased. Meanwhile Marius, with the tears running down his face, begged them to save him, and the masters of the ship, after they had gone through several changes of mind in a short space of time, finally told the cavalry that they would not give Marius up. The cavalry then angrily rode away.

But now the sailors began to think differently once again. They put in towards the shore and anchored at the mouth of the Liris where the river overflows its banks and forms a marsh. Here they suggested to Marius that he should disembark so that he could take some food on land and regain his strength after his hardships while they were waiting for good sailing weather. This, they said, could be depended on at the usual time, when the wind from the sea died down and a stiffish breeze began to blow from the marshes. Marius followed their advice and the sailors brought him ashore, where he lay down to rest in a grassy place, with no suspicion at all of what was to happen next. The sailors then went back to their ship, weighed anchor immediately, and made off. It was not honourable, they thought, to surrender Marius, but it was not safe to keep him.

Marius was now deserted by everyone. For a long time he lay on the shore speechless. Finally he pulled himself together and with great difficulty went forward with no kind of path to guide him. Making his way through deep marshes and ditches full of mud and water, he came upon the hut of an old man who worked in the fens. Marius fell down at his feet and begged him to save and preserve one who, if only he escaped his present danger, would reward him beyond all his hopes. The old man had either known Marius in the past or else recognized in his face something which showed his greatness. He told him that, if he wanted to rest, then his cottage would be the best place; but if he were trying to escape from pursuers, he would hide him somewhere more out of the way. Marius begged him to do so and the old man took him into the marsh and told him to crouch down in a hollow by the river bank. He put on top of him a lot of reeds and sticks, enough to cover him and not heavy enough to hurt him.

38. Before long, however, he heard from the hut the noise of some kind of disturbance. What had happened was that Geminius had sent out from Terracina a number of men to search for him, and some of these, coming by chance to the hut, were now terrifying the old man and shouting at him for having harboured and hidden a public enemy. So Marius got out of his hiding place, took off his clothes and plunged into the thick muddy water of the marsh. Yet even here he could not escape his pursuers. He was dragged out all covered in mud, taken naked to Minturnae and handed over to the local magistrates. By this time every city had received instructions that a public search should be made for Marius and that whoever captured him should put him to death. Nevertheless the magistrates decided to discuss the matter first. So they placed Marius under arrest in the house of a woman called Fannia.

This Fannia was thought to be an enemy of Marius because of an old grievance she had against him. She had been married to a man called Titinnius and, when divorced from him, had demanded to be given back her dowry, which was considerable. Titinnius replied by accusing her of adultery, and the case had come up before Marius during his sixth consulship. In the course of the proceedings it became clear that Fannia had led a dissolute life, but that her husband had known this when he married her and during the long time that he had lived with her. Marius therefore took a severe view of both of them. He ordered the husband to pay back the dowry, and fined the woman four copper coins as a mark of disgrace.[55]

Now, however, Fannia did not behave like a woman who had been wronged. As soon as she saw Marius, far from showing any resentment, she did her best to look after him and tried to encourage him. Marius thanked her for her kindness and told her that he felt quite confident because he had met with a very good omen.

The omen was as follows. When he and his escort had stopped outside Fannia's house, the doors had been opened and a donkey had come running out to drink at a spring near by. This donkey had given one look at Marius full of impudence and jollity and had stopped directly in front of him. It had then given a tremendous bray and gone frisking past him in exultation. From this Marius drew the following conclusion. He maintained that heaven was showing him that his way of escape was by sea rather than by land; for the donkey had left his dry fodder untouched and had turned to the water instead. After he had told Fannia about this, Marius lay down to rest, ordering the door of his room to be closed.

39. Meanwhile the magistrates and town council of Minturnae had been discussing the situation and had decided to put Marius to death without any further delay. No citizen of the town would take on the job of executioner, so a cavalryman, either a Gaul or a Cimbrian (both versions of the story are current) took a sword and went to Marius' room. There was not much light in the part of the room where Marius happened to be lying; in fact it was almost dark and we are told that it seemed to the soldier that the eyes of Marius were darting flames at him and out of the darkness came a great voice: 'My man, do you dare to make an end of Gaius Marius?'

At this the foreigner threw down his sword and rushed straight out of the room. He ran out of doors crying out simply: 'I cannot kill Gaius Marius.'

There was general astonishment, and this soon gave way to pity and a change of heart. People began to reproach themselves for having come to so lawless and so ungrateful a decision about a man who had been the saviour of Italy. It was bad enough, they thought, not to give him positive assistance. 'Let him go,' they said, 'wherever he wishes into exile and meet his fate somewhere else. And let us pray that the gods will not be angry with us for thrusting Marius poor and naked out of our city.'

Such thoughts led to action. They came in a body to the house, pressed round Marius and began to escort him down to the sea. Everyone wanted to do something to help, but though they all made as much haste as they could, yet there was still likely to be some loss of time, since directly on their road to the sea lay a place called the grove of Marica – a place which the people there consider sacred and make it a point of religion that nothing which is carried into the grove can ever be carried out again. To have made a detour round this place would have meant losing much time; but in the end one of the older men cried out and said that if it were a question of saving the life of Marius, no road ought to be considered barred or forbidden. He himself took the initiative by picking up some article which was being carried to the ship and going with it right through the holy place.

40. Thanks to such willingness to help soon all was ready. A ship was provided for Marius by a man called Belaeus, who afterwards commissioned a picture of these events and dedicated it in the temple at the spot where Marius embarked and put to sea.

With the aid of a favourable wind he came by chance to the island of Aenaria where he found Granius and the rest of his friends. With them he set out for Africa, but, owing to shortage of drinking water, they were forced to put in at Erycina in Sicily. Here, as it happened, the Roman quaestor was on the look-out for them. He very nearly captured Marius himself on landing and killed about sixteen of his men who had gone to fetch water. So Marius hurriedly put to sea again and crossed to the island of Meninx where he heard for the first time that his son had got away safely with Cethegus and that they were on their way to Iampsas, the King of Numidia, to ask his help.[56] This news afforded Marius some relief, and he ventured to leave the island and go towards Carthage.

The Roman governor of Africa at this time was Sextilius,[57] a man who in the past had been neither helped nor harmed by Marius. It was expected that pity would induce him to give them some help, but as soon as Marius had landed with a few companions he was met by an officer who stood in front of him and said, 'Marius, the governor Sextilius forbids you to land in Africa. If you disobey him, he says that he will uphold the decrees of the senate and treat you as a public enemy.'

When Marius heard this, grief and indignation made him speechless. For a long time he stood there in silence, glaring at the officer, who finally asked him what he had to say and what answer should he take back to the governor. Marius then groaned aloud and said: 'Tell him that you have seen Gaius Marius sitting as a fugitive among the ruins of Carthage'[58] – thus quite cleverly putting together and comparing the fate of that city with the change in his own fortunes.

Meanwhile Iampsas, the King of Numidia, was playing a double game. He treated young Marius and his companions with every mark of honour, but when they wanted to leave always had some excuse for preventing them. It became clear that in constantly putting off their departure he was up to no good. However, something occurred, quite in the order of nature, which secured their safety. Young Marius was extremely good-looking, and one of the king's concubines was much touched to see him so badly treated. She began by pitying and ended in loving him. At first he declined her advances, but when he saw that this was the only way of escape and that she was moved by real affection rather than a mere desire to gratify her lust, he accepted her kindness; she then helped him to escape and both he and his friends got clear away and succeeded in rejoining his father.

When the father and son had embraced each other, they made their way along the seashore and here they came upon some scorpions fighting. Marius took this to be a bad omen and so they immediately boarded a fishing boat and crossed over to the island of Cercina, not far from the mainland. They had only just put to sea when they saw some cavalry sent by the king riding straight towards the place where they had embarked. So Marius escaped from a danger which, it seems, was as great as any with which he ever met.

41. Now at Rome the news was as follows: Sulla was engaged in fighting with the generals of Mithridates in Boeotia; meanwhile the quarrel between the two consuls had ended in open violence.[59] A battle had taken place in which Octavius had been victorious. Cinna, who had been trying to act like a dictator, had been driven from Rome and Octavius had made Cornelius Merula consul in his place.[60] Cinna had then raised forces from other parts of Italy and was renewing the war against them.

When Marius heard this, he decided to sail for Italy as soon as possible. He took with him some Moorish cavalry from Africa and some refugees from Italy (all together not more than a thousand) and so put to sea. He reached Italy at Telamon in Etruria and as soon as he landed made a proclamation offering freedom to the slaves. Many free men also, farmers and herdsmen of the district, drawn by his fame, came flocking down to the coast, and he persuaded the youngest and strongest of these to join him. So in a few days he got together a considerable force and manned forty ships.

He knew that, while Octavius was a thoroughly reputable character who wanted to hold power strictly in accordance with the laws, Cinna was distrusted by Sulla and was an open enemy of the established constitution. It was Cinna whom he decided to join and to bring his forces over with him. And so he sent a message to him to say that he was ready to obey him in everything as consul. Cinna welcomed the proposal, gave Marius the title of pro-consul and sent him the fasces and the other insignia of office. But Marius said that all these decorations were out of keeping with his own fortunes. He came to meet the consul walking slowly on foot, being now more than seventy years old, dressed in the poorest clothing and with his hair uncut since the day he went into exile. He wished, no doubt, to appear as an object of compassion, and people did pity him; but they noticed at the same time that the fierce expression which was natural to him had become fiercer still; and, downcast though his eyes might be, they still clearly showed a spirit which, so far from being humbled, had been made savage by the change in his condition.

42. After he had greeted Cinna and met the soldiers, he set to work at once and soon altered the whole situation. He began by using his fleet to intercept the ships carrying corn and to plunder the merchants, thus gaining control of the supplies going into Rome. Next he sailed against and captured various cities on the coast; and finally, with the help of treachery from inside, he seized Ostia itself. Here he ravaged the town, killed most of the inhabitants and, by throwing a bridge across the river, completely cut the enemy off from all sea-borne supplies. He then marched on Rome and occupied the Janiculan Hill.

Octavius had allowed things to come to such a pass not so much because he lacked ability as because of his too strict ideas of what was right and wrong, which led him to ruin the general cause by failing to do what was expedient. For instance, he was frequently urged to enlist the slaves under the promise of freedom, but said that he could not possibly give slaves those rights of citizenship which, in obedience to the law, he was withholding from Gaius Marius. And when Metellus (son of the Metellus who had held the command in Africa and had been exiled through the intrigues of Marius)[61] came to Rome and appeared to be a very much better general than Octavius, the soldiers left Octavius and came to him, begging him to take over the command and save the city; they would not only fight, they said, but win, if only they were led efficiently and energetically. But Metellus answered them angrily and told them to go back and report to the consul; upon which they went over to the enemy. And Metellus himself, despairing of the situation, left Rome.

Octavius, however, remained behind. A number of Chaldaean astrologers, professional inspectors of sacrifices and interpreters of the Sibylline books had induced him to believe that all would be well. Here was a man who seems to have been in other respects remarkable among the Romans for his good sense and particularly remarkable for upholding the dignity of the consular office free from fear and favour in accordance with the ancestral laws and customs which he regarded as immutable decrees; yet in this one direction he was unbalanced, spending more of his time with charlatans and soothsayers than with men of political or military distinction. What happened to him was that, before Marius entered Rome, he was dragged down from the public platform in the forum and butchered by men who had been sent on in advance. They say that a Chaldaean document was found on his person after the murder. It was something not very easy to explain – that one of these two famous leaders, Marius, did well through paying attention to prophecies, while the other, Octavius, was destroyed by them.

43. In this state of affairs the senate met and sent a deputation to Cinna and Marius, inviting them to enter the city and begging them to spare the lives of the citizens. Cinna, as consul, received the deputation seated on his chair of office and gave encouraging replies to the senate's representatives. Marius stood beside the consul's chair and, though he did not utter a word, the heavy anger in his face and the grimness of his expression made it clear all the time that, as soon as he could, he was going to fill the city with blood.

When the conference was over, they went on towards Rome. Cinna entered the city with his bodyguard, but Marius stopped at the gates. In his anger he indulged in a kind of sarcasm and announced that he was an exile, one who was debarred by law from entering his own country; if his presence was really required, then another vote must be taken to annul the sentence of banishment; for he personally respected the laws and the city to which he was returning was a free city. So the people were called together, and before more than three or four tribes had voted, he dropped all pretence, gave up this legalistic talk about being an exile, and entered the city with his bodyguard which consisted of a picked band of those slaves who had joined him and whom he called 'Bardyaei'. These men killed many of the citizens at his word and many simply at a nod of his head. Finally they cut down with their swords in front of Marius a senator and an ex-praetor, Ancharius,[62] who had come forward and not been spoken to. And after this whenever anyone greeted Marius and received no word of greeting in return, they took this for a sign and at once slaughtered such people in the streets, so that even his personal friends were full of terror and apprehension when they approached him to offer him their good wishes.

After numbers had been killed, Cinna had had enough of murder; his appetite was blunted. But Marius' rage and thirst for blood increased from day to day as he kept on killing all against whom he had even the remotest suspicion. Every road and every city was full of men pursuing and hunting down those who were trying to escape or who had gone into hiding. And it was made evident that in such a situation as this no security was to be found in the trust that men have in a host or in a friend; for there were few indeed who did not betray those who fled to them for shelter. All the more therefore one should praise and admire the behaviour of the slaves of Cornutus. They hid their master in his house and then put a rope round the neck of one of the numerous dead bodies, hung it up, set a gold ring on its finger and, after showing it to Marius' body-guard, they laid out the corpse and buried it just as if it were the body of Cornutus himself. No one suspected the deception and so Cornutus escaped and, with the help of his slaves, got away safely to Gaul.

44. The orator Marcus Antonius[63] also found a good friend, though this did not save him. The man was poor and a plebeian. Since he had received into his house one of the leading men in Rome he wanted to entertain him as well as he could and sent a slave to an innkeeper in the district to get some wine. As the slave took unusual care in tasting it and then ordered some wine of a better quality, the innkeeper asked him why it was that he was buying the expensive high quality wine instead of the new ordinary kind that he usually bought. The slave, who believed that he was dealing with an old and reliable acquaintance, said quite simply that Marcus Antonius was in hiding at

his master's house and his master was entertaining him. But the
innkeeper was a treacherous corrupt character and, as soon as
the slave had gone away, hurried off himself to find Marius
who was already at supper. When he was brought into his
presence he promised to betray Marcus Antonius to him, and
it is said that at this news Marius cried out aloud and clapped
his hands for joy. He was actually on the point of rising up
from his meal and hurrying round to the place himself, but he
was restrained by his friends and so sent Annius[64] instead with
some soldiers, ordering them to bring him the head of Antonius
as quickly as possible. When they came to the house Annius
stayed at the door while the soldiers climbed the stairs and
entered the room. Once they were face to face with Antonius,
each man tried to get someone else, other than himself, to do
the murder. Indeed it appears that the charm and grace of
Antonius' way of speaking were such that as soon as he began
to talk to them and to beg for his life, no one even dared to
look him in the face; instead they hung down their heads and
all burst into tears. As time was passing, Annius went upstairs,
where he saw Antonius in the middle of his speech and the
soldiers quite dumbfounded and melted by his words. After
cursing them for cowards he ran up to Antonius and with his
own hands cut off his head.

Then there was the case of Lutatius Catulus who had been
Marius' colleague in the consulship and had shared with him
the triumph over the Cimbri. The only answer that Marius
would give to those who pleaded for him and begged that he
should be spared was 'He must die'. So Catulus shut himself in
a room, made a great fire of charcoal and committed suicide by
suffocation.

The sight of headless bodies thrown out on the streets and
trampled underfoot excited not so much pity as a general fear
and trembling. What the people found hardest of all to bear
was the atrocious conduct of the Bardyaei, as they were called.
These men butchered fathers of families in their own homes,
outraged their children and raped their wives. They went about
plundering and murdering, with no check on them at all until
Cinna and Sertorius[65] concerted measures between themselves

and, bringing their troops up while they were asleep in their camp, killed every one of them with volleys of javelins.

45. Meanwhile, to show, as it were, a change in the direction of the wind, news kept on coming in from all sides that Sulla had finished the war with Mithridates, that he had won back the lost provinces, that he was sailing against Italy with a large force. All this produced a very slight respite and intermission of these unspeakable calamities, since people believed that they were now on the brink of war. So Marius was elected consul for the seventh time.[66] He took office on the very first day of January (the beginning of the year) and had a man called Sextus Lucinus hurled down from the Tarpeian Rock. This was considered a most significant omen of the evils which were to fall once more on the party of Marius and on Rome herself.

But Marius himself was now an exhausted man. He was, as it were, afloat on a sea of anxieties and utterly tired out. It was too much for him to have to think once more of yet another war, and to imagine new struggles, fears which he knew from experience to be well-founded, and the weariness of it all. His spirits sank at the prospect and he could not raise them. He reflected too that what he now had to face was not an Octavius or a Merula commanding a heterogeneous and riotous mob of riff-raff; instead it was Sulla himself who was approaching, the same Sulla who in the past had driven him from Rome and who had now forced Mithridates back to the shores of the Euxine Sea. Such thoughts as these caused a kind of breakdown; he recalled his long wanderings, his flights and all the dangers he had undergone as he was driven over land and sea; and so he fell into a state of terrible despair; his nights were full of fear and were visited by dreadful dreams in which he seemed constantly to be hearing a voice saying:

> Dangerous is the lion's lair
> Even when the lion's not there.

Above all things he feared the sleepless nights and so he indulged in heavy bouts of drinking at all hours of the day and in a manner most unsuitable to his age, trying to induce sleep as a refuge from his own thoughts. Finally, when a messenger had arrived with news from the sea, fresh terrors came crowding upon him and so, fearing the future, burdened and sated with the present, it did not require much to make him ill and he contracted pleurisy, according to the account of Posidonius the philosopher who says that he went in personally and spoke to Marius on the subject of his embassy when Marius was ill. But Gaius Piso, an historian, gives a different account.[67] He says that Marius, while walking with his friends after dinner, began to talk about his life; beginning from his early youth he dwelt on all the changes for good or ill which had occurred and concluded by saying that a sensible man ought not to trust himself any longer to fortune. After this he said goodbye to his friends, took to his bed and, after seven days, died.

Others say that during his illness his passion for distinction was openly revealed by an absurd delusion into which he fell. He imagined that he was the commander-in-chief in the war with Mithridates and then behaved just as he used to do when really in action, throwing himself into all sorts of attitudes, going through various movements with piercing shouts and constantly yelling out his battle cry. So terribly and inexorably was he held in the grip of that passion of his for employment in that war – a passion which proceeded from his own envious nature and lust for power. Though he had lived for seventy years, was the first man in history to be elected consul seven times, though he had wealth and an establishment sufficient for many kingdoms at once, still he lamented his own fate in having to die before he had attained each and every object of his desires.

46. How different was the behaviour of Plato who when he was at the point of death, offered up thanks to his guardian spirit and to fortune because, in the first place, he had been born a man and not an irrational animal; then because he was a Greek and not a foreigner; and then because his birth had taken place in the times of Socrates. There is also the case of Antipater of Tarsus who, they say, when he was in the same

way near death, counted up all the blessings of his life and did not even forget to mention the good weather he had had on his voyage out to Athens, thus showing how deeply grateful he was to a benevolent fortune for every one of her gifts, and how he had laid them up safely in that most secure of human treasure-houses, the memory, to the very end. Thoughtless and forgetful people, on the other hand, let everything that happens to them slip away as time passes. And so, laying hold of and retaining nothing, real good always eludes them; instead they fill themselves with hopes, and neglect the present while they fix their eyes on the future. Yet what happens in the future is subject to fortune, whereas the present cannot be taken away. But still these people throw away the present gift of fortune as though it did not belong to them, and do nothing but dream of the future which is quite uncertain. Nor is there anything surprising in this. For dealing with the blessings which come to us from outside we need a firm foundation based on reason and education; without this foundation, people keep on seeking these blessings and heaping them up but can never satisfy the insatiable appetites of their souls.

So Marius died, seventeen days after entering upon his seventh consulship. In Rome there was immediately a feeling of joy and confidence. It seemed that the city had been freed from a harsh and savage tyranny. But in a few days people realized that they had only changed an old master for a young and vigorous one. For Marius the son now revealed his bitter, cruel nature by putting to death the noblest and most distinguished men in Rome.[68] His daring in war and his total disregard of danger had won him a great reputation and at first he was called 'the son of Mars'; but soon his true character was shown by his actions and he was called instead 'the son of Venus'. In the end he was blockaded in Praeneste by Sulla and, after many unsuccessful attempts to save his life, when the city was captured and there was no possibility of escape, he killed himself.[69]

2

SULLA

[138–78 BC]

The nature of the tradition about Sulla is largely determined by
two facts: Sulla won his civil war and wrote copious memoirs.
On the numerous occasions when Plutarch cites the autobiography, he usually does so for matters of no great importance:
obscure anecdotes or details that merely decorate a narrative.
There can be no doubt, however, that Plutarch often follows
the Sullan line even when this is not specifically recorded. His
strikingly violent denunciation of Sulpicius is particularly significant in this respect – we may contrast the more measured
judgement of Cicero – and he also presents the Sullan view of
Cinna, Carbo and Flaccus without giving any hint that other
opinions were possible. Nevertheless he is not entirely uncriti-
cal of the memoirs and is at least aware that not everyone
approved of the Peace of Dardanus. As usual he is happiest
in the retailing of improving anecdotes and the non-technical
narration of military campaigns. The disastrous significance of
Sulla's first march on Rome is passed over in silence, as are the
circumstances that made it possible, though here Plutarch does
show himself aware of the change in the relationship between
generals and their armies that had come about with the reforms
of Marius. It is in the account of the dictatorship that his defects
are most manifest. It was one of Sulla's principal objectives to
prevent the recurrence of various phenomena that had troubled
the established order over the last fifty years: the activities of
the popular tribunes, the struggle between senate and *equites*
for control of the courts, and the repeated consulships of his
rivals Marius, Cinna and Carbo. To this end he abolished the
legislative powers of the tribunate and debarred those who held

it from higher office, restored the courts to the senate and revived the *lex annalis*. But the chief danger to the republic was, as Sulla's own career had shown, the rebellious proconsul at the head of an army more loyal to himself than to Rome, and it was Sulla's total failure to check this menace that contributed most to the rapid collapse of his system. Not until Augustus did a Roman politician make a serious effort to ensure that no man should ever be able to achieve again the kind of coup d'état he had succeeded in bringing off himself. But these facts and their significance must, alas, be sought elsewhere than in the pages of Plutarch.

1. Lucius Cornelius Sulla came of a patrician (or noble) family. One of his ancestors, Rufinus,[1] is said to have held the consulship, though he is better known for falling into disgrace than for holding this honour. It was discovered that he owned, contrary to the law, more than ten pounds of silver plate and he was therefore expelled from the senate. After him the family went rapidly down in the world and remained obscure. There was nothing grand about Sulla's own domestic background, and when he was a young man he lived in cheap lodgings. He was reproached with this in later years when people thought that he had become more prosperous than he ought to be.

For instance, after the African campaign[2] when he was boasting of his achievements and giving himself airs we are told that one member of the aristocracy said to him: 'There is certainly something wrong about you, who have become so rich when your father left you nothing at all.' For, though the age of pure and upright manners had passed and people had degenerated and given way to their appetites for luxury and extravagance, yet they still thought that to forsake one's hereditary poverty was just as disgraceful as to squander a fortune that one had inherited. And afterwards when he had finally seized power and was putting numbers of people to death, a former slave who was supposed to be hiding one of those on the proscription lists and was therefore sentenced to be hurled down from the Tarpeian Rock, reproached Sulla with the fact that for a long time they had lived together in the same lodging house. The ex-slave had rented the upper rooms for 2,000 sesterces, and Sulla had paid 3,000 for the lower rooms. The difference between their fortunes was thus only 1,000 sesterces, the equivalent of 250 Attic drachmas. So much for the accounts of Sulla's fortunes in his early days.

2. As for his personal appearance, one can get a good general idea of it from the statues. But the terribly sharp and dominating glare of his blue eyes was made still more dreadful by the complexion of his face in which the pale skin was covered with angry blotches of red. It was because of this, they say, that he got the name 'Sulla'; and one of the street jokers at Athens made a verse on the subject:

'Sulla's face is a mulberry with oatmeal scattered on it.'

Evidence from such sources as this can be used quite appropriately of Sulla who was himself, they say, naturally prone to buffoonery. When he was still young and unknown he used to spend his time with ballet dancers and comedians and shared their dissolute way of life; and when he had won supreme power he was always organizing parties of the most impudently outspoken characters from the stage with whom he used to drink and exchange witticisms, with the result that people thought that he was acting in a manner very ill-suited to his age; and he not only cheapened the reputation of his high office but actually neglected much business which required attention. Once Sulla had sat down to dinner he found it quite impossible to take anything seriously. At other times he was a hard worker and used to wear a particularly forbidding expression, but he became completely transformed from the moment when he joined any social gathering or drinking party. On these occasions comedians and professional dancers found him perfectly tractable, a ready listener and willing to oblige anyone. Because of this habit of relaxation he seems to have been almost pathologically prone to sexual indulgence, being quite without restraint in his passion for pleasure. It was a passion which he continued to gratify even in old age. He remained attached from his early youth to an actor called Metrobius. Another experience of his was with Nicopolis, a woman rather easily accessible, but well off. He began by falling in love with her, but as she got used to his society and to the charm he had in his youth it ended in her falling in love with him and making him her heir when she died. He also inherited the fortune of his step-mother who loved him as though he were her own son. These legacies made him moderately well off.

3. He was appointed quaestor to Marius in his first consulship and sailed with him to Africa to make war on Jugurtha.[3] He was made responsible for the administration of the camp and in this post won a good name for himself. In particular he made full use of an opportunity which occurred of gaining the friendship of Bocchus, the King of Numidia. Some ambassadors of the king were fleeing from a band of Numidian robbers and Sulla offered them hospitality and sent them on their way with gifts and a safe escort. Bocchus had for a long time hated and feared his son-in-law Jugurtha; now, when Jugurtha had been defeated and taken refuge at his court, he was planning to betray him and called in Sulla to help, since he wanted the seizure and surrender of Jugurtha to be organized by Sulla rather than by himself. Sulla informed Marius of the proposal and, taking a few soldiers with him, put himself into very great danger; he was trusting the word of a native who had shown himself to be untrustworthy even to his closest relations, and in order to secure the surrender of someone else, he was putting his own life into this native's hands. And once Bocchus had both Jugurtha and Sulla in his power he was faced with the necessity of having to break his word to one or other of them and for a long time hesitated between the two alternatives. In the end, however, he made up his mind to proceed with his original plan of treachery and handed over Jugurtha to Sulla.

It was Marius who held the triumph for ending the war with Jugurtha, but those who envied him claimed that it was Sulla who deserved the credit, and Marius, though he said nothing, was still annoyed. Sulla too was naturally a boastful man. Now that he had emerged for the first time from his poverty and

obscurity and had become a person of some importance among
his fellow-citizens and was enjoying the sensation of being
honoured, he went so far in his passion for distinction as to have
a signet-ring made with a representation of his achievement.
He used this ring ever afterwards with its device of Bocchus
surrendering Jugurtha and himself receiving the surrender.

4. Marius was undoubtedly upset by this; but, as he still thought
Sulla not important enough for him to envy, he continued to
employ him in his campaigns – as a staff officer in his second
consulship, and as a colonel in his third.[4] Many useful things
were done by his means. For instance, in his first appointment
he captured Copillus, the chief of the Tectosages, and in his
second he persuaded the great and populous nation of the Marsi
to become the friends and allies of Rome.

He found, however, that as a result of this Marius was casting
a jealous eye on him and, so far from being glad to give him
further opportunities to distinguish himself, was standing in
the way of his advancement. He therefore attached himself
to Catulus, Marius' colleague in the consulship, who was an
excellent man though somewhat lacking in energy when it came
to fighting. By Catulus he was entrusted with really important
enterprises, so that both his power and his reputation increased.
As a commander in the field he subdued most of the native
tribes in the Alps; and, when there was a shortage of provisions,
he undertook the task of supplying them and accomplished this
task so successfully that the soldiers of Catulus not only had
plenty for themselves but some to spare for the soldiers of
Marius. Sulla himself states that Marius was extremely upset
by this. Certainly the hatred between the two of them was
originally based on slight and childish causes like these; yet
later it led them on, through the shedding of blood in civil
war and irreconcilable antagonisms, to tyranny and the utter
confusion of the whole state. This proves how wise Euripides
was and how well he knew the pathology of politics when he
recommended us to beware of ambition, which he calls the
most destructive of all powers and the most damaging to those
who worship her.

5. Sulla now thought that the reputation which he had won in war entitled him to turn to politics. He gave up campaigning and entered upon public life. However, when he stood as candidate for the city praetorship, he was not elected and, according to his own account this was because of the attitude of the people, who knew that he was a friend of Bocchus and looked forward, if he were made aedile before becoming praetor, to being treated to some particularly fine hunting shows and combats with wild animals from Africa; they therefore appointed other candidates as praetors so as to force him to stand for the aedileship.[5] It appears, however, from subsequent events that Sulla is disguising the real reason for his failure. For he was elected praetor in the following year, having won the support of the people partly by flattery and partly also by bribery.[6] So, during his praetorship, he was once angry with Caesar and said: 'I shall have to make use of my own authority against you,' at which Caesar laughed and replied: 'Considering that you bought it, you are absolutely right to call it your own.'

After his praetorship he was sent out to Cappadocia, ostensibly to reinstate Ariobarzanes, but really to keep a check on Mithridates who was busy with his intrigues and doubling the territory and power which he controlled already.[7] Sulla took out only a small force of his own, but was able to make use of the allies who were eager to be of help. After killing many of the native Cappadocians and still more of the Armenians who came to help them, he drove out Gordius and reinstated Ariobarzanes as king.

He spent some time by the Euphrates and while he was there he received a visit from Orobazus, a Parthian, who came as an ambassador from King Arsaces. Up to this time there had been no relations of any kind between Rome and Parthia, and the fact that Sulla was the first Roman ever to be approached by the Parthians with requests for alliance and friendship seems to be another example of his extraordinary good luck. It is said too that on this occasion Sulla ordered three chairs to be brought out – one for Ariobarzanes, one for Orobazus and one for himself – and that he himself sat on the middle chair and so gave them audience. As the result of this the King of Parthia

afterwards put Orobazus to death. As for Sulla, while some
people praised him for making the natives eat humble pie,
others regarded his behaviour as a vulgar and ill-timed display
of arrogance. There is also the story of a Chaldaean who was
one of the party of Orobazus. This Chaldaean is said to have
closely scrutinized Sulla's face and to have made a serious study
of his mental and physical reactions so as to find out his true
character by applying the principles of Chaldaean science. He
then said: 'It is impossible for this man not to be the greatest in
the world. What surprises me is that even now he abstains from
taking the first place among men.'

When Sulla returned to Rome he was prosecuted by
Censorinus[8] for corrupt financial practices. Censorinus alleged
that he had illegally raised large sums of money from a friendly
and allied kingdom. However, when the day of the trial came
Censorinus failed to put in an appearance and dropped the
charge.

6. The quarrel between Sulla and Marius now broke out again.
The new occasion for this was provided by the ambition of
Bocchus who, in order to please the Roman people and at the
same time to do Sulla a kindness, set up and dedicated on
the Capitol some figures carrying trophies and alongside them
gilded statues of Jugurtha being surrendered by him to Sulla.
Marius was furious at this and attempted to have the statues
removed; others, however, were quite prepared to aid Sulla in
resisting him. It seemed certain that Rome would be set aflame
between the two of them, but the long smouldering hostility of
Rome's Italian allies now blazed up into open war against the
city and this put an end to their quarrel for the time being.[9]

The war was on a great scale, had various changes of fortune,
did enormous damage to Rome, and brought her into the
utmost danger. In the course of it Marius was unable to do
anything really important, thus proving that one cannot be a
great general unless one is at the peak of one's health and
strength. Sulla on the other hand performed a number of memorable actions. Among the citizens his reputation was that of
a great commander: his friends considered him the greatest

commander of all, while even his enemies admitted that he
was the luckiest. Here his attitude was different from that of
Timotheus, the son of Conon, whose enemies attributed all his
successes to luck and had a picture painted in which he was
represented as lying asleep while Fortune was casting her net
over the enemy cities. Timotheus behaved rudely and angrily
to those who had done this, thinking that he was being deprived
by them of the credit due to his achievements; and on one
occasion, when he had returned from a campaign in which he
was thought to have done well, he said to the people: 'Here at
least, men of Athens, is a campaign in which Fortune has played
no part' – a childish enough outburst of vanity for which, we
are told, heaven requited him, since from that time on, so far
from doing anything brilliant, Timotheus failed in every one of
his undertakings, lost favour with the people and, in the end,
was exiled. Sulla, on the other hand, was delighted when he
was congratulated and praised for being lucky; he joined with
others in emphasizing the part played by providence in what
he had done and accepted his dependence on Fortune. This may
have been a form of boastfulness, or he may genuinely have
held this conviction about divine providence. Certainly in his
Memoirs he writes that when he considers all those occasions
on which he appears to have made wise decisions he finds that
the most successful actions were those upon which he entered
boldly and on the spur of the moment rather than after due
deliberation. He says too that he was born with natural endow-
ments not so much for war as for Fortune, and from this it
appears that he attributes more to Fortune than to his own
superior ability. Indeed he makes himself a pawn in the hand
of providence. He even regards the good feeling that existed
between himself and Metellus,[10] a man of equal rank and a
relation by marriage, as an example of supernaturally contrived
good fortune; for he had expected that Metellus would make
difficulties for him as a colleague in office, and actually found
him most willing to oblige. Then too in the dedication of the
Memoirs to Lucullus[11] he advises him to treat those dreams
which a divine power sends to advise us by night as the most
reliable of all things. He says also that when he was sent out

with an army to the war against the Italian allies a great chasm
in the earth opened near Laverna and out of the chasm came
much fire and one bright flame that shot up to the sky. The
soothsayers then foretold that a man of great qualities and of a
most remarkably striking appearance would take the government upon himself and free Rome from her present troubles.
Sulla says that he himself was this man; the golden colour of
his hair made him an extraordinary-looking man, and as for
his great qualities, he need not blush to mention them himself
after all the distinguished and important actions of his life.

So much for his views on the supernatural. In other respects
he seems to have had a character that was very irregular and
full of inconsistencies. His rapacity was great, but his generosity
was greater; he gave promotion for no apparent reason and
was just as unreasonable in the way in which he would insult
people; he was deferential to those whose help he needed and
arrogant to those who needed his help; so that one cannot say
whether in his true nature pride or servility predominated. In
his punishments and his reactions to injury the same inconsist-
ency is to be observed. He would have a man beaten to death
for some inconsiderable offence; yet on other occasions he
would meekly put up with really serious misdeeds. He would
cheerfully become reconciled to people who had done him quite
unforgivable injuries, and in other cases because of some trifling
misdemeanour the punishment would be death or confiscation
of goods. From this we may conclude that he was by nature
savage and unforgiving, but was capable of controlling his
natural severity by considerations of self-interest. For instance,
in this war between Rome and the Italian allies his soldiers
clubbed and stoned to death a legate of praetorian rank
(Albinus by name).[12] So far from punishing a crime of such
gravity Sulla did nothing about it except to issue a pompous
proclamation to the effect that he could now count upon an
improvement in his men's morale, since they would wish to
atone for their fault by showing their courage. Those who
complained were disregarded by him; for he had already
decided to break the power of Marius and, since it looked as

though the war with the allies was nearly over, to get himself appointed general against Mithridates. Consequently he pampered the troops under his command.

On his return to Rome he was elected consul with Quintus Pompeius.[13] He was now in his fiftieth year and made a very brilliant match by marrying Caecilia, the daughter of Metellus the chief pontiff.[14] There were a number of popular songs composed on the subject of this marriage and many members of the aristocracy showed their disapproval of it, thinking, as Livy says, that Sulla was not good enough for such a wife though he was good enough to be consul. This was not Sulla's only marriage. First, when he was still very young, he married Ilia, who bore him a daughter. Then, after her, he married Aelia, and thirdly Cloelia whom he divorced on the grounds of her sterility.[15] The divorce was arranged in an honourable manner and Sulla not only commended his ex-wife in speech but gave her gifts as well. But since he married Caecilia only a few days afterwards, people thought that he had not acted very well in making the accusation against Cloelia. However, he was always anxious to please Caecilia in everything and it was to Caecilia that the Roman people applied for help when they wished the exiles of Marius' party to be recalled and Sulla was refusing to allow this. It was thought too that when he captured Athens he treated the population all the more savagely because they had been in the habit of shouting out obscene jokes about Caecilia from the walls. All this, however, happened later.

7. At the time of which I am speaking Sulla regarded his consulship as a very minor matter compared with future events. What fired his imagination was the thought of the war against Mithridates. Here, however, he found himself opposed by Marius who, under the influence of those never ageing passions, love of distinction and a mania for fame, had set his heart on foreign war across the sea in spite of the fact that he had now grown unwieldy in body and had only recently retired from military service on account of his age.[16] While Sulla set out for his camp to attend to various matters which still required his attention,

Marius stayed at home and busied himself with contriving that terrible outbreak of civil violence which did more damage to Rome than all her wars put together. There were many supernatural warnings of what was to come. Fire broke out of its own accord from under the staves of the ensigns and was only got under control with great difficulty; three ravens brought their young out into the road and after eating them, carried back the remains to their nest; mice gnawed at some consecrated gold in a temple and when the keepers had caught one of them, a female, in a trap, she gave birth in the trap itself to five young and ate up three of them. But the most striking phenomenon of all was when the sound of a trumpet rang out from a perfectly clear and cloudless sky with a shrill, prolonged and dismal note so loud that people were driven half crazy with terror. The Etruscan wise men declared that this portent foretold a change over into a new age and a total revolution in the world. According to them there are eight ages in all. In each age the lives and manners of men are different and God has established for each age a definite span of time which is determined by the circuit of the Great Year. Whenever this circuit comes to an end and another begins some marvellous sign appears either on earth or in the heavens so that it becomes at once clear to those who have made a thorough study of the subject that men of a different character and way of life have now come into the world and the gods will be either more or less concerned with this new race than they were with their predecessors. All sorts of changes occur, they say, as one age succeeds another and in particular with regard to the art of divination one can observe that there are times when it rises in prestige and its predictions are accurate because clear and unmistakable signs are sent from heaven; and then again in another age it is not held in much honour, since for the most part its practitioners are relying on mere guesswork and are trying to grasp the future with senses that have become blunt and dim. This, at all events, was the story told by the wisest men among the Etruscans who were thought to know more than most about such things. And while the senate was sitting in the temple of Bellona and consulting with the soothsayers about these portents, a sparrow flew in in front of everyone with a grasshopper in its bill; it threw down part of the grasshopper and left it there and then flew away with the other part. This was interpreted by the professionals to mean that there would be quarrels and political disturbances between the great landowners and the common people of the city; for the common townspeople are loud and voluble like the grasshopper, while the sparrow might represent 'those who live on the land'.

8. Marius now formed an alliance with the tribune Sulpicius,[17] a man so thoroughly bad as to be quite exceptional; one tended to inquire not what others he surpassed, but on what occasions he surpassed himself in wickedness. He was cruel, reckless and grasping and showed himself to be so quite shamelessly and with a total lack of scruple – actually putting up the rights of Roman citizenship for sale by public auction to ex-slaves and aliens and counting out the money at a table specially set up in the forum. He maintained a private army of 3,000 swordsmen and went about accompanied by large bands of young men from the equestrian order, who were ready for anything and whom he used to call his Anti-senate. Though he got a law passed which forbade any senator to incur debts of more than 2,000 drachmas, he himself died owing three million. This was the man who was now let loose on the people by Marius and who by violence and armed force threw everything into confusion. He put forward a number of dangerous laws and in particular a proposal for giving the command against Mithridates to Marius. To prevent these proposals from being put to the vote the consuls decreed a suspension of all public business, whereupon Sulpicius led a disorderly mob against them while they were holding an assembly near the temple of Castor and Pollux. Among many others he killed the young son of the consul Pompeius in the forum. Pompeius himself succeeded in getting away unobserved, but Sulla was chased into the house of Marius and then forced to come out and to announce that the decree for the suspension of public business was cancelled. Because of this Sulpicius did not deprive Sulla of the consulship, though he did depose Pompeius. He contented himself with

transferring the command against Mithridates from Sulla to Marius. He also sent military tribunes immediately to Nola to take command of the army and bring it over to Marius.[18]

9. Sulla, however, escaped from Rome and got to the camp first. When his soldiers heard what had happened they stoned the tribunes to death, upon which the party of Marius in Rome began to put to death the friends of Sulla and to make away with their property. Numbers of people fled and changed from one side to the other, some making their way to Rome from the camp, others going over to the camp from Rome. The senate, no longer its own master, did what it was told to do by Marius and Sulpicius. When it was informed that Sulla was marching on Rome, it sent two of the praetors, Brutus and Servilius,[19] to forbid him to advance further. These praetors spoke somewhat abruptly to Sulla and for this the soldiers were quite prepared to kill them; instead they broke their rods of office, stripped them of their purple-bordered robes, and, after subjecting them to many other insults, turned them out of the camp. In Rome there was the greatest despondency among the citizens when they saw their magistrates stripped of their badges of office and heard them report that between the two parties things had now gone too far for there to be any hope of appeasement.

Marius and his party now began to make ready and Sulla with his colleague in the consulship moved forward from Nola with six legions, all at full strength. He saw that his army was eager to march directly on Rome, but he still hesitated in his own mind, fearing the dangers involved. But at a sacrifice which he was making the soothsayer Postumius, after inspecting the entrails, stretched out both his hands to him and asked to be put in chains and kept a prisoner until after the battle, saying that he was prepared to suffer any sort of punishment if Sulla did not enjoy a speedy and complete success. It is said also that there appeared to Sulla himself in dreams the goddess whose cult came to Rome from Cappadocia and who may be called either the Moon, or Athena, or Bellona. It seemed to Sulla that this goddess stood beside him and put a thunderbolt into his hands; she then named his enemies one by one and told him to strike them; and, after he had hurled the thunderbolt, they all fell down and vanished. Sulla was encouraged by this vision and, when he had told it to his colleague, led his army forward at daybreak against Rome.

At Pictae he was met by a deputation from the city who begged him not to go forward immediately to the attack, since the senate had voted that he should have all his due rights. Sulla then agreed to camp where he was and ordered his officers to mark out the ground for a camp, as was the usual thing to do, so that the deputation believed what he said and returned to Rome. But as soon as they had gone, he sent forward Lucius Basillus and Gaius Mummius,[20] who seized for him the city gate and the walls on the side of the Esquiline hill; he himself followed after them, marching with all the speed possible. Basillus and his men successfully forced their way into the city, but were then held up by showers of stones and tiles hurled down on them from the roofs by the unarmed city population and were forced back to the wall. But by this time Sulla had arrived. Seeing what was happening he shouted out to his men to set fire to the houses and, seizing hold of a burning torch, was himself the first to do so. At the same time he ordered his archers to make use of their fire-arrows and shoot them at the tops of the houses. The action was quite unconsidered and the result of mere passion. In his anger he had lost control of his actions; all that he could see was his enemies and he gave no consideration to friends, relations and old acquaintances; no feeling of pity moved him as he made his entry into the city by means of fire, which knew no distinction between the innocent and the guilty. Meanwhile Marius was driven back to the temple of Tellus. Here he issued a proclamation offering freedom to the slaves in return for their support. But he was not able to check the enemy's advance and so fled from the city.

10. Sulla now called a meeting of the senate and had the death sentence passed on Marius himself and a few others including the tribune Sulpicius. As for Sulpicius, he was betrayed by one of his servants and killed. Sulla first rewarded this servant by giving him his freedom and then had him hurled down from

the Tarpeian Rock. But in putting a price on the head of Marius, Sulla was acting neither generously nor, from a political point of view, wisely. Only a little time ago he had been himself in the power of Marius, having surrendered himself to him at his house, and had been allowed to go safely. Yet if Marius had then, instead of letting him go, handed him over to Sulpicius to be killed, he might have won supreme power. In spite of this Marius spared his life, and, after a few days, received very different treatment from Sulla who was now in the same position as he had been. The senate disliked these proceedings, though they kept their feelings hidden. The people, on the other hand, showed openly by their actions the hatred and indignation which they felt against Sulla. For instance, they not only ignominiously rejected his candidates for offices (Nonius,[21] his nephew, and Servius), but elected others whom they thought he would be least pleased to see thus honoured. Sulla, however, pretended to be delighted, making out that it was because of him that the people enjoyed the freedom of doing as they wished. And by way of appeasing the general hatred he allowed Lucius Cinna,[22] a man of the opposite party, to become consul, though first he made him promise and swear to support his own policy. Cinna went up to the Capitol with a stone in his hand and took the required oath; then, praying that, if he failed to preserve his goodwill for Sulla, he might be thrown out of Rome as the stone was thrown out of his hand, he threw the stone to the ground in front of a number of witnesses. But as soon as he came into office he attempted to undermine the existing order of things. He prepared a case against Sulla and appointed Virginius,[23] one of the tribunes, to act as prosecutor. Sulla, however, ignored both Virginius and the law courts. He now set out against Mithridates.

11. It is said that about the time when Sulla was setting out with his forces from Italy, Mithridates, who was then staying at Pergamum, received a number of warnings from heaven. For instance, there was a statue of Victory, holding a crown in her hand, which by some kind of machinery was being lowered down on him from above by the people of Pergamum; when it

was just on the point of touching his head, it broke in pieces
and the crown came tumbling down into the middle of the
theatre where it was shattered on the ground. Everyone
trembled at the sight and Mithridates himself was profoundly
discouraged, although at the time things were going better with
him than he could have hoped; for he had conquered Asia from
the Romans, Bithynia and Cappadocia from their kings, and
was now established in Pergamum, where he was distributing
wealth and provinces and kingdoms to his friends; one of his
sons was in Pontus and Bosporus in undisturbed possession of
the ancient realm as far as the deserts beyond Lake Maeotis;
another son, Ariarathes, with a large army of invasion was
reducing Thrace and Macedonia; and other places were being
subdued by the forces of his generals. The greatest of these was
Archelaus, whose fleet gave him complete mastery of the sea.
He was now subjugating the Cyclades and the other islands to
the east of Cape Malea and had occupied Euboea itself. From
his base in Athens he was bringing about the revolt from Rome
of all the peoples of Greece as far as Thessaly. He did, however, encounter a slight setback at Chaeronea. Here he was
opposed by Bruttius Sura, a legate of Sentius the governor of
Macedonia,[24] and a man of remarkable daring and intelligence.
As Archelaus came sweeping through Boeotia like a torrent,
Sura stood firmly in his path, fought three battles with him at
Chaeronea, forced him back, and made him retire again to the
sea. But he was ordered by Lucius Lucullus[25] to give way to
Sulla who was approaching and to leave the war to the man
who had been made responsible for it by decree of the senate.
Sura then immediately abandoned Boeotia and marched back
to Sentius, although things were going better with him than
he could have hoped and Greece, as the result of his gallant
behaviour, was becoming favourably disposed to the idea of
changing back again to the side of Rome. As for Bruttius, these
were the most brilliant achievements of his career.

12. As soon as Sulla arrived he received deputations and
requests for help from the other cities; but Athens was forced
by the tyrant Aristion to side with Mithridates. Sulla therefore

brought his whole force to bear against Athens; he invested Piraeus and began a regular siege, bringing up all kinds of mechanical devices and trying all methods of assault. Yet if he had been prepared to wait a little longer he could have captured the upper city without running any risks at all, since it was without supplies and was already reduced by famine to the last extremity. But Sulla was in a hurry to get back to Rome; he was alarmed by the revolution which had taken place there; and so at great risk, with continual fighting and at vast expense he pushed on with the war. Apart from all the rest of his military equipment, 10,000 pairs of mules were needed for the operation of his siege engines and were employed every day on this job. When timber grew scarce (since many of the works were destroyed through breaking down under their own weight and many were burned by the enemy's fire-missiles to which they were constantly exposed) he laid hands on the sacred groves and cut down the trees of the Academy, which was the most wooded of the suburbs, and of the Lyceum. He needed great sums of money also for the war and made off with the sacred treasures of Greece, sending for the most beautiful and valuable of the offerings deposited both in Epidaurus and at Olympia. He also wrote to the Amphictyons at Delphi, saying that it would be better to have the treasure of the god brought to him, since it would be safer in his keeping, if he did keep it, and, if he spent it, he would give back an equivalent value later. He sent a friend of his, Caphis the Phocian, with this message and ordered him to receive each item and have it weighed. Caphis arrived at Delphi, but was most reluctant to touch the holy things, and in the presence of the Amphictyons burst into tears at the necessity of having to do so. Some of them then declared that they could hear from the inner shrine the sound of a lyre being played, and Caphis, either because he believed them or because he wished to put some fear of the gods into Sulla, sent him news of this. Sulla, however, made a joke of it and wrote back to say that he was surprised that Caphis did not realize that singing was a sign not of anger, but of joy; he ordered him therefore to go in and take the treasure boldly, since the god was evidently delighted at the idea of handing it over.

So the treasures were sent away and certainly most of the Greeks did not know what was happening. But the silver jar, the last of the royal gifts still in existence, was too large and heavy for the baggage animals to carry and the Amphictyons were compelled to cut it into pieces. As they did so they called to mind the names of Titus Flamininus and Manius Acilius and Aemilius Paulus too. One of these had driven Antiochus out of Greece and the others had conquered the Kings of Macedonia.[26] And these men had not only kept their hands off the temples of the Greeks, but had endowed them and honoured them and done much to add to the general respect in which they were held. But these, they reflected, were the lawfully constituted commanders of disciplined troops who had learned to obey orders without a murmur; they were kingly in soul, but moderate in their personal outlay, keeping their expenditure to the ordinary fixed allowances of the time; and they thought that to show subservience to their own soldiers was more disgraceful than to show fear in the face of the enemy. But now the generals of this later period were men who had risen to the top by violence rather than by merit; they needed armies to fight against one another rather than against the public enemy; and so they were forced to combine the arts of the demagogue with the authority of the general. They spent money on making life easy for their soldiers and then, after purchasing their labour in this way, failed to observe that they had made their whole country a thing for sale and had put themselves in a position where they had to be the slaves of the worst sort of people in order to become the masters of the better. This was what caused the exile of Marius and this was what brought him back again against Sulla. This was what made Cinna's party murder Octavius and Fimbria's party murder Flaccus.[27] And here it was Sulla more than anyone else who set the example. In order to corrupt and win over to himself the soldiers of other generals, he gave his own troops a good time and spent money lavishly on them. He was thus at the same time encouraging the others to treachery and his own men to debauchery. All this required much money and especially was it required for this siege.

13. For there was something terrible and quite inexorable about Sulla's lust to capture Athens. Perhaps it was some spirit of envious emulation which drove him to fight as it were with the shadow of the city's former greatness; perhaps he had been made angry by the insults and vulgar abuse which were constantly hurled at him and at Metella from the walls by the tyrant Aristion, who would accompany his foul language with the most obscene gestures.

Aristion had a character which was compounded of cruelty and licentiousness. He was like a sink into which had run all the worst of the vicious and diseased qualities of Mithridates and now, like some fatal malady, he had fastened himself on Athens in these last days of hers – a city which in the past had survived innumerable wars and many periods of dictatorship and civil strife. This man, at a time when a bushel of wheat was being sold in the city at 1,000 drachmas, when people were subsisting on the feverfew which grew on the acropolis and were boiling down shoes and leather oil flasks to eat, was himself spending his time in continual drinking parties and revels in broad daylight, or showing off his steps in a war dance, or making jokes about the enemy. Meanwhile he allowed the sacred lamp of the goddess to go out for want of oil; and when the chief priestess asked him for a twelfth of a bushel of wheat, he sent her pepper instead. When the members of the Council and the priests came to him as suppliants and begged him to take pity on the city and come to terms with Sulla, he drove them off with a volley of arrows. Finally, when things had already gone too far, with much ado he sent out two or three of his drinking companions to negotiate a peace. These men made no proposals that could be of any help to Athens, but instead went off into long dissertations about Theseus and Eumolpus and the Persian wars. They were interrupted by Sulla who said: 'My friends, you can pack up your speeches and be off. Rome did not send me to Athens to study ancient history. My task is to subdue rebels.'

14. Meanwhile Sulla received news from some soldiers of his who had overheard in the Cerameicus some old men talking

together and abusing the tyrant for not guarding the approach
to the wall at the Heptachalcum, at which point alone it was
not only possible but easy for the enemy to force an entry. Sulla
took this information seriously. He came down to the place by
night, satisfied himself that it could be taken and went into
action immediately. He says himself in his *Memoirs* that the
first man to scale the wall was Marcus Ateius, who was opposed
by one of the enemy and, cutting downwards at him with his
sword, broke the sword on the man's helmet; nevertheless he
stood firm and held his ground without giving way. Certainly
it was at this point that the city was taken, as used to be reported
by the oldest of the Athenians.

Sulla himself entered the city at midnight, after having
thrown down and levelled with the ground the fortifications
between the Piraic and the Sacred Gate. It was a moment made
the more terrible by the blowing of trumpets, the blasts of
bugles and the shouting and yelling of his troops who were
now let loose by him to pillage and to slaughter and who poured
down the narrow alleyways with drawn swords in their hands.
There was thus no counting of the slain; to this day their
numbers are estimated simply by the area of ground that was
covered with blood. The blood shed in the market place alone
(without counting the slaughter that took place in the rest of
the city) spread all through the Cerameicus inside the Double
Gate; in fact many people say that it flowed out through
the Gate and washed right over the suburb outside. And yet,
though many indeed perished in this way, equally numerous
were those who, out of pity and love for their native city, took
their own lives. They thought that their city was doomed to
extinction, and this it was that made the best of them give up
all hope and fear the prospect of survival, since they expected
from Sulla neither generosity nor ordinary humanity. Finally,
however, partly because of the exiles Midias and Calliphon,
who threw themselves at his feet and begged him to have
mercy, partly because of the Roman senators with the army
who also interceded for the city, Sulla, who was himself by
this time sated with vengeance, made a few remarks in praise
of the ancient Athenians and then announced, 'I forgive a few

for the sake of the many, the living for the sake of the dead.'

He took Athens, as he himself says in his *Memoirs*, on
1 March, a day which corresponds very nearly with the first
day of the month Anthesterion. It happens that in this month
the Athenians hold many ceremonies in commemoration of the
ruin and destruction caused by the Flood, believing that it was
at this time of the year that it once took place.

When the city was taken, the tyrant retreated to the acropolis
and Curio[28] was instructed to besiege him there. He held out
for some time, but was compelled in the end to surrender for
lack of water. A sign from heaven followed at once. For on the
same day and at the very hour when Curio brought him down
as a prisoner, clouds gathered in a clear sky and so much rain
fell that the acropolis was filled with water.

Soon afterwards Sulla captured Piraeus also. He burned most
of it, including that very famous work of architecture the
arsenal of Philo.

15. Meanwhile Mithridates' general Taxiles had moved south-
ward from Thrace and Macedonia. He had a force consisting
of 100,000 infantry, 10,000 cavalry, and 90 four-horse chariots
equipped with scythes on their wheels. He sent to Archelaus,
who was still at sea with his fleet off Munychia, and asked him
to join him; but Archelaus had no desire to come on land and
join battle with the Romans; he planned instead to let the war
drag on and to cut off their supplies. And now Sulla showed
that he had a much better grasp of the situation than Archelaus.
He moved out of a region that was infertile and scarcely able
to support its population even in peacetime and transferred his
whole force to Boeotia. Many people considered that he was
making a mistake in leaving the rough country of Attica which
was so unsuited to cavalry and in entering the plains and wide
open spaces of Boeotia, knowing, as he did, that the main
strength of the foreign enemy was in chariots and cavalry. But,
as has been stated, he was flying from famine and shortage of
supplies, and so was forced to accept the risk of battle. He was
also anxious about Hortensius,[29] a bold and capable commander, who was bringing troops to him from Thessaly and

who was likely to be attacked by the foreign forces while cross-ing the passes. These were the reasons which led Sulla to move into Boeotia. As for Hortensius, one of my fellow-countrymen called Caphis led him across Parnassus by a route unknown to the foreign army and brought him to a place just below Tithora. This was not so large a city as it is now; it was just a fortress set on precipitous cliffs. In ancient times those of the Phocians who were fleeing from the invasion of Xerxes saved their lives and property by retiring to it. Hortensius camped here and, after beating off enemy attacks by day, came down at night by a difficult route to Patronis where he joined forces with Sulla who had marched out to meet him.

16. Now that the two armies were united they occupied a fertile and well-wooded hill rising out of the middle of the plains of Elatea, and with a supply of water at its foot. The name of the place is Philoboeotus and Sulla speaks most highly of its natural advantages and of its situation. Encamped here the Romans seemed to the enemy a very small force indeed. They had no more than 1,500 cavalry and less than 15,000 infantry. So the other generals overruled the objections of Archelaus and drew up their forces for battle, filling the whole plain with their horses and chariots and shields and bucklers.

Meanwhile the air was rent with the din and shouting of so many different races all forming up together in battle order. At the same time the very pride and ostentation of their expensive equipment was far from being useless or ineffective as a means to inspire terror. As their ranks swung and surged to and fro they presented a fearful sight like a flaming fire, what with the flashing of their armour, all magnificently embellished with gold and silver, and the bright colours of their Median and Scythian tunics intermixed with the bronze and shining steel. It was something which made the Romans shrink back inside their entrenchments, and Sulla, finding it impossible to remove their fear by any words of his and being unwilling to force them to fight when all they wanted to do was to run away, had to sit still and put up as best he could with the sight of the foreign army insulting him with their boasting and their derision. Yet

in fact this did him more good than anything else. His opponents were not remarkable even at the best of times for obeying
their generals, of whom there were far too many. Now in their
contempt for Sulla they became thoroughly undisciplined; only
a few remained steadfastly within their fortifications, while the
great majority, lured on by hopes of plunder and rapine, were
scattered over the country many days' march away from their
camp. They are said to have destroyed the city of Panope and
to have sacked Lebadea and robbed the prophetic shrine there
– all without any orders from their generals.

Sulla, grieved and angry as he was to see cities being destroyed
under his eyes, did not allow his soldiers to remain idle. He led
them out and made them dig ditches and divert the course of
the River Cephisus. He gave them no rest and showed that he
was prepared to punish without mercy any cases of slackness,
his idea being to wear them out with hard work so that the
constant drudgery would make them welcome danger. And so,
indeed, it happened. On the third day of this hard labour, as
Sulla was passing by, the soldiers all shouted out to him and
begged him to lead them against the enemy. Sulla replied: 'What
you say does not mean that you want to fight. It only means
that you don't want to work. However, if you are really ready
for action, take your arms and get up there,' and he pointed
out to them the place that had once been the acropolis of
Parapotamii, though all that was left of it now that the city had
been destroyed was a hill with steep rocks on all sides. This hill
was separated from Mount Hedylium by the breadth of the
River Assus, which then, at the very foot of the mountain, flows
into the Cephisus, and sweeps along in a very turbulent stream,
making the citadel a strong position for a camp. Sulla therefore
wanted to be the first to occupy this place, particularly as he
saw that the enemy troops called 'the Bronze-shields' were
moving up towards it, and he succeeded in doing so, now that
he could depend on his soldiers' willingness to fight.

Then, when Archelaus, repulsed from this position, had
begun to move against Chaeronea, the Chaeroneans who were
serving with Sulla begged him not to abandon their city. Sulla
sent out a senior officer, Gabinius,[30] with one legion and gave

the Chaeroneans permission to go too. In spite of their wish
to reach the city before Gabinius, it was Gabinius who got
there first, thus showing himself to be an excellent soldier and
one even more anxious to preserve the place than those who
had begged to be preserved. (According to Juba,[31] it was not
Gabinius, but Ericius who was sent on this mission.) This was
certainly for my native city a very narrow escape indeed from
danger.

17. Meanwhile favourable predictions and prophecies of victory kept on coming to the Romans from Lebadea and the
oracle of Trophonius. One can get a fuller account of these
from the local inhabitants, but Sulla himself, in the tenth book
of his *Memoirs*, describes how Quintus Titius, a well-known
Roman businessman in Greece, came to him immediately after
his victory at Chaeronea, with the news that Trophonius prophesied that he would fight another victorious battle in the same
neighbourhood within a short time. And after him one of the
soldiers in the legions, Salvenius by name, brought a message
from the god telling him how affairs in Italy were going to turn
out. The two men gave the same account of the source of these
utterances; for they both said they had seen a figure which in
beauty and in stature was like Olympian Zeus.

Sulla now crossed the Assus, advanced to the foot of Mount
Hedylium, and camped near Archelaus, who had erected strong
defence works in the district known as 'the Assia', which is
between Mount Acontium and Mount Hedylium. The place
where he pitched his tents is still to this day called 'Archelaus'
after him. Sulla waited here for one day and then left Murena[32]
behind with one legion and two cohorts to make things difficult
for the enemy if they attempted to draw up in order of battle.
He himself first made a sacrifice on the banks of the Cephisus
and then, after the ceremony was over, marched towards
Chaeronea to pick up the forces stationed there and to make a
reconnaissance of the place called Thurium which had already
been occupied by the enemy. This is a cone-shaped hill with a
rocky peak (we call it Orthopagus) and at its foot is the River
Molus and a temple of Apollo Thurius. (The god received the

name 'Thurius' from Thuro, the mother of Chaeron who is
traditionally supposed to have been the founder of Chaeronea.
But according to another account it was here that the cow
appeared which was given to Cadmus by Apollo to be his guide,
and the name of the place is derived from her, 'thor' being the
Phoenician word for cow.)

When Sulla drew near to Chaeronea, his officer in command
there came out to meet him, with all the troops in full armour,
carrying a wreath of laurel in his hand. Sulla received the wreath
and made a speech of welcome to the soldiers, encouraging
them to face steadfastly the dangers ahead. He was then
approached by two men from Chaeronea, Homoloïchus and
Anaxidamus, who undertook to cut off the enemy in Thurium,
if he would give them a few soldiers. There was a path, they
said, out of sight of the foreign army, which led from the place
called 'Petrachus' past the Museum to a part of Thurium above
the enemy position. If they took this path, there would be
nothing to stop them from launching an attack and either
stoning the enemy to death from above or else forcing them
down into the plain. When Gabinius had guaranteed that the
men were both brave and trustworthy, Sulla ordered them to
proceed with their enterprise. He himself then drew up his line
of battle with the cavalry on either wing. He took command of
the right wing himself, and gave the left to Murena. His officers,
Galba[33] and Hortensius, with cohorts of reserves, were stationed on high ground in the rear to guard against enveloping
movements from the flanks. It could be seen that the enemy's
wing, with numbers of cavalry and light troops, was being
drawn up in a loose and flexible formation to allow for movement. Evidently they intended to extend this wing and sweep
round behind the Romans.

18. Meanwhile the Chaeroneans (Ericius had been put in command of them by Sulla) had got round Thurium without being
seen. Their sudden appearance caused a great disturbance and
panic among the foreign troops there. Indeed most of their
casualties were self-inflicted; for, instead of standing their
ground, they rushed down the steep hill, falling on their own

spears and crowding each other over the precipices, while their
enemies charged down on them from above, aiming their blows
at their defenceless bodies. So 3,000 of them fell at Thurium.
Of those who escaped some were cut off and killed by Murena,
whose line was already drawn up for battle when he encountered them, and others, who managed to force their way to the
camp of their friends, fell into the ranks in a disorderly mass,
causing much panic and confusion and making the generals
lose time at a moment when they could least afford to do so.
For while they were in this state of disturbance Sulla promptly
gave the order to attack, and by rapidly reducing the space
between the two armies brought it about that the scythe-bearing
chariots lost their power to do damage. These chariots are most
effective after they have been driven for some distance and have
got up the speed and impetus to break through a line; a short
start makes them feeble and ineffectual, like missiles with inadequate propelling power behind them. So it happened to the
foreign army on this occasion. The first chariots were driven
forward slowly and made no serious impact at all. The Romans
beat them off and then, laughing and clapping their hands,
shouted out, as they do at races in the Circus, 'Bring on more!'
Then the two infantry forces came together. The foreigners held
their pikes out in front of them at full length and, by locking
their shields together, tried to keep their line unbroken. The
Romans threw down their javelins, drew their swords, and
struggled to push the pikes aside so that they could get to close
quarters as soon as possible. They were enraged at seeing drawn
up in front of the enemy 15,000 slaves whom the king's generals
had set free by proclamation in the cities and had enrolled in the
heavy infantry. A Roman centurion is said to have remarked: 'I
have never heard of slaves behaving like free men except at the
Saturnalia.' However, these men stood solidly together in a
dense array and held their ground with a daring quite uncharac-
teristic of the slave nature, so that they were only gradually
pushed back by the Roman infantry; and it was the constant
stream of javelins and firebolts from the Roman rear ranks
which in the end caused them to lose contact with each other
and to give way.

19. Archelaus now extended his right wing in an enveloping
movement, and Hortensius sent out his cohorts at the double
in order to attack him in the flank. But Archelaus quickly
wheeled round upon him with his personal force of 2,000
cavalry, and Hortensius, borne back by weight of numbers,
found himself hemmed in against the higher ground, gradually
losing contact with the main body and being surrounded by
the enemy. Sulla, seeing what was happening, hurried to his
assistance from the right wing which had not yet gone into
action. Archelaus, however, guessed what he was doing when
he saw the cloud of dust raised by his troops. He therefore left
Hortensius alone, wheeled round and set off for the right wing
where Sulla had come from, in the hope of surprising it with
no one in command. Just as this very moment Taxiles also bore
down on Murena with his Bronze-shields, and Sulla, hearing
the shouts of battle from both directions as they echoed and
re-echoed from the surrounding hills, halted and found it difficult to decide to which quarter of the field he ought to go. He
concluded that it was best to go back to his original position
and so he sent Hortensius with four cohorts to the help of
Murena, and, ordering the fifth cohort to follow him, hurried
back to the right wing. Here he found that his men were already
standing up well to Archelaus, and now, when he appeared,
they pushed forward all along the line, overpowering the enemy
and driving them back in disorder to the river and to Mount
Acontium. Sulla, however, did not forget the danger that
Murena was in and set off to help him. Finding that Murena's
men were already victorious he joined them in the pursuit.

Large numbers of the foreigners were killed in the plain,
but they suffered their greatest losses in their rush to their
entrenchments. Out of their enormous army only 10,000
managed to escape to Chalcis. As for Sulla, he states that
fourteen of his soldiers were missing, and that afterwards,
towards evening, two of these rejoined their units. So on his
trophies he had inscribed the names of Mars, Victory and
Venus, believing that his success in the war was just as much
due to good fortune as to good generalship and force of arms.
This trophy for the battle in the plain stands by the brook

Molus, at the point where Archelaus' troops first gave way; but there is another one planted on the top of Thurium to commemorate the encirclement of the foreign detachment there and it has an inscription in Greek giving the credit for this action to Homoloïchus and Anaxidamus.

Sulla held his victory celebration for this battle at Thebes, and had a stage erected near the fountain of Oedipus. The judges, however, were Greeks who had been invited from other cities. Towards the Thebans Sulla was irreconcilably hostile. He took away from them half of their territory, and consecrated it to Pythian Apollo and Olympian Zeus, with orders that the revenues should be used to pay back to these gods what he himself had taken from them.

20. After this he received news that Flaccus, one of his political opponents, had been made consul and was crossing the Ionian Sea with an army which, though it was officially meant to operate against Mithridates, was really to be used against himself.[34] He therefore marched towards Thessaly to meet him; but, when he came to the city of Melitea, news came in from all sides of how the country in his rear was being laid waste by an army of the king quite as large as the one which he had just defeated. For Dorylaus had put into Chalcis with a large fleet, bringing 80,000 of the best trained and disciplined troops in Mithridates' army. He had immediately invaded and now occupied Boeotia. Disregarding the objections of Archelaus, he was eager to bring Sulla to battle, and had put about the story that in the previous battle such enormous casualties could not have occurred if there had not been some treachery. Sulla, however, rapidly turned south and made it clear to Dorylaus that Archelaus was a man of intelligence who had an excellent knowledge of Roman prowess. After a minor engagement with Sulla near Tilphossium, Dorylaus became the leading advocate for avoiding battle and for dragging out the war by means of delaying tactics and lavish expenditure of money. Nevertheless Archelaus gained a certain amount of confidence from the nature of the position near Orchomenus where they were encamped – an ideal battleground for a side that was superior

in cavalry. It is the largest and most beautiful of all the plains in Boeotia. It starts at the city of Orchomenus and spreads out in unbroken and treeless level as far as the marshes where the River Melas loses itself. The Melas rises near Orchomenus and is the only Greek river which is deep and navigable from its source. It increases, like the Nile, at the time of the summer solstice and produces vegetation very like that of the Nile though on a smaller scale and without fruit. But it only flows for a short distance. Most of it disappears almost at once in lakes without exit and marshy ground. A small branch, however, joins the Cephisus somewhere near the place where there is a lake which is supposed to produce the best reeds for flutes.

21. Now that the two armies were camped close to each other, Archelaus made no immediate move, but Sulla began to dig ditches on both sides, his idea being to cut the enemy off, if possible, from the hard ground that was suitable for their cavalry and to force them back towards the marshes. The enemy, however, reacted strongly against this. As soon as they received the word of command from their generals they charged out vigorously and in great numbers. Not only were Sulla's labourers swept aside, but the greater part of the regular troops posted there to protect them were thrown into confusion and took to flight. At this point Sulla himself leaped down from his horse, seized a standard, and pushed his way forward through the fugitives towards the enemy. As he went, he shouted out: 'As for me, Romans, I can die here with honour; but as for you, when you are asked where it was that you betrayed your commander-in-chief, remember and say: "It was at Orchomenus."' His words had the right effect. Those who were running away faced round again; two of the cohorts on the right wing came up in support, and Sulla led his men against the enemy and routed them. He then retired a short distance and, after giving his troops breakfast, resumed the work of blockading the enemy's camp with his ditches. Once more the enemy charged out on him, this time in better order than before. Archelaus' stepson, Diogenes, fought with the greatest distinc-

tion on the right wing and died very gallantly in action. Their archers, pressed back by the Romans and left with no room to draw their bows, took bunches of arrows in their hands and used them like swords, stabbing at close quarters; but in the end they were penned up in their fortifications where, with all their dead and wounded, they passed a miserable night.

Next day Sulla again led out his troops to the enemy camp and went on with the work of digging ditches. Most of them came out to give him battle and he engaged and routed them. This time in the general panic no resistance was made and he took their camp by storm. The marshes were filled with their blood and the lake with their dead bodies. Even to this day, though almost 200 years have passed since the battle, one may still find embedded in the mud bows and helmets of foreign make, swords and fragments of steel breastplates. These actions, then – at Chaeronea and Orchomenus – are said to have taken place as I have described.

22. Meanwhile in Rome the lawless and violent behaviour of Cinna and Carbo towards the most prominent people was making many of these flee to Sulla's camp, as to a harbour in a storm, so that before long he had about him what almost amounted to a senate.[35] Metella herself, not without great difficulty, had managed to escape with her children. She arrived with the news that Sulla's house in Rome and villas in the country had been burned down by his enemies, and she begged him to come to the help of his party in Italy. Sulla was in doubt as to what to do. He could hardly bear the thought of doing nothing to save his country from oppression: on the other hand, he did not see how he could go away and leave behind him still unfinished such an important task as this war with Mithridates. While he was in this state of uncertainty a merchant from Delos, Archelaus by name, came to him secretly with a message from Archelaus, the king's general, which looked hopeful. Nothing could have pleased Sulla more and he wanted to arrange for a personal interview with Archelaus as soon as possible. The meeting took place on the coast near Delium, where the temple of Apollo is. Archelaus opened the discussion and proposed

that Sulla should abandon Asia and Pontus and sail off to the war in Rome; in return, he would receive from the king money, triremes and as many troops as he wished. At this point Sulla interrupted and said: 'Forget about Mithridates. Take the crown for yourself. Become an ally of the Roman people and hand over your fleet to them.' Archelaus replied that he would not dream of committing such an act of treachery. 'So,' said Sulla, 'I observe that you, Archelaus, a Cappadocian, a slave or, if you prefer it, a friend of a barbarian king, cannot stand the idea of doing a disgraceful act for a great reward; but still you have the face to suggest treachery to me. I am a Roman and a general. My name happens to be Sulla. And you, unless I am mistaken, are the same Archelaus who fled from Chaeronea with the little that was left of a force of a hundred and twenty thousand, and who then hid for two days in the marshes of Orchomenus after you had made it impossible to travel through Boeotia because of the numbers of your dead.' After this Archelaus adopted a different attitude. He kneeled down and begged Sulla to make an end of the war and to come to terms with Mithridates. Sulla granted his request and the following conditions were agreed upon: Mithridates was to give up Asia and Paphlagonia, to restore Bithynia to Nicomedes, and Cappadocia to Ariobarzanes, to pay an indemnity of 2,000 talents and to hand over seventy bronze-armoured ships complete with their equipment; Sulla, in return, was to guarantee to Mithridates the rest of his dominions and to have a vote passed making him an ally of Rome.[36]

23. When these terms had been agreed upon Sulla turned northwards and marched towards the Hellespont through Thessaly and Macedonia. He kept Archelaus with him and treated him with great distinction. Indeed he stopped his march and looked after him as though he had been one of his own generals when he fell seriously ill at Larissa. This gave rise to suspicions that there had been foul play at the battle of Chaeronea; and it was also observed that, whereas Sulla had released all his other prisoners who had been friends of Mithridates, he had put the tyrant Aristion, a personal enemy of Archelaus, to death by

poison. Most suspicious circumstance of all was the fact that Sulla granted to the Cappadocian about 2,000 acres of land in Euboea and gave him the title of friend and ally of Rome. Certainly in his *Memoirs* Sulla takes the trouble to defend himself on all these points.

Ambassadors now arrived from Mithridates and said that, while all the other peace terms were acceptable, the king did not think that he should lose Paphlagonia and, so far as the ships were concerned, he could not make any agreement about them at all. Sulla was furious and exclaimed: 'What is this that you are saying? Mithridates thinks he has a right to Paphlagonia? He refuses to give up the ships? I thought that he would come and grovel at my feet if I allowed him to keep that right hand of his with which he has killed so many Romans. However, he will soon change his tune when I have crossed over into Asia. At the moment he is just sitting still in Pergamum and making arrangements about a war which he has never seen the sight of.'

The ambassadors were terrified and made no reply; but Archelaus approached Sulla humbly and, with tears in his eyes, took hold of his right hand and tried to mollify his anger. In the end he persuaded him to send him on a personal mission to Mithridates. He would either, he said, have the peace ratified on Sulla's terms, or, if he failed to obtain the king's consent, he would kill himself. Sulla therefore sent him to the king. He himself invaded the country of the Maedi and, after ravaging the greater part of it, turned back again into Macedonia. At Philippi he received Archelaus who had returned with the news that all was well, but that Mithridates was extremely anxious to have a personal interview with Sulla. The main reason for this lay in the activities of Fimbria who, after assassinating Flaccus, the commander of the anti-Sulla party, had conquered Mithridates' generals and was now marching against the king himself.[37] Mithridates was frightened at the prospect and so chose to try to make friends with Sulla.

24. The meeting took place at Dardanus in the Troad. Mithridates had with him there 200 oared ships, 20,000

heavy-armed infantry, 6,000 cavalry and great numbers of scythed chariots. Sulla had 4 cohorts and 200 cavalry. When Mithridates came forward to meet him and held out his hand, Sulla asked him if he would put an end to the war on the terms to which Archelaus had agreed. Mithridates remained silent, whereupon Sulla said: 'I should have thought that those who have something to ask should be the first to speak; it is the conqueror who is in the position of being able to keep silent.'

Mithridates then began to make a speech in his own defence. In the course of it he attempted to show that the responsibility for the war lay partly with the gods; and partly, he suggested, it was the Romans themselves who were to blame. Sulla cut him short and said that he had heard long ago from others that Mithridates was a remarkably gifted orator and now he could see for himself that the reputation was deserved; he appeared to find no difficulty in producing plausible arguments to justify conduct that had been thoroughly wicked and unjust. Then, after pronouncing a most bitter indictment of what he had done, he asked once again, would he abide by the agreement made through Archelaus. Mithridates said that he would and Sulla then stepped forward to welcome him and gave him a kiss. Later he introduced the two kings, Ariobarzanes and Nicomedes, and reconciled them with him. And so Mithridates handed over 70 ships and 500 archers and then sailed away to Pontus.

Sulla realized that the peace which he had made was far from popular with his troops. They thought it a monstrous thing that they should now see this king who had been their greatest enemy and who had organized the massacre on one single day of 150,000 Romans in Asia, go sailing away with his wealth and spoils from Asia, which for four years on end he had plundered and taxed. Sulla therefore defended himself to them by saying that, if Fimbria and Mithridates had joined forces against him, he could not possibly have fought them both together.

25. He then set out from there against Fimbria who was in camp near Thyateira. He halted near by and began to fortify

his own camp. But Fimbria's men came out unarmed from
their camp, welcomed Sulla's soldiers and willingly helped
them in their work. Fimbria saw how they were changing
sides; he was frightened of Sulla who, he was convinced,
would prove irreconcilable; and so he committed suicide in
his camp.[38]

Sulla now imposed on Asia as a whole an indemnity of
20,000 talents. At the same time private families were entirely
ruined by the brutal behaviour and extortion of the troops
quartered on them. Orders were issued that every host should
give his guest four tetradrachms a day and should provide for
him an evening meal to which he might invite as many of
his friends as he liked; a military tribune should receive fifty
drachmas a day and two suits of clothes, one to wear at home
and one to wear when he went out.

26. Sulla put to sea from Ephesus with all his ships and on the
third day afterwards came to anchor in Piraeus. He was initiated into the mysteries and he seized for himself the library of
Apellicon the Teian. This library contained most of the works
of Aristotle and Theophrastus, which were then not yet in
general circulation. It is said that when the library had been
brought to Rome, most of the works in it were put in order
by the grammarian Tyrannio, and that it was from him that
Andronicus the Rhodian received copies of the manuscripts.
Andronicus published these and drew up the catalogues now
current. The elder Peripatetics, though they were certainly most
accomplished scholars themselves, do not appear to have possessed either a wide or an exact knowledge of the writings of
Aristotle and Theophrastus. This was because the estate of
Neleus of Scepsis, to whom Theophrastus bequeathed his
books, came into the hands of illiterate people who had no
notion of their value.

During Sulla's stay at Athens, he was afflicted by a feeling of
numbness and heaviness in the feet, which, according to Strabo,
is the first symptom of gout. He therefore sailed across to
Aedepsus to take the hot-water cure there, at the same time
enjoying a complete rest and passing his time in the society of

those who worked in the theatre. Here, while he was walking by the sea, some fishermen brought him some very fine fish. He was delighted with the gift and when he found out from them that they came from Halae he exclaimed: 'What! Is there a man of Halae still in existence?' For in the pursuit of the enemy after his victory at Orchomenus he had destroyed three cities of Boeotia at the same time – Anthedon, Larymna and Halae. The men were too frightened to open their mouths, but Sulla smiled at them and told them to go away and not worry. 'You have arrived', he said, 'with most excellent representatives who cannot be despised.' The men of Halae say that as a result of this they all plucked up courage and went back again to live in their city.

27. After marching through Thessaly and Macedonia, Sulla came down to the sea and prepared to cross over from Dyrrachium to Brundisium with 1,200 ships. Nearby is Apollonia and near Apollonia is the Nymphaeum, a holy piece of ground with meadows and a green dell where at various points there spring up streams of perpetually flowing fire. Here they say that a satyr, just like those represented by sculptors and painters, was caught while asleep and was brought to Sulla. The satyr was asked through many interpreters who he was, but could scarcely speak at all and could certainly say nothing intelligible. He could only let out a harsh cry something between the neighing of a horse and the bleating of a goat. Sulla was horrified and ordered the creature to be taken out of his sight.

Now when on the point of transporting his soldiers across the sea, Sulla feared that, once they got to Italy, they might all make off to their own cities. But in the first place they took an oath of their own accord, promising to stand by him and to do no damage in Italy except by his orders. Then, seeing that he was in need of a great deal of money, they made a voluntary contribution from among themselves, each man paying in proportion to what he possessed. Sulla, however, refused to accept this gift of theirs. He thanked them warmly and, after saying what he could to encourage them, crossed the sea, as he himself writes, to confront 15 enemy commanders and 450 cohorts –

though not without having received from Heaven the most
unmistakable signs that he would be successful. At Tarentum,
for instance, where he made a sacrifice as soon as he had landed,
the liver of the sacrificed animal was observed to have on it a
mark like a crown of laurel complete with the two woollen
triumphal bands hanging down from it. And just before he
crossed over from Greece there were seen in Campania near
Mount Tifatum, in the daytime, two huge he-goats charging
together and behaving just as men do in battle. This proved to
be an apparition; the fighting figures rose gradually upwards
from the earth, then appeared as vague insubstantial forms in
different parts of the sky and finally vanished altogether. It was
in this very place that not long afterwards great forces were
brought up against Sulla by Marius the younger and the consul
Norbanus.[39] On this occasion Sulla gave out no regular order
of battle, nor did he form up his army in their proper companies.
Relying simply on the force of a general enthusiasm among his
troops and on the daring which swept them forward, he routed
the enemy and shut up Norbanus in the city of Capua, after
having killed 7,000 of his men. It was because of this, he says,
that his soldiers, instead of dispersing to their own cities, stuck
together and despised their enemies, even though these were
many times more numerous than they were. He says too that
at Silvium a servant of Pontius in a state of divine possession
came up to him and declared that he brought him from Bellona
the domination of war and victory, but that, if he did not
make haste, the Capitol would be burned. And this actually
happened, he says, on the day which the man predicted, which
was the sixth of the month Quintilis, which we now call July.
Then there was the case of Marcus Lucullus, one of Sulla's
commanders, who was at Fidentia and with sixteen cohorts
was facing fifty cohorts of the enemy. Lucullus was confident
enough in his men's morale, but, since most of them were
unarmed, he hesitated to attack. However, while he considered
the position and deferred action, a gentle breeze blew from the
meadows of the plain nearby and carried with it numbers of
the meadow flowers, scattering them down upon his army; the
flowers settled of their own accord in wreaths upon the shields

and helmets of the soldiers, so that they looked to the enemy
as though they were all crowned with garlands. Thus they
became all the more eager to fight. They joined battle and
defeated the enemy, killing 18,000 of them and capturing
their camp. This Lucullus was the brother of the Lucullus who
afterwards conquered Mithridates and Tigranes.[40]

28. Sulla, however, saw that he was still surrounded on all sides
by his enemies who had many armies and large resources at
their disposal. He therefore used deceit as well as force in order
to gain power. He invited Scipio,[41] the other consul, to discuss
peace terms and, when Scipio agreed to do so, a number of
meetings and conferences took place. Sulla, however, constantly found some pretext or other for dragging out the discussions, and in the meantime was working on the loyalty of
Scipio's soldiers by means of his own men, who, like their
general, were practised in the use of deceit and all kinds of
trickery. On this occasion they went into the enemy's camp and
mixed with the men inside. Some they won over immediately
to Sulla's side by bribery, and others by promises, by soft words
and by arguments. In the end Sulla came close up to the camp
with twenty cohorts; his men greeted Scipio's men, and Scipio's
men returned their greetings and came over to them. Scipio,
entirely deserted, was captured in his tent, but then let go; and
Sulla, who, by using his twenty cohorts as decoy-birds, had
trapped forty cohorts of the enemy, led the whole lot of them
back to his camp. On this occasion too Carbo is said to have
remarked that in making war on Sulla he had to deal with one
who had both a fox and a lion in his heart, and that what
chiefly worried him was the fox.

After this, at Signia, Marius with eighty-five cohorts offered
him battle, and Sulla himself was only too glad to fight a decisive
battle on that day, because he had seen a vision in his sleep,
which was as follows: he seemed to see the elder Marius, who
had died some time ago, advising his son Marius to beware of
the following day, since it would bring him great misfortune.
Sulla was therefore eager enough to fight and was trying to get
Dolabella,[42] who was encamped some distance away, to join

him. The enemy, however, were in control of the roads and kept Sulla closely pent in, and his soldiers were worn out by their efforts to force a way through. Then in the middle of their operations there came a heavy fall of rain which made their state all the worse, so that the tribunes came to Sulla and begged him to wait before going into battle. They pointed out how the soldiers were utterly prostrated by their exertions and how they had laid their shields down on the ground and were resting on them. Sulla reluctantly agreed with his officers and gave orders to pitch a camp. But just as his men were beginning to dig the trench and throw up the rampart in front of it, Marius came riding up at the head of his troops and charged down on them confidently, hoping to scatter them before him while they were in this confused and disordered state. And now Heaven fulfilled the words which Sulla had heard in his sleep. His soldiers were filled with the same rage which he felt himself; they left off their work, planted their javelins in the trench, drew their swords and, shouting out all together, engaged the enemy at close quarters. The enemy's resistance did not last long; they were routed and great numbers of them were killed. Marius fled to Praeneste. Here he found that the gates were already closed, but a rope was thrown down to him and, after he had fastened it round his waist, he was hauled up to the top of the wall. According to other authorities (of whom Fenestella is one) Marius did not even know that the battle was taking place. Because of sleeplessness and exhaustion he had lain down on the ground in the shade and had abandoned himself to sleep at the time when the signal for battle was given; he was only woken up with difficulty later, when the rout had already taken place.

In this battle Sulla claims that his own losses amounted to only 23, while he killed 20,000 of the enemy and took 8,000 prisoners. Equally successful actions were carried out in other areas by his generals – Pompey, Crassus, Metellus and Servilius.[43] In an almost unbroken series of victories these commanders annihilated large forces of the enemy, and in the end Carbo, the leading figure in the opposite party,[44] ran away from his own army by night and sailed off to Africa.

29. In the final struggle, however, Telesinus the Samnite, like the wrestler who has been sitting by and then takes on the weary winner of the previous bout, nearly tripped Sulla up and gave him a fall at the very gates of Rome.[45] With Lamponius the Lucanian he had got together a large force and was hurrying to the relief of Marius who was besieged in Praeneste. He found, however, that Sulla was hurrying up on him from the front and Pompey from the rear. He was a great soldier and had had much experience in important actions; so now, finding his freedom of movement impeded both before and behind, he broke camp by night and with his whole army marched directly upon Rome. The city was virtually unguarded and he very nearly succeeded in breaking in. As it was, the place where he bivouacked before the city was about a mile from the Colline Gate and here he was indeed confident and full of hope as he reflected on how he had outgeneralled so many great commanders. At dawn next day the most distinguished young men in Rome rode out against him, and he overthrew many of them, including Appius Claudius, who came from an excellent family and was a good man himself.[46] In the city, as was natural, everything was in an uproar, what with the shrieking of the women and the running hither and thither, just as though it was already being taken by storm. The first to appear of Sulla's men was Balbus,[47] who came riding up at full speed with 700 cavalry. He halted just long enough to let the sweat dry off the horses, then bridled them again as quickly as possible and engaged the enemy.

At this point Sulla himself appeared on the scene. He ordered his leading contingents to take their food at once and then formed them up in order of battle. Dolabella and Torquatus[48] urgently begged him to wait and not to risk everything with forces who were worn out with fatigue and who would now have to fight, not with a Carbo or a Marius but with Samnites and Lucanians, races who hated Rome to the uttermost and who were the most warlike tribes in Italy. Sulla, however, put aside their objections. It was already about four o'clock in the afternoon, but he ordered the trumpets to sound the charge. The fight which followed was the hardest of all. The right wing, where Crassus was posted, won a brilliant victory, but the left

wing was being pressed back and doing badly when Sulla came
to its help, riding on a white horse which was a most spirited
animal and a very fast runner. Two of the enemy recognized
Sulla by his horse and poised their spears ready to hurl them at
him. Sulla himself never noticed this, but his groom did and
gave the horse a touch of the whip, so that Sulla just got past
in time and the spear-points, after grazing the horse's tail, stuck
in the ground. It is said too that Sulla had a little golden image
of Apollo from Delphi which he always carried with him into
battle inside his tunic, but that on this occasion he covered the
image with kisses and cried out: 'O Pythian Apollo, you who
in so many fights have raised me up – me, Sulla the Fortunate,
Sulla of the Cornelii – and made me great and famous, will you
now cast me down? Will you allow me to perish disgracefully
with my own countrymen, now that you have brought me to
the gates of my native place?'

So, they say, Sulla called upon the god. As for his men he
tried to deal with them by entreaties, by threats and by holding
them back with his own hands. In the end, however, the left
wing was completely broken and, in the general rout, he took
refuge in his camp, after having lost a number of his own friends
and acquaintances. Numbers also of those who had come out
from Rome to watch the battle were killed and trodden underfoot. It was generally believed that, so far as the city was
concerned, all was over, and that the siege of Marius in Praeneste was virtually at an end. In fact many of those who had
escaped from the rout made their way there and told Lucretius
Ofella, the officer in charge of the siege operations, to break up
his camp immediately, since Sulla was dead and Rome was in
enemy hands.

30. However, when it was already late at night there came to
Sulla's camp messengers from Crassus to fetch food for Crassus
himself and for his soldiers. For they had defeated the enemy,
pursued them to Antennae, and were now in camp there. When
Sulla heard this and heard also that most of the enemy had
been destroyed, he came to Antennae at dawn. Here 3,000 of
those left inside sent a deputation to him to ask for terms, and

Sulla promised that he would guarantee their safety if, before coming over to him, they would do some harm to the rest of his enemies. They trusted his word and set upon the others, and there was a great slaughter on both sides. This, however, did not prevent Sulla from collecting together into the circus at Rome the survivors both of the original 3,000 and of the rest, about 6,000 in all. He then summoned the senate to meet in the Temple of Bellona, and at the same moment as he himself rose up to speak those who had been given the job began to butcher the 6,000 in the circus. The noise of their shrieks – so many men being massacred in so small a space – was, as might be expected, easily audible and the senators were dumbfounded. Sulla, however, continued to speak with the same calm and unmoved expression. He told the senators to listen to what he had to say and not to bother their heads with what was going on outside. 'Some of the criminals', he said, 'are receiving correction. It is being done by my orders.'

This made it clear at once to the dullest-witted man in Rome that, so far from having escaped from tyranny, they had only exchanged one tyrant for another. As for the elder Marius, he had always had a savage character, and power had intensified, not altered his natural disposition. Sulla, on the other hand, had used his good fortune moderately at first and had behaved like a normal person; he had acquired the reputation of being a leader who was both an aristocrat and a friend of the people; then too from his earliest days he had been one who loved laughter and one who, so far from disguising his tenderer feelings, would often burst into tears. It was natural therefore that his behaviour should cast a certain suspicion on the very idea of high office and should make people think that these great powers bring about a change in the previous characters of their holders – a change in the direction of overexcitability, pomposity and inhumanity. However, I should have to write another essay altogether to determine the point whether this is a real change and revolution in a man's nature, brought about by fortune, or whether it is rather the case that when a man is in power the evil that has been latent in him reveals itself openly.

31. Sulla now devoted himself entirely to the work of butchery. The city was filled with murder and there was no counting the executions or setting a limit to them. Many people were killed because of purely personal enmities; they had no connection with Sulla in any way, but Sulla, in order to gratify members of his own party, permitted them to be done away with. Finally one of the younger men, Gaius Metellus,[49] ventured to ask Sulla in the senate at what point this terrible state of affairs was to end and how much further would he proceed before they could expect a cessation of what was now going on. 'We are not asking you,' he said, 'to pardon those whom you have decided to kill; all we ask is that you should free from suspense those whom you have decided not to kill.' Sulla replied that he was not sure yet whom he would spare, and Metellus at once said: 'Then let us know whom you intend to punish.' Sulla said that he would do this. According to some accounts this last speech was made not by Metellus, but by one of Sulla's creatures called Fufidius.[50]

Then immediately, and without consulting any magistrate, Sulla published a list of eighty men to be condemned.[51] Public opinion was outraged, but, after a single day's interval, he published another list containing 220 more names, and next day a third list with the same number of names on it. And in a public speech which he made on the subject he said that he was publishing the names of all those whom he happened to remember: those who escaped his memory for the moment would have their names put up later. He also condemned anyone who sheltered or attempted to save a person whose name was on the lists. Death was the penalty for such acts of humanity, and there were no exceptions in the cases of brothers, sons or parents. On the other hand, the reward for murder was two talents, and this sum was paid to anyone who killed a condemned man, even though it was a slave who killed his master or a son his father. Also (and this was regarded as the greatest injustice of all) he took away all civil rights from the sons and grandsons of those on the lists and confiscated the property of all of them.[52] These lists were published not only in Rome but in every city of Italy. No place remained undefiled

by murder – neither temple of god, nor hearth of hospitality, nor
ancestral home. Husbands were slaughtered in the embraces of
their wedded wives, sons in the arms of their mothers. And
those who were killed in the passion of the moment or because
of some private hatred were as nothing compared with those
who were butchered for the sake of their property. In fact it
became a regular thing to say among the executioners that
'So-and-so was killed by his big mansion, so-and-so by his
gardens, so-and-so by his hot-water installation.' There was,
for instance, Quintus Aurelius, a man who had nothing to do
with politics and who imagined that he was only connected
with these disastrous events in so far as he sympathized with
others who were in distress. He went into the forum and,
reading through the list of condemned, came upon his own
name. 'Things are bad for me,' he said; 'I am being hunted
down by my Alban estate.' And he had not gone far before he
was cut down by someone who had in fact been hunting after
him.

32. Meanwhile the younger Marius had killed himself when he
was at the point of being taken prisoner. Sulla came to Praeneste
and at first gave every man there a separate trial before execut-
ing him. Finally, however, not having sufficient time at his
disposal, he herded them all together into one place and gave
orders that the whole lot of them, 12,000 in all, should be
slaughtered. The single exception he made was a man who had
been his host; but this man acted nobly indeed. He told Sulla
that he would never, for the sake of his own life, be under an
obligation to a man who was the murderer of his native place,
and, joining in voluntarily with the rest of his countrymen, he
was cut down with them.

But the behaviour of Lucius Catiline[53] was considered to have
surpassed everything. He had murdered his brother before the
civil war was over, and now he asked Sulla to add his brother's
name to the list of the condemned, as though the man were still
alive. Sulla did this for him and, by way of showing his gratitude, Catiline killed a man of the opposite party called Marcus
Marius and brought his head to Sulla as he was sitting in the

forum. He then went to the water nearby which was sacred to Apollo and washed the blood off his hands.

33. Apart altogether from the massacres, the rest of Sulla's conduct also caused offence. He proclaimed himself dictator, thus reviving a type of authority which had not been used for the last 120 years. A decree was passed giving him immunity for all his past acts, while for the future he was to have the power of life and death, the power to confiscate property, to found colonies, to found new cities or to demolish existing ones, to take away or to bestow kingdoms at his pleasure.[54] In conducting the sales of confiscated estates, which he did sitting raised up on a platform, he behaved in such an arrogant and tyrannical way that he became more hated for his gifts than for his depredations. Good-looking women, musicians, ballet dancers, ex-slaves of the lowest possible type received at his hands the territories of nations and the revenues of cities, and women were forced to marry some of these creatures of his. Then there was the case of Pompey the Great with whom Sulla wished to establish a family connection.[55] Sulla ordered Pompey to divorce the wife he had and then forced Aemilia, the daughter of his own wife Metella and Scaurus, to leave her husband Manius Glabrio,[56] though she was pregnant by him, and to go and live as Pompey's wife. The young woman died in childbirth at Pompey's house. Then there was his behaviour to Lucretius Ofella, the man who had successfully carried out the siege of Marius.[57] Ofella wished to stand for the consulship and at first Sulla tried to prevent him. But Ofella appeared in the forum accompanied by a large crowd of his supporters. Sulla then sent one of the centurions of his bodyguard and had Ofella killed: he himself meanwhile was sitting on a raised platform in the temple of Castor and watched the murder from above. And when the people in the forum seized the centurion and brought him before the platform, Sulla told them to stop making a disturbance and to let the centurion go, since he had given the order himself.

34. His triumph, however, which was gorgeous enough because of the richness and rarity of the spoils taken from the king,

included something greater still.[58] This was the noble sight of the returned exiles. The most distinguished and most powerful men in Rome, with garlands on their heads, went in the procession, calling Sulla 'saviour' and 'father', since it was because of him that they were returning to their native city and bringing their wives and children with them. And finally, when the whole ceremony was over, he made a speech to the people, giving a full account of everything which he had done. In this speech he was just as anxious to show examples of his good fortune as of his actual ability and at the end of it he ordained that he be given the title of 'Fortunate' as a surname. This is the nearest equivalent of the word 'Felix'.[59] Though he himself when writing to the Greeks on official business called himself 'Epaphroditus' or 'Favourite of Venus', and on his trophies in Greece his name is inscribed as: LUCIUS CORNELIUS SULLA EPAPHRODITUS. And then when Metella bore him twins he called the male child Faustus and the female Fausta, the Roman adjective for what is fortunate and joyful.

In fact he showed so much more confidence in his good fortune than in his own powers that, in spite of the great numbers of people who had been killed by him and the great changes and innovations which he had made in the constitution, he laid down his dictatorship and gave back to the people the right of electing consuls.[60] In these elections he took no active part himself, and he went about in the forum like an ordinary citizen, unguarded, so that anyone who liked could call him to account. Things did not turn out as he had planned, and a violent character who was a personal enemy of his seemed likely to be elected consul.[61] This was Marcus Lepidus, who owed this position not so much to his own merits as to the active help which he received in his canvassing from Pompey, who was much favoured by the people. So, when Sulla saw Pompey going away from the polls, delighted with the victory of his candidate, he called him to him and said: 'This is a fine piece of statesmanship of yours, young man – getting Lepidus elected instead of Catulus,[62] when Catulus is the soundest man in the world and Lepidus the most certain to lose his head. I should advise you to be on the look-out, now that you have given your opponent greater power to do you harm.' Sulla showed a prophetic instinct in making this remark; for Lepidus very soon abandoned all restraint and went to war with Pompey's party.[63]

35. At the time when he consecrated the tenth part of his entire property to Hercules, Sulla entertained the people to some magnificent banquets. So much more was provided than what was necessary that every day great quantities of meat were thrown into the river and the wines drunk were of forty years old and upwards. The feasting lasted for many days and in the middle of it Metella fell mortally ill. The priests forbade Sulla to go near her or to have his house polluted by her funeral, and so he sent her a letter of divorce and ordered her to be carried to another house while she was still alive. In this case superstition made him follow the strict letter of the law; but he spared no expense at her funeral, thus disobeying the law which he himself had introduced for the limitation of such expenditure.[64] He also failed to abide by his own regulations for limiting the cost of banquets and tried to get over his grief by indulging in drinking bouts and expensive parties with vulgar entertainers.

A few months later there was a show of gladiators and since at this time men and women used to sit all together in the theatre, with no separate seating accommodation for the sexes, there happened to be sitting near Sulla a very beautiful woman of a most distinguished family. Her name was Valeria;[65] she was the daughter of Messalla and of a sister of Hortensius, the orator; and it so happened that she had recently been divorced from her husband. As she passed behind Sulla, she rested her hand on him, pulled off a little piece of wool from his toga and then went on to her seat. When Sulla looked round at her in surprise, she said: 'There's no reason to be surprised, Dictator. I only want to have a little bit of your good luck for myself.'

Sulla was far from displeased by this remark; indeed it was obvious at once that his amatory propensities had been stirred. He sent someone to ask discreetly what her name was and inquired about her family and past history. After this they kept glancing at each other, constantly turning their heads to look, and exchanging smiles. And in the end negotiations began for marriage. This was all innocent enough, perhaps, on her part; but, however chaste and worthy a character she may have been, Sulla's motive in marrying her was neither chaste nor virtuous; he was carried away, like a boy might have been, by a good-looking face and a saucy manner – just what naturally excites the most disgraceful and shameless sort of passion.

36. Nevertheless, even though he had her as his wife at home, he still kept company with women who were ballet dancers or harpists and with people from the theatre. They used to lie drinking together on couches all day long. Those who were at this time most influential with him were the following: Roscius the comedian,[66] Sorex the leading ballet dancer and Metrobius the female impersonator. Metrobius was now past his prime, but Sulla throughout everything continued to insist that he was in love with him. By living in this way he aggravated a disease which had not been serious in its early stages, and for a long time he was not aware that he had ulcers in the intestines. This resulted in the whole flesh being corrupted and turning into worms. Many people were employed day and night in removing these worms, but they increased far more quickly than they could be removed. Indeed they came swarming out in such numbers that all his clothing, baths, handbasins and food became infected with the corruption and flux. He tried to clean and scour himself by having frequent baths throughout the day; but it was no use: the flesh changed into worms too quickly and no washing away could keep pace with their numbers.

It is said that in very ancient times Acastus the son of Pelias died of this disease and in later times Alcman the lyric poet, Pherecydes the theologian, Callisthenes of Olynthus (who died in prison) and also Mucius the jurist.[67] And, if we may mention undistinguished but still notorious names, it is said that Eunus, the escaped slave who was leader in the Sicilian slave war,[68] died of being eaten by worms after he had been captured and brought to Rome.

37. Sulla not only foresaw his death, but may be said actually to have written about it. In the twenty-second book of his

Memoirs, which he finished writing two days before he died, he says that the Chaldaeans prophesied to him that he should have a life full of honour and that he should end his life when he was at the height of his good fortune. He says too that his son, who had died just before Metella, appeared to him in his dreams and, standing beside him in poor-looking clothes, begged his father not to have any more worries and to come with him to his mother Metella to live with her in peace and quietness. However, he continued to occupy himself with public affairs. Ten days before he died he reconciled the opposing parties in Dicaearchia and drafted laws to regulate the way in which the city should be governed. And on the very day before he died he discovered that the magistrate there, Granius, on the expectation of his death was refusing to pay a debt that he owed to the public treasury; he had Granius brought to his room, surrounded him with his servants and ordered them to strangle him; but in shouting out the orders he strained himself and, breaking the ulcer inside him, lost a quantity of blood. As a result his strength began to fail; he passed a wretched night and died on the next day. He left behind him two young children by Metella. It was after his death that Valeria gave birth to his daughter who was called Postuma – the name given by the Romans to children who are born after their father's death.

38. There were many people now who eagerly sided with Lepidus and supported his plan to deprive the dead body of the usual funeral honours. But Pompey, in spite of the fact that he was offended with Sulla (he was the only one of Sulla's friends not mentioned in his will) prevented the plan from being carried out, partly by using his influence and by methods of persuasion, partly by the threat of force. So he brought the body to Rome and made sure that it should have not only a safe but an honourable funeral. It is said that the women of Rome contributed such great quantities of spices that, apart from what was carried in 210 litters, there was enough left to make out of costly frankincense and cinnamon a large figure of Sulla himself and another figure of a lictor. The day was cloudy in the morning and, as they expected it would rain, they did not lay the

corpse on the pyre till the middle of the afternoon. Then a strong wind came and blew upon the pyre, raising a huge flame. They just had time to collect the bones, while the pyre was smouldering and the fire nearly out, when rain began to fall heavily and continued falling until night. It would seem, then, that his good fortune never left him and indeed actually took part in his funeral.[69]

His monument is in the Field of Mars and they say that the inscription on it is one that he wrote for it himself. The substance of it is that he had not been outdone by any of his friends in doing good or by any of his enemies in doing harm.

COMPARISON OF
LYSANDER AND SULLA

1. Since we have completed this life also, let us now come to the comparison. One thing they had in common was that both were founders of their own greatness. But it was peculiar to Lysander that he obtained all his offices with the consent of his fellow-citizens at a time when their affairs were in a healthy condition; he did not extract anything from them against their will, nor did he achieve power in contravention of the laws.

'But in a time of sedition the base man too is held in honour,' and so in Rome at that time, since the people was corrupt and the government in an unhealthy state, men of various origins rose to power. And it was no wonder that Sulla held office, when a Glaucia and a Saturninus drove a Metellus from the city, when sons of consuls were butchered in assemblies, when soldiers and arms were bought with gold and silver, and men passed laws by fire and steel, silencing opposition by violence. I do not blame the man who, in such conditions, succeeded in acquiring supreme power. But I cannot regard his becoming first man, when the city was in such a sorry state, as proof that he was also the best. Lysander on the other hand, since Sparta was at the height of good government and sobriety when she sent him out on the greatest commands and missions, was pretty much held to be the first of the first and the best of the best. So, though he often surrendered his power to his fellow-citizens, he just as often received it back again, since the honour accorded to his merits continued to be the highest in the state. But Sulla, when once he had been chosen to command an army, remained in arms for ten years together, making himself now consul, now dictator, but always being a tyrant.

2. Lysander did indeed attempt, as I have said, to change the form of government, but by milder and more legal means than Sulla: by persuasion, not by force of arms, and not by subverting everything at once, as Sulla did, but by improving only the appointment of the kings. Indeed it seemed to be natural justice, in a way, that in a city which had the leadership in Greece the best of the best should rule by virtue of excellence, not of noble birth. For just as a hunter looks for a dog, not the whelp of a particular bitch, and a horseman for a horse, not the foal of a particular mare – for what if the foal should turn out to be a mule? – so the statesman is completely mistaken if he inquires, not what kind of man the ruler is, but from whom he is descended. And indeed the Spartans themselves deposed some of their kings on the grounds that they were not kingly men but insignificant nonentities. And if vice is dishonourable even when conjoined with high birth, then virtue is to be honoured on its own account, not because of nobility.

Moreover, the acts of injustice which the one committed were on behalf of his friends, while the other's extended even to his friends. For it is agreed that Lysander perpetrated most of his transgressions for the sake of his comrades and carried out most of his massacres to maintain them in absolute power. But Sulla reduced the number of Pompey's soldiers out of jealousy and tried to take away from Dolabella the naval command he had given him, and when Lucretius Ofella[1] laid claim to the consulship as a reward for many great services, he ordered him to be cut down before his eyes, instilling in all men a fear and horror at his murder of his dearest friends.

3. Even more does their pursuit of riches and pleasures reveal that the one's behaviour was that of a commander, the other's that of a tyrant. For Lysander appears to have perpetrated no act of wantonness or youthful folly while he enjoyed such great authority and power. Indeed, if any man ever did, he avoided the praise and reproach of the proverbial 'Lions at home, foxes

abroad', so sober, Spartan and restrained was the way of life he everywhere displayed. But Sulla allowed neither his poverty in youth nor his years in old age to moderate his desires, but continued to bring in marital and sumptuary laws for the citizens while he himself, as Sallust says, was playing the lover and adulterer. In so doing he so beggared the city and emptied it of its wealth that he sold to allied and friendly cities freedom and autonomy for cash, while he was daily confiscating and selling at auction the largest and richest estates. Indeed, there was no measuring what he lavishly squandered and threw away upon his flatterers. For what calculation or economy was there likely to be in his drinking parties and entertainments, when on a public occasion, with the people standing by, at the sale of a large property, he ordered the auctioneer to knock it down to one of his friends at a nominal price, and when another bidder raised the price and the auctioneer announced the advance, he flew into a rage, saying 'It is a terrible and a tyrannical thing, my dear citizens, if I am not allowed to dispose of my own spoils as I wish.' But Lysander sent home for public use even the presents which had been given to him along with the rest of his booty. Not that I commend what he did. For perhaps by acquiring money for Sparta, he did her more harm than Sulla did to Rome by robbing her of it. But I offer this as evidence of the man's indifference to riches. Moreover, each had a curious experience with his own city. Sulla, who knew no restraint in his extravagance, tried to impose moderation on the citizens, while Lysander filled his city with the passions from which he himself was free. Sulla was therefore at fault in falling below the standard set by his own laws, Lysander in making the citizens fall below that he set himself, since he taught Sparta to want what he himself had learned not to covet. So much for their influence as statesmen.

4. But as regards contests in war, achievements in generalship, numbers of trophies and magnitude of dangers faced, Sulla is beyond compare. Lysander, it is true, won two victories in two naval battles, and I will add in his siege of Athens, which was not in fact a great affair, though its renown was most

dazzling. What occurred at Haliartus in Boeotia was due perhaps to a degree of ill fortune, but he seems guilty of bad
planning in not waiting for the king's large force, which had all
but arrived from Plataea. Instead, driven by resentment and
ambition, he made an inopportune assault on the walls, with
the result that a nondescript body of insignificant men made
a sortie and overwhelmed him. For he received his fatal
wound, not as Cleombrotus did at Leuctra, standing firm
against the enemy's attacks, nor as Cyrus did, or Epaminondas,
rallying his retreating men and guaranteeing them victory.
They all died like kings and generals. But Lysander threw
away his life ingloriously, like a mere targeteer or skirmisher,
and demonstrated that the Spartans of old did well to avoid
assaults on walled cities, in which not only an ordinary man
but even a child or a woman may happen to strike down the
greatest warrior, as Achilles, they say, was killed by Paris at
the gates.

   In Sulla's case it is not easy even to enumerate the pitched
battles he won and the myriads of enemies he destroyed. Rome
itself he captured twice, and he took the Piraeus of Athens, not
by starvation, as Lysander did, but by a number of great battles,
after he had driven Archelaus from the land to the sea. It is
important, too, to bear in mind the nature of their antagonists.
For I think it was mere child's play to win a naval battle
against Antiochus, Alcibiades' pilot, or to outwit Philocles, the
Athenian demagogue,

   'Inglorious man, armed only with a sharp tongue'.

These Mithridates would not have deigned to compare with
one of his grooms, nor Marius with one of his lictors. But of
the dynasts, consuls, generals and demagogues who faced Sulla,
to pass over the rest, who among the Romans was more formidable than Marius? What king was more powerful than
Mithridates? Who among the Italians was more warlike than
Lamponius and Telesinus? Yet Sulla drove out the first of them,
subdued the second and killed the other two.

5. But what is more important, in my opinion, than anything I have yet mentioned is this. Lysander achieved all his successes with the cooperation of the authorities at home, whereas Sulla set up his trophy at a time when he had been overcome by his enemies and forced into exile, when his wife was being driven from home, his house demolished and his friends killed, and when he himself was facing countless hordes of enemies in Boeotia and risking his life for his country. But not even when Mithridates offered him an alliance and forces to deploy against his enemies did he make any kind of concession or friendly gesture. Indeed, he would not even speak to him or offer him his hand until he heard him say in person that he would give up Asia, hand over his ships and restore Bithynia and Cappadocia to their rightful kings. Nothing that Sulla did seems more noble than this, or inspired by a loftier spirit, because he set the public interest before his own, and, like dogs of good breed, did not relax his bite or let go his grip until his adversary had yielded. Only then did he set out to avenge his private wrongs. And besides all this, their treatment of Athens is of some weight in a comparison of their characters. After taking the city, although it had fought against him in support of the power and supremacy of Mithridates, Sulla left it free and independent. But Lysander, though Athens had fallen from such a height of imperial power, showed it no pity, but abolished the democracy and appointed most savage and lawless men as tyrants.

It is time to consider whether we shall stray very far from the truth if we proclaim that Sulla won more successes, while Lysander had fewer failings, and give Lysander the prize for self-control and moderation, Sulla that for generalship and courage.

3
CRASSUS
[ABOUT 112–53 BC]

The coalition of Pompey, Caesar and Crassus played a major part in Roman politics between 60 and Crassus' death in 53. About two of its members, Pompey and Caesar, we know a great deal, about Crassus very little. Plutarch does not seem to have been much better off. The life is not a long one, and well over half is devoted to a detailed narrative of the campaign of Carrhae. Moreover, Plutarch offers a full account of the rebellion of Spartacus, the relevance of most of which might well be questioned. The reasons for this imbalance are twofold. First, the nature of Crassus' influence. Plutarch gives an admirable brief general statement of the sources of Crassus' wealth and the ways in which he used it to win power. We should of course like to know more, but with material of this kind there can be no happy medium. The only real alternative to Plutarch's kind of treatment would be a full list of those whom Crassus aided, with copious extracts from his account-books, and for such an approach Plutarch would have had no inclination, even if the sources had existed. Secondly, Plutarch had no taste for the complex details of political intrigue, as is painfully revealed not only by his *Crassus* but equally by the *Pompey* and the *Caesar*. Hence he gives no information on what Crassus' interests were in 59 and skips from Caesar's consulship to the conference of Luca without any attempt to untangle the intricacies of the shifting relations between the three dynasts and the efforts of their opponents to detach them from one another. So in general the life leaps from one landmark to the next: Spartacus, the consulship, the coalition, the second consulship and finally Carrhae. To understand Crassus' place in the history of Rome we should have to know what he was doing in between.

1. Marcus Crassus' father had held the office of censor and had been honoured with a triumph; but Crassus himself, with his two brothers, was brought up in a small house.[1] His two brothers were married while their parents were still alive and the whole family had their meals together; this may well have been one of the chief reasons why Crassus was so temperate and moderate in his own way of life. When one of his brothers died, he married the widow and had children by her; and indeed with regard to his relations with women his conduct was as exemplary as that of anyone in Rome. He was indeed in his later years accused of having had an affair with Licinia, one of the Vestal Virgins, and Licinia was actually prosecuted by a man called Plotius.[2] She was the owner of a very attractive house in the suburbs which Crassus wanted to get hold of at a low price, and it was for this reason that he was always hovering about Licinia and paying his attentions to her, thus provoking a scandal. And, in a sense, it was his avarice which cleared him of the charge of having corrupted the lady. He was acquitted by the court, but he did not let Licinia alone until he had acquired the property.

2. Certainly the Romans say that in the case of Crassus many virtues were obscured by one vice, namely avarice; and it did seem that he only had one vice, since it was such a predominant one that other evil propensities which he may have had were scarcely noticeable. How avaricious he was can be best proved by considering the vastness of his fortune and the ways in which he acquired it. He started with not more than 300 talents; then, during his consulship,[3] he dedicated a tenth of his property to Hercules, he provided a banquet for the people, and he gave out of his own funds to every Roman citizen enough to live on for three months; yet after all this, when he made up his accounts before setting out on the expedition to Parthia,[4] he found that he was worth 7,100 talents. And, since one must tell the truth, however damaging, he amassed most of this property

by means of fire and war; public calamities were his principal source of revenue.

He was conspicuous for the way in which he never once refused to accept or to buy up property at the time when Sulla, after his occupation of Rome, was selling the goods of those whom he had put to death.[5] Sulla considered and indeed called this property the spoils of war, and was anxious that as many and as influential people as possible should share the burden of his own guilt. Crassus also observed what frequent and every-day occurrences in Rome were fire and the collapse of buildings owing to their size and their close proximity to each other.[6] He therefore bought slaves who were architects and builders, and then, when he had more than 500 of them, he would buy up houses that were either on fire themselves or near the scene of the fire; the owners of these properties, in the terror and uncertainty of the moment, would let them go for next to nothing. In this way most of Rome came into his possession. Yet though he owned so many workmen, he built no houses for himself except the one in which he lived. In fact he used to say that people who were fond of building needed no enemies; they would ruin themselves by themselves.

He owned countless silver mines, large areas of valuable land and labourers to work it for him, yet all this, one may say, was nothing compared with the value of his slaves. There were great numbers of them and they were of the highest quality – readers, secretaries, silversmiths, stewards, waiters. He used to direct their education himself and take part in it by giving them personal instructions. Altogether his view was that the chief duty of a master is to care for his slaves, who are, in fact, the living tools for the management of a household. And in this he was in the right, if, as he used to say, he believed that the slaves should do the work, but he should direct the slaves. For we observe that the management of a household is a financial activity in so far as it deals with lifeless things; but it becomes a political activity when it deals with human beings. Crassus was not right, however, in thinking and in actually saying that no one could be called rich who could not support an army out of his income; for, as King Archidamus observed, 'there is no rationing scheme for war', and therefore it is impossible to fix a limit for the amount of wealth which war may require. Certainly Marius held a very different view. He, finding that, after he had distributed fourteen acres of land to each of his veterans, the men wanted more, said: 'May no Roman ever think that he has not got enough land, if he has enough to support himself.'

3. It must be admitted, however, that Crassus was eager to show kindness and hospitality. His house was open to all; and he used to lend money to his friends without interest; but when the time came for repayment, he was quite relentless about demanding it back from the borrower, so that his interest-free loans often proved more burdensome than the payment of heavy interest would have been. The people he invited to his dinner parties were usually ordinary people and not members of the great families; and these meals were not expensive, but they were good and there was a friendliness about them which made them more agreeable than more lavish entertainments.

So far as his general culture was concerned, he gave most attention to the art of speaking and to those aspects of it which would be useful in dealing with numbers of people. He became one of the best speakers in Rome and, by care and application, was able to surpass those who were more highly gifted by nature. He never appeared in the law courts without having prepared his speech beforehand, however small or inconsiderable the case might be with which he was dealing; and often when Pompey and Cicero and Caesar were reluctant to speak, he undertook the whole management of the case himself, thereby gaining an advantage over them in popularity, since people thought of him as a man willing to take trouble and to help others. Another thing which made him popular was the courteous unaffected way in which he greeted people and spoke to them. However humble and obscure a man might be, Crassus, on meeting him, would invariably return his greeting and address him by name. He is said to have been well read in history and also to have been something of a philosopher, attaching himself to the doctrines of Aristotle. His teacher in philosophy was Alexander, who in his relations with Crassus showed a remarkable good nature and mildness of disposition. Indeed it would be hard to say whether he was poorer before or after he got to know him. Certainly he was the only one of Crassus' friends who always used to accompany him when he went abroad; he would then be given a cloak for the journey which he would be asked to return when the journey was over. This, however, was at a later period in Crassus' life.

4. At the time when Cinna and Marius seized power,[7] it was at once evident that their purpose in re-entering the city was not to do good to their country but simply to wipe out and destroy the party of the nobility. They killed as many of these as they could lay their hands on, Crassus' father and brother among them.[8] Crassus himself, who was very young, escaped for the time being, but he saw himself surrounded on all sides and likely to be hunted down by the tyrants, and so, with three friends and ten servants, he fled to Spain, travelling with the greatest possible speed. He had been in Spain before, when his father was praetor there, and he had made friends in the country.[9] However, he found a general state of panic, with everyone terrified of the cruelty of Marius, as though he were actually standing over them in person, and he did not dare to approach anyone openly. Instead he went off the road into some fields along the seashore which belonged to Vibius Paciacus. Here there was a large cave in which he hid. However, as his provisions began to run out, he sent one slave to Vibius to sound him. When Vibius received the message, he was delighted to know that Crassus had escaped. He inquired how many were with him and where they were hidden, and then, though he did not come to see them personally, he took the bailiff of his farm near to the place and ordered him to bring a good meal there every day, to leave it near the cliff and then to go away without saying anything to anyone, and without busying himself with making further inquiries; he was threatened with death if he did start interfering in any way, and was promised his freedom if he cooperated loyally.

The cave is not far from the sea; there are cliffs all round it and the path that leads inside is narrow and difficult to find; but once one is inside, it opens up to an amazing height and at each side there are spacious chambers opening out of each other. There is plenty of water and light, since a spring of beautifully clear water comes out of the base of the cliff, and in the rock, at points where the different strata are close together, there are natural fissures which let in the light from outside, so that in the daytime the place is quite bright. The thickness of the rock makes the air inside dry and pure, all dampness and dripping water being carried away into the spring.

5. Here Crassus lived and every day the man came with the food. He never saw the people in the cave himself and had no idea who they were, but they saw him, since they knew about him and were on the watch for his arrival. The meals were plentiful and well prepared, so as to please the taste as well as to satisfy the appetite. Vibius in fact had made up his mind to treat Crassus in as friendly a way as possible; it even occurred to him to think of his age; Crassus, he reflected, was a very young man and some provision ought to be made for the pleasures natural to youth; merely to give what was necessary seemed to him to show a sort of enforced kindness rather than genuine goodwill. So he took with him two good-looking female slaves and went down to the sea. When he came to the right place, he pointed out to them the path which led up to the cave and told them to go inside and not to be afraid. Crassus, seeing them coming, feared that news had got about and that the place had been discovered. He asked them who they were and what they wanted, and they, as they had been told to do, replied that they were looking for a master who was hidden there. Crassus then realized that this was a kindly meant piece of pleasantry on the part of Vibius. He took the girls in and they stayed with him for the rest of the time that he was there, carrying messages to Vibius, when required to do so. Fenestella[10] says that he saw one of these slaves himself. By that time she was an old woman, and he often heard her describe this episode. She used to tell the story with the greatest pleasure.

6. Crassus spent eight months here in hiding; but as soon as he heard that Cinna was dead,[11] he came into the open, and great numbers of people volunteered to join him. Out of these he selected a body of 2,500 men and went round the various cities. One city, Malaca, was sacked by him according to many authorities, though they state also that Crassus himself denied this charge and always protested strongly when it was mentioned. After this he got together some ships and crossed to Africa where he joined Metellus Pius, a well-known man who had raised a considerable army.[12] However, he quarrelled with Metellus and, after only a short stay in Africa, set out to join Sulla, who treated him with every mark of distinction. When Sulla had crossed over to Italy, he wanted all the young men who were with him to take an active part in the campaign and gave each of them some special task to perform. Crassus, who was sent to raise an army amongst the Marsi, asked to be given an escort, since his way lay through country occupied by the enemy. Sulla was angry at this request and spoke to him sharply. 'I give you as an escort,' he said, 'your father, your brother, your friends, and your relations who have been put to death without law or justice and whose murderers I am pursuing.' Stung by this rebuke, Crassus set out at once and forced his way resolutely through the enemy. He raised a considerable army and in all Sulla's campaigns showed a most active spirit.

It was in the course of these campaigns, they say, that there first began that jealous rivalry for distinction which he felt towards Pompey. Pompey was the younger man and his father had had a bad reputation in Rome, being indeed quite exceptionally disliked by his fellow citizens;[13] yet in the events of this time Pompey stood out as conspicuously great, so much so that Sulla treated him with a respect that he seldom showed even to older men or to his own equals in rank; he would rise at his approach and uncover his head, and he saluted him by the title of 'Imperator'.[14] All this had a most mortifying effect on Crassus and made him jealous, though in fact Sulla had excellent reasons for preferring Pompey to him, since Crassus was lacking in experience and allowed the lustre of his achievements to be tarnished by his two innate vices of avarice and meanness. When, for example, he captured the city of Tuder in Umbria, it was believed that he appropriated most of the spoil for himself, and information to this effect was laid before Sulla. But in the last and greatest battle of all, which took place at the gates of Rome, while Sulla was defeated and his army driven back in disorder, Crassus with the right wing was victorious. He pursued the enemy until nightfall, and then sent a messenger to Sulla to tell him of the success and to ask for food for his soldiers. However, during the period of the proscriptions and of the selling up of confiscated property he again got himself a bad name by demanding gifts and by buying up large estates for low prices. It is said that in Bruttium he actually added a man's name to the proscription lists purely in order to get hold of his property and with no authority from Sulla; and that Sulla was so indignant at this that he never employed him again in public affairs. Yet Crassus was remarkably clever at flattering all types of people and getting them on his side; on the other hand he could easily be taken in himself by anyone who flattered him. Another trait of his which has been observed was that, though he was the most avaricious person in the world, he particularly disliked and was constantly abusing others who were also avaricious.

7. He was much annoyed by Pompey's successes as a commander, by the triumph which he held before becoming a senator, and by the title of 'Magnus' or 'The Great' which he received from his fellow citizens.[15] On one occasion when someone said: 'Pompey the Great is coming,' Crassus merely laughed and asked, 'As great as what?' Giving up, therefore, all attempts to equal Pompey in military matters, Crassus devoted himself to politics. Here by taking pains, by helping people in the law courts or with loans, or in the canvassing and questioning which has to be done and undergone by candidates for office, he acquired an influence and a reputation equal to that which Pompey had won by all his great military expeditions. Each of the two, in fact, had a peculiar position of his own. Pompey, because of his military campaigns, was more talked about and

more powerful in Rome when he was away; when he was present, he was often less important than Crassus. This was because there was a certain arrogance and haughtiness about Pompey's way of life. He avoided crowds, scarcely appeared in the forum, gave his help to only a few of those who asked him for it, and even then not very willingly. In this way he aimed at preserving his influence intact for use in his own interests. Crassus, on the other hand, was continually ready to be of use to people, always available and easy to be found; he had a hand in everything that was going on, and by the kindness which he was prepared to show to everyone he made himself more influential than Pompey was able to do with his high-handed manners. So far as dignity of appearance, persuasiveness of language, and attractiveness of face are concerned, there was, so it is said, nothing to choose between them.

However, this spirit of rivalry did not result in Crassus feeling anything that could be called hatred or ill-will. He did not like to see Pompey and Caesar more honoured than himself, but this passion for distinction of his was free from hostility and malice. It is true that when Caesar was captured and held prisoner by the pirates in Asia, he exclaimed: 'How pleased you will be, Crassus, when you hear that I have been captured!'[16] Later, however, they were undoubtedly on very friendly terms. There was, for instance, the time when Caesar was on the point of setting out for Spain as praetor and had no money.[17] On this occasion his creditors descended on him and were for seizing his luggage; but Crassus stood by him and got him out of trouble by becoming his guarantor for a sum of 830 talents. And when all Rome was divided between three powerful parties, that of Pompey, that of Caesar and that of Crassus, it was the sober and conservative element in the city which followed Pompey, and the violent and easily unsettled types who hung on the hopes of Caesar, while Crassus took up a position between the two and made use of each. As for Cato, his reputation was greater than his power; he was rather looked up to than followed. As a politician Crassus was singularly inconsistent, neither a steadfast friend nor an implacable enemy. Where his self-interest was involved he found no difficulty in breaking off an attachment or in making up a quarrel. Indeed it often happened that, in a short space of time, he came forward both as the supporter and as the opponent of the same man and the same measures. He was strong because he was popular and because he was feared – particularly because he was feared. Certainly Sicinnius,[18] who gave more trouble than anyone else to the magistrates and popular leaders of his time, when he was asked why Crassus was the only person whom he left alone and did not attack, replied: 'Because he has hay on his horns' – it being a custom among the Romans to tie hay round the horns of dangerous bulls, so that people who met them might be on their guard.

8. The rising of the gladiators and their devastation of Italy, which is generally known as the war of Spartacus, began as follows.[19] A man called Lentulus Batiatus had an establishment for gladiators at Capua. Most of them were Gauls and Thracians. They had done nothing wrong, but, simply because of the cruelty of their owner, were kept in close confinement until the time came for them to engage in combat. Two hundred of them planned to escape, but their plan was betrayed and only seventy-eight, who realized this, managed to act in time and get away, armed with choppers and spits which they seized from some cookhouse. On the road they came across some wagons which were carrying arms for gladiators to another city, and they took these arms for their own use. They then occupied a strong position and elected three leaders. The first of these was Spartacus. He was a Thracian from the nomadic tribes and not only had a great spirit and great physical strength, but was, much more than one would expect from his condition, most intelligent and cultured, being more like a Greek than a Thracian. They say that when he was first taken to Rome to be sold, a snake was seen coiled round his head while he was asleep and his wife, who came from the same tribe and was a prophetess subject to possession by the frenzy of Dionysus, declared that this sign meant that he would have a great and terrible power which would end in misfortune. This woman shared in his escape and was then living with him.

9. First, then, the gladiators repulsed those who came out against them from Capua. In this engagement they got hold of proper arms and gladly took them in exchange for their own gladiatorial equipment which they threw away, as being barbarous and dishonourable weapons to use. Then the praetor Clodius,[20] with 3,000 soldiers, was sent out against them from Rome. He laid siege to them in a position which they took up on a hill. There was only one way up this hill, and that was a narrow and difficult one, and was closely guarded by Clodius; in every other direction there was nothing but sheer precipitous cliffs. The top of the hill, however, was covered with wild vines and from these they cut off all the branches that they needed, and then twisted them into strong ladders which were long enough to reach from the top, where they were fastened, right down the cliff face to the plain below. They all got down safely by means of these ladders except for one man who stayed at the top to deal with their arms, and he, once the rest had got down, began to drop the arms down to them, and, when he had finished his task, descended last and reached the plain in safety. The Romans knew nothing of all this, and so the gladiators were able to get round behind them and to throw them into confusion by the unexpectedness of the attack, first routing them and then capturing their camp. And now they were joined by numbers of herdsmen and shepherds of those parts, all sturdy men and fast on their feet. Some of these they armed as regular infantrymen and made use of others as scouts and light troops.

The second expedition against them was led by the praetor Publius Varinus. First they engaged and routed a force of 2,000 men under his deputy commander, Furius by name; then came the turn of Cossinius,[21] who had been sent out with a large force to advise Varinus and to share with him the responsibility of the command. Spartacus watched his movements closely and very nearly captured him as he was bathing near Salinae. He only just managed to escape, and Spartacus immediately seized all his baggage and then pressed on hard after him and captured his camp. There was a great slaughter and Cossinius was among those who fell. Next Spartacus defeated the praetor himself in

a number of engagements and finally captured his lictors and
the very horse that he rode. By this time Spartacus had grown
to be a great and formidable power, but he showed no signs of
losing his head. He could not expect to prove superior to the
whole power of Rome, and so he began to lead his army towards
the Alps His view was that they should cross the mountains
and then disperse to their own homes, some to Thrace and
some to Gaul. His men, however, would not listen to him. They
were strong in numbers and full of confidence, and they went
about Italy ravaging everything in their way.

There was now more to disturb the senate than just the
shame and the disgrace of the revolt. The situation had become
dangerous enough to inspire real fear, and as a result both
consuls[22] were sent out to deal with what was considered a
major war and a most difficult one to fight. One of the consuls,
Gellius, fell suddenly upon and entirely destroyed the German
contingent of Spartacus' troops, who in their insolent self-
confidence had marched off on their own and lost contact with
the rest; but when Lentulus, the other consul, had surrounded
him with large forces, Spartacus turned to the attack, joined
battle, defeated the legates of Lentulus and captured all their
equipment. He then pushed on towards the Alps and was confronted by Cassius,[23] the governor of Cisalpine Gaul, with an
army of 10,000 men. In the battle that followed Cassius was
defeated and, after losing many of his men, only just managed
to escape with his own life.

10. This news roused the senate to anger. The consuls were
told to return to civilian life, and Crassus was appointed to the
supreme command of the war.[24] Because of his reputation or
because of their friendship with him large numbers of the nobility volunteered to serve with him. Spartacus was now bearing
down on Picenum, and Crassus himself took up a position on
the borders of the district with the intention of meeting the
attack there. He ordered one of his subordinate commanders,
Mummius,[25] with two legions to march round by another route
and instructed him to follow the enemy, but not to join battle
with them or even to do any skirmishing. Mummius, however,

as soon as he saw what appeared to him a good opportunity, offered battle and was defeated. Many of his men were killed and many saved their lives by throwing away their arms and running for it. Crassus gave Mummius himself a very rough reception after this. He re-armed his soldiers and made them give guarantees that in future they would preserve the arms in their possession. Then he took 500 of those who had been the first to fly and had shown themselves the greatest cowards, and, dividing them into fifty squads of ten men each, put to death one man, chosen by lot, from each squad. This was a traditional method of punishing soldiers, now revived by Crassus after having been out of use for many years. Those who are punished in this way not only lose their lives but are also disgraced, since the whole army is there to watch, and the actual circumstances of the execution are very savage and repulsive.

After employing this method of conversion on his men, Crassus led them against the enemy. But Spartacus slipped away from him and marched through Lucania to the sea. At the Straits he fell in with some pirate ships from Cilicia and formed the plan of landing 2,000 men in Sicily and seizing the island; he would be able, he thought, to start another revolt of the slaves there, since the previous slave war had recently died down and only needed a little fuel to make it blaze out again. However, the Cilicians, after agreeing to his proposals and receiving gifts from him, failed to keep their promises and sailed off. So Spartacus marched back again from the sea and established his army in the peninsula of Rhegium. At this point Crassus came up. His observation of the place made him see what should be done, and he began to build fortifications right across the isthmus. In this way he was able at the same time to keep his own soldiers busy and to deprive the enemy of supplies. The task which he had set himself was neither easy nor inconsiderable, but he finished it and, contrary to all expectation, had it done in a very short time. A ditch, nearly forty miles long and fifteen feet wide and deep, was carried across the neck of land from sea to sea; and above the ditch he constructed a wall which was astonishingly high and strong. At first Spartacus despised these fortifications and did not take them seriously; but soon he found himself short of plunder and, when he wanted to break out from the peninsula, he realized that he was walled in and could get no more supplies where he was. So he waited for a night when it was snowing and a wintry storm had got up, and then, after filling up a small section of the ditch with earth and timber and branches of trees, managed to get a third of his army across.

11. Crassus was now alarmed, thinking that Spartacus might conceive the idea of marching directly on Rome. But he was relieved from his anxiety when he saw that, as the result of some disagreement, many of Spartacus' men had left him and were encamped as an independent force by themselves near a lake in Lucania, which, they say, changes from time to time, being sometimes full of fresh water and sometimes having water which is too salt to drink. Crassus fell upon this division of the enemy and dislodged them from their positions by the lake, but at this point Spartacus suddenly appeared and stopped their flight, so that he was prevented from following them up and slaughtering them.

Crassus now regretted that he had previously written to the senate to ask them to send for Lucullus from Thrace and Pompey from Spain. He made all the haste he could to finish the war before these generals arrived, knowing that the credit for the success would be likely to go not to himself but to the commander who appeared on the scene with reinforcements. In the first place, then, he decided to attack the enemy force under Gaius Canicius and Castus, who had separated themselves from the rest and were operating on their own. With this intention he sent out 6,000 men to occupy some high ground before the enemy could do so and he told them to try to do this without being observed. They, however, though they attempted to elude observation by covering up their helmets, were seen by two women who were sacrificing for the enemy, and they would have been in great danger if Crassus had not quickly appeared and joined battle. This was the most stubbornly contested battle of all. In it Crassus' troops killed 12,300 men, but he only found two of them who were wounded in the back. All the rest died standing in the ranks and fighting back against the Romans.

After this force had been defeated, Spartacus retired to the mountains of Petelia. One of Crassus' officers called Quintus,[26] and the quaestor Scrofa followed closely in his tracks. But when Spartacus turned on his pursuers, the Romans were entirely routed and they only just managed to drag the quaestor, who had been wounded, into safety. This success turned out to be the undoing of Spartacus, since it filled his slaves with overconfidence. They refused any longer to avoid battle and would not even obey their officers. Instead they surrounded them with arms in their hands as soon as they began to march and forced them to lead them back through Lucania against the Romans. This was precisely what Crassus most wanted them to do. It had already been reported that Pompey was on his way, and in fact a number of people were already loudly proclaiming that the victory in this war belonged to him; it only remained for him to come and fight a battle, they said, and the war would be over. Crassus, therefore, was very eager to fight the decisive engagement himself and he camped close by the enemy. Here, as his men were digging a trench, the slaves came out, jumped into the trench and began to fight with those who were digging. More men from both sides kept on coming up, and Spartacus, realizing that he had no alternative, drew up his whole army in order of battle.

First, when his horse was brought to him, he drew his sword and killed it, saying that the enemy had plenty of good horses which would be his if he won, and, if he lost, he would not need a horse at all. Then he made straight for Crassus himself, charging forward through the press of weapons and wounded men, and, though he did not reach Crassus, he cut down two centurions who fell on him together. Finally, when his own men had taken to flight, he himself, surrounded by enemies, still stood his ground and died fighting to the last.

Crassus had had good fortune, had shown excellent generalship and had risked his own life in the fighting; nevertheless the success of Crassus served to increase the fame of Pompey. The fugitives from the battle fell in with Pompey's troops and were destroyed, so that Pompey, in his dispatch to the senate, was able to say that, while Crassus certainly had conquered the slaves in open battle, he himself had dug the war up by the roots. Pompey then celebrated a magnificent triumph for his victories against Sertorius and for the war in Spain,[27] while Crassus, much as he may have wanted to do so, did not venture to ask for a proper triumph; indeed it was thought that he acted rather meanly and discreditably when he accepted, for a war fought against slaves, the minor honour of a procession on foot, called the 'ovation'. I have described in my *Life of Marcellus* how the ovation differs from the triumph and why it is called an 'ovation'.

12. After this Pompey was at once asked to stand for the consulship,[28] and Crassus, who had hopes of becoming consul at the same time, did not hesitate to ask Pompey for his help. Pompey was very glad to be asked. He wanted to have Crassus in one way or other always under an obligation to him for some favour, and he did his best to help him in his candidature. In the end, when speaking to an assembly of the people, he said that if they gave him Crassus as a colleague he would be as grateful for that as for the consulship itself.

These friendly relations, however, were not maintained once they came into office. In fact they differed on practically every point that came up; they were constantly quarrelling, each trying to get the better of the other, and, as a result, they made themselves as consuls politically ineffective and achieved nothing – except that Crassus made a great sacrifice in honour of Hercules and gave a feast to the people at which 10,000 tables were set out and each man was presented with an allowance of grain enough to last for three months. When, in the end, their year of office was nearly over and they were speaking to an assembly of the people, they were interrupted by a man called Onatius Aurelius, not a member of the nobility, but a member of the equestrian order and somewhat rough and ready in his manners. He jumped on to the platform and related to the assembly a vision which had appeared to him in his sleep. 'Jupiter,' he said, 'appeared to me and told me to say in public that you must not allow the consuls to lay down their office until they have become friends.' When he said this, the people urged them to become reconciled, but Pompey stood still, without making a sign. Crassus, however, took the initiative. He clasped Pompey's hand and said: 'My friends, I do not think that I am lowering or demeaning myself in any way if I take the first step in the direction of friendship and goodwill towards Pompey, a man to whom you gave the title of "the Great" when he had scarcely a hair on his chin, and whom you honoured with a triumph before he was even a member of the senate.'[29]

13. So far as his consulship is concerned, these were the memorable events. When he was censor, he accomplished literally nothing at all.[30] There was no revision of the list of senators, no review of the propertied classes who had served in war, and no census of the population, though he had as his colleague Lutatius Catulus,[31] who should have been one of the easiest people possible to get on with. They say, however, that Catulus strongly objected to Crassus' dangerous and provocative policy of annexing Egypt to Rome, and that as a result of this the two censors quarrelled and both agreed to lay down their office.

At the time of the great conspiracy of Catiline which so nearly caused a revolution in Rome, Crassus was certainly suspected of being involved, and was actually named by one man as being one of the conspirators.[32] No one, however, believed this, though Cicero, in one of his speeches, definitely suggests that both Crassus and Caesar were implicated.[33] It is true that this speech was not published until both Crassus and Caesar were dead; but in his prose work on the subject of his consulship Cicero says that Crassus came to him in the night with a letter giving details of Catiline's plans, thus making it quite clear that the conspiracy really existed.[34] Because of this Crassus hated Cicero ever afterwards, but he was prevented from openly doing him harm by his son Publius, who was a keen student of literature and of all branches of learning and very much attached to Cicero.[35] In fact when Cicero changed into mourning at the time of his trial,[36] Publius did so too and induced the other young men to follow his example; and in the end he persuaded his father to become Cicero's friend.

14. We now come to the time when Caesar, on his return from his provincial governorship, was proposing to stand for the consulship.[37] He observed that Pompey and Crassus were once again on bad terms with each other and, while he had no wish to make an enemy of one of them by seeking support from the other, he felt that without the help of either of them his own prospects would be hopeless. He therefore set to work to reconcile them.[38] He was constantly pointing out to them that the effect of their attacks on each other merely increased the power of such people as Cicero, Catulus and Cato, all of whom would be quite negligible if only Crassus and Pompey would combine interests and join their parties together and direct the state with a single purpose and a united power. Caesar's arguments proved effective. He reconciled the two of them and brought them both over to his own side, thus forming out of this triumvirate a force that was irresistible and which he used to overthrow both the senate and the people. For it was not the case that by getting Crassus to support Pompey or Pompey to support Crassus he made either of them greater than before; instead, by using them he made himself greater than anyone. So, with the support of them both, he was at once brilliantly successful at the elections and became consul. During his consulship they had decrees passed which gave him the command of armies and put Gaul into his hands.[39] They had thus, as it were, established him in a position of strength, and no doubt thought in terms of quietly sharing out everything else among themselves, once they had seen to it that Caesar's command in the province that had been allotted to him was duly ratified.

In all this Pompey no doubt was actuated simply by his boundless love of power; but in the case of Crassus a new passion, in addition to his old weakness of avarice, began to show itself. The glorious exploits of Caesar made Crassus also long for trophies and triumphs – the one field of activity in which he was not, he considered, Caesar's superior. This passion of his gave him no rest or peace until it ended in an inglorious death and a national disaster.

When Caesar came south from Gaul to the city of Luca a great many Romans went there to meet him.[40] Among these were Pompey and Crassus. At the private conferences which the three men held together they decided to tighten their grip on public affairs and to take over the entire control of the state. Caesar was to retain his army and Pompey and Crassus were to have other provinces and armies. The only way to carry out this plan was to stand for a second consulship.[41] Pompey and Crassus were to put themselves forward as candidates, and Caesar was to cooperate by writing to his friends and sending back large numbers of his soldiers to support them at the elections.

15. Having reached this understanding, Pompey and Crassus returned to Rome. People at once suspected what their plans were and everywhere the view was expressed that this meeting of theirs with Caesar had been for no good. In the senate Marcellinus and Domitius[42] asked Pompey if he intended to stand for the consulship, and Pompey replied that the answer was perhaps 'yes' and perhaps 'no'. When further pressed, he said that what he wanted was the votes of the good elements in the state, not of the bad. Pompey, in these replies of his, gave an impression of pride and arrogance; but Crassus adopted a more moderate attitude and said, when questioned, that if it was in the best interests of Rome, he would stand for the consulship, otherwise he would not. As a result of this some people, amongst whom was Domitius, were bold enough to put their names forward as candidates. Most of these, however, grew frightened and withdrew when Pompey and Crassus openly announced that they were standing. But Cato encouraged Domitius, who was a relation and a friend of his, to fight the election.[43] He earnestly urged him not to abandon his hopes and to regard himself as the champion of the freedom of the whole community. It was a tyranny, he said, not a consulship which Pompey and Crassus wanted, and their actions showed that they were not thinking in terms of merely being elected to

an office, but of grabbing provinces and armies for themselves.

These were Cato's feelings and he expressed them with such effect that he practically forced Domitius to appear in the forum as a candidate for the consulship. Large numbers of people supported their party, and indeed there was a considerable body of opinion which was outraged by the behaviour of Pompey and Crassus. 'Why', it was asked, 'should these two want a second consulship? And why for a second time should they want to hold it together? Why should they not have other colleagues? Surely we have among us men who are quite good enough to share the office with either Pompey or Crassus.' This kind of talk alarmed the supporters of Crassus and Pompey who now lost all restraint and behaved in the most violent and disorderly manner possible. The climax was when they laid an ambush for Domitius as he was coming down into the forum with his followers before dawn. On this occasion they killed his torch-bearer and wounded many of the others, including Cato himself. So, with their opponents routed and forced to stay shut up in their houses, they had themselves proclaimed consuls. Soon afterwards they again surrounded a meeting of the assembly with bands of armed men, threw Cato out of the forum, killed others who resisted them, and then passed decrees by which Caesar's command in Gaul was prolonged for five years while they themselves had provinces and armies voted to them. These were divided by lot, Syria going to Crassus and the Spanish provinces to Pompey.[44]

16. Everyone was pleased at the way the lot had fallen out. Most people did not want Pompey to be a long way away from Rome, and Pompey, who was very much in love with his wife,[45] proposed to spend most of his time there. As for Crassus, as soon as the result of the lot was known, he showed by his evident delight that he regarded this as the best piece of good fortune that had ever come to him. Even in public and among people who did not know him he was scarcely capable of keeping quiet about it, and when he was in the company of his friends the language he used was empty, childish and boastful – indecorous at his age and quite at variance with his usual

character, since up to this time he had never been a vain or
boastful man. Now, however, he seemed to be transported right
out of his senses. He had no intention of making Syria or even
Parthia the limit of his successful enterprises. What he proposed
to do was to make the campaigns of Lucullus against Tigranes
and those of Pompey against Mithridates[46] appear as mere
child's play, and in his hopes he saw himself penetrating as far
as Bactria and India and the Outer Ocean.

This was in spite of the fact that in the law which was passed
giving him his command there was no reference at all to a war
with Parthia. Yet everyone knew that this was what Crassus'
mind was bent on; and Caesar wrote to him from Gaul expressing his approval of the project and encouraging him to enter
upon this war. One of the tribunes, Ateius by name,[47] did
threaten to oppose his leaving the city and indeed there was a
considerable party who objected strongly to the idea of a man
going out to make war on people who, so far from having done
any harm to the Romans, were bound to them by treaties of
friendship.[48] Crassus was alarmed by this attitude and asked
Pompey, who had such a great name among the general mass
of the people, to help him by coming to see him off from the
city. And though a large crowd was all prepared to raise a
disturbance and try to prevent Crassus from leaving, as soon
as they saw Pompey leading the way with a bright and cheerful
face, they calmed down and stood aside in silence to let them
pass. Ateius, however, stood in his way and at first tried to
stop him by verbal protests against his going forward; he then
ordered his attendant officer to arrest him and detain him. But
other tribunes would not allow this and so the attendant released Crassus. Ateius then ran on ahead to the city gate where
he set up a brazier with lighted fuel in it. When Crassus came
to the gate, he threw incense and libations on the brazier and
called down on him curses which were dreadful and frightening
enough in themselves and made still more dreadful by the names
of certain strange and terrible deities whom he called upon in
his invocations. The Romans believe that these mysterious and
ancient curses are so powerful that no one who has had them
laid upon him can escape from their effect – and that an evil

fate will also be in store for the man who utters them; consequently they are seldom made use of at all, and never lightly.
So on this occasion people blamed Ateius for what he had done;
he had been angry with Crassus for the sake of Rome, yet he
had involved Rome in these curses and in the terror which must
be felt of supernatural intervention.

17. Crassus went on his way and reached Brundisium. There
were still wintry storms and the sea was rough, but instead of
waiting he put to sea and lost a considerable number of ships.
Then, with what remained of his forces, he hurried on by land
through Galatia. Here he met King Deiotarus,[49] who was now
a very old man, and saw that he was founding a new city. 'Your
majesty,' said Crassus, by way of raising a laugh, 'I observe
that you are starting your building at the twelfth hour.' The
Galatian laughed and replied: 'But you yourself, Imperator, I
observe, are none too early in marching against the Parthians.'
Crassus was in fact over sixty and looked older.

When he reached the scene of operations, things at first went
as he had hoped. He had no difficulty in bridging the Euphrates;
he led his army across without loss, and occupied a number of
cities in Mesopotamia which came over to him of their own
accord. At one city, however, a hundred of his soldiers were
killed. (It was ruled over by the tyrant Apollonius and its Greek
name was Zenodotia.) Crassus then brought up his forces,
overpowered the defences, plundered the valuables and sold the
inhabitants as slaves. For the capture of this place he allowed his
soldiers to salute him as 'Imperator', which was not an action
that at all redounded to his credit. To be so pleased with such
a trifling success seemed to show a very mean spirit and a lack
of confidence for the greater exploits that lay ahead.

He then employed 7,000 infantry and 1,000 cavalry to garrison the cities that had come over to him, and retired to Syria
himself. Here he took up winter quarters and waited for his son
who was coming to him from Caesar's army in Gaul. The young
man had received a number of decorations for his gallantry in
war and was bringing with him 1,000 first-class cavalry.[50]

Here, it seemed, Crassus made his first mistake – apart from the original and greatest mistake, which was in undertaking the expedition at all. He should have gone forward and made contact with the cities of Babylon and Seleucia, which had always been hostile to the Parthians; but instead of doing this he gave the enemy time to make their preparations. He was also blamed for acting more like a business man than a general during the time he spent in Syria. There were no regular roll-calls for the troops and he did nothing about organizing athletic contests for them. Instead he was working out what revenue could be drawn from the various cities; many days were spent over scales and balances while he weighed the treasures of the goddess at Hierapolis; he sent demands for fixed numbers of troops to areas in the neighbourhood and to local rulers, and then, as soon as he was offered money, cancelled these demands, thus losing his credit and becoming an object of contempt. It was here that he received the first sign from heaven, from that goddess whom some call Aphrodite and others Hera, while others regard her as the natural cause which produces out of moisture the first principles and seeds of everything, and conveys to mankind the first knowledge of all that is good. As they were going out of her temple, first young Crassus, the son, stumbled and fell down at the gate, and then his father fell down on top of him.

18. As soon as Crassus had begun to concentrate his troops after their period in winter quarters, ambassadors came to him from Arsaces. Their message was a short one. If, they said, this army had been sent out by the Roman people, then it meant war to the bitter end with no question of negotiations. But if, as they had been informed, the fact was that Crassus, for his own private profit and against the wishes of his countrymen, had invaded Parthia and occupied Parthian territory, then Arsaces was prepared to adopt a reasonable attitude: he would take pity on Crassus as an old man, and as for his soldiers, who were rather in the position of Crassus' prisoners than his protectors, he would allow them to go back to Rome.

Crassus boastfully replied that he would give them his answer in Seleucia, and the eldest of the ambassadors, Vagises, burst out laughing and, pointing to the palm of his upturned hand, said: 'Hair will grow here, Crassus, before you set eyes on Seleucia.' They then rode away to King Hyrodes, to tell him that it was war.

And now information which deserved to be taken seriously began to come in from various people who had been in the Mesopotamian cities garrisoned by the Romans and who, at great risk, had managed to make their way out. They had seen with their own eyes how large the enemy forces were and what methods of warfare they employed in their attacks on the cities. As usually happens, their reports made things appear even more terrible than they really were. 'These people,' they said, 'are impossible to shake off if they are in pursuit, and impossible to overtake if they are in flight; they employ a new kind of missile which travels faster than sight and pierces through whatever is in the way before one can see who is discharging these weapons; and their armoured cavalry has weapons of offence which will cut through everything and defensive equipment which will stand up to any blow.'

This news had a most depressing effect on the soldiers' spirits. Up to now they had believed that the Parthians were just the same as the Armenians or even the Cappadocians whom Lucullus had gone on plundering until he was tired of it, and they had imagined that the main difficulties of the campaign would be the long journey and the pursuing of troops who would not come to close quarters; now, however, they found themselves in the unexpected position of having to face real fighting and great danger. Some of the officers, amongst whom was Cassius the quaestor,[51] thought that Crassus ought to call a halt and reconsider the whole undertaking. The professional prophets also quietly spread the news that at their sacrifices the omens for Crassus were invariably bad and inauspicious. But Crassus paid no attention to them or to anyone else who gave any advice other than to press forward.

19. He was particularly encouraged by Artavasdes, the King of Armenia, who came to his camp with 6,000 cavalry. These were said to be merely the king's personal guard and escort, and

in addition to them he promised to produce 10,000 armoured cavalry and 30,000 infantry to be maintained by himself. He urged Crassus to invade Parthia by way of Armenia, pointing out that, if he did so, he would not only be leading his army through country which was well supplied (the king himself would see to that), but would also be marching in safety, since the Parthians' one strong point was their cavalry and here Crassus would have the protection of mountains, continuous lines of hills, and country generally unsuited for cavalry operations. Crassus, without showing any great enthusiasm, welcomed the king's support and the splendid reinforcements that he offered, but as for his route he said that he would march through Mesopotamia where he had left many brave Roman soldiers. The King of Armenia then rode away.

While Crassus was taking his army over the Euphrates at Zeugma peals of thunder of an extraordinary violence crashed all round them, lightning flashed in the soldiers' faces, and a wind like a cloud but of hurricane force fell upon their raft, broke it up and carried parts of it away. Also two thunderbolts fell upon the place where he was intending to make his camp. And one of the general's horses, beautifully harnessed and caparisoned, dragged off its groom and disappeared with him under the surface of the river. It is also said that the eagle on the first standard raised faced about of its own accord. Then, when the soldiers were given their rations after crossing the river, the first things to be issued were lentils and salt, which are considered by the Romans to be signs of mourning and are used by them for the offerings which they make to the dead. Crassus himself too, when he was addressing the troops, let fall a phrase that had a most frightening effect on the men. 'I propose to break down the bridge,' he said, 'so that not a single one of you can get back.' Of course he should have corrected himself as soon as he realized how ill chosen his words were and should, seeing his hearers so alarmed, have explained what he really meant; but he was too stubborn and obstinate to do so. And finally, when he was conducting the customary service of purification for the army and the prophet placed the entrails of the sacrificed animal in his hands, he let them fall on to the ground. Seeing how very much alarmed everyone was at this, he smiled and said: 'This is what comes of being old. But no weapon will fall from my hands.'

20. He then marched along the river with seven legions, nearly 4,000 cavalry, and about the same number of light troops. His scouts had been making a reconnaissance and some of them now came back and reported that there were no men to be seen in the area, but that they had come across the tracks of a great number of horses which appeared to have wheeled round and to have fled when pursued. This news made Crassus himself even more confident than before, and the soldiers too began to feel the utmost contempt for the Parthians, imagining that they would never come to close quarters. Cassius, however, had another interview with Crassus and told him that in his opinion the best plan was to give the army a breathing space in one of the cities occupied by the Romans until they received some reliable information about the enemy; or, if he would not do this, then they should advance to Seleucia, keeping all the time close to the river. In this way they would be certain of their supplies, since boats would be able to put in wherever they camped, and they would have the river to prevent them being surrounded, so that, in any fighting, the enemy would have to face them from in front and fight on equal terms.

21. Crassus was still considering and weighing up these arguments when an Arab chieftain called Ariamnes put in an appearance. This Ariamnes was a sly treacherous character; indeed he played the greatest and the most decisive part in all that combination of evil which fortune had designed for the destruction of the Romans. Some of the soldiers who had served in the east with Pompey knew that he had benefited from Pompey's kindness and that he was supposed to be pro-Roman. In fact he was acting in collusion with the king's generals and was trying to worm his way into the confidence of Crassus with the idea of getting him to turn away as far as possible from the river and the foothills and to bring him down into the wide open plain where he could be surrounded. For the Parthians

had not the least intention of engaging the Romans face to face
in regular battle.

This native, then, who also had the gift of speaking plausibly,
came to Crassus. He began by expressing his admiration for his
benefactor Pompey, and by congratulating Crassus on his own
army. He criticized him, however, for wasting so much time in
making his preparations; what Crassus needed, he said, was
not a great weight of armament but quick hands and very quick
feet to catch up with an enemy who, for some time now, had
been trying to get together all their most valuable property
and slaves and to fly with them into the depths of Scythia or
Hyrcania. 'And yet,' he said, 'if you do intend to fight, you
ought to do so quickly before all the king's forces are concentrated into one place and the king gets back his courage. At the
moment there are just advance guards under the Surena and
Sillaces put there to check your pursuit, while the king himself
has simply disappeared.'

The whole of this story was untrue. In fact Hyrodes had at
once divided his army into two parts. He himself with one part
was now devastating Armenia to punish Artavasdes and he had
sent the Surena with the other part against the Romans. This
was not, as some say, because he despised them. It scarcely
makes sense to suppose that he looked down upon Crassus, the
foremost man in Rome, as an antagonist and chose rather to
make war on Artavasdes, raiding and destroying villages in
Armenia. It is more probable that he took the danger very
seriously and was holding himself in reserve waiting to see what
would happen, meanwhile sending the Surena forward to test
the enemy forces in battle and to interfere with their movements. And the Surena himself was an extremely distinguished
man. In wealth, birth and in the honour paid to him he ranked
next after the king; in courage and ability he was the foremost
Parthian of his time; and in stature and personal beauty he had
no equal. When he travelled about the country on his own
affairs he was always accompanied by a baggage train of 1,000
camels; 200 wagons carried his harem; 1,000 armoured cavalry
and still more light armed cavalry acted as his escort. The total
number of his cavalry, his vassals and his slaves came to at least

10,000 men. He had, as an ancient privilege of his family, the right to be the first to set the crown on the head of a King of Parthia at the coronation. And when this particular King Hyrodes had been driven out, it was the Surena who restored him to his throne and captured for him the city of Seleucia the Great. In this operation he was the first man to scale the city walls and had beaten back the defenders fighting with them hand to hand. At this time he was not yet thirty years old, but he had the highest reputation for careful planning and for intelligence. Indeed it was largely by means of these qualities that he destroyed Crassus, whom he found perfectly easy to take in, first because he was proud and overconfident, and subsequently because he was cowed by his calamities.

22. Now Ariamnes succeeded in getting him to do as he wished. He drew him away from the river and led him right into the open plains. At first the route was a good one and the going was easy; soon, however, the march became difficult as they entered a district where there was deep sand underfoot, a level plain with no trees and no water, going on, so far as the eye could see, for ever. The men were not only exhausted by thirst and by the difficulties of the march; they were also overcome by a kind of sullen despair when they looked around them; for there was not a single growing thing in sight, not a stream, not a sign of any rising ground, not a blade of grass; there was a sea of sand and nothing else, and the desert billows of this sea were sweeping around the army on every side. This in itself was enough to make them suspect that they were being tricked. Soon, also, messengers arrived from Artavasdes the Armenian. Their news was that Artavasdes was engaged in heavy fighting with Hyrodes who had invaded his country in force; he was therefore unable to send any help to Crassus, but he advised him to march towards Armenia, to join forces with the Armenians and then give battle to Hyrodes; this, in his view, was the best plan; but, if Crassus would not follow it, he urged him, wherever he marched or camped, to keep near the mountains where cavalry could not operate easily. To this message Crassus sent no written reply. In his angry mood and

his obstinate perversity he merely told the messengers that at present he had no time for the Armenians, but later on he would come there and make Artavasdes pay for his treachery.

Cassius once again strongly disapproved. Seeing that his attitude only annoyed Crassus, he gave up trying to advise him. But he took the native chieftain aside and spoke to him without mincing his words. 'What evil spirit brought you to us, you villain?' he said. 'What drugs and sorceries have you been using to persuade Crassus to pour his army into a great yawning wilderness and to follow a route that is better fitted for a captain of Arabian robbers than for a Roman imperator?' The native, however, was full of cunning. Putting on the most humble air, he tried to encourage them and begged them to endure for a little longer. He would run along beside the soldiers, helping them with their tasks, laughing and making jokes. 'Do you think that you are marching through Campania?' he would say. 'Are you longing for the fountains and streams there, and the shady places, yes, and the baths and the taverns? Oh, no, you must remember that the country you are going through is the border land between Assyria and Arabia.' So the native managed the Romans as if they were children, and rode off himself before his treachery was discovered. He went with the full knowledge of Crassus. In fact he had actually persuaded Crassus that he was going to work in his interests by sowing confusion in the minds of the enemy.

23. It is said that on this day Crassus, instead of wearing the purple robe which Roman generals normally wear, appeared dressed in a black robe. He changed this as soon as he realized his mistake. Then some of the standard bearers had the greatest difficulty in raising their standards, which seemed to have got fixed into the earth. Crassus took none of this seriously. He marched as fast as possible, making the infantry keep pace with the cavalry, and so hurried forward until a few of his scouts returned and told him that the rest of them had been killed by the enemy, that they themselves had only just managed to escape, and that a Parthian force in very great numbers and

showing every sign of confidence was coming up prepared to give battle. This news, naturally enough, had a disturbing effect on everyone. Crassus himself was absolutely thunderstruck. He began to make his dispositions hurriedly and without much consistency. First he followed the advice of Cassius and, with a view to preventing the enemy from surrounding them, extended his line of infantry as far as possible across the plain, without giving it much depth, and dividing all the cavalry between the two wings. Then he changed his mind and concentrated his forces into a compact body, forming them up in a hollow square, ready to face in four directions, and with twelve cohorts on each side. To each cohort a squadron of cavalry was assigned, so that no part of the line might be without the support of cavalry, and the whole force could advance with equal protection everywhere. He put Cassius in command of one of the wings and young Crassus in command of the other, while he himself took up his position in the centre.

In this formation they marched forward until they came to a stream called the Balissus. It was a small stream in any case and now there was not much water in it, but by this time it was a pleasant enough sight to the soldiers who were hot and thirsty after their hard march without water at all. It was therefore the opinion of most of the officers that they should camp there for the night and, after finding out what they could about the numbers of the enemy and their order of battle, advance against them at dawn. Crassus, however, was carried away by the eagerness of his son and of the cavalry who were with him and who were all in favour of pressing on and engaging the enemy. He therefore gave orders that those who needed to do so should eat and drink standing as they were in their ranks, and, even before they had all had time to do this, he again led them forward. Instead of making them march slowly and halting from time to time, as is usual when on the way to battle, he kept up a quick pace until the enemy came into sight. The Romans were surprised to observe that they were neither so numerous nor so splendidly armed as they had expected. This was, in fact, because the Surena had hidden his main force behind the front ranks and had ordered them to cover themselves with coats and skins so as to conceal the glittering of their armour.

Now, when they were near the Romans and their general gave the signal, first of all the whole plain was filled with a deep and terrifying roaring sound. For the Parthians, instead of having horns or trumpets to sound the attack, make use of hollow drums of stretched hide to which bronze bells are attached. They beat on these drums all at once in many different parts of the field and the sound produced is most eerie and terrifying, like the roaring of wild animals with something of the sharpness of a peal of thunder. They have, it seems, correctly observed that the sense of hearing has the most disturbing effect on us of all our senses, most quickly arouses our emotions and most effectively overpowers our judgement.

24. Before the Romans had recovered from their consternation at this din, the enemy suddenly dropped the coverings of their armour. Now they could be seen clearly, their helmets and breastplates blazing like fire, their Margianian steel glittering keen and bright, their horses armoured with plates of bronze and steel. The tallest and best looking of them all was the Surena himself, though his beauty had a kind of feminine quality which did not exactly fit in with his reputation for physical courage. He was dressed rather in the Median way, with his face painted and with parted hair, while the rest of the Parthians still wore their hair long and bunched up over their foreheads in the Scythian fashion so as to make themselves look more formidable.

Their original plan was to charge the Romans with their lances and force their way through their front ranks. But when they saw the depth of the wall of shields with which they were confronted and how steadfastly and firmly the men were standing, they drew back again and, while giving the impression that they were breaking their ranks and losing all cohesion, actually succeeded in surrounding the hollow square before the Romans realized what was happening. Crassus ordered his light-armed troops to make a charge, but they were unable to make much progress. They ran into a shower of arrows and soon gave in, hurrying back for shelter to the lines of the regular infantry among whom they began to cause some disorder and terror, since the men could now see how strong and fast these Parthian arrows were, which could pierce armour and go through every kind of defensive covering, hard or soft alike.

The Parthians now spread out and began to shoot their arrows from all sides at once. There was no attempt at accurate marksmanship, since the Romans were so densely crowded together that it was impossible to miss the target even if one wished to do so. They merely kept on shooting with their great strong bows, curved so as to give the maximum impetus to the arrows, and the blows fell powerfully and heavily upon the Romans. Thus the position of the Romans was, from the first, a very awkward one. If they stayed in their ranks they were wounded one after the other; if they attempted to come to close quarters, they were still unable to do the enemy any harm and suffered just as much themselves. For the Parthians shot as they fled, being, indeed, more adept at this than anyone else except the Scythians; and it is certainly a very clever manoeuvre – to fight and to look after one's own safety at the same time, so that there is no dishonour in running away.

25. The Romans endured all this so long as they had hopes that, once the Parthians had used up all their arrows, they would either break off the engagement or come to close quarters. But when they realized that a large number of camels loaded with arrows was standing by and that those who had first surrounded them were getting fresh supplies of ammunition from the camels, then Crassus saw no end to it all and began to lose heart. He sent a message to his son informing him of the situation and asking him to join battle with the enemy before he was entirely surrounded; for it was in his part of the field that the enemy cavalry were making their most vigorous attacks and they were sweeping round his flank with the idea of getting in his rear.

So the young man took 1,300 cavalry, 1,000 of which had come from Caesar, 500 archers and 8 cohorts from the infantry which were nearest to him and led them forward to the attack. But the Parthians who were trying to encircle Crassus, either because, as some say, they found themselves on marshy ground or because they deliberately planned to draw Publius as far as possible from his father and then attack him, wheeled their horses round and made off. Publius then shouted out: 'They are on the run,' and charged after them. With him were two friends of his of about the same age as he, Censorinus, who was of senatorial rank and a very good speaker, and Megabacchus, who was greatly distinguished for his courage and his physical strength.[52] The cavalry followed after and even the infantry managed to keep up. Hope had filled them with eagerness and joy; they imagined they were victorious and were engaged in a pursuit until, after they had gone a long way forward, they realized the trick that had been played on them. Now those who had appeared to be running away wheeled about again and at the same time were joined by fresh troops in even greater numbers. The Romans halted, expecting that the enemy would come to close quarters with them, since there were so few of them. However, the Parthians merely stationed their armoured cavalry in front of the Romans and with the rest of their cavalry, in loose order, rode all round them, tearing up the plain with their horses' hooves, and raising great masses of sand which fell from the air in a continual shower so that the Romans could scarcely see or speak. Huddled together in a narrow space and getting into each others' way, they were shot down by the arrows. Nor did death come to them either easily or quickly. In the convulsion and agony of their pain they would writhe as the arrows struck them; they would break them off in their wounds and then lacerate and disfigure their own bodies by trying to tear out by main force the barbed arrow heads that had pierced through their veins and muscles.

Many died in this way, and even the survivors were in no state to fight. When Publius called on them to attack the enemy's armoured cavalry, they showed him hands pinioned to their shields, feet nailed through into the ground, so that they were incapable of either running away or of defending themselves.

Publius therefore urged on his cavalry, charged forward with
them boldly and came to grips with the enemy. But both in
defence and attack the odds were against him. The small light
spears of his Gauls came up against tough breastplates of raw
hide or of steel, whereas they, with their unprotected and lightly
armoured bodies, had to face the thrusts of long pikes. It was
on his Gallic cavalry that Publius chiefly relied and indeed he
did wonders with them. They grasped the long spears of the
Parthians in their hands, grappled with the riders and pulled
them down, clumsy with all their weight of armour, from their
horses. Many of them too abandoned their own horses and,
crawling under those of the enemy, stabbed them in the belly.
The horses would then rear up in agony and die trampling
indiscriminately under their feet the bodies of their riders and
of their attackers alike. However, the Gauls, who were not
accustomed to either heat or thirst, suffered very intensely from
both. They had lost most of their horses through driving them
on to the long spears. And so they were forced to fall back
towards the infantry, taking with them Publius, who was now
badly wounded. Seeing a small hill of sand near by they all
retired to it, fastened their horses in the centre, and made a ring
of locked shields on the outside. They imagined that in this
formation they would best be able to resist the attacks of the
natives, but it turned out in just the opposite way. On level
ground the front ranks do afford a certain amount of protection
to those behind; but here the rising ground made them stand,
as it were, in tiers, the man behind being always higher up than
the man in front of him. There was thus no escaping the arrows
which rained down on all of them alike as they stood there in
misery at having reached this inglorious and ineffectual end.

With Publius were two Greeks, Hieronymus and Nicomachus,
who lived near by at Carrhae. They both urged him to slip
away with them and escape to the city of Ichnae which was
friendly to the Romans, and not far off. But Publius said that
there was no death so terrible that, for fear of it, he would
abandon men who were dying on his account. He bade them
farewell and told them to look after their own safety. Then,
since he was unable to use his hand, which had been pierced

through with an arrow, he presented his side to his shield-bearer and ordered him to run him through with his sword. Censorinus, they say, died in the same way. Megabacchus killed himself, as did the others who were of most note. The survivors fought on until the Parthians came up the hill and rode them down with their long spears. Not more than 500, they say, were taken prisoners. The Parthians then cut off Publius' head and at once rode off against Crassus.

26. His situation was as follows. After he had ordered his son to charge the Parthians he received news that there had been a great rout of the enemy and that they were being hotly pursued. He observed too that there was a slackening off in the attacks made on his own part of the front. (This was because most of his attackers had gone riding off in the direction where Publius was.) Crassus therefore regained some of his confidence. He put his army into regular order and posted it on sloping ground where he waited, expecting that at any moment his son would return from the pursuit. Meanwhile Publius, as soon as he found himself in danger, had been sending messengers back to his father. Of these the first ones had been intercepted by the natives and killed; others, however, managed with great diffi-culty to get through and reported that unless Publius received quick and full support from Crassus, it was all over with him. Crassus was now pulled in different directions by his feelings. He was no longer capable of judging anything in a rational manner. He feared for his whole army and he longed for his son; and so he was at one moment for giving help, and at the next for refusing it. Finally, however, he began to move forward with his forces.

Just at this moment the enemy came bearing down on them again with shouts and cries of battle which were even more terrible than before. Numbers of their drums again roared out round the Romans, who stood there waiting for a second battle to begin. Then came the men who were carrying the head of Publius fixed on the point of a spear. They rode close up, showing the head, and insolently inquired who the parents could be and what family he came from. For it was impossible, they said, that such a brave and gallant soldier could be the son of such a miserable coward as Crassus. This sight, more than all the other dreadful things that had happened, broke the spirit and paralysed the energies of the Romans. It might have been expected to rouse in them feelings of anger and revenge, but instead of this it merely filled them with fear and trembling. Yet Crassus, they say, at this moment of his suffering, behaved more admirably than ever before in his life. He went up and down the ranks, shouting out to the men: 'Romans, this grief is a private thing of my own. But in you abide the great fortune and glory of Rome, unbroken and undefeated. And now, if you feel any pity for me, who have lost the best son that any father has ever had, show it in the fury with which you face the enemy. Take away their joy; make them suffer for their cruelty; do not be downhearted at what has happened; remember that if one aims at great things, one must expect great sufferings. Those were no bloodless victories which Lucullus won over Tigranes or Scipio over Antiochus.[53] And in the old days our ancestors lost a thousand ships off Sicily and many imperators and generals in Italy. Yet not one of these losses prevented them in the end from overthrowing their conquerors. Rome became great not by good fortune but by courage and endurance in the face of danger.'

27. Even while he was speaking these words of encouragement, Crassus could see how few there were who were listening to him with any enthusiasm; and when he told them to raise their battle cry, he recognized how abject was now the spirit of his army. They only succeeded in raising a weak, feeble and unsteady shout, while the shout coming from the native army rang out clear and bold. The enemy then got to work. Their light cavalry rode round the flanks, shooting their arrows in on the Romans, while their armoured cavalry attacking from in front with their long spears kept driving them closer and closer together. Some, indeed, to avoid death from the arrows found the courage to dash out recklessly against their attackers, but they did little damage and soon died, since the spears used by the Parthians against the horses were heavily weighted with

steel and made great and mortal wounds, often having enough impetus to transfix two men at once.

So they fought until nightfall and then the Parthians withdrew, saying that they were prepared to be generous to Crassus and would give him one night in which to mourn for his son, unless he showed a better sense for his own interests and would agree to go to Arsaces rather than be carried to him. They then made camp close by, full of hope and confidence.

But for the Romans the night was a bitter one. They did nothing about burying their dead or taking care of the wounded and dying. Each man spent the time in lamenting his own fate; for escape seemed equally impossible whether they stayed there waiting for daybreak, or whether in the hours of darkness they plunged off into the vast desert. And they were at a loss what to do with their wounded; if they took them with them, it would slow down the speed of their flight, and if they left them behind, their cries would let the enemy know that they were running away. As for Crassus, though they held him responsible for everything, they still longed to see his face and to hear his voice. But Crassus had covered up his face and was lying by himself in the dark. The ordinary mind will see in his plight an example of the fickleness of fortune, but to the wise it will seem rather an example of reckless ambition. Because of this he was not content to be first and greatest among many millions; simply from the fact that two men were judged superior to him, he concluded that he had nothing at all.

Now his legate Octavius and Cassius tried to make him get up and to put some heart into him. They found, however, that he was in a state of utter despair and so, on their own responsibility, they called a meeting of the captains and centurions. After discussing matters they decided not to stay where they were and they got the army on the move without using any trumpet signals and, at first, in silence. Soon, however, the disabled men realized that they were being left behind; there were shouts and cries for help and the whole camp was filled with terrible disorder and panic. Then, as they moved forward, fear would come over them and they would fall into disorder, as they imagined that the enemy were bearing down on them.

They frequently altered the direction of their march and frequently formed up in order of battle; some of the wounded who followed after them were taken up and carried, others were laid down and abandoned. So the whole army was delayed except for 300 cavalry under Egnatius who reached Carrhae about midnight. Egnatius called out in Latin to the sentries on the walls, and, when they answered him, told them to inform their commander, Coponius, that there had been a great battle between Crassus and the Parthians. Then, without another word and without even saying who he was, he rode off to Zeugma. So he saved himself and his men, but got a bad name for having deserted his general. However, the message which he had shouted out to Coponius certainly proved valuable to Crassus. Coponius came to the conclusion that no one with good tidings to tell would deliver a message so hurriedly and in so few words. He immediately ordered his soldiers to take up their arms and, as soon as he found out that Crassus was marching in his direction, he went out to meet him and, escorting him with his own troops, brought the army inside the city.

28. During the night the Parthians, though they knew that the Romans were in flight, had made no attempt to pursue them. At dawn, however, they swept down on those who had been left behind in the camp (there were at least 4,000) and slaughtered the whole lot of them. They then rode over the plain and picked up a number of stragglers. The legate Vargunteius with four cohorts had got separated from the main body while it was still dark and had missed the way. This force was surrounded by the Parthians on a small hill and, fighting back against its attackers, was entirely destroyed, except for twenty men. These men tried to force their way through the enemy with drawn swords and the Parthians, admiring their courage, opened their ranks and let them march quietly on their way to Carrhae.[54]

The Surena now received a false report to the effect that Crassus and all the most distinguished Romans had got away, and that those who had fled into Carrhae were merely a mixed-up crowd of insignificant people who were scarcely

worth his attention. This made him fear that he had lost the
crowning achievement of his victory, but he was still not sure
and wished to find out the truth, so that he could either stay
there and besiege Crassus or else go after him in pursuit and
leave Carrhae alone. So he sent one of his men who could speak
both languages up to the walls and told him to call out in Latin
for Crassus himself or for Cassius and to say that the Surena
wished to have a conference with them. The man did so, and
when the message was reported to Crassus he accepted the
invitation. Soon afterwards some Arabs from the native army
came up. They knew Crassus and Cassius well by sight, since
they had been in the Roman camp before the battle, and, when
they saw Cassius on the wall, they said that the Surena was
willing to make peace and to allow them to go in safety, if they
would make a treaty with the king and leave Mesopotamia;
this, they said, seemed more to the advantage of both parties
than to go on fighting to the bitter end. Cassius accepted the
proposal and asked that a time and place should be fixed for a
meeting between the Surena and Crassus. The Arabs said that
they would arrange for this and then rode away.

29. The Surena was delighted to find that the men he wanted
were there and could be besieged. At daybreak he led his
Parthians up against the city. With all sorts of insulting words
they told the Romans that, if they wanted a truce, they must
hand over to them Crassus and Cassius in chains. The Romans,
angry at finding themselves deceived, told Crassus to give up
any vain and distant hopes he might have of getting help from
the Armenians, and decided on flight. None of the people of
Carrhae were supposed to know of this decision of theirs
beforehand; but Andromachus, the least trustworthy person
of them all, was fully informed. Crassus not only confided
the secret to him, but appointed him to be the guide on their
march. So the Parthians knew exactly what was happening,
since Andromachus reported every detail to them.

Since the Parthians are not used to night operations and so
find them difficult, it was by night that Crassus set out. But
Andromachus, so that the pursuers should not be left too far

behind, led the army now in one direction, now in another, finally bringing them into a marshy area full of ditches where those who were following him found it difficult to march and had to make a number of detours. Meanwhile some of the Romans had come to the conclusion that there was something definitely wrong about all this twisting and turning of Andromachus and had decided to follow him no further. Cassius went right back to Carrhae. Here his Arab guides advised him to wait until the moon had got past the sign of the Scorpion, but Cassius replied: 'Personally I am more frightened of the Archer than the Scorpion,' and rode off to Syria with 500 cavalry. Others also, who had reliable guides, reached a hilly district called Sinnaca and took up a strong position there before day came. There were about 5,000 of them and their commander Octavius was a good and brave soldier.

Day found Crassus, however, still being cheated by Andromachus and still in the difficult marshy area. He had with him four cohorts of infantry, very few cavalry altogether and five lictors. With these he got back after much difficulty on to the right road, and now the enemy came down upon him. He was still about a mile and a half away from Octavius and so unable to make contact with him. He therefore took refuge on another hill which was not so strong a position as that held by Octavius and not so well adapted for defence against cavalry. However, it was situated below Sinnaca and was connected with it by a long ridge that ran through the middle of the plain. Those who were with Octavius could therefore see in what danger Crassus was. First of all Octavius himself with a few others ran down from the higher ground to help him. Then all the rest, cursing themselves for their cowardice, charged down too, fell upon the enemy and dislodged them from the hill. They came all round Crassus and covered him with their shields, proudly declaring that there was no arrow in Parthia that should touch the body of their imperator, so long as there was one of them left alive to fight in his defence.

30. The Surena now saw that his own men were becoming less eager to face danger. He realized that, if night came on and the

Romans succeeded in getting to the mountains, they would be entirely beyond his reach. So he resorted to deception. He set free some of his prisoners who, while in his camp, had heard deliberately framed conversations among the natives to the effect that the king had no wish to be involved in an irreconcilable struggle with the Romans and that what he wanted to do was to regain their friendship by going out of his way to treat Crassus kindly. After this the natives stopped fighting and the Surena, with the chief men in his army, rode quietly up the hill. He unstrung his bow, held out his hand, and invited Crassus to come to an understanding. 'It is against the king's wishes,' he said, 'that we have been testing the courage and power of your soldiers. In reality he has no harsh feelings towards you and wants of his own accord to prove his friendship by offering you a truce if you will withdraw and by allowing you to go away in safety.'

The Roman soldiers were overjoyed at hearing these words from the Surena and were eager to accept his offer. Crassus, however, was not impressed. Every defeat which he had suffered at the hands of the natives had been due to treachery, and this sudden change in their attitude did not seem to him to make sense. He therefore wished to reflect on the matter. But the soldiers kept on shouting and urging him to accept; then they began to abuse him, and say what a cowardly thing it was for him to force them to fight in battle with an enemy whom he himself was afraid to meet even for the purpose of conversation and when they had no arms in their hands. At first Crassus tried entreaties. If only, he said, they would hold out for what was left of the day, they could reach the mountains and the rough country during the night; he pointed out the way to them and begged them not to give up hope when they were so close to safety. But the soldiers were infuriated with him; they began to clash their shields together and to threaten him. Crassus was terrified and began to go towards the Surena. As he went, he turned round and spoke simply these words: 'Octavius and Petronius and all you other Roman officers present, you see that I am being forced to go this way. You are eye-witnesses of the shameful and violent treatment which I have received. But if you escape and get safely home tell them all there that Crassus died because he was deceived by the enemy, not because he was handed over to the enemy by his own countrymen.'

31. Octavius, however, and his immediate friends would not stay behind. They went down the hill with Crassus. The lictors were following, but Crassus ordered them back. The first of the natives to meet them were two half-breed Greeks, who leaped from their horses and bowed down to the ground before Crassus. Then they spoke to him in Greek and asked him to send some of his party on ahead so that the Surena could show them that he and his own party were coming to the meeting without armour and without swords. Crassus replied that if he had even considered the question of his own life, he would never have put himself in their hands at all; nevertheless he sent on the two brothers Roscii[55] to find out what were the arrangements for the meeting and how many on each side should take part in it. The two brothers were immediately seized by the Surena and kept under arrest. And now the Surena himself, with the chief men of his army, came forward on horseback. 'What is this?' he said. 'The Roman imperator on foot, and we mounted?' And he ordered his men to bring Crassus a horse. Crassus replied that neither of them was at fault in this; each was merely following the custom of his own country. The Surena then said that from now on a state of peace existed between King Hyrodes and the Romans; it was necessary, however, to go forward as far as the river and have the terms of the agreement put into writing. 'We find,' he added, 'that you Romans have not got very good memories about the terms of treaties.' He held out his right hand to Crassus and, when Crassus proposed to send for a horse, said: 'There is no need to do that. The king makes you a present of this one.' At the same time a horse with its bridle all decked with gold was brought forward and the grooms lifted Crassus up into the saddle and then ran along beside him, whipping the horse to make it go faster. Octavius was the first to seize hold of the bridle, and after him one of the military tribunes, Petronius; then the rest of the Romans who were there gathered round,

trying to stop the horse and dragging away those who on
both sides of him were forcing Crassus forward. Pushing and
struggling with each other, they soon came to blows. Octavius
drew his sword and killed a groom belonging to one of the
natives, but was himself struck down from behind by another
of them. Petronius had no sword with him; he was struck, however, on his breastplate, and leaped down from his horse un-
wounded. Crassus was killed by a Parthian called Pomaxathres,
though, according to other accounts, it was not he but another
Parthian who killed him and cut off his head and right hand as
he lay on the ground. This, however, is conjecture rather than
certain knowledge. Of the Romans who were present some
were killed fighting around Crassus and the rest fled back to
the hill. Here the Parthians came up to them and told them that
Crassus had met the fate which he deserved, but the Surena
ordered the rest of them to come down from the hill and to
have no fear. Some of them then came down and surrendered;
others scattered in different directions during the night and of
these only a very few reached safety; most were hunted down
by the Arabs, captured and killed. In the whole campaign it is
said that 20,000 were killed and 10,000 taken prisoner.

32. The Surena took the head and hand of Crassus and sent
them to Hyrodes in Armenia. Then he sent messengers to
Seleucia to say that he was bringing Crassus there alive and he
organized a kind of mock procession which, in his insolence,
he called a triumph. The one of his prisoners who looked
most like Crassus was Gaius Paccianus. He was made to put
on the dress of a queen, was instructed to answer, when
addressed, to the names of 'Crassus' and 'Imperator' and so
was led along on horseback. In front of him rode trumpeters
and a few lictors who were mounted on camels; purses were
hung from the lictors' bundles of rods and to their axes were
fastened the heads of Romans which had just been cut off;
behind them came the courtesans and singing women of
Seleucia, singing all sorts of vulgar and obscene songs on the
theme of the effeminacy and cowardice of Crassus.

All this was for everybody to see. But the Surena also

assembled the senate of Seleucia and brought to their notice the obscene books called the 'Milesian Tales' of Aristides. Here, at least, he was not deceiving people, since the books had been discovered in the luggage of Roscius. They afforded the Surena an opportunity for making a number of insulting jokes about the Romans who, he said, even when they were going into battle could not leave this sort of topic and this kind of literature alone. The people of Seleucia, however, realized how wise Aesop was in his fable about the wallets. They saw the Surena carrying in front of him a bag full of Milesian obscenities, but trailing behind him all the luxury of a Parthian Sybaris in wagonload after wagonload of concubines. Indeed his army was like those fabulous snakes (the echidnae and scytalae) which people talk about: what was in front and what immediately met the eye was fearful and savage enough with all the spears and bows and horsemen; but the columns ended in a tail consisting of dances, cymbals, lutes and all-night revelry with loose women. Certainly one cannot excuse Roscius; but the Parthians, considering that many of their kings of the royal line of Arsacidae have sprung from Milesian and Ionian courtesans, were rather lacking in a sense of proportion when they took umbrage at the 'Milesian Tales'.

33. While this was going on Hyrodes had made peace with Artavasdes of Armenia and had agreed to receive the sister of Artavasdes as wife for his son Pacorus. The two kings gave banquets and organized drinking parties for each other, and in the course of these many Greek compositions were produced. Hyrodes knew Greek and was well versed in Greek literature, and Artavasdes actually composed tragedies and wrote speeches and works of history, some of which are still extant.

When the head of Crassus was brought to the king's door, the tables had been taken away and a tragic actor, called Jason of Tralles, was singing the scene in Euripides' *Bacchae* just before the entrance of Agave. While he was still being applauded, Sillaces, who stood at the door of the banqueting hall, bowed down low before the king and then threw the head of Crassus into the centre of the company. Clapping their hands and shouting with joy, the Parthians lifted the head up, and, at the king's command, Sillaces was given a seat at the banquet. Then Jason handed to one of the chorus the costume which he had been wearing for the part of Pentheus, seized hold of Crassus' head, and, assuming the part of a woman inspired by Bacchus, sang in a rapturous way the verses:

> 'We bring from the mountain
> fresh-cut a shoot to the palace,
> O happy our hunting!'

Everyone was delighted with this. But when he got to the dialogue with the chorus:

> (CHORUS): 'Who killed him?'
> (AGAVE): 'The honour is mine.'

Pomaxathres, who happened to be present at the banquet, sprang up and seized hold of the head. 'This is for me to say,' he said, 'not him.' The king was overjoyed. He gave to Pomaxathres the customary gifts and to Jason he gave a talent. This, they say, was the finale to the tragedy of Crassus' expedition.

However, Hyrodes was justly requited for his cruelty and the Surena for his treachery. Not long afterwards Hyrodes, jealous of the reputation of the Surena, put him to death. Then Hyrodes himself, after losing his son Pacorus who was defeated in battle by the Romans,[56] grew ill and his disease turned into a dropsy. His son Phraates was plotting against him and tried to poison him with aconite, but the disease absorbed the poison and nullified its effects, so that the king began to recover. Phraates then took the shortest way and strangled him.[57]

COMPARISON OF NICIAS
AND CRASSUS

1. By comparison, first the wealth of Nicias was acquired in a more respectable manner than that of Crassus. For although the exploitation of mines cannot be highly regarded, since it is largely carried on by employing criminals or barbarians, some of whom are kept in chains and worked to death in dank and disease-ridden places, it will appear in a more favourable light when compared with the public confiscations of Sulla and the making of contracts at the scene of a conflagration. For Crassus openly utilized these expedients as men do agriculture and money-lending. As for the practices he denied when questioned, taking bribes for speaking in the senate, wronging the allies, seducing women with his flatteries and helping villains to cover up their crimes, no such charges, even false ones, were ever made against Nicias; he was rather laughed at for spending his money to buy off informers out of cowardice, a practice unbecoming perhaps in a Pericles or an Aristides, but necessary for him, since he was not very courageous by nature. And concerning this practice Lycurgus the orator, in later times, spoke bluntly to the people when accused of buying off one of these informers. 'I am delighted,' he said, 'if after such a long political career among you, I have been caught out in giving, rather than in taking money.'

In the outlay of money Nicias was more public-spirited in his pursuit of honour through offerings to the gods, the provision of gymnastic exhibitions and the training of choruses. Yet his whole estate, together with his outgoings, was a mere fraction of what Crassus laid out when he feasted so many myriads of men at once and then furnished them with food afterwards. I

am therefore amazed that anyone should fail to perceive that
vice is a sort of inequality and incongruity of character, when
he sees men amassing money without shame and squandering
it to no purpose.

2. So much for their wealth. In their political careers no chican-
ery, injustice, violence or harshness attaches to Nicias; he was
rather deceived by Alcibiades and approached the people with
too much caution. But Crassus is accused of much ungenerous
faithlessness in his vacillations between friendship and enmity.
As for violence, he himself did not deny that when he was
standing for the consulship he hired men to lay hands on Cato
and Domitius. And in the assembly which voted on the assign-
ment of the provinces, many were wounded and four killed,
and Crassus himself (a fact which escaped us in the account of
his life), when L. Annalius, a senator, was speaking against it,
punched him in the face with his fist and drove him bleeding
from the scene.

But if Crassus was violent and tyrannical in these matters,
Nicias' timidity and cowardice in public life and his subservience to the basest men deserve the severest censure. Crassus,
indeed, showed a certain largeness and loftiness of spirit in
this sphere, for he competed not with men like Cleon and
Hyperbolus but with the brilliant Caesar and Pompey with his
three triumphs. Nor did he avoid confrontation, but met the
power of each head on, and in achieving the honour of the
censorship he outdid even Pompey. For at the highest level in
politics one must not choose a course which arouses no envy
but one which is dazzling, and throw envy into the shade by
the greatness of one's power. But if you set your heart above
all else on security and quiet, and fear Alcibiades in the
assembly, the Spartans at Pylos and Perdiccas in Thrace, then
there is ample room in the city where you can withdraw and
sit at leisure, 'weaving for yourself,' as some sophists say, 'a
garland of tranquillity'. Nicias' love of peace, indeed, was truly
godlike, and his putting a stop to the war was a political achievement of the greatest benefit to Greece. And because he did this,
Crassus is not worthy of comparison with him, nor would he

be even if he had extended the frontiers of the Roman empire to the Caspian Sea or the Indian Ocean.

3. When, however, a man wields superior power in a city which is responsive to virtue, he should not give houseroom to the base, or command to those incapable of command, or trust to those unworthy of trust. But this is what Nicias did when, on his own initiative, he put Cleon in command of the army, a man who was nothing more in the city than a shameless bawler from the rostrum. I do not indeed commend Crassus, in the rising of Spartacus, for pressing on to finish the war with more speed than safety, although it was natural for a man of ambition to be afraid that Pompey would come to rob him of the glory, just as Mummius had robbed Metellus of Corinth. But the conduct of Nicias was utterly strange and bizarre. For it was not when it afforded him hopes of an easy victory that he yielded the honour of command to his enemy, but when he suspected that it would involve him in great peril, then he was content to betray the common good for the sake of his own safety. And yet Themistocles, during the Persian wars, to keep a worthless and foolish man from ruining the city as a general, paid him to step down from office, while Cato stood for the tribunate precisely when he saw that it would involve him in the greatest toils and dangers on behalf of the city. Nicias, on the other hand, retained the command against Minoa, Cythera and the hapless Melians, but when it was necessary to fight the Spartans, stripped off his general's cloak, handed over to the inexperience and rashness of Cleon ships, men, arms and a mission requiring the utmost experience, and so betrayed not only his own reputation but the security and safety of his country. In consequence he was later forced, very much against his will, to make war on Syracuse, for it was thought to be not through calculation of what was expedient but merely through love of ease and lack of spirit that he did all he could to deprive the city of Sicily.

There is, however, a proof of his great reasonableness. Although he was always averse to war and tried to avoid military command, the Athenians never stopped electing him to it, believing him to be their most experienced and best general. Crassus, on the other hand, was constantly eager for command, but did not succeed in getting it except in the servile war, and even then only out of necessity, because Pompey, Metellus and both the Luculli were away. And yet by that time he enjoyed the greatest honour and influence. But it would seem that even his supporters thought him, in the words of the comic poet, 'the bravest everywhere but in the field'. Even so this did not prevent the Romans from being overwhelmed by his ambitious desire for command. For the Athenians sent Nicias out to the war against his will, but the Romans were led out by Crassus against theirs. It was thanks to Crassus that his city, to his city that Nicias came to grief.

4. However, in this there is more reason to praise Nicias than to blame Crassus. Nicias deployed the experience and calculation of a wise leader and did not share the deceitful hopes of his fellow-citizens, but insisted that it was beyond his powers to take Sicily, whereas Crassus made the mistake of embarking on the Parthian war as if it were a very easy undertaking. Nevertheless his aims were high. While Caesar was subduing the West – Gaul, Germany and Britain – he was bent on marching to the East and the Indian Ocean, to complete the subjection of Asia, to which Lucullus had aspired and which Pompey had undertaken. Now they were men of good intentions and honourably disposed towards all, and yet they chose the same course as Crassus and adopted the same principles. For Pompey met with opposition from the senate when his province was being assigned to him, and when Caesar routed 300,000 Germans, Cato proposed in the senate that he should be handed over to those he had defeated, so as to bring upon his own head the punishment for his breach of faith. But the people contemptuously dismissed Cato's proposal, sacrificed to the gods for fifteen days in thanksgiving for Caesar's victory and were full of joy. What then would have been their feelings and for how many days would they have sacrificed to the gods, if Crassus had written to them from Babylon that he was victorious and had then overrun Media, Persia, Hyrcania, Susa and

Bactria and declared them Roman provinces? 'For if wrong must be done,' as Euripides says, when men cannot remain quiet and do not know how to rest content with the blessings they already have, then let it not be in raiding Scandeia or Mende or in hunting out exiled Aeginetans, who have abandoned their own territory and hidden themselves away like birds in another land. Let a high price be set on wrongdoing and let justice not be cast aside lightly or on trivial grounds, as if it were some small or insignificant thing. Those who praise Alexander's expedition but criticize that of Crassus unfairly judge the enterprise by its outcome.

5. As to the actual conduct of their campaigns, Nicias has not a little to his credit, for he defeated his enemies in many battles and came close to taking Syracuse. Nor were all his failures his own fault; they might be ascribed to his ill health and to the jealousy of the citizens at home. But Crassus made so many mistakes that he gave fortune no chance to favour him. It is a wonder, therefore, not that his folly succumbed to the power of the Parthians, but rather that it overcame the good fortune of the Romans.

Since one of them was wholly given over to divination and the other wholly disregarded it, yet both alike perished, it is hard to draw a sound conclusion from the evidence. But failure due to caution, supported by old-established and widely held opinion, is more reasonable than lawlessness and obstinacy.

In his death, however, Crassus was the less worthy of reproach. He did not give himself up, nor was he bound, nor yet beguiled, but yielded to the entreaties of his friends and was betrayed by the ill faith of the enemy, whereas Nicias was led by the hope of a shameful and inglorious safety to entrust himself to the enemy and so made his death a source of greater disgrace to himself.

4
POMPEY

[106–48 BC]

The life of Pompey is a curious mixture. The opening remarks
on Pompey's character are surprising to say the least: the
Pompey who emerges from the pages of Cicero is hardly tactful,
easy of manner and free from conceit. Yet Plutarch later makes
several more pertinent observations. He recognizes Pompey's
tendency to throw his weight around, as evidenced by his treatment of Lucullus and Metellus Creticus, and is aware of his
extreme sensitivity to criticism and his constant yearning for
popular approval. He also fully appreciates certain aspects of
Pompey's career. The extraordinary nature of Pompey's rise,
the skill with which he developed his *clientelae* in Sicily, Africa
and the East, and his brilliant capacity for organizing large-scale
campaigns, as against the pirates, are all given due notice. But
as always Plutarch is deterred by the complexities of internal
politics. He remarks on Pompey's lack of political success on
his return from the Mithridatic War, but the account of the
decade before the Civil War leaves much to be desired. Plutarch
obviously did not understand Pompey's attitude to Cicero's
exile and recall, and he pays no attention at all to relations
between Pompey and the *boni* either before or after Luca, or to
Pompey's infinitely devious efforts to play off Caesar against
the *boni* in the late fifties. On the credit side he gives proper
weight to the deaths of first Julia and then Crassus, and is
excellent on Pompey's exploitation of growing anarchy and on
the factors that secured him his third consulship. The narrative
of the Civil War is lacking in any discussion of Pompey's contro-
versial strategy, but by way of compensation it contains one of
the biographer's rare political insights, for Plutarch is conscious

that the *boni* were using Pompey and that, if Pompey once got
rid of Caesar for them, he would find himself put on the shelf,
if not liquidated.

1. From the very beginning the Roman people seem to have
felt for Pompey the same feelings as those expressed by the
Prometheus of Aeschylus for Heracles when, after Heracles had
delivered him, he says:

'I hate the father, but I dearly love this son of his.' For the
Romans never hated any of their generals so much and so
bitterly as they hated Pompey's father, Strabo.[1] While he was
alive they stood in awe of his military power (and he was
certainly a most formidable soldier); but when he was killed by
a thunderbolt, they insulted his dead body and dragged it from
the bier as it was being carried to the funeral. On the other
hand no Roman was ever held in such affection by the people
as Pompey was, and no Roman enjoyed an affection which
started so early in his career, which reached such a height in his
prosperity, and which remained so constant in his time of
adversity. There was one reason and one only for the hatred
felt against Strabo, namely his insatiable love of money; but
there were many reasons for loving Pompey: his modest way
of life, his record as a soldier, his eloquence, his trustworthy
character and the easy tactful way he had of dealing with
people.[2] No one ever asked favours with less offence or granted
them with more grace. For among his many charms he possessed the ability to give without arrogance and to receive
without loss of dignity.

2. At the beginning of his career too he had an appearance
which seemed to plead for him before he opened his mouth,
and this was a great help to him in winning people's affections.
He was attractive certainly, but part of his attractiveness lay in
a kind of dignity and sweetness of disposition; and at the height
and flower of his youthful beauty there was apparent at the
same time the majesty and the kingliness of his nature. His
hair swept back in a kind of wave from the forehead and the
configuration of his face round the eyes gave him a melting

look, so that he was supposed (though the resemblance was not a close one) to resemble the statues of King Alexander. It was a name often given to him in his early youth and Pompey himself was not averse from it, so that some people soon applied the word 'Alexander' to him in mockery. It was because of this too that Lucius Philippus,[3] a man of consular rank, when speaking for Pompey in the courts, said that there was nothing strange in the fact that he, being Philip, should love Alexander.

They say that Flora the courtesan, when she was getting on in years, was always delighted to tell people about her early intimacy with Pompey: she always had the marks of his bites on her, she said, when she went away after having made love with him. She would also describe how one of Pompey's friends, called Geminius,[4] fell in love with her. The advances he made to her annoyed her greatly and she told him that she must refuse him because of Pompey. Geminius then approached Pompey and Pompey turned her over to Geminius, but afterwards he would never have anything to do with her or even meet her, although it was thought that he was very much in love with her; and she herself, far from taking this as a courtesan might be expected to do, was ill for a long time with grief and longing for him. And yet she was so famous for her good looks that when Caecilius Metellus[5] was decorating the temple of Castor and Pollux with statues and paintings, he had a portrait of her painted and dedicated it with the other offerings because of her remarkable beauty.

Pompey also treated the wife of his ex-slave Demetrius,[6] a man who had much influence with him and who left an estate of 4,000 talents, with a rudeness and lack of generosity which were quite unlike him, because he was afraid of getting the reputation of being under the spell of her beauty which was very famous and supposed to be irresistible. Yet in spite of all his caution and circumspection in these matters, he did not avoid the censure of his enemies. He was accused of having relations with married women and of neglecting public business and betraying public interests in order to gratify them.

There was a story told of him which illustrates his simple

tastes with regard to the pleasures of the table. Once when he was ill and had lost his appetite a doctor prescribed a thrush for him. Since it was the wrong season his servants could not find one for sale, and someone said they could be obtained at Lucullus', as thrushes were kept there all the year round. 'So,' said Pompey, 'if Lucullus was not a gourmet, I should have had to die,' and, without paying any attention to the doctor's advice, he took something which could be easily procured. This, however, happened at a later date.

3. When he was still a very young man and was serving with his father in a campaign against Cinna[7] he had a friend called Lucius Terentius who shared his tent with him. This man was bribed by Cinna to murder Pompey while others were to set fire to the general's tent. Pompey was informed of the conspiracy while he was at supper. He showed no sign of disturbance; in fact he drank more than usual and was particularly friendly to Terentius. After retiring to rest, he slipped out of the tent without being seen, put a guard round his father's tent and waited. Terentius, when he thought that the proper time had come, got up with his sword drawn, went to Pompey's bedside and stabbed the bedclothes again and again, supposing him to be lying there. After this there was a great uproar. In their hatred of the general the soldiers broke out into mutiny, tearing down the tents and seizing their arms. The general meanwhile, in all this disturbance, was afraid to show himself; but Pompey went about in the middle of it all, weeping and pleading with the soldiers, and finally he threw himself down on his face in front of the gate of the camp and lay there blocking up the passageway, crying out aloud and telling the soldiers to trample over his body if they wanted to go out. As a result everyone drew back in shame and all except 800 changed their minds and were reconciled to their general.

4. Directly after Strabo's death,[8] Pompey, as his heir, was put on trial for misappropriation of public funds. So far as most of the thefts were concerned Pompey was able to prove to the

magistrates that they had been the work of one of his father's
ex-slaves called Alexander; but he was still charged himself with
being in possession of hunting nets and books from the booty
taken at Asculum.[9] He had in fact received these things from
his father after he had captured Asculum, but he had lost them
later, when, after his father had returned to Rome, the house
had been broken into and pillaged by Cinna's bodyguard. In
the preliminary investigation before the lawsuit began Pompey
was often confronted with his accuser, and on all these occasions he showed a keen intelligence and a balance that was
remarkable in one so young, and won great credit and favour,
so that Antistius who, as praetor,[10] was judge in the case,
became very fond of him, offered him his daughter in marriage
and negotiated about the marriage with his friends. Pompey
accepted the offer and an engagement was made privately.
However, from the partiality shown by Antistius to Pompey in
the case, people were able to guess what was going on, and in
the end, when Antistius announced that the verdict of the jury
was 'not guilty', the people, as though they had been waiting
for the signal, all shouted out: 'Talasio' – which is the ancient
and traditional greeting used at weddings.

They say that the custom originated in the following way. At
the time when the daughters of the Sabines came to Rome to
see the games there and were violently abducted by the most
distinguished Romans to be their wives, some quite unknown
people – labourers and herdsmen – seized hold of a fine beautiful girl and began to carry her off. In case any of their betters
should meet them and take away their prize, they all shouted
out as they ran: 'For Talasius' – Talasius being a well-known
and influential person. And so all who heard the name clapped
their hands and shouted out too by way of expressing their
approval and congratulating the lucky man. It was from this
event, they say (since the marriage was certainly a fortunate
one for Talasius), that the word came to be used in a merry
joyful way as a greeting to the newly wed. This is the most
credible of the accounts given of the 'Talasio' invocation. In
any case, a few days after the trial, Pompey married Antistia.

5. He then joined Cinna's army, but finding that various accusations and suggestions were being made against him, he grew afraid and took himself speedily and secretly out of the way. His disappearance caused a lot of talk and a rumour got about in the army that Cinna had killed the young man. As a result of this all those who had for a long time hated Cinna and felt oppressed by him now rose up against him. Cinna attempted to escape, but was seized by a centurion who followed after him with his sword drawn. Falling at this man's knees, Cinna held out to him his seal-ring which was a very valuable one. But the centurion very insolently said: 'I have not come here to seal documents, but to punish a wicked lawless tyrant,' and with these words he killed him.[11]

After Cinna had come to this end, Carbo, a still more violent and irresponsible tyrant, took over and kept the supreme power.[12] Sulla, however, was approaching and most people longed for him to come, since things were so bad already that they thought that even a change of masters would be a positive benefit. The disasters that had fallen upon Rome had brought her to such a pass that, there being no hope of freedom, people longed only for a milder form of slavery.

6. At this time Pompey was staying in the district of Picenum in Italy, partly because he had estates there, but mainly because he liked the towns in this part of the country where, as his father's son, he had many friends and many people attached to him. He saw how all the best and most distinguished people in the neighbourhood were leaving their homes and flying from all sides to Sulla's camp, as though to a haven of refuge. But he decided that instead of going there as an empty-handed fugitive asking for help, he would join Sulla with an army of his own, would do Sulla some service first and in doing so would win honour for himself. And so he started an agitation among the people of Picenum, urging them to revolt from the government in Rome. They listened to him with enthusiasm and would have nothing to do with the agents sent into the district by Carbo. In fact when a man called Vedius said that Pompey ought to be in school rather than trying to give lessons to the people, they

were so angry that they immediately fell upon Vedius and killed him.

After this Pompey, who was only twenty-three years old and had never been appointed general by anyone, appointed himself to the command. He set up his tribunal in the market place of the large city of Auximum and issued an edict ordering the chief men there (two brothers called Ventidius) who were acting against him in Carbo's interest to leave the city. He then proceeded to raise troops, appointed centurions and officers for them, all in accordance with the correct military form, and went on to make a circuit of the other cities, in all of which he acted in the same way. Members of Carbo's party were unable to make head against him and took to flight; the rest gladly volunteered their services and in a short time he had succeeded in raising three whole legions[13] at full strength and had provided them with food, transport animals, wagons and all other necessary equipment. With this force he set out to march to Sulla. He was in no hurry and showed no desire to escape observation. Instead he took time on the march, doing what harm he could to the enemy on the way, and trying to detach from Carbo every part of Italy through which he passed.

7. It was natural that he should be opposed and in fact three enemy generals, Carrinas, Cloelius and Brutus,[14] came against him at once. They did not stand directly in his way nor combine their forces into one; instead they surrounded him with three separate armies and planned to annihilate him. This did not alarm Pompey. He collected his own troops together into one body and immediately attacked one of the enemy armies – the one commanded by Brutus. He stationed his cavalry, in which he was himself, at the front and when from the enemy's army also the Celtic cavalry rode out to engage him, he at once closed with the foremost and the strongest one of them and with a blow of his spear struck him down from his horse. The rest turned and fled, throwing the infantry also into confusion so that there was a general rout. After this the other two generals quarrelled among themselves and retreated, each on his own, and the cities in that area came over to Pompey, assuming that

his enemies had got out of the way because they were afraid of him. Next he was opposed by the consul Scipio,[15] but before the two lines were within range of each other's javelins Scipio's men shouted greetings to Pompey's and came over to their side. Scipio himself took to flight. And finally when Carbo himself sent many squadrons of cavalry against him near the River Arsis, Pompey met the attack gallantly, routed the enemy force, and in his pursuit drove them on to ground where it was impossible for cavalry to operate. Here, when they saw there was no hope of escape, they surrendered with their arms and their horses.

8. Sulla had not yet heard of these successes. In fact when the first news of Pompey's movements reached him he had been alarmed at the prospect of his having to face so many and such experienced enemy commanders and was hurrying to his help. When Pompey realized that he was near, he ordered his officers to see to it that the troops were fully armed and drawn up in their proper formations so that they might make a really fine and brilliant impression on the commander-in-chief. He expected, no doubt, to receive great honours from him, but he received more than he expected. For when Sulla saw him approaching with such a fine army of young strong men, all happy and elated with their successes, he dismounted from his horse and, after he had been saluted, as was right, by the title of 'Imperator', he greeted Pompey in return by calling him 'Imperator' too. To win this title Sulla was at war with such men as Scipio and Marius[16] and no one could have imagined that he would award it to a young man who was not yet even a member of the senate. His subsequent behaviour too was in accord with this first show of goodwill. He would rise to his feet when Pompey approached and would uncover his head – things which one would hardly ever see him doing for anyone else, although he had a number of distinguished people in his entourage.

All this, however, did not make Pompey conceited. In fact, when Sulla proposed to send him at once to Gaul, where Metellus[17] was in command but was considered to be doing less

than he could do with the forces at his disposal, Pompey said
that it would not be right for him to take over the command
from a man of great reputation who was his senior; he would
willingly, however, join Metellus and help him in the war, if
Metellus wanted him and asked him to do so. Metellus accepted
this proposal and wrote asking him to come. Pompey then
hurried off to Gaul, where he not only did wonders himself
but put fresh fire and spirit into Metellus, whose vigour and
enterprise in war were, in a way, dying down in his old age. So,
when a stream of molten bronze is poured on to metal which
is cold and solid, it is said to soften it and melt it down even
more successfully than fire does.

However, just as athletes who have won all the men's events
and been awarded prizes at all the games do not make much of
or even record the victories they won when they were boys,
so it is with the deeds of Pompey at this time. They were
extraordinary in themselves but were quite blotted out by the
number and the importance of his later achievements in war,
and I am afraid to do more than touch upon them lest I should
take up too much space on these early deeds and so leave myself
insufficient room for those actions and experiences of his which
were the greatest ones and the ones best suited to illustrate his
character.

9. When Sulla had gained control of Italy and had been proclaimed Dictator he rewarded his officers and generals by
making them rich, by appointing them to official posts, and by
granting them willingly and without reserve every favour that
they asked for. Pompey, however, was one whom Sulla admired
for his good qualities and whom he regarded as highly useful
to him in his administration. He therefore wished to attach him
closely to himself by some kind of marriage alliance. His wife
Metella was also in favour of this plan, and she and Sulla
together persuaded Pompey to divorce Antistia and to marry
Aemilia, the step-daughter of Sulla and daughter of Metella by
her previous husband Scaurus. Aemilia already had a husband[18]
and was with child by him at the time. The marriage was
therefore imposed dictatorially and was made rather in the

interests of Sulla than in accordance with the character of Pompey. Aemilia was wedded to him when she was pregnant by another man, and Antistia was divorced in a way that was dishonourable and also pathetic, since because of Pompey she had just lost her father Antistius, who had been murdered[19] in the senate house because he was thought to be on Sulla's side for the sake of Pompey. Her mother also, faced with all this, took her own life, so adding another calamity to the tragedy of this second marriage; and, to make the tragedy complete, Aemilia herself died in childbirth almost as soon as she had come to live in Pompey's house.

10. After this, news reached Sulla that Perpenna[20] was in process of occupying Sicily and making the island into a base for the survivors of the opposite party; that Carbo was cruising off Sicily with a fleet; that Domitius[21] had invaded Africa and that numbers of other important exiles – all, in fact, who had succeeded in escaping his proscriptions[22] – were gathering together in those parts. Pompey, with a large force, was sent to deal with them. Perpenna at once abandoned Sicily to him. Pompey took over the cities there, which had been badly treated by Perpenna, and acted with great humanity towards all of them except for the Mamertines in Messana.[23] These people objected to his jurisdiction and authority, claiming that it was contrary to an ancient law established by the Romans. To this Pompey replied: 'Stop quoting the laws to us. We carry swords.' He was also thought to have behaved rudely and with a lack of common humanity to Carbo in his misfortunes. It may well have been necessary for him to put Carbo to death, but this should have been done immediately he had been captured, and then it would have been the act of whoever gave the order. As it was, however, Pompey had led before him in chains a Roman who had been three times consul; he forced him to stand in front of the tribunal where he himself was sitting, and subjected him to a lengthy examination, to the distress and indignation of all who were present; he then ordered him to be taken away and put to death.[24] They say that after Carbo was led off to execution and when he saw the sword already drawn, he asked

for a short delay and a convenient place to relieve himself, since he was troubled by a looseness of the bowels. And Gaius Oppius,[25] the friend of Caesar, says that Pompey also behaved very inhumanly in the case of Quintus Valerius. He knew that Valerius was a remarkably learned and scholarly man and, when he was brought before him, Pompey took him aside, walked up and down with him, and, after he had asked him questions and found out what he wanted to know, ordered his servants to take the man away and put him to death at once.

However, one must be very careful about believing everything that Oppius says when he is dealing with the enemies or the friends of Caesar. It was a matter of necessity for Pompey to punish those of Sulla's enemies who were most important in themselves and whose capture was generally known to have taken place. With regard to the others, he allowed as many as he could to get away and in some cases he actually helped them to escape. One must admire also his conduct with regard to Himera. This city had sided with the enemy and Pompey had decided to punish it, but Sthenius,[26] the popular leader there, asked for an audience with him and said that he would not be acting rightly if he were to let the guilty go and destroy the innocent. Pompey asked him whom he meant by the guilty, and Sthenius said that it was himself he meant, since he had persuaded his friends and forced his opponents among the citizens to act as they had done. Pompey, admiring the man's frankness of speech and nobility of character, first pardoned him and then all the rest. Also, when he heard that his soldiers on their marches had been behaving in a disorderly way, he had their swords sealed up in their scabbards and whoever broke the seal was punished for it.

11. While he was still engaged in dealing with the situation in Sicily he received a decree of the senate and a letter from Sulla ordering him to sail to Africa and bring his whole force into action against Domitius. In Africa Domitius had got together a much larger army than that which Marius had raised when, not so long ago,[27] he had crossed over from there to Italy and with its aid had brought about a revolution in Rome and

made himself a tyrant instead of an exile. So Pompey made his preparations quickly; he left his sister's husband, Memmius,[28] in charge of Sicily and put to sea with 120 warships and 800 transports carrying provisions, ammunition, money and siege equipment. Part of this force put in at Utica and part at Carthage, and, as soon as he landed, 7,000 of the enemy deserted and came over to him. His own army consisted of six legions at full strength.

Here, they say, a rather absurd thing happened to him. It seems that some of his soldiers came across some hidden treasure and got a considerable amount of money. The story of this got abroad and all the rest of the army fancied that the place must be full of money which had been buried by the Carthaginians at some time of calamity. And so for many days Pompey could do nothing at all with his soldiers who were all busy looking for treasure. He merely went about laughing at the sight of so many thousands of men together digging up the ground and turning it over, until in the end they got tired of it and asked him to lead them wherever he liked; they had already, they said, suffered enough for their foolishness.

12. Domitius now drew up his army against Pompey in a position where there was a dried-up river bed in front of him which was steep and difficult to cross. A storm of rain began in the morning and, as it continued raining, he gave up the idea of fighting on that day and ordered a retreat. Pompey, however, seized the opportunity, advanced directly to the attack and crossed the watercourse. The enemy were in disorder and confusion when they met his attack; they were not all together and they put up no united resistance; and at the same time the wind veered round and drove the rain into their faces. The storm troubled the Romans too, since they could not see each other clearly and Pompey himself had a narrow escape from death when he was not recognized and was rather slow in replying to a soldier who asked him for the password.

Nevertheless, they routed the enemy with great slaughter. It is said that out of 20,000 only 3,000 escaped. The soldiers then saluted Pompey with the title of 'Imperator', but Pompey said that he could not accept this honour so long as the enemy camp remained standing; if they thought him worthy of the title, then they must first destroy that. They then immediately made an assault on the ramparts and Pompey, to avoid the same danger as that from which he had just escaped, fought without a helmet. The camp was soon taken and Domitius was killed. The cities either submitted to Pompey at once or were taken by storm. Pompey also captured King Iarbas, who had been in alliance with Domitius, and gave his kingdom to Hiempsal. Next, making full use of his good fortune and of the impetus with which his army was moving forward, he invaded Numidia. He marched through the country for many days, conquered all with whom he came in contact, and made the natives feel again, what they had almost forgotten, a healthy fear of and respect for the Romans. The very animals, he said, who lived in Africa ought to have some experience of Roman strength and Roman daring; and so he devoted a few days to the hunting of lions and elephants. Altogether, they say, it took him only forty days to annihilate the enemy army, to gain control of Africa, and to settle the relations of its kings; and this was when he was twenty-four years old.

13. On his return to Utica he was given a letter from Sulla instructing him to send his army back to Italy except for one legion with which he was to remain himself in Africa until another general came out to supersede him.[29] This was a message which grieved and distressed Pompey very much, but he did not show his feelings openly. His army, on the other hand, made their indignation perfectly clear. When Pompey urged them to go home before him, they shouted out against Sulla, and, declaring that they would never forsake their general, told Pompey not to trust himself to the tyrant. As for Pompey, he tried at first to calm the men down by speaking to them in a reasonable way; but when this had no effect on them he came down from the platform where he stood and retired to his tent in tears. The soldiers, however, seized hold of him and made him stand on the platform again, and so it went on for a long time with the army urging him to stay there in command and

Pompey begging them to obey orders and not to start a mutiny. Finally, as they became more and more urgent and noisy in their demands, Pompey swore solemnly that he would kill himself if they forced him to act as they wished; and even then the clamour only gradually died down.

The first news of this that came to Sulla was to the effect that Pompey had revolted and he remarked to his friends that he was evidently fated, now that he was an old man, to have boys for his antagonists. He said this because Marius too,[30] who was quite a young man, had caused him much trouble and involved him in very great danger. However, when he learned the truth and saw that everyone was hurrying out of Rome to welcome Pompey and to show their goodwill by escorting him back to the city, he quickly decided to outdo them all. He went out himself to meet him and, after greeting him in the warmest possible manner, addressed him in a loud voice with the name of 'Magnus' or 'the Great', and told all those who were present to salute him in the same way. Others say that this title was first given to him in Africa by the whole army and that Sulla's confirmation of it merely gave it weight and force. Pompey himself, however, was the last of all to make use of it. It was only after a long time, when he was sent to Spain as pro-consul to operate against Sertorius,[31] that he began to sign letters and decrees as 'Pompeius Magnus'. By this time the title had become well known and the use of it could not cause offence.

In this connection one cannot help feeling respect and admiration for the ancient Romans; these titles and surnames of theirs were not only given as a reward for successes in war or in military leadership; achievements in civil life and the abilities of statesmen were also honoured by them. In two such cases the title of 'Maximus' or 'the Greatest' was bestowed by the people – on Valerius for his services in bringing the people and the senate together when there was a rift between them, and on Fabius Rullus[32] because he expelled from the senate a number of people who were descended from ex-slaves and had got themselves enrolled as senators because of their wealth.

14. Pompey now asked for a triumph. The request was opposed by Sulla who pointed out that legally this was an honour which could be given to a consul or a praetor, but to no one else. For this reason the first of the Scipios, after his victorious actions against the Carthaginians in Spain – actions which were on a bigger scale and more important than anything which Pompey had done – did not ask for a triumph, because he was neither a consul nor a praetor.[33] And if Pompey, who had scarcely grown a beard as yet, and was too young even to be a senator, were to ride into Rome in a triumphal procession, people would be angry not only with Sulla's government but also with Pompey himself for receiving such an honour. Therefore, so Sulla said to Pompey, his request could not be allowed and he would oppose him and put a stop to his ambitious plans if he refused to give way.

Pompey, however, was not in the least frightened. He asked Sulla to bear in mind the fact that more people worshipped the rising than the setting sun, implying that while his own power was on the increase that of Sulla was growing less and less. Sulla did not hear these words distinctly, but the looks and gestures of those who had heard them showed him how astonished they were and he asked what it was that had been said. When he was told what it was he was astounded at Pompey's audacity and cried out twice in succession: 'Let him have his triumph!' Others too were angry and indignant at the idea, and in order to annoy them all the more Pompey is said to have planned to make his triumphal entry in a chariot drawn by four elephants. (He had brought over from Africa a number of elephants which he had captured from the kings.) However, the city gate was too narrow and so he had to give up this idea and fall back on the conventional horses. And when his soldiers, who had not got as large rewards as they expected, showed a tendency to mutiny and to disturb the proceedings, Pompey declared that it was a matter of complete indifference to him: he would rather forgo his triumph than try to curry favour with his troops. It was on this occasion that Servilius,[34] a man of great distinction and one who had been very much opposed to Pompey's triumph, said: 'Now I see that Pompey really is great and does deserve his triumph.'

It is clear too that at this time Pompey could easily have become a member of the senate, if he had wished to do so. But Pompey was not anxious for this; his pursuit of glory, as they say, always took an unlikely or an unusual course. And in fact there would not have been anything very surprising in his becoming a senator before he had reached the proper age; the really dazzling honour was to have a triumph when he was not a senator at all. This was something which had a considerable effect in making him popular among the ordinary people, who were delighted to find that after his triumph he was still officially included among the equestrian order.

15. Sulla was far from pleased when he saw how Pompey's reputation and power were growing; but he was ashamed to interfere and so did nothing about it. He did show his annoyance, however, on one occasion. This was when, acting in direct opposition to Sulla's wishes, Pompey had got Lepidus elected to the consulship by helping him in his canvassing and using his own personal popularity to win the support of the people for Lepidus.[35] When Sulla saw Pompey leaving the forum with a great crowd following him, he said: 'Young man, I can see you are delighted with your victory. A wonderful thing indeed and a most generous action – to use your influence with the people so that Lepidus, one of the worst men living, should get more votes at the election than Catulus, who is one of the best. It is about time, however, that you woke up and gave your attention to what is happening. What you have done is to make your opponent stronger than yourself.'

But the clearest proof that Sulla gave of his ill-feeling against Pompey was in the writing of his will. There were legacies for all his other friends, some of whom were appointed guardians to his son,[36] but Pompey's name was not mentioned at all. Pompey, however, bore this in a very decent, sensible way. In fact, when Lepidus and others tried to prevent Sulla's body from being buried in the Field of Mars or even from having a state funeral at all, he intervened personally, and saw to it that the ceremony was not only carried out in security but with every mark of honour.[37]

16. Sulla's prophecies were fulfilled shortly after his death. Lepidus tried to grasp for himself the power which Sulla had held; nor did he go about it in any roundabout way or with any pretence of legality. He took up arms immediately, basing himself on a revival of the old factions now long enfeebled, or rather on what had been left of them by Sulla. His colleague Catulus, who could count on the support of the best and healthiest elements both in the senate and among the people, had a reputation for good sense and just dealing which was second to none of the Romans of his time; on the other hand he was thought to be more at home in political than in military leadership. Events themselves, therefore, seemed to call for Pompey, and Pompey was not slow in deciding which side to take. He attached himself to the cause of the nobility and was given command of an army to operate against Lepidus, who had already succeeded in making a large part of Italy revolt and who, with a force under Brutus, was in control of Cisalpine Gaul.[38]

Pompey attacked and subdued with ease most of the rebel forces; but at Mutina in Gaul he was engaged for a long time in besieging Brutus. During this time Lepidus had made a quick dash on Rome and had camped outside the city. He demanded a second consulship for himself and, with his huge crowd of followers, he brought the citizens to the verge of panic. Their fears were dispelled by a letter which arrived from Pompey stating that he had won the war without having to fight a battle. Whether Brutus betrayed his army or whether his army changed sides and betrayed him, we do not know. In any case Brutus surrendered to Pompey, and, after receiving from him a cavalry escort, retired to a small town on the Po. Here, after one day had passed, he was put to death by Geminius, who was acting under Pompey's instructions. Pompey was much blamed for this. For directly after Brutus' army had changed sides, he wrote to the senate to say that Brutus had come over to him of his own accord; and then in a second letter, after Brutus had been killed, he produced evidence against him. This Brutus was the father of the Brutus who, with Cassius, killed Caesar. Neither in his wars nor in the manner of his death was the son like the father, as may be read in his 'Life'.

As for Lepidus, he was driven out of Italy and crossed over to Sardinia.[39] There he fell ill and died of despair. The despair was not, apparently, caused by the failure of his policy but was due to his coming upon a letter which proved that his wife[40] had been unfaithful to him.

17. Meanwhile there hung over Rome like a cloud the menace of Sertorius, a very different sort of general from Lepidus. Sertorius was now in control of Spain. The poison of the civil wars had, as it were, come to a head in him and he represented the last stages of the disease. He had already put an end to the careers of many inferior commanders and was now engaged with Metellus Pius,[41] who was a distinguished man and a good soldier but was considered to be handicapped by his age, no longer quick to seize the opportunities of war and liable to be left behind by events when they occurred quickly and suddenly. For the methods of Sertorius were those of a robber chieftain; his unconventional attacks, his ambushes and his flanking movements had a disturbing effect on a man whose whole training was in regular pitched battles and who commanded troops which were heavily armed and lacking in mobility. Pompey therefore kept his army together and tried to arrange to have himself sent out to reinforce Metellus. Catulus ordered him to disband his troops, but instead of doing so he kept on making one excuse or another and remained under arms near the city until the senate gave him the command on the motion of Lucius Philippus.[42] They say that on this occasion someone in the senate expressed surprise at the proposal and asked whether Philippus really thought it necessary for Pompey to be sent out with the status and power of a consul. 'Not of a consul,' replied Philippus, 'but of the consuls' – implying that in his view both of the consuls for that year were quite useless.

18. Pompey's arrival in Spain produced the effects which normally follow the appearance of a new commander with a great reputation. The troops on the spot, with something fresh to look forward to, became changed men; the Spanish tribes which

were not bound by very close alliances to Sertorius began to
grow restless and to show signs of deserting his cause. Sertorius
therefore began to make and to publicize a number of con-
temptuous references to Pompey. 'I should only need,' he said
mockingly, 'a cane and whip to deal with this boy, if I were not
afraid of that old woman' – Metellus being the old woman. In
fact, however, he watched Pompey closely and out of fear for
him showed much more caution than previously in his general
conduct of the campaign. As for Metellus (though no one would
have expected this of him), he had become very luxury-loving
and had given himself up entirely to his pleasures; his whole
character had suddenly undergone an alteration and he was
now both extravagant and ostentatious. These defects in
Metellus served to increase Pompey's reputation and made him
extraordinarily popular, since his own way of life was a model
of simplicity; not that this cost him much effort; he was naturally a temperate character and was in complete control of his
desires.

There were many changes of fortune in this war. What upset
Pompey most of all was the capture of Lauro by Sertorius. He
had imagined that the enemy was surrounded and had boasted
of the fact; it then suddenly appeared that he was surrounded
himself; he was afraid to move and had to look on while the
city was burned before his eyes. However, he won a victory
near Valentia against Herennius and Perpenna,[43] Roman exiles
who had joined Sertorius and been given command of armies
by him, and killed more than 10,000 of their men.

19. Flushed with this success and full of confidence, he then
hastened to engage Sertorius himself, being eager to win a
victory without Metellus having any share in it. The two forces
joined battle near the River Sucro late in the day and both
generals were anxious for Metellus not to appear – Pompey,
because he wanted to fight without anyone to help him, Sertorius because he wanted to fight without anyone to help his
opponent. As it happened, the battle was indecisive; on each
side one wing won and one lost. But, so far as the two generals
were concerned, Sertorius had the better of it. The troops under

his personal command routed those who were opposed to them. Pompey was less successful. He was fighting on horseback and was attacked by a tall man who was fighting on foot. Charging at each other they came to close quarters and each struck the other on the hand with his sword. The sword strokes, however, were not of equal force. Pompey was merely wounded, but the hand of his antagonist was cut right off. But now enemy troops in still greater numbers bore down on him; his own troops were already routed. He made his escape from what seemed to be a hopeless position by abandoning his horse to the enemy. The horse had golden ornaments on its head and other trappings of great value, and, while the enemy fought with each other over the division of the spoil, Pompey himself got away. At dawn on the following day both armies formed up with the intention of making certain of the victory that had so far eluded them. By now, however, Metellus was approaching: Sertorius retired and his army scattered in different directions. These were his usual tactics – a total dispersal of his forces followed by a rapid mobilization – so that at times Sertorius would be moving about the country entirely on his own and at other times would take the field with an army of 150,000 men, like a winter torrent suddenly swollen with rain.

When Pompey, after this battle, went to meet Metellus and they drew near to each other, he ordered his lictors to lower their fasces to show his respect for Metellus as his superior in rank. Metellus, however, would not allow this, and in every other way, too, treated Pompey with the greatest consideration. Though a man of consular rank and Pompey's senior, he claimed no special rights for himself, except that, when both armies were encamped together, the watchword was issued to the whole camp from his tent. Usually, though, they encamped apart from each other, and indeed they were constantly finding their communications cut and their forces separated as a result of the unpredictable tactics of Sertorius who had a genius for appearing almost at the same moment in a number of different places and forcing them to fight now here now there. In the end, by cutting off their supplies, by laying the country waste, and by gaining control of the sea he drove them both out of his own area of Spain and forced them to retreat to other provinces because of lack of provisions.

20. By his expenses on this war Pompey had already run through most of his private fortune. He now asked the senate for money and threatened to come back with his army to Italy if his request was not granted.[44] Lucullus was consul at this time. He was not on good terms with Pompey, but he did everything that he could to have the money sent. This was because he was trying to get himself appointed to the command against Mithridates and he was afraid of giving Pompey any excuse for returning home, since Pompey would have liked to have left Sertorius alone and gone out against Mithridates himself; it would be a command that would bring him much honour, and Mithridates seemed a much easier proposition than Sertorius. About this time,[45] however, Sertorius was treacherously murdered by members of his own party. Perpenna was the leader of these and he now attempted to take Sertorius' place. But, though he had the advantage of the same army and the same resources, he had none of Sertorius' talent and ability in making use of them. Pompey took the field against him immediately and, finding that his strategy was entirely haphazard, lured him into a trap. He sent out ten cohorts and ordered them to scatter over the plain in loose order. Perpenna attacked them and was beginning to pursue them when Pompey appeared on the scene with his entire army. Battle was joined and Pompey won a complete victory. Most of Perpenna's officers were killed in the battle: Perpenna himself was brought to Pompey alive and Pompey ordered him to be put to death. Some people criticize Pompey for this, saying that he was lacking in gratitude and had forgotten what had happened in Sicily; in fact, however, he was showing excellent judgement and a most valuable sense of the public interest. Perpenna had come into possession of Sertorius' correspondence and offered to produce letters from some of the most important people in Rome who, wishing to start a revolution and change the existing form of government, had written to Sertorius inviting him to march on Italy. Pompey, however, was afraid that this evidence would simply

be the occasion for greater wars than the ones now ended; and so he put Perpenna to death and burned the letters without even reading them himself.

21. After this he stayed in Spain long enough to put down any sort of disorder which was on a really big scale, and to arrange appropriate settlements dealing with the more explosive elements in the situation. He then led his army back to Italy where he happened to arrive just at the height of the Slave War.[46] Because of this Crassus, who was in command against the slaves, precipitated the decisive battle at some risk to himself. The venture turned out successfully and he killed 12,300 of the enemy. Even in this success, however, fortune somehow or other managed to give Pompey a share; 5,000 fugitives from the battle fell into his hands; he killed them all, and then, anticipating Crassus' own dispatches, wrote to the senate to say that, while Crassus had certainly defeated the gladiators in a pitched battle, he himself had finished the war off utterly and entirely. So popular was he in Rome that everyone liked hearing and repeating this remark, and so far as Spain and Sertorius were concerned, no one even in jest would maintain that the entire credit was due to anyone except Pompey.

Yet in all this general desire to see him and to do him honour there were also present feelings of suspicion and of fear; it was thought that, instead of disbanding his army, he might go straight ahead and, by the use of military force and absolutism, make himself into another Sulla. And so of all those who ran out of the city to greet him on his return just as many were actuated by fear as by goodwill. Pompey, however, soon put an end to these suspicions by announcing that he would disband his army as soon as his triumph was over. There was now only one fault that his enemies could find in him, namely that he was paying more attention to the people than to the senate and that, in order to do the people a favour, he had decided to restore to the tribunes the powers which Sulla had taken away from them.[47] This was indeed the case. To see the tribunes once more enjoying their former powers was the one thing above all others which the Roman people most frantically desired and most eagerly longed for; and Pompey on his side thought himself extremely lucky to have the opportunity of passing this particular measure, since if some other statesman had anticipated him in this, he could never have found an equally good way of expressing his thanks to the people for the goodwill which they had shown him.

22. So he was awarded a second triumph and was declared consul.[48] It was not so much for this, however, that men admired him and thought him great; what seemed the most remarkable proof of his extraordinary distinction was that Crassus, the richest statesman of the time, the best orator and the greatest man, Crassus, who looked down upon Pompey and everyone else, had not ventured to put himself forward as a candidate for the consulship until he had first asked Pompey to support him. Pompey was delighted to do so; he had always wanted to do Crassus a good turn and so he very readily agreed to his request, used his influence with the people to help Crassus' candidature, and gave out that he should be as grateful to them if they gave him Crassus as a colleague as he would be for the consulship itself. In spite of this, however, once they had been elected consuls, they disagreed on every single point and were constantly in opposition to each other. In the senate Crassus was the more influential of the two, but Pompey had great power with the people. He had given them back their tribunes, and he allowed a bill to be passed to give once more to the equestrian order the right of serving on the juries in the law courts.[49]

But perhaps the most enjoyable of all spectacles to the people was the one which Pompey afforded himself when he appeared in person to ask for his discharge from military service. It is an old custom at Rome that those who belong to the cavalry should, at the conclusion of the legal period of their military service, come into the forum, each leading his horse, and appear before the two officials called censors. Each man gives the names of the generals and imperators under whom he has served, and some account of his own actions in war, and then receives his discharge. According to his record he receives from the censors words either of praise or blame.

On this occasion the censors Gellius and Lentulus[50] were sitting in state, and the gentlemen with their horses were passing in review in front of them when Pompey was seen coming down the hill into the forum. He had all the insignia of a consul, but he was leading his horse with his own hand. When he came nearer so that he could be seen by everyone, he ordered his lictors to make way for him and then led his horse up to the bench where the censors were sitting. The people were amazed and stood in complete silence; the censors too were awed and also delighted at the sight. Then the senior censor questioned him, 'Pompey the Great, I require you to tell me whether you have taken part in all the military campaigns that the law demands.' And in a loud voice Pompey replied: 'I have taken part in all of them, and all under myself as imperator.' These words were greeted with a great shout from the people, and indeed it became quite impossible to restrain their rapturous applause; the censors rose from their seats and led the procession escorting Pompey home, this giving great pleasure to the people who followed behind, shouting and clapping.

23. When Pompey's term of office was nearly over and his differences with Crassus were getting greater and greater, a man of the name of Gaius Aurelius, who, though belonging to the equestrian order, had never taken any part in politics, got up on to the speaker's platform at an assembly of the people and came forward to say that Jupiter had appeared to him in a dream and had instructed him to tell the consuls that they must not lay down their office until they had made friends with each other. At these words Pompey stood still without making a sign. It was Crassus who made the first move by clasping Pompey's hand and speaking to him politely. He then said to the people: 'My friends, I do not think that I am lowering or demeaning myself in any way if I take the initiative here. In giving way to Pompey, I am giving way to one whom you were pleased to call "the Great" when he had still scarcely a hair on

his chin, and for whom you decreed two triumphs before he was even a member of the senate.' They then became reconciled together, and afterwards laid down their office.

Crassus now went back to the way of life which he had adopted from the beginning of his career; but Pompey began to appear less and less frequently as a speaker in the courts and gradually withdrew himself from the forum; he only rarely showed himself in public, though when he did he was always accompanied by a large crowd. In fact unless when he was surrounded by people it was soon difficult to meet him at all or even to see him; what he liked best was to make his appearance with great numbers crowding all round him at once, thus giving the impression of a majesty and pomp surrounding him; evidently he thought that he ought to keep his dignity intact and not risk losing it in the conversations and familiarities of ordinary common life. And it is true that civilian life can have a very damaging effect on the reputations of those who have won great names for themselves in war and who are not well adapted to the kind of equality which one finds in a democracy. Such people think that they ought to enjoy the same supremacy in civilian life as that to which they are used when in command of armies; whereas the others, who have not had such distinguished records in war, are not prepared to put up with a situation in which they do not have any advantages in civil life either. And so when they find a man with a brilliant reputation for his campaigns and his triumphs taking a full part in peacetime activities, they do their best to undermine his position and to humiliate him; if, on the other hand, he renounces these activities and withdraws into private life, they cease to envy him and leave his military power and reputation intact. How true this is was soon shown by events.

24. The power of the pirates was originally based on Cilicia and at first the pirate fleets employed hit-and-run tactics. They gained confidence and daring during the period of the Mithridatic war when they took subsidies from the king and served in his interest. Then while Romans were fighting each other in civil wars at the gates of Rome, the sea was left

unguarded and so the pirates were gradually enticed further and further on until, instead of confining their operations to attacks on navigation, they began to lay waste islands and cities on the coasts. Soon men of wealth and of good family, men who would claim for themselves exceptional intelligence, began to join the pirate fleets and to share in their enterprises, regarding piracy as a profession in which honour could be gained and ambition satisfied. In many places too there were regular fortified harbours and signal stations for the use of the pirates, and the fleets which put in at these places were admirably equipped for their own work with fine crews, expert pilots, and light, fast ships. They were certainly formidable enough; but what excited most indignation was the odious arrogance of it all – the gilded sails, the purple awnings, the silvered oars – the general impression that they were delighting in this way of life and priding themselves on their evil deeds. Roman supremacy was brought into contempt by their flute-playing, their stringed instruments, their drunken revels along every coast, their seizures of high-ranking officials, and the ransoms which they demanded for captured cities. It may be stated as a fact that the pirates had in service more than 1,000 ships and that the cities captured by them amounted to 400. They also attacked and plundered sanctuaries and holy places which had never been violated before: Claros, for example, Didyma and Samothrace; the temple of Chthonian Earth at Hermione; the temple of Asclepius at Epidaurus; the temples of Poseidon at the Isthmus, at Taenarum and at Calauria; the temples of Apollo at Actium and Leucas; and the temples of Hera at Samos, at Argos and at Lacinium. They themselves offered strange sacrifices of their own at Olympus, where they celebrated secret rites or mysteries, among which were those of Mithras. These Mithraic rites, first celebrated by the pirates, are still celebrated today.

But it was the Romans who suffered most from the insolence of the pirates, who would even march inland up the Roman roads from the sea, plundering the country and sacking the country houses on their way. There was one occasion when they captured two praetors, Sextilius and Bellienus,[51] in their official purple-edged robes and carried them off together with their servants and their lictors. Then there was the case of the daughter of Antonius, a man who had celebrated a triumph.[52] She was captured by the pirates while she was on her way into the country and a large ransom had to be paid for her release. But the way in which they treated their prisoners was the most outrageous thing of all. If a prisoner cried out that he was a Roman and gave his name, they would pretend to be absolutely terrified; they would smite their thighs with their hands, and fall down at his feet, begging him to forgive them. The prisoner, seeing them so humble and hearing their entreaties, would believe that they meant what they said. They would then put Roman boots on his feet and clothe him in a Roman toga in order, they said, that there should be no mistake about his identity in the future. And so they would play with him for some time, getting all the amusement possible out of him until, in the end, they would let down a ship's ladder when they were far out to sea and tell him that he was quite free to go and that they wished him a pleasant journey. If he objected, then they threw him overboard themselves and drowned him.

25. The power of the pirates extended over the whole area of our Mediterranean sea. The result was that all navigation and all commerce were at a standstill; and it was this aspect of the situation which caused the Romans, who were already short of provisions and expected a real breakdown in supplies, to send out Pompey with a commission to drive the pirates off the seas. Gabinius,[53] one of Pompey's friends, drew up a law by which Pompey was to be given not only the supreme naval command but what amounted in fact to an absolute authority and uncontrolled power over everyone. The law provided that his command should extend over the sea as far as the pillars of Hercules and over all the mainland to the distance of fifty miles from the sea. There were not many places in the Roman world which were not included within these limits; and inside the area also were a number of great nations and of powerful kings. Then he was to be given power to choose from the senate fifteen subordinate commanders to whom he would assign their special tasks, to take from the treasury and from the tax-farmers as

much money as he wanted, to raise a fleet of 200 ships, and to arrange personally for the levying of troops and sailors in whatever numbers he thought fit.

The provisions of the proposed law were read out before the assembly and were received by the people with the greatest enthusiasm. The most important and influential men in the senate, however, thought that such power, without restrictions and without limits, while it might be too great to be envied, was still something to be feared. And so, with the single exception of Caesar, they all opposed the law. Caesar spoke in favour of it, not at all out of any consideration for Pompey, but because from the beginning of his career he was trying to steal into the people's hearts and make use of them for his own interests. All the rest attacked Pompey violently; and one of the consuls[54] only narrowly escaped being torn to pieces by the people when he told Pompey that, if he wanted to be another Romulus he would not escape Romulus' fate. Catulus,[55] however, was treated with respect when he came forward to speak against the law. The people listened to him in silence while he paid a long and generous tribute to Pompey's abilities and then gave his advice, which was to use sparingly a man of such value and not to keep on exposing him to new dangers and new wars. 'If you lost Pompey,' he said, 'whom would you have to take his place?' At this they all shouted out together: 'We should have you.' So Catulus, having failed to get his advice accepted, retired from the speaker's platform. But when Roscius[56] came forward to speak, no one would listen to him at all. He therefore made signs with his fingers indicating that he was against the idea of there being just one commander-in-chief, and thought that a second one should be chosen to work in cooperation with Pompey. The people were furious at this suggestion and, so it is said, raised such a shout that a raven which was flying over the forum was stunned by it and fell down into the crowd. This incident seems to show that when birds fall down in this way it is not due to the air being as it were broken and torn apart so as to make a vacuum, but that they are actually struck by the impact of the voice, which, when it rises up loud and strong, produces in the air a kind of wave or billow.

26. So for the time being the assembly was adjourned. When the day came for voting on the law, Pompey went quietly out of the city into the country. There he was informed that the law had been passed and he came back into the city by night so as to avoid the envy that would be occasioned by crowds of people coming out to meet him and congratulate him. When it was day he appeared in public and offered a sacrifice. An assembly was held for him and at this he arranged to have given him still greater powers than those which had been voted to him already. In fact his forces were practically doubled. Five hundred ships were manned for him and an army was raised consisting of 120,000 regular infantry and 5,000 cavalry. Twenty-four men who had been in command of armies or held the office of praetor were chosen by him out of the senate to act as his lieutenants, and in addition he had two quaestors. There was now a sudden drop in all the prices of foodstuffs and this enabled the delighted people to say that the very name of Pompey had put an end to the war.

Pompey, however, went on with his task. He divided the Mediterranean and the adjacent coasts into thirteen separate areas each of which was entrusted to a commander with a fixed number of ships.[57] This dispersal of his forces throughout the sea enabled him to surround entire fleets of pirate ships which he hunted down and brought into harbour. Others managed to slip off on their own or in small detachments and from all directions hurried back as it were to their hive in Cilicia. Pompey with his sixty best ships proposed to sail against them himself. But he did not set out against them until he had entirely cleared of pirates the Tyrrhenian Sea, the Libyan Sea and the seas about Sardinia, Corsica and Sicily. All this was done in the space of forty days and was the result of his own tireless energy and the enthusiastic support which he received from his subordinate officers.

27. In Rome, however, the consul Piso, who hated and envied Pompey, was weakening the efficiency of his forces by discharging the crews of his ships before their time.[58] So Pompey sent his fleet round to Brundisium and went overland himself through

Tuscany to Rome. As soon as it was known that he was coming, everyone came pouring out of the city to meet him, just as if they had not done the same thing only a few days before when they were seeing him off. What made them so happy was the way in which the whole situation had changed more quickly than anyone could have expected; the markets were now full to overflowing. As a result Piso was in danger of being deprived of his consulship. Gabinius had a law to this effect already drawn up; but Pompey would not allow it to be put forward, and in all other respects too behaved with the greatest moderation. Once he had arranged everything to his own satisfaction he left Rome for Brundisium and put to sea.

He had no wish to lose time and opportunity, and so he sailed past the cities on his route without stopping. Athens, however, he could not pass by. He went up from the coast to the city, sacrificed to the gods, and made a speech to the people. Just as he was leaving, he read two inscriptions, each of a single verse, which had been addressed to him. One was inside the gate and was as follows:

'Knowing that you are mortal, you are all the more divine.' And the other one outside the gate: 'We awaited, we saluted, we have seen, we wish you well.' Some of the pirate bands still at sea and operating away from their bases now asked for mercy. Pompey treated them very humanely; he took over their ships and made prisoners of the men, but inflicted no further punishment. This encouraged the rest also to hope for forgiveness and, avoiding his other commanders, they came out with their wives and children and surrendered to him. He spared all of them and it was chiefly through their help that he was able to track down, seize and punish those who were still in hiding because they were conscious of having committed crimes too great to be forgiven.

28. The majority, however, which included the most formidable of the pirates, had brought their families, their property and all who were unfit for military service into castles and fortresses near the Taurus mountains; they themselves manned their ships and waited to give battle to Pompey near the headland of

Coracesium in Cilicia. In the engagement which followed the
pirates were defeated and were then besieged. Finally they
begged for mercy and surrendered themselves together with all
the cities and islands which they controlled and which they had
fortified, making them very difficult to take by storm and indeed
almost inaccessible. And so the war was brought to an end. In
less than three months piracy had been completely driven from
the seas. Among the many ships surrendered to Pompey were
ninety warships with brazen rams. There were more than
20,000 prisoners.

As regards the prisoners Pompey never even entertained the
idea of putting them to death; on the other hand there were
great numbers of them, they were poor and used to war; so that
he did not think it would be wise to let them go and allow them
to disperse or else to reorganize themselves again in bands. He
reflected, therefore, that by nature man neither is nor becomes
a wild or unsocial creature; it is rather the case that the habit
of vice makes him become something which by nature he is
not, and on the other hand he can be made civilized again by
precept and example and by a change of place and of occupation; in fact even wild beasts, given a measure of gentle treatment, lose their savage and intractable qualities. With all this
in mind, he decided to transfer the men from the sea to the
land, to give them a taste of civilized life and to get them used
to living in cities and cultivating the land. Some of them were
received by the small and half-populated cities of Cilicia which,
on admitting them to citizenship, were given additional land.
Many were settled by Pompey in the city of Soli which had
recently been devastated by King Tigranes of Armenia and
which he now restored. Most of them, however, were given a
place to live in at Dyme in Achaea, which was at that time very
underpopulated and had a lot of good land.

29. Those who looked on Pompey with an envious eye found
fault with these measures of his; but even his best friends disapproved of the way in which he treated Metellus in Crete.[59]
This Metellus was a relation of the Metellus who had been
Pompey's colleague in Spain, and had been sent out as governor

to Crete before Pompey had received his own command. Crete was the second source of pirates after Cilicia, and Metellus, having surrounded many of them, was busy in rooting them out and destroying them. But those who still survived and were being besieged sent humble messages to Pompey, inviting him to come to Crete which, they said, was part of his province since all of it fell within the fifty-mile limit from the sea. Pompey accepted the invitation and wrote to Metellus telling him to cease hostilities. He also wrote to the cities instructing them that they need pay no further attention to Metellus and he sent out to them to act as their commander one of his own officers called Lucius Octavius.[60] Octavius, by joining in with the besieged pirates, entering their fortresses, and fighting on their side succeeded in making Pompey hated as an oppressor. He also made him look ridiculous, since, purely out of his envious desire to outshine Metellus, he was lending his name to be used in the cause of ruffians who had no respect for gods or men and was fastening his own reputation round their necks like a kind of amulet to keep them from harm. Even Achilles, one must admit, was acting not like a man but like a mere boy entirely crazy and mad for distinction, when he made signs to the others, preventing them from striking at Hector, 'Lest another win the glory and himself take second place.'

But in the present instance it appeared that Pompey was actually fighting on the side of the common enemy and was saving their lives simply in order to prevent another general from enjoying a triumph which he had worked hard to earn. Metellus, however, was not daunted. He got the pirates into his hands and dealt with them in his own way. As for Octavius, he sent him off after using very violent and insulting language to him in front of the whole army.

30. When it was announced in Rome that the war against the pirates was over and that Pompey, having no further business on his hands, was engaged in visiting the cities of the east, Manilius, one of the tribunes of the people, proposed a law by which Pompey should be given all the territory and forces then under the command of Lucullus, together with Bithynia, which

was under the command of Glabrio, and that he should be
entrusted with the task of making war on the Kings Mithridates
and Tigranes.[61] With this commission he was still to retain his
naval forces and the authority over the seas which he had
already. In practice this meant putting the whole of the Roman
empire into one man's hands. The only provinces which could
be held to be outside his authority by the terms of the previous
law were Phrygia, Lycaonia, Galatia, Cappadocia, Cilicia,
Upper Colchis and Armenia: now these too were handed over
to him together with the forces and equipment which Lucullus
had used in his conquest of Mithridates and Tigranes.

Lucullus in this way was being robbed of the glory which he
had earned by his achievements and was being replaced by
someone who would merely reap the honour of a triumph
rather than undertake the difficulties of a war. The aristocratic
party in Rome, however, though they did recognize that Lucullus was being treated unjustly and ungratefully, were not so
much concerned about him; what they found difficult to bear
was the thought of so much power being given to Pompey; it
amounted, they thought, to the setting up of a tyranny and in
all their private conversations they encouraged and urged each
other on to do all they could to prevent the law being passed
and not to surrender their liberty. However, when the time came
for voting on the law their hearts failed them, so frightened were
they of the people, and no one said a word against it except
Catulus, who made a long speech attacking both the law and
the tribune who was proposing it. Finding that his words had
no effect whatever on the people, he turned to the senate, crying
out to them from the speaker's platform and urging them again
and again to act as their forefathers had done and find some
mountain or desolate rock to which they could retire and preserve their liberty. However, the law was passed, and passed,
so we are told, by a unanimous vote of all the tribes. So Pompey,
who was not even in Rome at the time, was vested with powers
almost as great as those which Sulla had exercised after he had
conquered the city by force of arms.

When Pompey received the letters telling him that the law
had been passed, his friends crowded round him to congratulate

him, but he himself, so it is said, frowned and struck himself
on the thigh and then said, in the voice of one who was already
overburdened with power and weary of exercising it, 'How sad
it makes me, this constant succession of labours! Really I would
rather be one of those people whom no one has heard about, if
I am never to have any relief from military service, and never
to be able to escape from being envied so that I can live quietly
in the country with my wife.' Even Pompey's best friends found
this sort of language, which was in fact mere play-acting, rather
insupportable. They knew perfectly well that he hated Lucullus
and that this feeling was acting as a stimulus to his natural
passion for distinction and love of power, so that he was all the
more delighted with what had happened.

31. In fact his actions soon unmasked him. He sent out procla-
mations far and wide commanding the soldiers to join him and
summoned all the subject kings and princes into his presence;
and as he went through the country he altered every single
arrangement that had been made by Lucullus, remitting many
penalties, taking away many rewards and indeed, out of pure
jealousy, doing everything he could to show the admirers of
Lucullus that he was now entirely without power. Lucullus,
through his friends, protested at this behaviour. It was decided
that there should be a meeting between the two generals and
this meeting took place in Galatia. As both were great generals
with great successes to their names, the lictors on both sides
had their rods wreathed with laurel when they met. Lucullus,
however, had been coming through well-wooded country
where there was plenty of vegetation, while Pompey had been
marching for a long way over parched treeless ground. So when
Lucullus' lictors saw that Pompey's laurels were all dry and
withered, they took some of their own fresh laurels and decorated his rods with wreaths of them. This was considered as an
omen indicating that Pompey was coming to take away from
Lucullus the rewards and the glory of his victories.

Lucullus had been consul before Pompey and was the elder
man; Pompey had the advantage over him in having been
honoured with two triumphs.[62] Nevertheless, their first meeting

was as friendly and polite as could be; each spoke in the highest
terms of the other's achievements and congratulated him on his
successes. In subsequent discussions, however, they failed to
reach any kind of reasonable or moderate agreement. Harsh
words began to be spoken – Pompey attacking Lucullus for
being too fond of money, and Lucullus attacking Pompey for
being too fond of power – and their friends had some difficulty
in parting them. Lucullus then, still remaining in Galatia, made
distributions of the conquered land and gave presents to whatever people he wished. Pompey, camping a little distance away
from him, stopped his orders being carried out and detached
from him all his troops except 1,600 who, being in a mutinous
state of mind, would be, he thought, ill-disposed to Lucullus
and no use to himself. He would also quite openly speak in
slighting terms of what Lucullus had done. Lucullus, he said,
had been fighting against kings who amounted to nothing more
than painted scenery on the stage, whereas he himself had a
real war to deal with and a real army, disciplined by defeat,
since now Mithridates had started to use shields, swords and
horses. To this Lucullus retorted that Pompey was going out to
fight a war that was no war at all but only the shadow of one,
and that in so doing he was following his usual custom of
settling down, like some lazy carrion bird, on the bodies that
had been killed by others and tearing to pieces the scattered
remains of wars. It was in just this way that he had appropriated
to himself the victories over Sertorius, Lepidus and the followers
of Spartacus, though in fact these victories had been won by
Metellus, Catulus and Crassus. There was therefore no reason
to be surprised at his present plan of seizing for himself the
glory of the Pontic and Armenian wars; was he not a man who
had somehow managed by hook or by crook to get himself a
triumph on the strength of having defeated runaway slaves?

32. After this Lucullus withdrew from Galatia. Pompey employed his whole fleet in patrolling the sea between Phoenicia
and the Bosporus and himself marched against Mithridates
who, with a fighting force of 30,000 infantry and 2,000 cavalry,
still did not dare to offer battle. Mithridates first camped in a

strong position on a mountain which would have been very difficult to attack, but, assuming that there was no water there, he abandoned it. Pompey then occupied this same mountain. From the nature of the vegetation and from the channels in the ground he conjectured that there must be springs in the place and he ordered his men to dig wells all over the area. Water was discovered immediately and in ample quantity to supply the whole camp, so that it seemed most surprising that Mithridates, in all the time that he had been there, had been ignorant of the fact. Pompey's next move was to invest the king's camp and surround it with fortified works; but, after being besieged for forty-five days Mithridates succeeded in slipping away with the best part of his army; he killed those who were sick or unfit for service. Next, however, Pompey caught up with him near the River Euphrates and camped close by him. Fearing that he might give him the slip again by crossing the river first, he drew up his army and led it forward about midnight. At this time Mithridates is said to have had a dream showing him what was going to happen. He dreamed that he was sailing on the Pontic Sea with a fair wind behind him, that he was already in sight of the Bosporus and was talking gaily with his fellow passengers, as one might be expected to do in one's pleasure in finding oneself really and certainly safe; and then suddenly he seemed to see himself, with all his companions gone, being tossed about on the sea clinging to a small piece of wreckage. While he was still dreaming and feeling the effects of his dream, his friends came to his bed and woke him up with the news that Pompey was attacking. There was nothing to be done except to fight in defence of the camp, and so his generals led out their forces and put them in order of battle.

When Pompey saw that they were all ready to meet him, he was reluctant to take the risk of fighting in the darkness. Instead he proposed simply to surround them so that they could not escape, and then when it was day to join battle with the advantage of numbers on his side. His senior officers, however, urgently pressed him to attack at once and it was their counsels which prevailed. It was not, in fact, entirely dark. The moon had not yet set and gave sufficient light for people to be able to distinguish each other. Indeed it was the moonlight which did more harm than anything else to the king's troops. For the Romans had the light at their backs as they advanced, and since the moon was now close to the horizon, the shadows thrown by their bodies reached far forward towards the enemy, who, being unable to estimate correctly how far they were away, imagined that they were at close quarters already and hurled their javelins before anyone was in range, doing no harm whatever. Seeing this, the Romans raised a great shout and charged down on them. The king's troops no longer had the courage to stand their ground; they panicked and fled and were cut down by the Romans. Many more than 10,000 of them were killed and the camp was captured.

Mithridates himself, however, with 800 cavalry had, at the very beginning of the attack, cut his way right through the Romans and made his escape. His escort soon scattered in different directions and he was left with three companions. Among these was his concubine Hypsicrateia, a girl who had always shown the spirit of a man and always been ready to take any risk. For this reason the king used to give her the masculine name of Hypsicrates. On this occasion she was mounted and dressed like a Persian. In all the king's flight she was never wearied by the long journeys and constantly attended to the king's person and to his horse too, until they came to a place called Sinora, which was full of money and treasure belonging to the king. From his stores here Mithridates took suits of costly clothing and distributed them amongst those who had come together to join him after his flight. He also gave to each of his friends deadly poison to carry with them, so that no one need fall into the hands of the enemy against his will. His intention was to set out from here and go to Armenia to join Tigranes, but Tigranes forbade him to come and put out a proclamation offering 100 talents for his person. He therefore made his way past the sources of the Euphrates and continued his flight through the country of Colchis.

33. Pompey next invaded Armenia. He was invited into the country by young Tigranes who was now in revolt against his

father and who met Pompey by the River Araxes. This river rises in the same area as the Euphrates, but then turns eastward and flows into the Caspian Sea. The two of them then marched forward together, receiving the submission of the cities on their way. But King Tigranes, who had recently suffered very heavily in the war with Lucullus, once he learned that Pompey was of a mild and forgiving disposition, received a Roman garrison in his palace and, with all his friends and relations, set out in person to surrender himself to Pompey. He rode up to the Roman camp on horseback, and here was met by two of Pompey's lictors who ordered him to dismount and to proceed on foot; it was unprecedented, they said, for anyone to appear on horseback in a Roman camp. Tigranes not only submitted to this but unloosed his sword and handed that over too. And finally, when he came before Pompey himself, he took off his royal diadem and made as if to lay it at his feet, and, worst of all, was ready to prostrate himself and to clasp Pompey's knees in supplication. But before he could do so, Pompey took him by the hand and drew him forward. He gave him a seat near himself and, placing his son on the other side, told him that, as for what he had lost, that was the responsibility of Lucullus, who had in fact taken from him Syria, Phoenicia, Cilicia, Galatia and Sophene; but he could continue to hold what he still possessed if he paid 6,000 talents to the Romans as an indemnity for his acts of aggression; and his son should have the kingdom of Sophene. Tigranes was perfectly satisfied with these terms, and when the Romans saluted him as king he was overjoyed and promised to give half a mina of silver to each soldier, ten minas to each centurion, and a talent to each military tribune. His son, however, was dissatisfied and, when he was invited to supper, he replied that he had no need to depend on Pompey for this sort of hospitality; he could easily find some other Roman to dine with, if he wanted. Upon this he was put into chains and kept under guard until he could appear in Pompey's triumph.[63] Not long afterwards Phraates, the Parthian, sent to Pompey asking to have the young man given to him on the grounds that he was his son-in-law; he also suggested that the Euphrates should be considered the boundary between his empire and that of the Romans. Pompey replied that, so far as Tigranes was concerned, he belonged more to his father than his father-in-law; and, with regard to the boundary, that the one adopted would be a just one.

34. Leaving Afranius[64] in charge of Armenia, Pompey himself now went after Mithridates, following the only possible route which was through the tribes living round the Caucasus mountains. The largest of those nations are the Albanians and the Iberians. The Iberians extend to the Moschian mountains and the Euxine Sea; the Albanians lie more to the east in the direction of the Caspian. At first these Albanians agreed to Pompey's request to be allowed to pass through their land freely; but winter came on while the Romans were still in their country and, while the Roman army was busy celebrating the Saturnalia, the Albanians mustered a force of no less than 40,000 men, crossed the River Cyrnus, and attacked. (The Cyrnus rises in the Iberian mountains, is joined by the Araxes as it flows out of Armenia, and finally, through twelve mouths, empties itself into the Caspian. Though according to other accounts the Araxes does not join the Cyrnus; it flows in a course of its own and enters the Caspian near the mouths of the Cyrnus.) Though it would have been quite possible for Pompey to have opposed the enemy's passage of the river, he allowed them to cross without interference. He then led his army against them and routed them with very great loss. But when their king sent a deputation to beg for mercy, Pompey forgave him his misdeeds and made a treaty with him. He then marched against the Iberians, who were as numerous as the others and better soldiers; they were also strong partisans of Mithridates and wished to gratify the king by driving Pompey out of the country. (They had not been subject either to the Medes or the Persians, and had not even formed part of the Macedonian empire, since Alexander had made a very hurried march back from Hyrcania.) These people too, however, were routed by Pompey in a great battle in which 9,000 of them were killed and more than 10,000 taken prisoner. Pompey then invaded Colchis and

at the River Phasis was met by Servilius[65] with the fleet with which he was patrolling the Euxine.

35. Mithridates had now gone into hiding among the tribes living about the Bosporus and the Maeotic Sea. To pursue him further would have been an operation of great difficulty. Pompey also received the news that the Albanians had once again broken out into revolt. This news made him angry. He was determined that they should not get the better of him, and so he turned back and crossed the Cyrnus again. The crossing of the river was a difficult and hazardous undertaking, since the natives had erected palisades along long stretches of the banks. He then had to march for a great distance through waterless and difficult country. For this march he had 10,000 skins filled with water, and so advanced on the enemy and found them drawn up ready for battle by the River Abas. They had 60,000 infantry and 12,000 cavalry, but were badly armed and most of them were clothed only in the skins of wild beasts. They were led by a brother of their king, called Cosis, who, when the armies were close together charged at Pompey himself and struck him with a javelin at the joint of his breastplate; but Pompey ran him through the body and killed him.

It is said that Amazons also were fighting with the native troops in this battle and that they had come down from the mountainous area of the River Thermodon. Certainly when the Romans were gathering in the spoil from the barbarians after the battle they came across shields and buskins of the Amazon type; but no women's bodies were found. The Amazons live in the parts of the Caucasus range that slope down to the Hyrcanian Sea; they do not share the same frontier with the Albanians; the Gelae and the Leges are in between, and the Amazons every year meet these people near the River Thermodon and keep company with them for two months, after which they go away and live on their own.

36. After the battle Pompey set out on a march to the Hyrcanian and Caspian Sea, but when he was only three days' march away

from it he was forced to turn back because of the numbers of
deadly snakes which were found. He then retired to Lesser
Armenia, where the kings of the Elymaeans and the Medes sent
ambassadors to him. He replied to them by letter in friendly
terms. The King of Parthia, however, had invaded Gordyene
and was plundering the subjects of Tigranes. Pompey sent a
force against him under the command of Afranius, who drove
him out of Gordyene and pursued him as far as the district
round Arbela.

A number of Mithridates' concubines were brought to
Pompey, but he took none of them for himself and sent them
all back to their parents and relations, most of them being in
fact the wives or daughters of generals or princes. The exception
was Stratonice, who was honoured more than all the others by
the king and was in charge of the richest of his castles. She, it
seems, was the daughter of an impoverished old man who was
a harpist. She played to Mithridates once while he was sitting
over his wine and made such a rapid conquest of him that he
took her away to bed with him. Her old father, who had been
dismissed without so much as a kind word, was greatly upset.
In the morning, however, when he woke up, he found his house
full of tables covered with gold and silver goblets; there was
a great crowd of servants; there were eunuchs and pages bringing him expensive clothes to wear; and outside his door was
standing a horse richly caparisoned like those belonging to the
king's friends. At first the old man thought that all this was
some sort of a practical joke which people were playing on him
and he started to run out of doors; but the servants kept him
back and told him that the king had bestowed on him the huge
estate of a rich man who had died recently and that all this was
merely a foretaste or specimen of what was to come. They had
some difficulty in persuading him that this was true, but, once
he believed it, he put on his purple robes, jumped on his horse
and went riding through the city, shouting out: 'Mine, it's all
mine!' When people laughed at him, he told them not to be
surprised at his behaviour; what was really surprising, he said,
was that, considering how mad he was with joy, he did not
throw stones at everyone he met. This was the sort of family

from which Stratonice came. She now surrendered this fortress of hers to Pompey and brought him many gifts in addition. Of these he only accepted what could be used to adorn the temples in Rome or to add splendour to his triumph; the rest he left to her and told her that she was welcome to use them as she pleased. Also when the King of the Iberians sent him a bed, a table and a throne, all of gold, and begged him to accept them, he handed them all over to the quaestors for the public treasury.

37. In the castle of Caenum Pompey also discovered secret documents belonging to Mithridates. He had an enjoyable time reading them, since they threw a good deal of light on the king's character. There were memoranda, for instance, which proved that Mithridates had poisoned, among many others, his son Ariarathes. He had also poisoned Alcaeus of Sardis simply because he had done better than Mithridates himself in a horse race. Then there were written interpretations of dreams, some of his own and some of dreams dreamed by his wives. There were letters written in very lascivious language from Monime to him and from him to her. According to Theophanes there was also discovered an address of Rutilius inciting him to the massacre of the Romans in Asia.[66] Most authorities, however, seem to be right in supposing that this was merely a malicious invention on the part of Theophanes, perhaps because he hated Rutilius, whose character was certainly very unlike his own, or, very probably, because he wanted to please Pompey whose father had been described by Rutilius in his histories as one of the worst men living.

38. From Caenum Pompey went on to Amisus. Here he was led by his passion for glory to act in a way that really seemed as though he were bringing a punishment on himself. He had often and bitterly reproached Lucullus on the grounds that, while the enemy was still alive, he nevertheless went on issuing edicts and distributing gifts and honours – things, according to Pompey, which it is only normal to do when one is victorious and the war is over and done with. Yet now, while Mithridates was in

undisputed control of the Bosporus and had got together a considerable force, Pompey himself proceeded to act in exactly the same way, making regulations for the various provinces and distributing gifts, as if the whole war had been brought to a conclusion. Twelve of the local monarchs had come to visit him, together with numbers of chieftains and princes; and it was to gratify them that, in replying to a letter from the King of Parthia, he refused to address him by his usual title of King of Kings. He had also a consuming passion to conquer Syria and march through Arabia to the Red Sea, so that he might extend his conquests to the ocean which surrounds the world on all sides. Already in Africa he had been the first to go forward victoriously as far as the Outer Sea; in Spain too he had carried the power of Rome up to the Atlantic; and thirdly, in his recent pursuit of the Albanians he had very nearly reached the Hyrcanian Sea. By reaching the Red Sea he would, as it were, round off the circuit of his military expeditions and, with this end in view, he got his army again on the move. It was also true that he recognized the difficulties involved in hunting Mithridates down with a regular army and considered him harder to deal with when he was on the run than when he was prepared to give battle.

39. He therefore declared that for Mithridates he was leaving behind a stronger opponent than himself – namely famine, and he instructed his fleet to blockade the Bosporus and to intercept all merchants sailing there. Death was to be the penalty for all who were caught.

He then started on his search, taking with him nearly the whole of his army. On his way he came to the place where lay the still unburied bodies of the troops of Triarius[67] who had fallen in their disastrous action against Mithridates. Pompey now gave them all a particularly fine funeral with all proper honours. It seems that the chief reason why Lucullus was so hated was that he had neglected to do this. Through the operations of his subordinate officer Afranius he subdued the Arabians round Amanus, and himself marched down to Syria. Since this country had no legitimate kings of its own, he made

it into a province and declared it to be a possession of the
Roman people. He next conquered Judaea and took the King
Aristobulus prisoner. He founded new cities and he gave their
liberty to others after punishing the tyrants who had been in
control of them. But he spent most of his time in judicial
business, settling the disputes of kings and cities. When he was
not able to go personally to deal with these cases, he sent his
friends to act for him, as happened when he sent three judges
to arbitrate between the Armenians and Parthians, who had
referred to him the decision over a disputed piece of territory.
His military power gave him a great enough name; but he was
equally respected for his natural good qualities and for his
merciful disposition. This indeed served as a cover for very
many of the faults of his friends and intimates, since it was not
in his nature either to prevent them doing wrong or to punish
them afterwards. However, all who had dealings with him
personally found him so helpful that they gladly put up with
the rapacity and overbearing conduct of his friends.

40. Of these friends the one who had most influence with him
was Demetrius, an ex-slave, and a young man who was far
from unintelligent, though his good fortune went too much
to his head. The following story is told about him. Cato the
philosopher,[68] who was then still a young man, though he
already had a great reputation and the highest ideals, went up
to Antioch with the intention of seeing the sights. Pompey was
not in the city at the time. According to this story Cato himself
was walking on foot, as he always did, while the friends who
were travelling with him were on horseback. In front of the
gate of the city he observed a great crowd of men all wearing
white, and by the road there were youths drawn up on one side
and boys on the other. Cato assumed that all this was done in
order to show deference and respect to him, and he was annoyed
by it, since he had no wish for anything of the kind. Nevertheless, he told his friends to dismount and to proceed on foot
with him. But when they drew near, the organizer of all these
ceremonies, with a wreath on his head and a wand in his
hand, came to meet them and asked them where they had left

Demetrius and when could he be expected to arrive. Cato's friends all burst out laughing, but Cato merely said: 'Alas! poor city,' and went on without making any other reply.

Nevertheless, Pompey succeeded in making Demetrius rather less obnoxious to other people by the way in which he calmly put up with his impertinence. It is said, for instance, that at entertainments, while Pompey was waiting to receive his other guests, Demetrius was often to be seen already reclining at the table, perfectly at his ease and with the hood of his toga pulled down over his ears. Even before he had returned to Italy he had bought up one of the pleasantest pieces of property in the suburbs of Rome with most delightful walks and facilities for entertainment, and there were gardens, purchased for a great sum of money, called 'the Demetrian gardens'; whereas Pompey himself lived in a simple inexpensive house until the time of his third triumph.[69] Afterwards, certainly, when he was building the beautiful and famous theatre which is called after him, he constructed close by it, like a small boat attached to a big ship, a house for himself which was grander than the one he had before; but even this one was not grand enough to excite envy. In fact, so the story goes, when the person who came into possession of the house after Pompey first entered it he was quite surprised and asked, 'Where did Pompey the Great hold his dinner parties?'

41. The King of the Arabs round Petra had up to this time thought nothing of the power of Rome. Now, however, he became seriously alarmed and wrote to say that he had decided to make his submission and would do whatever he was told to do. So Pompey, who wished to keep him up to this resolution, marched towards Petra. Most people were inclined to blame him for making this expedition; it seemed to be an evasion of the pursuit of Mithridates, and they thought that the army ought rather to be used against that inveterate enemy of Rome who was once more stirring up trouble and was reported to be planning to lead an army through Scythia and Paeonia against Italy. Pompey, however, thought it would be easier to destroy the king's forces in actual war than to secure the king's person

while he was on the run; he had no wish to wear out his own troops in a vain pursuit; and so he let the time drag on and in the meanwhile employed himself on other enterprises.

As it was, fortune resolved the difficulty. He was already not far from Petra and, having pitched his camp for the day, was exercising himself on horseback near the rampart, when dispatch bearers rode up bringing good news from Pontus. Such messengers can be recognized immediately, since they have laurels twined round the tips of their spears, and, as soon as the soldiers saw them, they all rushed in a crowd to Pompey. At first Pompey wanted to finish his exercise, but he gave in to their shouts and entreaties, dismounted from his horse, took the dispatches and led the way into the camp. There was no regular tribunal and not even that military substitute for one which the soldiers make with their own hands by cutting thick sods of earth and piling them on top of each other. So in the urgency and excitement of the moment they brought together the saddles of the baggage animals and raised a sort of platform out of them. Pompey got up on to it and announced to the army that Mithridates was dead; he had killed himself when his son Pharnaces had revolted; all the power in those parts had come into the hands of Pharnaces, and Pharnaces had written to say that he was acting in his own name and in that of the Romans.

42. This news naturally enough filled the army with joy. Sacrifices were made to the gods; there was feasting and merrymaking. The death of Mithridates[70] seemed to them like the death of 10,000 enemies.

So, with much less difficulty than could have been expected, Pompey had put the finishing touch to his great actions and his campaigns. He immediately withdrew from Arabia, marched quickly through the provinces on the way and came to Amisus. Here he found a number of gifts which had been sent to him by Pharnaces, also many dead bodies of the royal family including the dead body of Mithridates himself. The body was not easy to recognize by the face, since the embalmers had neglected to remove the brain; but those who cared to see the sight could recognize him by his scars. Pompey could not bring himself to look upon the actual corpse; he sent it away to Sinope in order to propitiate the jealousy of heaven. But he was amazed at the size and the splendour of the arms and the clothes which Mithridates used to wear. The swordbelt, nevertheless, which cost 400 talents, was stolen by Publius and sold to Ariarathes; and the tiara, a piece of wonderful workmanship, was secretly handed over at his request to Faustus, the son of Sulla, by Mithridates' foster-brother Gaius. Pompey knew nothing of this at the time, but Pharnaces found out about it afterwards and punished the thieves.

Having settled the affairs of the east and made what arrangements seemed good to him, Pompey started on his journey home. He now travelled with much more pomp and ceremony than before. For example, when he came to Mitylene, he gave the city its freedom for the sake of Theophanes, and he was a spectator of the traditional competition held there for poets who, this time, had only one theme, which was the exploits of Pompey. He was very pleased with the theatre itself and had sketches and plans of it made for him, with the intention of building one like it in Rome, only larger and more magnificent. And when he was at Rhodes he listened to all the professors there and gave each one of them a gift of a talent. Poseidonius has actually published the speech which he made before him; he was disputing against the rhetorician Hermagoras, and his theme was The Principles of Investigation. At Athens Pompey behaved in just the same way to the philosophers, and also gave fifty talents to the city to help with its restoration. He hoped therefore that he would return to Italy with the most brilliant reputation in the world and that his family would be longing to see him as much as he was longing to see them. However, that divine power whose task it is always to mingle a certain proportion of evil with the greatest and most glorious gifts of fortune had for some time been secretly at work to make his homecoming less joyful than it might have been. During his absence his wife Mucia had been living a very loose life. So long as he was far away, Pompey had paid no attention to the stories about her; but now that he was getting near to Italy and

had time, it seems, to examine more carefully the charges
against her, he sent her a notice of divorce. Neither then nor
subsequently did he openly reveal the reasons why he was
divorcing her. The reason is stated, however, in Cicero's
letters.[71]

43. Before Pompey arrived all sorts of rumours about him
were current in Rome and there were scenes of considerable
disturbance. It was thought that he would immediately lead his
army against the city and make sure of absolute power for
himself. Crassus secretly left Rome taking his money and children with him, either because he was genuinely afraid or, as
seemed more likely, because he wished to make the calumnies
against Pompey seem more credible and to increase the ill-will
felt against him. Because of these rumours Pompey, as soon as
he landed in Italy, held an assembly of his soldiers and, after
making an appropriate speech in which he expressed his warm
feelings towards them, told them to disperse to their own cities
and go back to their homes, not forgetting to be ready to come
together again for the celebration of his triumph. Once his
army had been disbanded and everyone knew about it, a most
remarkable thing happened. The spectacle of Pompey the Great
travelling unarmed and accompanied by only a few of his intimate friends, as though he were returning from some holiday
abroad, so affected the cities on his route that all the inhabitants
came pouring out to show their goodwill to him and escorted
him on his way to Rome. There were more of them than there
had been in the army which he had disbanded, so that, if
he had at that time been planning any sort of revolutionary
measures, he would not have needed his army at all.

44. It was against the law for a general to enter the city before
his triumph had taken place. Pompey sent a message to the
senate requesting a postponement of the consular elections and
asking them to do him this favour so that he might be able
to be present in person to help Piso[72] in his canvassing. This
request was opposed by Cato and was refused. Nevertheless,
Pompey admired Cato for the way in which he spoke his mind

and for being the only man who would openly take a firm stand
on behalf of what was right. He very much wanted somehow
or other to win him over to his side and, since Cato had two
nieces, he wanted to marry one of them himself and have the
other one married to his son.[73] Cato, however, saw through the
design. The proposed marriage alliance seemed to him a form
of bribery and the whole scheme an attempt to corrupt him –
though his sister and his wife were far from pleased at his
turning down the chance of having Pompey the Great as a
kinsman. In the meantime, however, Pompey, in his desire to
have Afranius elected consul,[74] was spending large sums on his
behalf among the voters in the tribes. They used actually to go
down to Pompey's gardens to collect their money and the thing
became much talked about. Pompey himself was severely
criticized; the consulship, it was said, was the highest office of
all and Pompey himself had been rewarded with it because of
his successes in war; yet now he was treating it as something
which could be bought and given to those who could not attain
it by their merits. 'Now we,' said Cato to the women of his
family, 'should have had to take our share of this ill fame if we
had allied ourselves to Pompey.' The women had to acknowledge the truth of his words and to admit that he had been a
better judge than they of what was right and proper.

45. His triumph was on such a scale that, although two separate
days were devoted to it,[75] the time was still not long enough,
and much of what had been got ready for it – in fact enough
to equip another triumphal procession altogether – was not
included in the actual spectacle. In front of the procession were
carried placards with the names of the countries over which he
was triumphing. These were: Pontus, Armenia, Cappadocia,
Paphlagonia, Media, Colchis, Iberia, Albania, Syria, Cilicia,
Mesopotamia, Phoenicia, Palestine, Judaea and Arabia; there
was also the power of the pirates, overthrown both by sea and
on land. In the course of these campaigns it was shown that he
had captured no less than 1,000 fortified places, nearly 900
cities and 800 pirate ships; he had founded 39 cities. The
inscriptions also showed that whereas in the past the public

revenue from taxation used to be 50 million drachmas, they were now receiving from the additions to the empire made by Pompey a total of 85 million; and that he was bringing into the public treasury in coined money and in gold and silver plate 20,000 talents, apart altogether from the money which had been given to his soldiers, none of whom had received less than 1,500 drachmas. The prisoners led in the procession were, apart from the pirate chiefs, the son of Tigranes of Armenia with his wife and daughter, Zosime, a wife of King Tigranes himself, Aristobulus, King of the Jews, a sister and five children of Mithridates, some Scythian women and hostages given by the Iberians, by the Albanians and by the King of Commagene; there were also great numbers of trophies, one for every battle in which he had been victorious, either in person or in the persons of his lieutenants. But what seemed to be the greatest glory of all and one quite unprecedented in Roman history was that this third triumph of his was over the third continent. Others before him had celebrated three triumphs; but his first had been over Africa, his second over Europe, and now this last one was over Asia, so that in his three triumphs he seemed in a sense to have led the whole world captive.

46. Those who go out of their way to find an exact and precise parallel between Pompey and Alexander in everything claim that at this time he was under thirty-four years old. In fact he was nearly forty. And it would have been well for him if his life had ended at this point, up to which he had enjoyed Alexander's good fortune, since in the years that were to come his successes only made him hated and his failures were irretrievable. The great power in the city which was rightly his was used by him wrongly in the interests of others; as he strengthened them, so he weakened his own reputation, till, before he realized what was happening, he found himself ruined by the very force and greatness of his own power. When the strongest parts of a city's defences are captured the enemy becomes all the stronger through having them in his possession. Just so it was through Pompey's power and influence that Caesar was able to challenge Rome, and in the end to overthrow and ruin the very man by

whose aid he had become strong enough to rise above the rest. The sequence of events was as follows.

Lucullus had been treated outrageously by Pompey in Asia, and as soon as he returned to Rome was given a magnificent reception by the senate. When Pompey also got back, the senate, wishing to curtail his great reputation, were all the more urgent in encouraging Lucullus to take an active part in politics. By this time Lucullus had abandoned himself to the pleasures of an easy life and to the enjoyment of his wealth; most things made little impression on him and he seemed to have lost all zest for action. However, in the case of Pompey he plunged straight into the fray. He made a vigorous and indeed over-whelming attack on him in connection with those administrat-ive arrangements of his own which Pompey had cancelled, and, with the support of Cato, gained a majority in the senate for his own views.[76] Pompey, defeated and harried as he was, found it necessary to look for support to popular tribunes and young adventurers. Of these much the most unpleasant and most unscrupulous character was Clodius.[77] One may say that Clodius took Pompey up and threw him down at the people's feet, causing him to roll about ignominiously in the dirt of the forum. He carried Pompey about with him, using him as a means to give weight and authority to his own speeches and proposals all of which were made simply to gratify and flatter the mob. He even went so far as to ask to be paid for his services, as though he were doing Pompey good instead of bringing him into disgrace; and later he got his reward, when Pompey betrayed Cicero, who was his friend and indeed had done more for him in politics than had anyone else. Now, when Cicero was in danger and implored Pompey to help him, Pompey would not even meet him face to face; he kept his front door barred against those who came on Cicero's behalf and slipped out himself by a back entrance. After this Cicero, fearing the result of his trial, secretly fled from Rome.[78]

47. Caesar had now returned from his province[79] and had begun to adopt a line of policy which, while it gave him personally very great popularity at the time and power for the future, did

the utmost harm both to Pompey and to Rome. Caesar was standing for his first consulship. He saw that while Pompey and Crassus were at daggers drawn, he could only make a friend of one of them at the cost of making an enemy of the other. He therefore attempted to bring about a reconciliation between them – an admirable thing in itself and even a patriotic action, but one that was undertaken by Caesar for the wrong motives and with all the skill of a practised master of intrigue. A city, like a ship, can gain stability from opposed forces which together prevent it rocking one way or the other; but now these forces were united into one and there was nothing to stop the movement of violent party interest from overthrowing everything. Certainly Cato's remark is to the point here. When people were saying that the whole state had been overturned by the quarrel which broke out afterwards between Caesar and Pompey, Cato pointed out that they were wrong; they were merely putting the blame on to what had happened last; the first disaster and the worst had been, not the quarrel and split between Caesar and Pompey, but the friendship and harmony that had existed between them.

Caesar, then, was elected consul. He immediately began to work in favour of the poor and distressed classes by proposing measures for the founding of new cities and for the distribution of land.[80] This was a lowering of his great office. He was behaving as consul as though he were a tribune, and he was opposed by his colleague Bibulus.[81] Cato too was ready to support Bibulus with all his might. Caesar therefore brought Pompey out openly in front of the people on the speaker's platform in the forum and asked him whether he approved of the new laws. Pompey said that he did. 'Then,' said Caesar, 'if there is any violent resistance made to these laws, will you come to the help of the people?' 'Certainly I will,' Pompey replied. 'And against those who threaten to use swords I shall bring both a sword and a shield.' Never in his life had Pompey said or done anything so stupid and vulgar, as was generally admitted. Even his friends apologized for him and said that these words must have been spoken carelessly and on the spur of the moment. Nevertheless, his subsequent actions made it clear enough that he had now entirely given himself up to be used as Caesar wished. To everyone's surprise Pompey now married Caesar's daughter, Julia, though she was engaged to Caepio[82] and was supposed to be going to marry him in a few days' time. To soften the anger of Caepio, Pompey promised him his own daughter, although she too was already engaged to Faustus, the son of Sulla. Caesar himself married Calpurnia, the daughter of Piso.[83]

48. After this Pompey filled the city with soldiers and held everyone down by force. As the consul Bibulus, accompanied by Lucullus and Cato, was going down to the forum, he was set upon by the crowd who broke the fasces of his lictors in pieces; someone emptied a basket of dung over Bibulus' head; and two of the tribunes who were escorting him were wounded. Having thus cleared the forum of their opponents, they proceeded to pass the law providing for the distribution of land. The people were caught by the bait and now became thoroughly tame and subservient. They were prepared to support any project, made no fuss at all, merely voted quietly for whatever was proposed. So those settlements made by Pompey which had been challenged by Lucullus were now ratified; Caesar received the two Gauls and Illyricum for five years together with four legions at full strength;[84] and it was arranged that the consuls for the following year should be Piso, who was Caesar's father-in-law, and Gabinius,[85] who was the most conspicuous amongst Pompey's flatterers.

While all this was going on, Bibulus shut himself up in his house and for the remaining eight months of his consulship never appeared in public, though he continued to issue edicts attacking Pompey and Caesar in the most violent terms. Cato, like an inspired man possessed with the spirit of prophecy, foretold in the senate what the future would bring to Rome and to Pompey. Lucullus gave up the struggle and retired to his easy way of life, saying that he was now too old for politics. This occasioned Pompey's remark that if one is too old for politics one ought also to be too old for living like a Sybarite. Nevertheless, Pompey himself soon allowed himself to be weakly seduced by his passion for his young wife; he spent all his time with her in country houses and pleasure gardens, and paid no attention to what was going on in the forum. The result was that even Clodius, who was now tribune of the people,[86] began to despise him and to venture upon the most outrageous actions. He had driven Cicero into exile, and had got Cato sent to Cyprus on the pretext of a military commission.[87] Caesar had already gone off to Gaul. So finding that the people were devoted to him, since everything he had done in politics had been designed to please them, Clodius now attempted to repeal some of the measures passed by Pompey; he rescued Pompey's prisoner Tigranes and kept him in his own company;[88] and he instituted prosecutions against some of Pompey's friends, using them as a means for estimating what Pompey's real power was. Finally, when Pompey appeared at a case which was being tried in the courts, Clodius, leading a gang of the vilest and most foul-mouthed characters, took up a position in a conspicuous place and kept shouting out such questions as these: 'What's the name of the lecherous imperator? What's the name of the man who is trying to find a man? Who is it who scratches his head with one finger?' After each question he would make a sign by shaking the folds of his toga, and the mob, like a trained chorus, would all roar out the answer: 'Pompey.'

49. All this was undoubtedly very annoying to Pompey. He was quite unused to hearing any ill spoken of him, and in this sort of warfare he had no experience at all. But he was still more distressed when he saw that the senate were delighted to see him being insulted in this way, regarding it as no more than he deserved for having betrayed Cicero. Soon it came to fighting and even bloodshed in the forum, and one of Clodius' servants was discovered with a sword in his hand creeping through the crowd towards Pompey.[89] This served Pompey as an excuse, though he was also terrified of facing Clodius' vulgar abuse, and, for the rest of Clodius' term of office, he kept out of the forum altogether and stayed at home, constantly discussing with his friends means by which he could mollify the hard feelings felt against him by the senate and the nobility. Culleo[90]

recommended him to divorce Julia, to break off relations with
Caesar and to make friends with the senate instead; but Pompey
would have none of this. On the other hand, he did agree with
those who thought that he ought to bring back Cicero, who
hated Clodius and was loved by the senate. So with a large
force he escorted Cicero's brother,[91] who was petitioning for
his recall, into the forum. Here, though some people were
wounded and some killed, he got the better of Clodius. So the
law was passed for Cicero's recall,[92] and Cicero, as soon as he
returned to Rome, reconciled Pompey with the senate; then, by
speaking in favour of the law for the organization of the corn
supply, he made Pompey once again virtually the master of all
Roman possessions by sea and land.[93] Pompey was put in control of all ports and trading centres, with authority to arrange
the distribution of foodstuffs: so, to put it briefly, his power
extended over everything carried by sea or produced on land.
These measures were attacked by Clodius who said that the
law had not been made because of the scarcity of grain, but the
scarcity of grain had been artificially produced so that the law
might be passed, and that the only object of the law was to give
Pompey a new office so that that power of his which was, as it
were, withering away as a result of his failing spirits, might
revive again and gather strength. Others maintain that the law
was a piece of trickery on the part of the consul Spinther whose
plan was to keep Pompey out of the way in a higher office, so
that he himself might be sent out to give assistance to King
Ptolemy.[94] However, the tribune Canidius did propose a law
by which Pompey, without an army and attended by two lictors,
was to go out and act as a mediator between the king and his
subjects in Alexandria. Pompey too was thought to be not at
all averse from the proposal; but the senate rejected it on the
reasonably plausible grounds that they feared for his safety.
There were also various writings found scattered about the
forum and near the senate house stating that Ptolemy's own
wish was to have Pompey given to him as a commander rather
than Spinther. And Timagenes actually says that there was no
really compelling reason for Ptolemy to have left Egypt at all,
and that he only did so as a result of pressure brought to bear

on him by Theophanes who was scheming to get Pompey a new command and a new opportunity for making money. As for this story, the bad character of Theophanes may be used as evidence for its truth; but stronger evidence against it is to be found in Pompey's own nature: he was certainly ambitious, but never in such a mean or unworthy way.

50. Now that he was appointed director and administrator of the grain trade, Pompey sent out his agents and friends in various directions, and set sail himself to Sicily, Sardinia and Africa, collecting grain in all these places. When he was ready to start on his voyage home a great storm blew up over the sea and the captains of the ships were reluctant to set sail; but he led the way on board himself and ordered them to weigh anchor, shouting out to them: 'We have to sail; we do not have to live.' So, with good fortune assisting his own daring and energy, he filled the sea with ships and the markets with grain. In fact he provided so much of it that there was a surplus left over for the use of people outside Italy, the supply overflowing, as it were from a welling fountain, in all directions.

51. All this time Caesar was growing great and famous as a result of his wars in Gaul. Though he seemed to be very far away from Rome and wholly taken up with the Belgae, the Suevi and the Britons, in fact he was secretly and with great cleverness at work in the heart of the city and in all important matters was undermining Pompey's position. He was making his army into something which he controlled as though it were his own body; these native tribes were not the main point; he was merely using his campaigns against them as a form of training, as it might be hunting exercise, with the final aim of creating a force of his own which would be both alarming and invincible. Meanwhile he was sending back to Rome quantities of gold and silver, spoils of battle and all the other wealth which was coming in to him from his many wars; by bribery, by helping with the expenses of aediles, praetors, consuls and their wives, he was building up a great party of his own. So, when he crossed the Alps and spent the winter at Luca, huge

crowds of all sorts of people, men and women, came there to see him, struggling as to who could get there first; and in addition to these there were 200 members of the senate, including Pompey and Crassus; and 120 fasces of proconsuls and praetors were to be seen at Caesar's doors.[95]

These visitors of his were all sent away by Caesar full of hopes and loaded with money; but with Crassus and Pompey he came to the following understanding: they were to stand for the consulship and Caesar was to help them by sending large numbers of his soldiers home to vote for them; and as soon as they were elected, they were to arrange for provinces and armies to be allotted to themselves, and to confirm Caesar in the command of the provinces he had already for another period of five years.

When all this became generally known it aroused great indignation among the leading men in Rome. At an assembly of the people Marcellinus[96] stood up and asked Pompey and Crassus to their faces whether they intended to stand for the consulship or not. The people urged them to reply and Pompey, who spoke first, said that the answer was perhaps 'yes' and perhaps 'no'. Crassus made a more statesmanlike answer, saying that his course of action would depend on what he thought would be the best thing for the commonwealth. Marcellinus then proceeded with his attack on Pompey and was making, it was thought, a strong speech, when Pompey interrupted him by saying: 'Marcellinus is the unfairest man I know. He ought to be grateful to me for giving him something to say when he was always so tongue-tied. He used to be starved of words and now he is positively choking over them.'

52. Nevertheless, although most of the possible candidates for the consulship now declined to stand, Cato's active encouragement induced Lucius Domitius[97] not to give in. 'We are not fighting,' said Cato, 'merely for office, but for liberty against our oppressors.' Pompey's party, however, who were afraid that Cato's firmness, backed up as it was by the whole of the senate, might have the effect of winning over the more decent elements among the people and making them change sides,

prevented Domitius from going down into the forum. They organized a band of armed men who killed his torchbearer as he was leading the way and put all the rest to flight. Cato was the last to retire, after having received a wound in his right arm while defending Domitius.

So by such methods as these Pompey and Crassus made their way to the consulship; nor did they behave any better when they were in office. First of all, when the people were voting for the election of Cato to the praetorship, Pompey alleged that some inauspicious omen had been seen and dissolved the assembly. They then bribed the voters in the tribes and proclaimed Vatinius praetor instead of Cato. Next, through the agency of the tribune Trebonius,[98] they brought forward laws which, according to the agreement already reached, gave to Caesar an additional five years' command in his provinces, to Crassus Syria and the command against the Parthians, and to Pompey himself the whole of Africa, both the Spanish provinces and four legions. Two of these legions he lent to Caesar, at his request, for the war in Gaul.

Crassus went out to his province at the end of his year of office as consul. Pompey, however, stayed behind to open his theatre, at the dedication of which he held athletic sports and musical contests and provided wild animal fights in which 500 lions were killed. The most remarkable show of all – indeed a most horrifying spectacle – was an elephant fight.

53. All this added to his prestige and increased his popularity. On the other hand, the resentment felt against him also increased. This was because he handed over his provinces and his armies to subordinate commanders who were friends of his, while he himself spent all his time with his wife, going about Italy from one pleasure resort to another, whether because he was so deeply in love with her or (this reason also is given) because she was so much in love with him that he could not bear to leave her. Certainly the young wife's fondness for her husband was notorious, and Pompey, at his age, scarcely seemed to be a fit object for such passionate devotion. The reason for it seems to have lain in his constancy as a husband

(since he remained entirely faithful to his own wife), and also in his ability to unbend from his dignity and to become really charming in personal relationships – a quality of his which was particularly attractive to women, as may be shown even from the evidence, which is far from unreliable, of the courtesan Flora. Once it happened that during the elections for the aedileships a fight broke out and numbers of people were killed near the place where Pompey was standing. As he was covered with their blood he changed his clothes. His servants ran to his house with the blood-stained garments, making a great noise, and his young wife, who was pregnant at the time, fainted at the sight of the toga all covered with blood, and was only brought back to life again with great difficulty. As it was, the shock to her feelings caused a miscarriage. It was natural, therefore, that even those who most disapproved of Pompey because of his friendship with Caesar could not blame him for the love he felt for his wife. Later, however, she conceived again and gave birth to a daughter; but she died in the process of giving birth and the child only survived her for a few days.[99] Pompey made preparations to have her buried at his country estate near Alba, but the people insisted on taking the body down to the Field of Mars to be buried there. They did this rather out of pity for the young woman than as a mark of favour to either Pompey or Caesar. Yet so far as these two were concerned, it appeared that the people were more inclined to honour Caesar, who was absent, than Pompey, who was present.

For now immediately the city began, as it were, to roll and heave like the sea before a storm. Everything was in a state of agitation and every speech that was made tended towards division, now that there no longer existed between the two men this marriage relationship which hitherto had disguised rather than restrained their rival ambitions. Before long, too, the news arrived of how Crassus had lost his life in Parthia.[100] So was removed another factor which had been an important obstacle to the outbreak of civil war, since it was largely through fear of Crassus that up to now Pompey and Caesar had continued to behave reasonably correctly to each other. Now, however, that fortune had, as it were, removed from the ring the third com-

petitor, who might have taken on whichever was the winner
out of the other two, the words of the comic poet immediately
became very much to the point:

'now each prepares for each,
   bodies with oil all smeared and hands made rough with dust.'

What a small thing, when compared with human nature, is
good fortune, and how incapable of satisfying its demands! All
the extent of that great and far-flung empire could not satisfy
the ambition of two men. They had heard and read of how the
gods

'Divided all that is in three, and each received his share,'

yet they, who were only two, did not think the Roman empire
big enough to contain them both.

54. Pompey did, in fact, once say in a speech to the people that
he had always come into office earlier than he had expected
and had always laid his offices down more quickly than others
had expected. And certainly he could always point to the way
in which he had disbanded his armies to prove the truth of this.
Now, however, he thought that Caesar was not going to dismiss
his forces, and he tried to make himself secure against him by
means of the magistracies in Rome. Apart from this he took no
exceptional or revolutionary measures, and tried to give the
impression, not of distrusting Caesar, but rather of tolerating
him and not taking him seriously. He soon saw, however, that,
since the citizens were bribed, the magistracies were not going
at all the way he wished, and he allowed a state of affairs to
come into existence where there was no government at all.
People at once began to talk of the necessity for a dictatorship,
and the tribune Lucilius first ventured to bring the subject
forward, openly advising the people to choose Pompey as dictator.[101] This proposal was attacked by Cato, and Lucilius very
nearly lost his tribuneship, while on Pompey's behalf many of
his friends came forward and stated that he neither asked to be

nor wanted to be dictator. Cato then made a speech congratulating Pompey and urging him to support the cause of law and
order. As a result of this moral pressure Pompey, for the time
being, did so and Domitius and Messalla were made consuls.[102]
Later, however, Rome was again without a government, and
people began to be still more outspoken in agitating for a
dictatorship. Cato and his party, fearing that they might be
forced to give way to this agitation, decided to let Pompey have
a kind of office which was defined by law, so as to keep him
out of the absolute power and authority which would be his as
a dictator. So Bibulus, who was no friend to Pompey, first
proposed in the senate that Pompey should be chosen as sole
consul;[103] in this way, he said, Rome would either be saved
from the present state of anarchy or, if subjected, would at least
be subjected to her ablest citizen. The proposal, coming from
Bibulus, seemed strange enough. Cato then rose to speak and
led everyone to expect that he would speak against it; but, when
silence was made for him, he said that he personally would not
have proposed the motion before the house, but, now that it
had been proposed by someone else, he recommended them to
adopt it, since, in his view, any government was better than
none and he thought that Pompey, in such disturbed times, was
likely to govern better than anyone else. The senate accepted
the proposal and decreed that Pompey, if elected consul, should
hold the office alone, but that if he himself should desire a
colleague, he should be empowered, after the expiry of two
months, to choose whomsoever he thought fit.

In this way Pompey became consul and was declared so by
Sulpicius the interrex.[104] Pompey then made friendly overtures
to Cato, expressing his great gratitude to him for what he had
done, and inviting him to give advice in a private capacity on
how the government should be run. Cato, however, would not
admit that Pompey had any reason to be grateful to him; his
speech, he said, had been made entirely in the interests of Rome
and not at all for Pompey's sake; as for advice, he was quite
prepared to give it, if asked, in a private capacity, and, if he
were not asked, he would certainly say what he thought in
public. This was typical of Cato.

55. Pompey now entered Rome and married Cornelia, a daughter of Metellus Scipio.[105] She was not a virgin, but had recently been left a widow by her first husband Publius, the son of Crassus, who had been killed in Parthia. The young woman had many charming qualities apart from her youth and beauty. She had a good knowledge of literature, of playing the lyre and of geometry; and she was a regular and intelligent listener to lectures on philosophy. Moreover her character was quite free of that gracelessness and pretentiousness which too often affect young women who possess such accomplishments. No fault could be found with her father's family or reputation. Nevertheless, there were some who disapproved of the marriage because of the disparity in years, Cornelia being more of an age to marry one of Pompey's sons. Pompey also came in for some criticism for neglecting his responsibilities to the city at such a time. Rome had chosen him as her physician and put herself into his sole charge; yet here he was with garlands on his head celebrating a wedding, when he ought to have considered that his very consulship was a public calamity, since it would never have been given to him in such an illegal way if his country had been prosperous. Then there was his conduct in presiding over the courts dealing with bribery and corruption and in introducing laws regulating the procedure at the trials.[106] Here, in general, his behaviour as an arbiter was dignified and beyond reproach; his presence in the courts with an armed force had the effect of making the courtrooms safe, orderly and quiet. Yet when his father-in-law Scipio was put on trial, he summoned the 360 members of the jury to his own house and asked them to acquit the defendant, and the prosecutor abandoned the case when he saw Scipio being escorted out of the forum by the jury.

So once again Pompey found that he was being badly spoken of. Things became still worse when, after he had passed a law putting an end to the practice of making speeches in praise of people under trial, he himself came into court to make a speech in praise of Plancus.[107] Cato happened to be a member of the jury on this occasion, and he clapped his hands over his ears, saying that it was not right for him to listen to these speeches of praise when they were illegal. As a result Cato was removed

from the jury, before he had the chance of voting, but, nevertheless, Plancus was convicted by the other votes, much to the
discredit of Pompey. A few days afterwards Hypsaeus, a man
of consular rank,[108] who was being prosecuted in the courts,
waited for Pompey to return from his bath to his supper and
then fell down before him, clasped his knees, and implored him
for his help; but Pompey passed by him disdainfully and said
that, apart from spoiling his supper, he was achieving nothing.
This gave him the reputation of being anything but impartial,
and he was much blamed for it.

In all other respects, however, he did well and succeeded in
getting the situation under control. For the last five months of
his year of office he chose his father-in-law to be his colleague.
It was also voted that he should keep his provinces for another
period of four years and that he should receive 1,000 talents
each year for the payment and general organization of his
armies.[109]

56. It was this that gave occasion to some of Caesar's friends
to claim that for Caesar too, who was fighting so continuously
for the empire, some consideration ought to be shown. Either,
they said, he ought to have another consulship, or else his
command ought to be prolonged, so that he, who had done the
work, should continue in power and enjoy his honours in peace
instead of being deprived of all his glory by some successor
who might be appointed. There was a conflict of opinion over
this, and Pompey, giving the impression that out of goodwill to
Caesar he was trying to calm down any ill-feeling that might
exist towards him, said that he had letters from Caesar which
showed that he wanted to be relieved of his command and be
replaced by a successor; it would be only right, however, that
he should be allowed to stand for the consulship even in his
absence. Cato and his party opposed this suggestion. Caesar,
they said, must lay down his arms and become an ordinary
citizen before securing any favour from his fellow-citizens.
Pompey raised no great objections to this, but behaved rather
as though he had been overruled, and as a result increased
people's suspicions of what his real feelings towards Caesar

were. He also sent to Caesar and, on the pretext of the Parthian war, asked for the return of the troops which he had lent him. Caesar knew well enough why these soldiers were being asked for, but he sent them back after having given them very generous rewards for their services.

57. About this time Pompey had a serious illness in Naples. When he recovered the Neapolitans, on the motion of Praxagoras, offered sacrifices of thanksgiving for his preservation. Their example was followed by other towns in the neighbourhood, and so it went on spreading through the whole of Italy; every city, big or small, held its festival for days on end. There was no containing the great crowds that thronged to meet him from every direction; roads, villages and harbours were all filled with people sacrificing and feasting. Numbers of people too, with garlands on their heads and torches in their hands, welcomed him and escorted him on his way, pelting him with flowers, so that this return journey of his to Rome was a most splendid and beautiful sight. Yet this is said to have been one of the main causes which led to the war. The effect of this enormous public rejoicing was that Pompey began to feel a kind of overconfidence in himself, which went far beyond considerations based on real facts. So far his caution had always given him security in his great and successful actions; now he threw this caution to the winds, and plunged into a mood of unlimited confidence; for Caesar's power he felt nothing but contempt; to deal with him, he thought, it would not be necessary to have an army or to make any preparations which would involve any effort; he could, in fact, pull him down much more easily than he had originally set him up. Another factor working in the same direction was the arrival of Appius[110] who brought from Gaul the troops which Pompey had lent to Caesar. Appius constantly belittled Caesar's achievements there and told a number of damaging stories about Caesar himself. He declared that Pompey must be quite ignorant of his own power and reputation if he thought that he needed the support of any other troops against Caesar; Caesar's own would be quite enough to put Caesar down, once Pompey appeared upon the scene, so

much did they hate Caesar and so much did they love Pompey. This kind of language put Pompey into a state of exaltation. His confidence filled him with such a supreme contempt for his adversary that he simply laughed at those who feared a war. When someone said that, supposing Caesar were to march on Rome, it was not clear with what forces the city could be defended, Pompey merely smiled and, speaking with the utmost calm, told him that there was no need to be at all concerned. 'Anywhere in Italy,' he said, 'I have only to stamp my foot upon the ground, and there will rise up armies of infantry and armies of cavalry.'

58. And now, on the other side, Caesar was intervening more actively in public affairs. He remained himself quite close to the frontiers of Italy and was always sending his soldiers back to Rome to take part in the elections. Many of the magistrates were now in his pay or being corrupted by him. Among these was the consul Paulus, who was won over by a bribe of 1,500 talents; also the tribune Curio,[111] who was hopelessly in debt and had his debts paid off by Caesar; also Mark Antony, who was a friend of Curio and had thus become involved in his debts. And there was a story told of one of Caesar's centurions who had come back to Rome and, standing outside the senate house, heard the news that the senate was refusing to prolong the period of Caesar's command. The centurion then clapped his hand upon his sword and said: 'Well then, this will do it for him.' And in fact all the moves which Caesar was making and all his preparations seemed to have this sort of an end in view.

Nevertheless, the claims and demands put forward by Curio on behalf of Caesar looked fair enough.[112] He demanded one of two things; either Pompey also should be required to lay down his military commands, or else Caesar should retain his. The argument was that if both of them became private citizens on fair and equal terms, or if they stayed as they were, equally matched with the forces they had at their disposal, they would remain quiet; but to weaken only one of them would double the power of which men stood in fear.

To this the consul Marcellus[113] replied that Caesar was merely a robber and that, if he failed to lay down his arms, he should be declared a public enemy. Curio, however, with the support of Antony and Piso,[114] pressed his case strongly and succeeded in having the matter put up to the senate to be voted upon. He asked that all those should withdraw to one side who were of the opinion that Caesar alone should lay down his arms and that Pompey should retain his own command. The majority of the senators withdrew. When, however, he next proposed that all those should withdraw who were of the opinion that both should lay down their arms and neither retain their commands, only twenty-two voted for Pompey and all the rest sided with Curio. Assuming that he had won the day, Curio rushed off, beaming with delight, to a meeting of the people who loudly applauded him, put garlands round his head, and pelted him with flowers. Pompey had not been present at the meeting of the senate, since commanders of armies are not allowed inside the city. Marcellus, however, rose from his place and said that, since he could see ten legions already looming up over the Alps and marching on Rome, he was not going to sit there listening to speeches; instead he would, on his own authority, send out a man to oppose these legions and to act in defence of the fatherland.

59. At this the city put on mourning as though for a public calamity. Marcellus went to see Pompey. He marched through the forum with the senators all following him and, standing in front of Pompey, said: 'I order you, Pompey, to come to the help of your country. You are to make use of the forces now ready for action and to raise others.' Lentulus,[115] who was one of the consuls elected for the following year, said the same thing. But when Pompey began to recruit troops, some refused to obey the orders for calling up, and those who did come in came reluctantly and without any enthusiasm.[116] The general demand was that some settlement should be arranged. One reason for this was that Antony, in defiance of the senate, had read out at an assembly a letter from Caesar which contained proposals which were likely to be found attractive by the people. He suggested that both he and Pompey should give up

their provinces, disband their armies, and then submit themselves to the people's judgement, each giving an account of
what he had done. But Lentulus, who by this time had become
consul, refused to convene a meeting of the senate. Cicero,
however, who had just returned from Cilicia, did his best to
arrange a settlement by proposing that Caesar should give up
Gaul and the majority of his forces, but should retain Illyricum
and two legions while waiting for his second consulship. When
Pompey objected to this plan, Caesar's friends were prepared
to agree that Caesar should dismiss one of the two legions; but
Lentulus would have none of this and Cato shouted out that
Pompey was blundering again and allowing himself to be taken
in; and so the proposed settlement came to nothing.

60. And now came the news that Caesar had occupied the large
Italian city of Ariminum and was marching straight on Rome
with his whole army. This was not true. In fact he had with
him on the march no more than 300 cavalry and 5,000 regular
infantry; the rest of his forces were on the other side of the
Alps, and he was not waiting for them since he wanted to
fall suddenly upon his enemies, while they were in a state of
confusion and not expecting him, rather than to give them time
and then fight when they were ready for him. He had reached
the River Rubicon, which was the boundary of his own legal
province,[117] and there he had stood still in silence, delaying the
moment of crossing while he considered in his own mind, as
was natural enough, what a prodigious enterprise it was that
he was undertaking. Then, like one who throws himself over a
precipice into some vast abyss, he shut his eyes, as it were, to
the light of reasoned calculation, blinded himself to the idea of
danger, and, with these words only, which he spoke in Greek
to those who were near him, 'Let the die be cast!' he led his
army across the river.

The news fell on Rome like a blow and immediately the city
was filled with uproar, consternation and terror such as had
never been known before. The senate, with all the magistrates,
at once hurried in a body to Pompey. Tullus asked him what
military forces were available, and Pompey, after some hesita-

tion, replied in a manner that was far from confident. He had ready for service at the moment, he said, the troops which had come from Caesar, but he thought that it would also be possible to mobilize out of those who had previously been called up an army of 30,000 men. Tullus then cried out aloud: 'Pompey, you have deceived us!' and advised sending a deputation to Caesar. Favonius,[118] who in many ways was not a bad man, though he used to imagine that by being rude and abusive he was copying Cato's straightforward way of speech, told Pompey to stamp his foot on the ground and produce the promised armies. The witticism was out of place, but Pompey bore it patiently, and, when Cato reminded him of what he had said to him about Caesar at the very beginning, he merely replied that Cato certainly had spoken like a prophet but he himself had acted like a friend.

61. Cato now advised that Pompey should be chosen as commander-in-chief, with unlimited powers, adding that those who are responsible for bringing about a desperate situation should also have the job of curing it. He then set out at once for Sicily, which was the province allotted to him, and the other senators too who had provincial commands went out to their respective districts.[119] However, since nearly the whole of Italy was in a state of disturbance, it was impossible to say what was going on. People from outside the city sought refuge there and came pouring into Rome from all directions, while the Romans themselves were hurrying out and abandoning the city, for the conditions there were so stormy and confused that the better element was quite powerless, while all the forces making for insubordination grew in strength and became most difficult for the magistrates to control. It was impossible to check the panic; no one would allow Pompey to use his own judgement and everyone rushed to him with whatever idea, proceeding from fear, distress or perplexity, happened to be his at the moment. In one and the same day quite contrary plans were decided upon; it was impossible for Pompey to get accurate information about the enemy, since people were constantly reporting to him every chance rumour that came along and were then furious

with him if he did not believe them. In the circumstances Pompey issued an edict declaring a state of civil war, ordered all the senators to follow him, gave notice that those who failed to do so would be regarded as partisans of Caesar, and, late in the evening, left the city. The consuls also fled, without even making the sacrifices that are usually made at the outbreak of war. Yet even in this terrible situation Pompey himself was a man to be envied, so great was the general affection in which he was held. Many found fault with his generalship, but no one hated the general. Indeed one would have found that the majority of those who fled from the city did so, not so much for the sake of liberty as because they could not bear to forsake Pompey.

62. A few days later Caesar entered and occupied Rome. He did what he could to calm people's fears and behaved with great moderation to everyone, except in the case of Metellus,[120] one of the tribunes, who tried to prevent him taking money out of the public treasury. Caesar threatened to have Metellus put to death and followed up the threat with language of even greater truculence; it was much easier for him, he said, to do this than to say it. So, with Metellus overruled in this way, Caesar took what he wanted from the treasury and then set out in pursuit of Pompey, since he wanted to drive him out of Italy before his forces in Spain could come to join him.

Meanwhile Pompey had occupied Brundisium. He found plenty of transports there and immediately put the consuls and thirty cohorts of soldiers on board the ships and sent them across before him to Dyrrhachium. He sent his father-in-law Scipio and his son Gnaeus to Syria to raise a fleet. He himself barricaded the gates, and stationed the most lightly armed soldiers on the walls. He told the citizens of Brundisium to stay quietly in their houses and then dig up all the ground inside the city, cutting trenches across the streets and filling them with stakes sunk in the earth – all except for two streets by which in the end he made his way down to the sea. He spent two days in embarking the main body of his troops in a quiet and orderly manner, and on the third day suddenly gave the signal to the men who were guarding the walls. They hurried down quickly, were taken aboard and brought across to Dyrrhachium. Caesar, seeing the walls unguarded, realized that Pompey was making his escape, and, in following closely after him, he nearly got his own troops entangled in the ditches and stakes. The people of Brundisium, however, warned him about them and so he kept clear of the city and wheeled round it to the harbour, where he found that all the transports had put to sea except two which had only a few soldiers on board.

63. Most people hold the view that this withdrawal of Pompey can be considered among his most remarkable military achievements. Caesar himself, however, was astonished that he abandoned and surrendered Italy when he was based on a strong city, was expecting his forces from Spain and had complete control of the seas. Cicero also finds fault with him for following the strategy of Themistocles rather than that of Pericles, when the position in which he found himself was like that of Pericles and not like that of Themistocles. And Caesar certainly showed by his actions that he very much feared the idea of a long war. For after he had captured Numerius,[121] a friend of Pompey, he sent him to Brundisium with an offer of peace and reconciliation on fair and equal terms. Numerius, however, sailed away with Pompey. Caesar, who without bloodshed had in sixty days become the master of the whole of Italy, would have liked to have followed after Pompey at once; but there were no transports available,[122] and so he turned back and marched into Spain, wishing to bring over to himself the soldiers of Pompey who were stationed there.

64. Meanwhile Pompey was getting together a very great force. On the sea he was quite irresistible. His navy consisted of 500 warships together with an enormous number of light craft and fast cruisers. As for his cavalry, it was the flower of Rome and of Italy; 7,000 men, well-born, rich and full of spirit. His infantry was a mixed lot and needed training. This training he gave to them at Beroea, and, far from just watching it, he took an active part himself in all their exercises, as though he were still

at the height of his own powers. And certainly it was a most encouraging and inspiring sight to see Pompey the Great, who was only two years short of the age of sixty, wearing full armour and vying with all the rest as an infantryman; and then again on horseback drawing his sword with no trouble at all while his horse was at full gallop and putting it back with perfect ease into its sheath. He showed too that in throwing the javelin he was not only accurate but vigorous. There were many of the young men who failed to throw as far as he did.

Kings and rulers of nations kept on coming to him and he had with him so many of the leading men of Rome that they were enough to constitute a full senate. Labienus[123] deserted Caesar, whose friend he had been and with whom he had served throughout the Gallic wars, and came over to Pompey. So also did Brutus, the son of that Brutus who had been put to death by Pompey in Gaul. He was a man of a high and great spirit. Up to this time he had never spoken to Pompey or even saluted him, since he regarded him as his father's murderer; but now he saw him as the defender of Roman liberty and so put himself under his command. Cicero too, though he had both written and spoken in favour of a different policy, nevertheless was ashamed not to be counted among those who were risking everything for their country. Another man who came to Pompey in Macedonia was Tidius Sextius. He was very old and lame in one leg, and the others laughed and jeered at him when he appeared. But when Pompey saw him he rose up and ran to meet him, thinking that it was a great testimony to himself when men who were too old and too weak for active service chose danger with him rather than security at home.

65. When their senate met a decree was passed, on the motion of Cato, that no Roman should be killed except in battle and that no city subject to Rome should be plundered. This made people still more attached to Pompey's party. Indeed even those who took no part in the war either because they lived too far away or were thought not strong enough to be of use, still, in their hearts at least, were on Pompey's side and, so far as words went, fought with him for the cause of justice. They considered

that anyone who did not want Pompey to win was an enemy to gods and men alike.

It must be admitted that Caesar also showed himself merciful as a conqueror.[124] After defeating and capturing the forces of Pompey in Spain, he freely released the commanders and took the soldiers into his own service. He then recrossed the Alps, marched quickly through Italy and reached Brundisium shortly after the winter solstice. After crossing the sea from there he put in himself at the port of Oricum, but sent Vibullius,[125] a friend of Pompey's whom he had with him as a prisoner, direct to Pompey with a proposal that they should hold a conference, disband all their forces within three days, renew their old friendship under oath and return to Italy. Pompey regarded this offer as merely another trick. He marched quickly down to the sea and occupied all strong points and all positions and sites suitable for defence by infantry, as well as all naval stations and landing places that were available to traffic by sea. The result was that every wind that blew brought Pompey grain or troops or money, while Caesar found himself in difficulties both by land and sea and had of necessity to seek a battle.[126] He was constantly attacking Pompey's fortifications and challenging him to come out in the open, and in most of these irregular engagements he had the better of things. Once, however, he was very close to disaster and nearly lost his whole army. Pompey had fought brilliantly and in the end routed Caesar's whole force, killing 2,000 of them. But either he was unable or else he feared to push on and force his way after the defeated army into their camp. It was this that led Caesar to say to his friends: 'Today the enemy would have won, if they had had a commander who was a winner.'

66. After this victory Pompey's followers were full of confidence and were eager to fight a battle that would decide the whole issue. But Pompey, although he wrote as though he had won the war to foreign kings and generals and cities, shrank from taking the risk of a pitched battle. He considered that he could subdue the enemy in the end simply by delaying matters and by imposing hardships on them; for the enemy were men who had

never been conquered by force of arms; they had long been used to winning battles fighting side by side; on the other hand, they were getting old and were not so fit for the other exigencies of military service – long marches, constantly moving camp, digging trenches and building fortifications; naturally, therefore, they wanted to come to close quarters and fight as soon as possible.

Up to now, in spite of all difficulties, Pompey had succeeded somehow or other in inducing his followers to restrain themselves; but after this battle, when Caesar was compelled by lack of supplies to break camp and march through Athamania into Thessaly, their confidence was such that there was no holding them in. The general cry was that Caesar was in flight; some were for following after him and hunting him down; some were for crossing over into Italy; and some sent their servants or their friends to Rome to rent houses near the forum, on the assumption that they would be almost at once standing for election to the various magistracies. Many, too, sailed out of their own accord to Lesbos, where Pompey had sent Cornelia so as to be in safety, and gave her the glad news that the war was already over.

A meeting of the senate was called and Afranius[127] said that in his view what they should do was to make sure of Italy; he pointed out that Italy was, in the end, what they were fighting for, and that whoever controlled Italy would also immediately come into control of Sicily, Sardinia, Corsica, Spain and the whole of Gaul; then, he said, Pompey's chief consideration was naturally his own country, and here was this country close by and stretching out her hands to him in supplication; it could not be right to allow her to be subjected to the insults and the domination of the slaves and flatterers of a tyrant. Pompey himself, however, considered that his own honour was involved; it would be disgraceful for him to run away from Caesar for a second time and to assume the role of the pursued when fortune had put him in the position of being the pursuer; he thought too that it would be morally wrong to abandon Scipio[128] and others of consular rank in Thessaly and in Greece, who would immediately come into Caesar's hands together

with the money and the considerable forces which they controlled; in his view the best way of showing affection for Rome
was to fight for her at the furthest possible distance from the
city, so that Rome herself might be spared both the sufferings
and the alarms of war and might await quietly the return of the
conqueror, whoever it might be.

67. Having reached this decision, Pompey set out in pursuit of
Caesar. He was determined to avoid battle and planned instead
to follow closely in his tracks, cutting his lines of communication and weakening him by depriving him of supplies. This
was, he thought, in any case the best plan, and he was also
influenced by being told that the common talk among the
cavalry was to the effect that, once they had defeated Caesar,
they must get rid of Pompey too. Some say that this was the
reason why Pompey never gave Cato any really important command; and that, even when he was marching against Caesar,
he left Cato behind at the coast in charge of the stores, because
he was afraid that, if Caesar were eliminated, Cato might insist
on him laying down his own command immediately.

So, while he quietly followed in the enemy's tracks, Pompey
found himself attacked and criticized from all sides. People said
that his strategy was directed not against Caesar but against his
country and the senate; it aimed simply at keeping himself
perpetually in power, so that he might never cease to have as
his guards and servants men who claimed for themselves the
right to rule the world. Domitius Ahenobarbus[129] added to his
unpopularity by nicknaming him 'Agamemnon' and 'King of
Kings'. And Favonius caused just as much displeasure to him
as those who attacked him more openly when, jesting at the
worst possible moment, he shouted out: 'Well, well, my friends,
this year too we shall get no figs from Tusculum.' And Lucius
Afranius, who had been accused of treachery after he had lost
his forces in Spain,[130] now that he saw that Pompey was avoiding battle, went about saying that he was indeed surprised to
find that those who were so ready to accuse him did not go out
themselves and fight this man who was supposed to be simply
a buyer of provinces.

This kind of talk, which was constantly going on, had its effect. Pompey was a slave to his own glory and could not bear to hear the reproaches of his friends, who now forced their will on him and dragged him along after them, so that he became the servant of their hopes and impulses and abandoned his own best-laid plans. Such weakness would have been disgraceful enough in a master of a ship; it was much more so in the case of a general in supreme command of so many nations and so many armies. Pompey himself approved of those doctors who never gratify the morbid longings of their patients; yet now he gave in to what amounted to a disease among his own followers and was frightened of taking measures to preserve them which would make him personally unpopular. Certainly it would be impossible to say that these followers of his were in a sound and healthy state. Some were already going about the army making electioneering speeches with the idea of securing consulships or praetorships for themselves; Spinther, Domitius and Scipio were quarrelling and scheming and forming parties as to which of them should succeed Caesar as chief pontiff;[131] all behaving as though their adversary was Tigranes the Armenian or some king of the Nabataeans, when in fact it was Caesar – Caesar and that army of his with which he had stormed 1,000 cities and subdued more than 300 nations; with which he had fought innumerable battles, always victorious, against the Germans and the Gauls, taking a million men prisoners and killing another million on the battlefield.

68. Forgetting all this, they kept on clamouring and urging Pompey on, and, when they came down into the plain of Pharsalia, they forced him to call a council of war. Labienus, the commander of the cavalry, rose to speak first and swore that he would not return from the battle unless he routed the enemy; the rest followed him and swore the same oath. That night Pompey dreamed that he was going into the theatre, that the people were clapping their hands and that he himself was offering all sorts of spoils of war to adorn the temple of Venus the Victorious. In some respects this vision encouraged him, but in another way it had a depressing effect. Caesar's family traced

its origin from Venus, and he feared that it might be that this
family would be glorified and made illustrious through him.
Also he was woken up in the night by various panic disturbances
which went sweeping through the camp. Then during the morning watch a great light shone out over Caesar's camp, which
was quiet, and out of it came a flame like a torch which darted
down upon the camp of Pompey. Caesar himself says that he
saw this while he was inspecting the sentry posts.

At dawn Caesar was intending to break camp and march
towards Scotussa. The soldiers were packing up the tents and
sending the baggage animals and the servants on ahead, when
the scouts came in and reported that they had seen a great
number of arms moving about in the enemy's camp, that there
was a general commotion there and a noise as though they were
coming out to battle. Soon afterwards other scouts came in with
the news that the front ranks were already forming in battle
order. Caesar immediately gave orders for the purple tunic to
be hung up in front of his tent – this being the Roman signal
for battle. 'The day which we have been waiting for has come,'
he said. 'We shall fight now against men instead of against want
and hunger.' His soldiers shouted with joy when they saw the
signal. They dropped the tents and hurried to arms. And as
their officers led them into position each man, as though he
were a trained member of a chorus, fell into line without fuss,
with an ease born of much practice.

69. Pompey himself, with the right wing, intended to oppose
Antony; he placed his father-in-law Scipio in the centre against
Lucius Calvinus,[132] the left wing was commanded by Lucius
Domitius and was supported by the main body of the cavalry.
Indeed nearly the entire cavalry force was collected here with
the intention of overwhelming Caesar and cutting the tenth
legion to pieces. This legion had the reputation of being the
most formidable of all and Caesar himself usually fought in its
ranks.

Caesar saw what a heavy weight of cavalry was supporting
the enemy's left and was alarmed at the brilliant show they
made. He sent for six cohorts from his reserves and stationed

them behind the tenth legion, with orders to stay there quietly and keep out of the enemy's sight; but whenever the cavalry charged, they were to run forward through the front ranks and, instead of hurling their javelins, as good soldiers usually do in their eagerness to draw their swords, they were to strike upwards with them, thrusting at the enemy's faces and eyes; 'These handsome young fellows,' he said, 'who are behaving as though they were in some kind of tattoo, will never endure the sight of steel right in their faces and will run away to save their good looks.'

While Caesar was engaged in this way, Pompey, on horseback, was observing the battle order of both armies. He saw that Caesar's army was lined up in a quiet and orderly way and the men were waiting for the moment of attack, whereas the greater part of his own army lacked this steadiness; owing to their inexperience they were surging this way and that and making a lot of noise. He was afraid that their lines would be entirely broken up at the very beginning of the battle, and so he issued an order that the front ranks, with their spears advanced, were to stand still in their places and so receive the enemy's charge. According to Caesar, Pompey made a mistake in adopting these tactics. He says that their effect was to deprive the blows of the force which they would have had if the soldiers had charged forward; that this running to meet the enemy, with the shouting and the actual physical motion, is usually the most important factor of all in promoting the right kind of enthusiasm and elan in battle; and that Pompey sacrificed these advantages by fixing his men to the spot where they were standing and so chilling their ardour. And yet Pompey had rather more than twice as many men as Caesar, whose force amounted to 22,000.

70. And now on both sides the signal was given. The trumpet called to the attack, and in most cases each man saw only what was in front of him. But there were a few Romans, the noblest of them, and there were some Greeks who were present without taking part in the battle who, now that the fearful moment had come, could not help reflecting upon the causes of all this – the

greed and the personal rivalry which had brought the empire
to such a pass. Here were opposed armies of the same kin,
ranks of brothers, identical standards; here the whole manhood
and might of a single state was involved in self-destruction – a
clear enough lesson of how blind and how mad a thing human
nature is when under the sway of passion. Had they only been
content quietly to govern and enjoy their conquests, the greatest
and best part of earth and sea was theirs to control. Or if they
still yearned and thirsted for more trophies and triumphs, they
could have had all the wars they wanted with Parthians or with
Germans. Scythia and India too still remained unconquered,
and in these cases they could have covered up their greed with
the not inglorious title of a civilizing mission. Certainly Scythia
could not produce the cavalry, or Parthia the archers, or India
the wealth to stand up to an invading army of 70,000 Romans
led by Pompey and by Caesar, whose names were known to
these peoples long before they had heard the name of Rome, so
remote and various and savage had been the nations already
conquered by these two. Now, however, they met together with
opposed arms; no tender feeling even for their own reputations
– since up to this day both had been called invincible – could
induce them to spare their country. The family relationship that
had existed between them, the charms of Julia, her marriage to
Pompey – all these could now be seen in their true light. They
had been the deceptive and suspected pledges of a treaty based
on self-interest; real friendship had never played any part in it.

71. So the plain of Pharsalia was filled with men and horses
and arms. On both sides the signal for battle was raised; and
from Caesar's army the first man to charge forward out of the
ranks was Gaius Crassianus, a centurion in command of 120
men.[133] He had promised Caesar much and he was keeping his
promise. For Crassianus had been the first man whom Caesar
saw as he came out of the camp that day, and Caesar had asked
him how he felt about the battle. Then Crassianus had stretched
out his right hand and shouted out: 'You are going to win,
Caesar, and win gloriously. And as for me, you shall praise
me today, whether I am alive or dead at the end of it.' Now

Crassianus kept these words of his in mind. He rushed forward, with many others following his example, and plunged into the middle of the enemy ranks. Close fighting with swords began immediately and many were killed; and so the centurion forced his way forward, cutting down the men in the front ranks until one of them stood up to him and drove his sword in at his mouth with such force that the point came through at the back of his neck.

After Crassianus had fallen the fighting remained evenly poised at that part of the field. But on the right Pompey was slow in bringing his men into action; he kept looking in the other direction, waiting to see how his cavalry was doing, and so lost time. And now the cavalry deployed their squadrons with the intention of encircling Caesar's flank and forcing back upon the main line of infantry the few cavalry which he had stationed in front of them. But at Caesar's signal his own cavalry withdrew and the cohorts, 3,000 men, who had been drawn up in order to deal with the enveloping movement, ran forward from the rear and met the enemy's charge. As they had been instructed to do, they stood close by the horses and thrust upwards with their javelins, aiming at the riders' faces. These cavalrymen of Pompey's had no experience of any kind of fighting, and were quite unprepared to meet this unanticipated form of attack. They lacked the courage to stand up to blows aimed at their mouths and eyes, and, covering their faces with their hands, they wheeled about and fled in the most disgraceful manner. Once they were in flight Caesar's soldiers took no further notice of them. They turned upon the enemy's infantry, attacking just at the point where the wing, because of the flight of the cavalry, was exposed and so could be outflanked and encircled. While they bore down upon the flank, the tenth legion attacked from the front. Pompey's men, who had expected that they were going to surround the enemy, saw that they were being surrounded themselves. Their resistance collapsed and they did not even preserve their order.

72. With his infantry routed in this way, Pompey now could conjecture from the cloud of dust which he saw what had

happened to his cavalry. What thoughts passed through his mind it would be hard to say; he looked beside himself and half-crazed and seemed utterly to have forgotten that he was Pompey the Great. Slowly and without saying a word to anyone he walked off towards his camp – as in Homer's description of Ajax:

> But Zeus the father, throned on high, in Ajax stirred up fear.
> He slung behind his back the shield of seven ox hides strong,
> And stood amazed and trembled as he peered among the throng.

So Pompey went to his tent and sat down there speechless. Finally a number of the victorious troops burst into the camp on the heels of the fugitives, and then Pompey said simply: 'What! Into the camp too?' and, without another word, got up, put on clothes suitable to the state of his fortunes, and made his escape. The rest of his legions also fled and in the camp itself there was a great slaughter of the servants and the men who were guarding the tents. Only 6,000 soldiers fell, according to Asinius Pollio[134] who fought in the battle on Caesar's side.

   When Caesar's troops captured the camp they could see before their eyes evidence of the vanity and folly of the enemy. Every tent was wreathed with boughs of myrtle and contained carefully laid out dining couches covered with flowers and tables with drinking vessels all set out; bowls of wine were there to hand and everything was beautifully arranged as though for some great feast following a sacrifice. There was no impression at all of men arming themselves for battle. Such had been the extent of their deluding hopes, and such the measure of their senseless confidence when they had gone out to war.

73. As for Pompey, when he had got a little distance from the camp, he gave his horse the rein. No one was pursuing him and so, with only a very few companions, he went quietly away. It is easy to imagine what was in his mind – a man who for thirty-four years had grown accustomed to victory and to supremacy in everything and who now, in his old age, was learning for the first time what defeat and flight meant. He

thought, no doubt, of how in one hour he had lost the glory and the power which he had won in so many wars and battles; a little while ago legions of infantry and squadrons of cavalry had been there to protect him, and now, shrunk to so small a state, so insignificantly attended, he was trying to escape the notice of his enemies who were in pursuit of him.

He went past Larissa and came to the Vale of Tempe. Here, since he was thirsty, he threw himself down on his face and drank out of the river. Then he rose up again and went on through Tempe until he came down to the sea. The rest of the night he spent in a fisherman's hut. At dawn he went aboard one of the river boats. He took with him only those of his followers who were free men. His slaves he dismissed, telling them to go back to Caesar and not to be afraid. He then went along the coast until he saw a good-sized merchant ship which was just about to put to sea. The captain of this ship was a Roman citizen, Peticius by name, who knew Pompey by sight, though he was not well acquainted with him. It so happened that on the previous night Peticius had had a dream in which Pompey was speaking to him, looking downcast and wretched and not at all like the Pompey whom he had so often seen. People are apt to make much of such dreams, especially if they have time on their hands; and so Peticius was just telling his shipmates of this dream of his when suddenly one of the sailors told him that he could see a river boat being rowed out from the shore and that there were men in it who were waving their cloaks and holding out their hands towards them. Peticius looked in that direction and immediately recognized Pompey, just as he had seen him in his dream. He smote himself on his head, ordered the sailors to bring the little boat alongside, and, stretching out his hand, called to Pompey by name. He could already tell from his altered appearance how his fortunes also had changed, and, without waiting for any words of entreaty, he took him on board with all those whom he wished to have with him and set sail. With Pompey were the two Lentuli[135] and Favonius. Shortly afterwards they saw the King Deiotarus trying to get out to them from the shore, and they took him on board too. When it was time for supper and the ship's captain had made what preparations he could for their entertainment, Favonius, seeing that Pompey, having no servants to attend him, was beginning to take off his own shoes, ran up to him, took off his shoes for him and helped him to anoint himself. And from that time on he continued to wait on him and do for him all the things that servants do, even down to washing his feet and preparing his meals. Indeed anyone who saw this generous service, so simple and unaffected, might well have quoted the line:

'How every action of a noble mind is fair!'

74. And so, after going along the coast to Amphipolis, Pompey crossed over from there to Mitylene, wishing to take Cornelia and his son on board. When he reached the shore of the island, he sent a messenger to the city, not at all the sort of messenger which Cornelia was expecting after all the glad tidings and letters which she had received. For she was hoping that the war had ended at Dyrrhachium and that now there was nothing left for Pompey to do except to pursue Caesar. The messenger found her still in this mood and could not bring himself to speak his words of salutation. It was by tears rather than by words that he made her see the extent of her calamity, and he merely told her to make haste if she wished to see Pompey who had come with one ship, and that ship not his own. On hearing this Cornelia flung herself down on the ground and lay there for a long time speechless and unconscious. Finally and with much difficulty she recovered consciousness and, realizing that this was no occasion for tears and lamentations, ran through the city to the sea. Here Pompey met her and caught her in his arms as she tottered and was about to fall. 'O my husband,' she said, 'it is because of my fortune, not yours, that I see you now reduced to one small ship, you who, before your marriage with Cornelia, had 500 ships with you when you sailed this sea. Why have you come to see me? Why did you not leave to her cruel fate the wife who has brought on you too such terrible misfortune? What a happy woman I should have been if I had died before hearing that Publius, whom I married as a maiden,

had been killed in Parthia! And how wise if, even after his death, I had done what I meant to do and put an end to my own life! But I was spared, it seems, to do still more harm and to be the ruin of Pompey the Great.'

75. Pompey, we are told, replied to these words of Cornelia as follows:

'It is true, Cornelia, that you have only known one side of my fortune, and that the better side. It has remained with me longer than is usual, and perhaps this fact has deceived you as well as me. But we are mortals. We must bear what has happened and again put fortune to the test. One may still hope that, just as I have fallen so low from such a height, so from these depths I may rise again.'

So his wife sent for her belongings and her servants from the city. The people of Mitylene welcomed Pompey and invited him to enter the city walls, but Pompey refused to do so. He told them that they too must submit to the conqueror and advised them not to be afraid since Caesar was a good man and would act humanely towards them. He himself then turned to the philosopher Cratippus, who had come down from the city to see him, and had a short discussion with him in which he made some criticisms of the idea of Providence. Cratippus made no very strenuous objections to Pompey's arguments and tried to lead him to better hopes. He had no wish to cause pain by arguing against him at such a time. Actually to the questions raised by Pompey about Providence Cratippus might have answered that it was because the state had been so badly administered that it now required to be governed by one man; and he might well have asked Pompey: 'How can we be convinced, Pompey, and what evidence have you to offer that, if you had been the winner, you would have made a better use of your fortune than Caesar?'

But I must not be led into a digression on this question of the divine ordering of events.

76. After taking on board his wife and his friends, Pompey set sail, not putting into any harbours except when he was com-

pelled to do so to take in food or water. The first city that he
entered was Attaleia in Pamphylia and here some triremes came
to him from Cilicia, some troops were got together and he once
again had senators round him – about sixty of them. He heard
too that his navy was still intact and that Cato had taken many
soldiers on board and was crossing over to Africa with them.
At this news he showed his distress to his friends and blamed
himself for having allowed himself to be forced to fight with
his land forces without making any use of his fleet, an arm in
which he had an unquestioned superiority, and had not even
kept his fleet close enough to him, so that, if defeated by land,
he could have reinforced himself by sea and so would again
have been almost at once at the head of forces powerful enough
to meet the enemy on even terms. And indeed it is perfectly
true that Pompey's greatest mistake and Caesar's cleverest
move was in having this battle fought so far away from naval
reinforcements.

However, Pompey had now to plan and act on the basis of
existing circumstances. He sent messengers to the various cities,
and sailed to some of them himself, asking for money and for
men to serve in his ships. But he knew the speed and energy
with which his enemy was likely to act and he was afraid
that Caesar might come upon him and surprise him before his
preparations had been made; and so he looked about for some
safe place to which he could retire temporarily. He discussed
this question with his followers and it was agreed that no
Roman province could afford them a safe refuge. As for foreign
kingdoms, Pompey himself said that he considered that Parthia
was the one most capable of both receiving and protecting them
in their present weakness and later of helping them to build up
their strength and sending them out to fight again with a large
force. Others who took part in the discussion suggested going
to Africa and to King Juba. But Theophanes the Lesbian pointed
out that Egypt was only three days' sail away and there was
Ptolemy, who was a mere boy and very much indebted to
Pompey for the friendship and kindness done by him to his
father.[136] In Theophanes' view it would be sheer madness for
Pompey to decide against Egypt and to put himself into the

power of the Parthians, who were the most treacherous people alive; to refuse to take the second place under a Roman, who had been a relation of his by marriage (and second after Caesar would still be first among all the rest), to refuse even to see whether Caesar would behave moderately or not, and yet to be willing to place himself at the mercy of Arsaces, which even Crassus would not do while he lived; finally to bring a young wife, of the family of the Scipios, among a nation of barbarians who measure power by the ability to commit outrage and to forget decency; even if she suffered no indignity there, but was only thought to have suffered it, her fate would still be cruel enough, since she would certainly be in the power of those who could harm her if they wished. This argument, they say, and this alone persuaded Pompey not to make the journey to the Euphrates – if indeed one may say that it was any calculation of Pompey's own, rather than some supernatural power which was guiding him on the journey which he now went.

77. It was decided, then, that they would seek refuge in Egypt. Pompey with his wife set sail in a Seleucian trireme from Cyprus. His companions sailed with him, some in warships like his own, others in merchant ships. He crossed the sea safely, but was then informed that Ptolemy with an army was established at Pelusium and was making war against his sister.[137] Pompey put in at Pelusium, and sent on a messenger to tell the king of his arrival and to ask for his protection.

Ptolemy himself was a very young man. It was Pothinus who managed everything for him, and Pothinus now called a council of the most influential people. Only those were influential whom Pothinus wished to be so. He asked each one for his opinion as to what was to be done. A terrible thought indeed – that the fate of Pompey the Great should be left to the discussion of Pothinus the eunuch, Theodotus of Chios, a professional teacher of rhetoric, and Achillas the Egyptian. These were the chief counsellors of the king, the rest of the council being made up of court officials and tutors. And it was from this sort of a court that Pompey, tossing at anchor some distance from the shore, was awaiting his verdict – Pompey, who thought it beneath him to have to thank Caesar for saving his life.

Different opinions were expressed.[138] Some were for driving Pompey out of the country, others were for inviting him in and welcoming him. Theodotus, however, giving a demonstration of his skill in argument and of his rhetorical prowess, came forward with the view that neither of these courses would be safe for them: if they received Pompey, they would make Caesar their enemy and Pompey their master; if they forced him to leave, they would offend Pompey by the order of expulsion, and Caesar by forcing him to continue his pursuit; the best thing to do, therefore, was to invite the man into the country and then kill him; in this way they would earn Caesar's gratitude and have nothing to fear from Pompey. He then smiled and, so we are told, added the words: 'Dead men don't bite.'

78. After deciding upon this plan, they entrusted the execution of it to Achillas. Achillas took with him a man called Septimius,[139] who had once been one of Pompey's centurions, another centurion called Salvius and three or four servants. With these he put to sea and sailed towards Pompey's ship. All the most distinguished of those who sailed with Pompey had gone on board his ship to see what was happening. When they saw that instead of there being anything regal or splendid about their reception or anything to justify the hopeful expectations of Theophanes, there were just a few men sailing towards them in a single fishing boat, they grew suspicious at this apparent lack of respect and advised Pompey to have his ship rowed back into the open sea while they were still out of range from the shore. By this time, however, the boat had drawn near. First Septimius rose to his feet and in Latin saluted Pompey as 'Imperator'; then Achillas greeted him in Greek and invited him to come aboard the boat, saying that in this part there was shallow water for a long distance from the shore, so that, owing to the shoals of sand, the sea was not navigable for a trireme. At the same time it could be seen that some of the king's ships were being manned and that the whole shore was full of

soldiers. Even if they changed their minds, there seemed to be no way of escape, and besides to show lack of confidence might merely provide the murderers with an excuse for the crime. So Pompey embraced Cornelia, who was weeping and lamenting for him as though he was already dead, and ordered two centurions to go into the boat before him, also an ex-slave of his called Philip and a servant called Scythes. Then, as Achillas was already stretching his hand out to him from the boat, he turned to his wife and son and quoted the verses of Sophocles:

> Whoever takes his way into a tyrant's court
> Becomes his slave, although he went there a free man.

79. These were the last words he spoke to his friends and after speaking them he went into the boat. It was some distance from the trireme to the land and Pompey, seeing that none of the company addressed a single friendly word to him, turned his eyes towards Septimius and said: 'Surely I am not mistaken. You and I have been comrades-in-arms together.' Septimius merely nodded his head, saying nothing and giving no sign of friendly feeling. Deep silence fell again, and Pompey took a small notebook in which he had written down in Greek the speech which he proposed to use in addressing Ptolemy, and began to look through it. As they drew near the shore Cornelia and his friends watched from the trireme to see what would happen. Cornelia was in a state of terrible anxiety, but she began to take heart when she saw great numbers of the king's people gathering together at the landing place, apparently to give him an honourable reception. But just then, as Pompey took Philip's hand so as to rise up more easily to his feet, Septimius ran him through the body with his sword from behind; then Salvius and then Achillas drew their daggers and stabbed him. And Pompey, drawing his toga down over his face with both hands, endured their blows; he neither said nor did anything unworthy of himself, only groaned a little, and so ended his life in his sixtieth year and only one day after his birthday.

80. When the people on the trireme saw the murder, they gave such a cry that it could be heard from the shore. Then they hurriedly weighed anchor and took to flight. A strong wind helped them as they ran out to sea and the Egyptians, though wishing to pursue them, turned back. But they cut off Pompey's head and threw the rest of his body naked out of the boat, leaving it there as a spectacle for those who desired to see such a sight. Philip, however, stayed by the body until they had had their fill of gazing at it. He then washed it in sea water and wrapped it in one of his own tunics. Then, since he had no materials, he searched up and down the coast until he found some broken planks of a small fishing boat, old and decaying, but enough to build a makeshift funeral pyre for a naked and mutilated body. As he was collecting the wood and building the pyre, an old man came up who was a Roman and who in his youth had served with Pompey in his first campaigns. 'Who are you,' he said, 'who are preparing the funeral for Pompey the Great?' Philip said that he was Pompey's ex-slave and the old man said: 'But you must not have this honour all to yourself. Let me too share in the pious work now that the chance has come to me. I shall not altogether regret my life in a foreign land if, in return for so many hardships, I find this happiness at last – to touch with my hands and to prepare for burial the body of the greatest Imperator that Rome has seen.' And so were performed the last rites for Pompey.

Next day Lucius Lentulus,[140] who knew nothing of what had happened, came sailing along the coast on his way from Cyprus, and saw a funeral pyre with Philip standing beside it. Before Philip had seen him he exclaimed: 'Who can it be who has ended his days and rests in this place?' Then, after a short pause, he groaned and said: 'But it may be you, you, Pompey the Great.' Soon he went ashore, where he was arrested and put to death.

So Pompey came to his end. Not long afterwards Caesar arrived in Egypt, a country polluted with this foul deed. When one of the Egyptians was sent to him with Pompey's head, he turned away from him with loathing, as from an assassin; and when he received Pompey's signet ring on which was engraved

FALL OF THE ROMAN REPUBLIC

a lion holding a sword in his paws, he burst into tears. Achillas
and Pothinus he put to death. King Ptolemy himself, after being
defeated in battle on the banks of the Nile, disappeared and was
not heard of again. The sophist Theodotus, however, escaped
Caesar's vengeance. He fled from Egypt and wandered about
living a wretched life and hated by everyone. But after Marcus
Brutus had killed Caesar and come into power,[141] he discovered
Theodotus in Asia and put him to death with every possible
torture. The ashes of Pompey were taken to Cornelia, who gave
them burial at his country house near Alba.

COMPARISON OF
AGESILAUS AND POMPEY

1. Now that their lives have been set out, let us briefly run over the points in which they differed, bringing them together side by side. They are as follows. First, it was in the justest fashion that Pompey came to power and fame, setting out on his own initiative and rendering many great services to Sulla when Sulla was freeing Italy from her tyrants. Agesilaus on the other hand appeared to get his kingship by offending against both gods and men, since he caused Leotychidas to be condemned as illegitimate, though his brother had recognized him as his legitimate son, and made light of the oracle concerning his own lameness. Secondly, Pompey not only continued to hold Sulla in honour while he lived, but also after his death gave his body funeral obsequies despite the opposition of Lepidus, and gave his own daughter in marriage to Sulla's son Faustus,[1] whereas Agesilaus displaced Lysander on the merest pretext and grossly insulted him. And yet Sulla got no less from Pompey than he gave him, while it was Lysander who made Agesilaus king of Sparta and general of all Greece. Thirdly, Pompey's transgressions against justice in his political life were due to his family connections, for he joined in most of the misdeeds of Caesar and Scipio because they were his relatives by marriage. But Agesilaus snatched Sphodrias from the death to which he had been condemned for wronging the Athenians merely to gratify his son's passion, and when Phoebidas broke the peace with Thebes, it was blatantly because of the crime itself that Agesilaus enthusiastically supported him. In a word, whatever harm Pompey was accused of bringing upon the Romans by deference to his friends or ignorance, Agesilaus brought as

much on the Spartans out of anger and resentment when he kindled the Boeotian war.

2. Moreover, if the disasters which overtook them are to be ascribed to any ill fortune of either, that of Pompey could not have been anticipated by the Romans, but Agesilaus would not allow the Spartans to guard against the 'lame sovereignty', though they had heard and knew about it beforehand. For even if Leotychidas had been proved ten thousand times a bastard and an alien, the Eurypontidae could easily have provided Sparta with a king of legitimate birth and sound of limb, if Lysander had not obscured the meaning of the oracle in the interests of Agesilaus.

On the other hand, there was never another political device like the remedy which Agesilaus applied after the disaster at Leuctra to the state's problem in dealing with those who had run away, when he urged that the laws should slumber for that day. Nor can we find anything similar in Pompey's career. On the contrary, he did not even think that he needed to abide by the laws that he himself had made, thus demonstrating the greatness of his power to his friends. But when Agesilaus confronted the necessity of breaking the laws to save his fellow-citizens, he devised a way by which the laws would not harm the citizens, nor yet be abrogated to avoid such harm. I attribute also to political virtue in Agesilaus that inimitable act of his when he abandoned his campaign in Asia on receipt of the message-stick. For he did not, like Pompey, help the commonwealth only by deeds that made him great, but with an eye to the welfare of his country he renounced such great power and fame as no man attained before or since, except Alexander.

3. And now under another rubric, their campaigns and achievements in war, the trophies of Pompey were so many, the forces led by him so vast, and the pitched battles in which he was victorious so innumerable, that not even Xenophon, I think, would compare the victories of Agesilaus, though by reason of his other excellent qualities he is specially privileged, as it were, to say and write whatever he pleases about the man. I think

also that in merciful behaviour towards their enemies the two men were different. For Agesilaus was so obsessed with enslaving Thebes and depopulating Messenia, Thebes the mother-city of his family and Messenia a sister-foundation to his own country, that he nearly lost Sparta and did lose her supremacy in Greece. But Pompey gave cities to those of the pirates who changed their mode of life, and when it was in his power to lead King Tigranes of Armenia in his triumphal procession he made him an ally instead, saying that he thought more of the future than of a single day.

If, however, it is to the greatest and most influential decisions and deeds in war that the palm of merit in a commander is to be awarded, then the Spartan far outstrips the Roman. For, in the first place, he did not desert or abandon his city, though the enemy attacked it with an army of 70,000 men, while he had only a few hoplites, and these recently defeated at Leuctra. But Pompey, after Caesar had occupied a single city of Italy with only 5,300 men, evacuated Rome in a panic, either yielding ignobly to so few, or falsely conjecturing that there were more. And though he took away with him his own wife and children, he left those of the other citizens defenceless and fled, when he ought to have either conquered in a battle for his country or accepted terms from the victor, who was his fellow-citizen and relation by marriage. But as it was, though he thought it a terrible thing to prolong his term of military command or vote him a consulship, he gave Caesar the opportunity to capture the city and say to Metellus that he considered him and all the rest of the citizens as his prisoners of war.

4. Moreover, the chief task of a good general is to force his enemies to give battle when he is superior to them and not to be forced to fight when his forces are inferior. By doing this Agesilaus always remained undefeated, whereas Caesar escaped injury at Pompey's hands when he was inferior to him and forced him to stake the whole issue on a battle with land forces, in which Caesar was superior, and suffer defeat. So Caesar instantly gained control of money, provisions and the sea, advantages by which he would have been brought down

without a battle if they had remained with his enemy. The excuse made for this failure is really a very grave accusation against such a general. For that a youthful commander should be disconcerted by tumults and outcries into cowardly weakness and abandon the safest course is natural and pardonable. But who could accept that Pompey the Great, whose camp the Romans called their country and his tent their senate, while they gave the name of traitors and rebels to the consuls and praetors and other magistrates at Rome, who was known to be under no man's command but to have served all his campaigns with the greatest success as commander-in-chief, should be almost forced by the gibes of Favonius and Domitius and the fear of being called Agamemnon to risk the supremacy and freedom of Rome? If he was concerned only with the immediate loss of reputation, then he ought to have made a stand at the beginning and fought to a finish for Rome, instead of calling his notorious flight a Themistoclean stratagem and afterwards counting it a disgraceful thing to delay before fighting in Thessaly. For surely God had not appointed that Pharsalian plain to be the stadium and theatre of their struggle for supremacy, nor was he summoned by a herald to go down and fight or leave the victor's wreath for another. His great resources at sea put at his disposal many plains, 10,000 cities and a whole earth if he wanted to imitate Maximus or Marius or Lucullus, or Agesilaus himself, who withstood no less disturbances in Sparta when the Spartans wanted to fight the Thebans in defence of their land, and in Egypt put up with many slanders, accusations and suspicions on the part of the king when he urged him to take no action. But he followed his own best counsels as he wished, and not only saved the Egyptians despite themselves and kept Sparta upright in the midst of so great a convulsion, but actually set up a trophy in the city for a victory over the Thebans, which he made possible later by keeping the Spartans from forcing their way to destruction. Therefore Agesilaus was afterwards commended by those he had compelled to take the path of safety, while Pompey, whom others had led into error, was accused by the very men to whom he had yielded. And yet some say that he was deceived by his father-in-law Scipio, who wanted to keep for himself the greater part of the funds he had brought from Asia and therefore hid it away, then hurried on the battle on the grounds that there was no money left. But even if this were true, a general ought not to allow himself to be so easily tricked into risking his greatest interests. In these matters, then, that is the view we take of each of them.

5. And as to their voyages to Egypt, one sailed there of necessity and in flight, the other for no honourable reason nor of necessity, but for money, so that what he got for serving the barbarians as commander might enable him to make war on the Greeks. Then again, as to the charges that we bring against the Egyptians for their treatment of Pompey, the Egyptians make the same charges against Agesilaus. For Pompey trusted them and was wronged by them, while Agesilaus was trusted by them, but abandoned them and went over to the enemies of those he had sailed to assist.

5

CAESAR

[100¹–44 BC]

The life of Caesar displays much the same merits and defects as that of Pompey. The intrigues that determined the shifting balance of power at Rome in the sixties and fifties are again neglected, but again Plutarch is admirable on such matters as the consequences of Julia's death, the growth of anarchy at Rome before the Civil War, and the increasing tactlessness shown by Caesar the dictator. In his accounts of Caesar's wars he is naturally heavily dependent on the *Bellum Gallicum*, the *Bellum Civile* and the other works of the Caesarian corpus, but it is to his credit that he also consulted other sources, including some, like Tanusius, hostile to Caesar. The most insidious feature of the work as a whole is the assumption, by no means of course peculiar to Plutarch, that Caesar had planned from the outset of his career to overthrow the republic and seize absolute power. This view has found favour in some countries at certain times, but there is nothing to be said for it. Caesar was always daring and ambitious – his social and financial circumstances were such that he had to be, if he was going to make a career at all. But until 59 his successes, though striking (especially his election as *pontifex maximus*), in no way strained the normal framework of Roman public life. As for his position after 59, it could hardly have come about, whatever his plans, had not Cato and his friends by their short-sighted opposition from 62 on driven Pompey into Caesar's arms. The belief that Caesar thought himself born to rule alone leads Plutarch into repeated exaggerations of his early importance and suppressions of his reliance on the help of others. In the sixties Caesar, like many more, climbed on the Pompeian bandwagon, but Plutarch says nothing of this. Later his belief in Caesar's monarchical designs makes him oversimplify the conflict between Pompey and Caesar and deters him from any discussion of what Caesar, as dictator, had in mind for the constitution and himself.

1. After Sulla had seized power, he wanted to make Caesar divorce his wife Cornelia, the daughter of Cinna, who had previously held the entire government in his hands; but he could not persuade Caesar to do this either by promises or by intimidation, and so he confiscated her dowry.[2] The reason for Caesar's hatred of Sulla was his relationship to Marius. Julia, a sister of Caesar's father, was the wife of the elder Marius and the mother of Marius the Younger, who was therefore Caesar's cousin.[3] At the beginning, when so many people were being killed[4] and there was so much to do, Caesar was overlooked by Sulla; but, instead of being content with this, he presented himself to the people as a candidate for a priesthood,[5] though he was still only a mere boy. Sulla, without openly objecting, took measures to see that he was not elected and discussed the question of whether or not to have him put to death. When some of his advisers said that there was no point in killing a boy like him, Sulla replied that they must be lacking in intelligence if they did not see that in this boy there were many Mariuses.

This remark was reported to Caesar and for some time he went into hiding, wandering from place to place in the Sabine country. In the end he became ill and while he was going from one house to another at night, he fell into the hands of some of Sulla's soldiers who were searching the district and arresting those who were in hiding there. With a bribe of two talents Caesar persuaded their leader, Cornelius, to let him go, and then went immediately to the sea and sailed to King Nicomedes in Bithynia. He stayed for a short time with the king and then on his voyage back was captured near the island of Pharmacusa by some of the pirates who even at that time controlled the seas with their large fleets of ships and innumerable smaller craft.[6]

2. First, when the pirates demanded a ransom of twenty talents, Caesar burst out laughing. They did not know, he said, who it

was that they had captured, and he volunteered to pay fifty. Then, when he had sent his followers to the various cities in order to raise the money and was left with one friend and two servants among these Cilicians, about the most bloodthirsty people in the world, he treated them so highhandedly that, whenever he wanted to sleep, he would send to them and tell them to stop talking. For thirty-eight days, with the greatest unconcern, he joined in all their games and exercises, just as if he was their leader instead of their prisoner. He also wrote poems and speeches which he read aloud to them, and if they failed to admire his work, he would call them to their faces illiterate savages, and would often laughingly threaten to have them all hanged. They were much taken with this and attributed his freedom of speech to a kind of simplicity in his character or boyish playfulness. However, the ransom arrived from Miletus and, as soon as he had paid it and been set free, he immediately manned some ships and set sail from the harbour of Miletus against the pirates. He found them still there, lying at anchor off the island, and he captured nearly all of them. He took their property as spoils of war and put the men themselves into the prison at Pergamum. He then went in person to Junius,[7] the governor of Asia, thinking it proper that he, as praetor in charge of the province, should see to the punishment of the prisoners. Junius, however, cast longing eyes at the money, which came to a considerable sum, and kept saying that he needed time to look into the case. Caesar paid no further attention to him. He went to Pergamum, took the pirates out of prison and crucified the lot of them, just as he had often told them he would do when he was on the island and they imagined that he was joking.

3. By this time Sulla's power was declining[8] and Caesar's friends were urging him to return. First, however, he set sail for Rhodes to study under Apollonius, the son of Molon. Cicero also had been a pupil of Apollonius, who was a famous master of oratory and had the reputation of being a very good man as well. It is said that Caesar's natural ability as a political speaker was of the highest order, and that he took the greatest pains to cultivate

it, so that in this field the second place was indisputably his. He did not aim higher than this, since his main efforts were directed towards becoming the first power in the state and the greatest soldier; and so, because of the campaigns and the political activities by means of which he made himself supreme, he never, as a speaker, reached the full height which nature intended him to reach. And he himself, at a later time, in his reply to Cicero's essay on Cato, begs his readers not to compare the plain style of a soldier with the eloquence of an orator who was not only naturally gifted but had had plenty of time to cultivate his gifts.

4. After he had returned to Rome, he prosecuted Dolabella for maladministration in his province and many of the Greek cities supplied him with evidence.[9] Dolabella was acquitted, but Caesar, in return for the support which he had received from the Greeks, acted as their advocate when they prosecuted Publius Antonius for corrupt practices before Marcus Lucullus, the praetor of Macedonia.[10] His intervention was so effective that Antonius appealed to the tribunes in Rome, claiming that he was not getting a fair trial in Greece with Greeks as his accusers.

In Rome Caesar won a brilliant reputation and great popularity by his eloquence in these trials. He had an ability to make himself liked which was remarkable in one of his age, and he was very much in the good graces of the ordinary citizen because of his easy manners and the friendly way in which he mixed with people. Then there were his dinner parties and entertainments and a certain splendour about his whole way of life; all this made him gradually more and more important politically. At first his enemies thought that this influence of his would soon come to nothing, once he stopped spending money, and they stood aside and watched it grow among the common people. Later, however, when it had become too great for anything to be done about it and was plainly aimed directly at a complete revolution in the state, they realized that it is always wrong to consider that something which begins in a small way cannot rapidly become important if it is left unchecked because of being underrated and so receives the advantage of continuity. Certainly Cicero, who is thought to have been the first to have

seen beneath the surface of Caesar's political programme and
to have feared it as one might fear the smiling surface of the
sea, and who understood how powerful a character was hidden
behind Caesar's agreeable, good-humoured manners, said that,
in general, he could detect in everything that Caesar planned
or undertook in politics a purpose that was aiming at absolute
power. 'On the other hand,' he said, 'when I notice how carefully arranged his hair is and when I watch him scratching
his head with one finger, I cannot imagine that this man could
conceive of such a wicked thing as to destroy the Roman
constitution.' This, however, belongs at a later date.

5. The first proof he had of the people's goodwill towards him
was when he stood for the post of military tribune at the same
time as Gaius Popilius and came out above him on the list.[11] A
second and clearer example of their favour appeared when,
after the death of his aunt Julia, the wife of Marius, he made a
brilliant public speech in praise of her in the forum, and was
bold enough to display in the funeral procession images of
Marius himself.[12] These had not been seen since the time that
Sulla came into power, Marius and his friends having been
branded as public enemies. On this occasion there were some
who shouted out against Caesar for what he had done, but
the people shouted them down in no uncertain manner. They
welcomed Caesar with loud applause and showed the greatest
admiration for him for having, after such a long time, brought
back to Rome, as it were from the dead, the honours due to
Marius.

It was an ancient Roman tradition to pronounce public
speeches at the funerals of elderly women; but it was not the
usual thing in the cases of young women, and Caesar was the
first to do it, when his own wife died.[13] This also was an action
which made him popular. It brought him much sympathy from
the people, who regarded him as a tender-hearted man, full of
feeling, and liked him for it.

After the funeral of his wife he went out to Spain as quaestor
to one of the praetors, called Vetus. He always had the greatest
respect for Vetus and gave his son the appointment of quaestor

under him, when he, in his turn, became praetor.[14] When he had completed his service in this post, he married Pompeia as his third wife.[15] (By Cornelia he had a daughter who was afterwards married to Pompey the Great.[16])

He spent money recklessly, and many people thought that he was purchasing a moment's brief fame at an enormous price, whereas in reality he was buying the greatest place in the world at inconsiderable expense. We are told, for instance, that before entering upon public office he was 1300 talents in debt. Then, on being appointed curator of the Appian Way, in addition to the official allowance he spent vast sums of his own money on it. And, when he was aedile,[17] he provided a show of 320 pairs of gladiators fighting in single combat, and what with this and all his other lavish expenditure on theatrical performances, processions and public banquets he threw into the shade all attempts at winning distinction in this way that had been made by previous holders of the office.[18] The result was to make the people so favourably disposed towards him that every man among them was trying to find new offices and new honours to bestow upon him in return for what he had done.

6. There were two parties in Rome – one that of Sulla, which, since his time had been all powerful, the other that of Marius, which was then in a very low state indeed, with its numbers all scattered and scarcely daring to show their heads.[19] It was this party which Caesar wished to revive and make his own; and so, during his aedileship, when these great personal displays of his were at their height, he had images of Marius made in secret and figures of Victory carrying trophies and brought them to the Capitol by night and had them set up there. When the sun rose all these figures could be seen glittering with gold and constructed with the most exquisite craftsmanship; there were inscriptions too commemorating Marius' victories over the Cimbri.[20] And all who saw them were amazed at the daring of the man who had set them up – it was quite obvious who he was. The news soon spread and brought everyone together to see the sight. There were some who shouted out that this revival of honours which by laws and decrees were properly dead and

done with was a sign that Caesar was aiming at securing supreme power in the state for himself; that, after he had previously softened up the people's feelings, he was now making this experiment to see whether, as a result of his lavish personal displays, they had become sufficiently tame to put up with his humour and to allow him to indulge in these innovations. On the other hand, Marius' party took heart and encouraged each other; it was amazing how many of them there were who suddenly showed themselves openly, and they filled the Capitol with the noise of their applause. Many burst into tears of joy at the sight of Marius' features; they praised Caesar to the skies and declared him to be, more than anyone, worthy to be Marius' relation. But when the senate met to discuss the matter, Lutatius Catulus,[21] who at that time was one of the most respected people in Rome, rose up and attacked Caesar. He ended his speech with the memorable words: 'You are no longer working underground, Caesar. Your artillery is planted in the open and it is there for the capture of the state.' Caesar, however, defended himself against these charges and convinced the senate that they were baseless. His admirers then became even more elated and urged him not to climb down for anybody's sake. The people, they said, would be glad to see him triumph over everyone and be the first man in the state.

7. It was at this time too that Metellus,[22] the chief pontiff, died. This priesthood was very much sought after and two of the most distinguished men in Rome with the greatest influence in the senate, Isauricus[23] and Catulus, were candidates for the office. Caesar, however, would not give way to them. He turned to the people and put himself forward as a rival candidate. Since there seemed to be very little in it so far as the feelings of the electors were concerned, Catulus, who, with his greater reputation in the first place was most disturbed at the prospect of this uncertainty, sent to Caesar and tried to bribe him with a large sum of money to stand down and abandon this project for putting himself in the public eye. Caesar replied that he would fight the election to the end, even if he had to borrow more money than Catulus had offered him.

On the day of the election Caesar's mother came with him in tears to the door of their house, and Caesar, after kissing her goodbye, said: 'Today, Mother, you will see your son either as high priest or as an exile.' The contest was a close one, but, when the votes were taken, Caesar came out on top, and this made the senate and the nobles afraid that he would go on to lead the people forward on a course of violent extremism.

This was why Piso[24] and Catulus found fault with Cicero for having spared Caesar when, at the time of Catiline's conspiracy, he had given his enemies a hold over him. Catiline[25] had planned not only to overthrow the constitution but to destroy the whole government and produce a state of complete chaos. He himself had been driven out of the city, this reverse being due to evidence against him of a minor character, before his final plans had come to light; but he left Lentulus and Cethegus behind to organize the conspiracy in his absence. Whether or not Caesar secretly gave these men any help or encouragement we do not know; but after they had been overwhelmingly proved guilty in front of the senate and Cicero, as consul, asked each senator to give his opinion on how they should be punished, all the other senators, until it came to the turn of Caesar, were in favour of the death penalty;[26] but Caesar rose up and, in a long and carefully worded speech, objected to this. He stated that, in his view, except in the case of the most extreme emergency, it was unprecedented and unjust to put to death without trial men of high rank and of famous families; what he recommended was that they should be put into chains and kept under arrest in whatever cities of Italy Cicero himself might select until the war against Catiline had been won; after that the senate, in a time of peace and in an atmosphere of calm, should decide what was best to be done in each individual case.

8. Caesar's views seemed so humane in themselves and the speech with which he backed them up was so powerful that not only did he win the support of subsequent speakers in the debate, but many too of those who had spoken before him took back the opinions which they had expressed previously and came over to his side – until it came round to Cato[27] and to

Catulus, who vigorously opposed him. Cato's very violent speech helped to fix suspicion on Caesar himself and the effect of his attack was that the conspirators were handed over to the executioner, and while Caesar was leaving the senate, many of the young men who at that time were acting as Cicero's bodyguard ran up with drawn swords ready to make an end of him. However, Curio,[28] so it is said, threw his toga round him, and got him away safely; and Cicero himself, when the young men looked at him to see what his wishes were, shook his head – either because he was frightened of the people or because he thought the murder would be entirely unjust and illegal.

As for this story, if it is a true one, I cannot understand why Cicero did not mention it in the book he wrote about his consulship. Certainly, however, he was blamed afterwards for not having made use of this best of all opportunities for getting rid of Caesar and for having shown excessive fear of the people, who were devoted to Caesar. In fact, a few days later, when Caesar attended a meeting of the senate and while attempting to clear himself of the suspicions felt against him met with a most hostile and noisy reception, the people, seeing that the session of the senate was lasting longer than usual, came up in a tumultuous mob and surrounded the senate house, shouting out for Caesar and demanding that he should be let go. This was why Cato, who feared above all things that there might be a revolution starting from the poorer classes who, with their hopes fixed on Caesar, were kindling a fire among the general population, persuaded the senate to give them a monthly ration of grain – which meant an addition to the expenditure of the state of 7½ million drachmas a year.[29] Nevertheless, this was a measure which definitely had the effect of removing the great fear that was felt at the time; it weakened and dispersed Caesar's power just at the right moment. He had been elected praetor for the next year[30] and could have been more formidable still in this office.

9. As it happened there were no disturbances during his praetorship.[31] There was only a somewhat unfortunate affair which concerned his domestic life. Publius Clodius came from a

patrician family and was distinguished both for his wealth and for his powers as an orator; but in his capacity for behaving quite outrageously he surpassed all the most notorious evil livers of his time. This man was in love with Caesar's wife Pompeia, who did not reject his advances. However, the women's part of the house was closely supervised and Caesar's mother, Aurelia,[32] was a person of strict respectability. She never let the young wife out of her sight and so made it difficult and dangerous for the lovers to meet.

The Romans have a goddess whom they call 'the Good Goddess', the same one as the Greeks call 'the Women's Goddess'. The Phrygians claim this goddess as their own and say that she was the mother of King Midas; the Romans say that she was one of the nymphs called Dryads and was married to Faunus; the Greeks say that she is that one of the mothers of Dionysus whose name must not be spoken. And this is why the women, when they are celebrating her festival, cover the tents with branches of vine and, in accordance with the myth, have a sacred snake enthroned at the goddess's side. It is not lawful for a man to be present at the rites nor even to be in the house where they are being celebrated. The women perform the sacred ceremonies by themselves and these ceremonies are said to be very much like those of the Orphics. When the time for the festival comes, the consul or praetor at whose house it is being held goes away, as does every male creature in the household. His wife then takes over the house and arranges the decorations. The most important ceremonies take place by night; the women play together among themselves during the night-long celebrations, and there is much music as well.

10. On this occasion, when Pompeia was in charge of the celebrations, Clodius, who was still beardless and therefore thought that he would escape notice, dressed himself up as a female flute-player and, looking just like a young woman, arrived at the house. He found the door open and was brought inside quite safely by the maid on duty who was in the secret. The maid then ran off to tell Pompeia; time passed and Clodius lacked the patience to stay where he had been left. He began to

wander about the house, which was a very large one, trying to avoid the lights, and was accosted by one of Aurelia's servants who, as one woman to another, asked him to come and play with her. When Clodius said 'no', she dragged him forward and asked him who he was and where he came from. Clodius said that he was waiting for Pompeia's girl, Abra (the name of the maid who had introduced him), but his voice gave him away. Aurelia's servant shrieked and ran off to where the lights and the crowd were, crying out that she had caught a man. The women were in a panic. Aurelia put a stop to the sacred rites of the goddess and covered up the holy things. She then ordered the doors to be shut and went all over the house with lighted torches in search of Clodius. He was found hiding in the room belonging to the maid who had let him into the house and, when it was discovered who he was, the women drove him out of doors. They then went away immediately while it was still night and told their husbands what had happened. As soon as it was day then word was going about the city that Clodius had committed sacrilege and owed satisfaction not only to those who had been outraged by his conduct but also to the city and to the gods. One of the tribunes,[33] therefore, officially indicted Clodius for sacrilege and the most influential members of the senate banded themselves together against him. They gave evidence of a number of shocking crimes which he had committed, among which was adultery with his sister, who was the wife of Lucullus.[34] The people, however, set themselves against this party of the nobility and their defence of Clodius was very useful to him so far as the jury were concerned, who took alarm and were terrified of the numbers of his supporters. Caesar divorced Pompeia at once, but when he was called as a witness at the trial, he said that he knew nothing about the charges against Clodius. This seemed a most surprising thing to say and the prosecuting counsel asked: 'In that case, why did you divorce your wife?' 'Because,' said Caesar, 'I considered that my wife ought not to be even suspected.' Some say that in giving this evidence Caesar really meant what he said; according to others he was acting in order to please the people, who were determined to save Clodius. At any rate Clodius was acquitted of the charge. Most of the jurymen handed in their votes in illegible writing so that they might avoid the risks both of violence from the people, if they condemned him, and of contempt from the nobility, if they acquitted him.

11. Directly after his praetorship Caesar received Spain as his province.[35] However, he found it very difficult to arrange matters with his creditors who tried to prevent him leaving the city and were extremely importunate. He therefore turned for help to Crassus, who was the richest man in Rome and who needed Caesar's vigour and fire for carrying out his own political campaign against Pompey. Crassus met the demands of those creditors who were most difficult to deal with and would not be put off any longer, and gave his personal guarantee for 830 talents. So Caesar was able to set out for his province.

There is a story that while he was crossing the Alps he came to a small native village with hardly any inhabitants and altogether a miserable-looking place. His friends were laughing and joking about it, saying: 'No doubt here too one would find people pushing themselves forward to gain office, and here too there are struggles to get the first place and jealous rivalries among the great men.' Caesar then said to them in all seriousness: 'As far as I am concerned, I would rather be the first man here than the second in Rome.'

It is also said that at another time when he was in Spain and had some leisure, he was reading some part of the history of Alexander and, after sitting for a long time lost in his own thoughts, burst into tears. His friends were surprised and asked him the reason. 'Don't you think,' he said, 'that I have something worth being sorry about, when I reflect that at my age Alexander was already king over so many peoples, while I have never yet achieved anything really remarkable?'

12. Certainly, as soon as he reached Spain he set to work immediately. In a few days he raised ten cohorts in addition to the force of twenty cohorts which was there already. He then marched against the Callaici and the Lusitani and, after conquering them, went on as far as the outer sea, subduing the

tribes which before then had been independent of Rome. These military successes of his were followed up by equally good work in civilian administration. He established good relations between the various cities. One of his most notable achievements was to solve the problem of the existing ill-feeling between debtors and creditors. He ordered that the creditor should take two-thirds annually of the debtor's income, and that the owner of the property should retain the use of the rest and so go on in this way until the whole debt was paid off. By these measures he had acquired a great reputation by the time he left his province. He had become rich himself and he had made his soldiers rich as a result of his campaigns, and he had been saluted by them as 'Imperator'.

13. The law was that those who desired the honour of a triumph had to wait outside the city, while candidates for the consulship had to be present in the city in person. Caesar, who arrived at Rome just at the time of the consular elections,[36] was therefore in a dilemma and sent to the senate asking permission for his name to be put forward for the consulship by his friends, while he himself remained outside the city.[37] Cato, however, first opposed the request by insisting that it was illegal, and then, when he saw that many senators had been won over by Caesar's attentions, managed to get a vote on the matter put off by wasting time and speaking for the entire day. Caesar then decided to forgo the triumph and to try for the consulship. He entered the city and immediately adopted a policy which deceived everyone except Cato. This was to effect a reconciliation between Pompey and Crassus, the two most powerful people in Rome. Caesar brought these men together, making them friends instead of enemies, and used their united power for the strengthening of himself. So before anyone was aware of it, he had, by an action which could be called a simple piece of kindness, succeeded in producing what was in effect a revolution. For the cause of the civil wars was not, as most people think, the quarrel between Caesar and Pompey; it was rather their friendship, since in the first place they worked together to destroy the power of the aristocracy and only when

this had been accomplished quarrelled amongst themselves. Cato often prophesied what would happen and at the time was considered merely bad-tempered and interfering; afterwards, however, he was thought to have been a wise counsellor, though an unsuccessful one.

14. So Caesar, armed and supported by the friendship of Pompey and Crassus, pressed on towards the consulship and, with Calpurnius Bibulus,[38] was triumphantly elected. As soon as he entered upon his office he proposed various measures for the allotment and redistribution of land – measures that would have come better from some revolutionary tribune of the people than from a consul.[39] He encountered stiff opposition from all the most respectable elements in the senate. This was just the excuse that he had long been looking for. He vigorously protested that it was against his will that he was being driven to put matters before the Assembly of the People, but that the senate's high-handed and stubborn behaviour left him no other course than to devote himself to the people's interest. He then hurried out of the senate and stood up to speak before the People's Assembly, with Crassus on one side of him and Pompey on the other. He asked them whether they approved of his laws and, when they said that they did, he called upon them to give him their help and to defend him against those who were threatening to resist him with their swords. This they promised to do, and Pompey actually added that, if it was a question of swords, he could produce a sword and a shield as well. The nobility were deeply offended by this mad and boyishly impulsive remark of Pompey's – so unworthy of his own dignity and so lacking in the respect properly due to the senate; the people, however, were delighted with it.

Caesar went on to gain a still firmer hold over Pompey's power and influence. He had a daughter, Julia, who was engaged to Servilius Caepio,[40] and he now engaged her to Pompey, saying that he would arrange that Servilius could marry Pompey's daughter – though she too was engaged already, having been promised to Faustus, the son of Sulla. And shortly afterwards Caesar married Calpurnia, a daughter of

Piso,[41] and got Piso elected as consul for the following year. At this Cato violently protested and exclaimed that it was an intolerable state of affairs to have the government prostituted by marriage alliances and to see men pushing each other forward to high positions and the commands of provinces and armies by the means of women.

As for Caesar's colleague Bibulus, so far from having any success in his efforts to obstruct Caesar's legislation, he, and Cato with him, was often in danger of being killed in the forum. So he shut himself up in his house and stayed there for the rest of his term of office. And Pompey, directly after his marriage, filled the forum with armed men and helped the people to pass Caesar's laws and to give him, as his consular province to be held for five years, Gaul on both sides of the Alps, together with Illyricum and an army of four legions.[42] Cato attempted to speak against these proposals, but Caesar had him led off to prison. He imagined that Cato would appeal to the tribunes, but he walked on his way without saying a word and when Caesar saw that not only were the nobility displeased but the people too, out of respect for Cato's good qualities, were following him in silence and with downcast eyes, he himself privately asked one of the tribunes to get him released.

Out of the whole number of senators, only a very few used to attend the meetings presided over by Caesar; the rest showed their hatred of his proceedings by staying away. There was a very old senator called Considius who told Caesar that his colleagues did not come to these meetings because they were afraid of his armed soldiers. 'Then why,' said Caesar, 'aren't you equally afraid and why don't you stay at home?' 'Because,' said Considius, 'old age has deprived me of fear. I do not have to give much consideration to the little amount of life that is left to me.'

But the most disgraceful political action of the time was considered to be the election to the tribuneship, during Caesar's consulship, of Clodius – the man who had attempted to seduce his wife and who had broken in on the secret nocturnal ceremonies. Clodius was elected in order that he might dispose of Cicero; and Caesar did not set out on his campaign until, with

the help of Clodius, he had raised a party against Cicero and
driven him out of Italy.[43]

15. So much for the accounts of Caesar's career before his
Gallic campaigns. After this he seems, as it were, to have made
a new start and to have entered upon a different way of life and
of achievement. And the period of the wars which he now
fought and of the campaigns by which he subjugated Gaul
proved him to be as good a soldier and a commander as any
of those who have been most admired for their leadership
and shown themselves to be the greatest generals. In fact, if
we compare him with such men as Fabius and Scipio and
Metellus,[44] or with those who were either his contemporaries
or lived a little before his time, such as Sulla, Marius, the two
Luculli, or even with Pompey himself, whose fame for every
kind of military excellence was, at this period, in full flower
and reaching up to the skies, we shall find that Caesar's achievements surpass them all. He may be considered superior to one
because of the difficulty of the country in which he fought; to
another because of the extent of his conquests; to another
because of the numbers and strength of the enemy forces which
he defeated; to another because of the savage treacherous
character of the tribes whose goodwill he won; to another
because of the reasonable and considerate way in which he
treated prisoners; to another because of the gifts he gave to his
soldiers and his acts of kindness to them; and he surpassed
them all in the fact that he fought more battles than any of
them and killed greater numbers of the enemy. For, though his
campaigns in Gaul did not last for as much as ten complete
years, in this time he took by storm more than 800 cities,
subdued 300 nations, and fought pitched battles at various
times with 3 million men, of whom he destroyed one million in
the actual fighting and took another million prisoners.

16. His ability to secure the affection of his men and to get
the best out of them was remarkable. Soldiers who in other
campaigns had not shown themselves to be any better than the
average became irresistible and invincible and ready to confront

any danger, once it was a question of fighting for Caesar's honour and glory. There are many examples of this: Acilius,[45] for instance, who in the naval battle off Marseilles boarded an enemy ship and had his right hand cut off with a sword, but still kept hold of his shield with the other hand and struck his enemies in the face with it till he drove them all back and got possession of the ship. Then there was Cassius Scaeva[46] who, in the battle of Dyrrhachium, had one eye shot out with an arrow, his shoulder transfixed with one javelin and his thigh with another; he had received on his shield 130 darts and javelins and then called out to the enemy as though he intended to surrender. When two of them came up to him, he cut off the shoulder of one of them with his sword, struck the other one in the face and forced him to run away, and got off safely himself with the help of his comrades. Then there was the occasion in Britain when some of the leading centurions had got themselves into a marshy place with water all round and were being set upon by the enemy. An ordinary soldier, while Caesar himself was watching the fighting, rushed into the thick of it and, after showing the utmost daring and gallantry, drove the natives off and rescued the centurions. Finally, with great difficulty, he made his own way back after all the rest, plunged into the muddy stream, and, without his shield, sometimes swimming and sometimes wading, just managed to get across. Caesar and those with him were full of admiration for the man and shouted out to him in joy as they came to meet him; but the soldier was thoroughly dejected and, with tears in his eyes, fell at Caesar's feet, and asked to be forgiven for having let go of his shield. Then, too, in Africa, Scipio[47] captured one of Caesar's ships in which Granius Petro,[48] who had been appointed quaestor, was sailing. Scipio gave the other passengers over to his soldiers as booty but told the quaestor that he would spare his life. Granius, however, said that with Caesar's soldiers the custom was to give, not to receive, mercy, and so plunged his sword into his body and killed himself.

17. It was Caesar himself who inspired and cultivated this spirit, this passion for distinction among his men. He did it in the first

place because he made it clear, by the ungrudging way in which he would distribute rewards and honours, that he was not amassing a great fortune from his wars in order to spend it on his personal pleasures or on any life of self-indulgence; instead he was keeping it, as it were, in trust, a fund open to all for the reward of valour, and his own share in all this wealth was no greater than what he bestowed on his soldiers who deserved it. And secondly, he showed that there was no danger which he was not willing to face, no form of hard work from which he excused himself. So far as his fondness for taking risks went, his men, who knew his passion for distinction, were not surprised at it; but they were amazed at the way in which he would undergo hardships which were, it seemed, beyond his physical strength to endure. For he was a slightly built man, had a soft and white skin, suffered from headaches and was subject to epileptic fits. (His first epileptic attack took place, it is said, in Corduba.) Yet so far from making his poor health an excuse for living an easy life, he used warfare as a tonic for his health. By long hard journeys, simple diet, sleeping night after night in the open and rough living he fought off his illness and made his body strong enough to resist all attacks. As a matter of fact, most of the sleep he got was in chariots or in litters: rest, for him, was something to be used for action; and in the day-time he would be carried round to the garrisons and cities and camps and have sitting with him one slave who was trained to write from dictation as he went along, and behind him a soldier standing with a sword. He travelled very fast. For instance on his first journey from Rome, he reached the Rhône in seven days.

He had been an expert rider from boyhood. He had trained himself to put his hands behind his back and then, keeping them tightly clasped, to put his horse to its full gallop. And in the Gallic campaigns he got himself into the habit of dictating letters on horseback, keeping two secretaries busy at once, or even more, according to Oppius.[49] It is said too that Caesar was the first to arrange for what amounted to conversations with his friends by letters, when, owing to the numbers of things he had to do or because of the very size of the city, he could not

spare the time to see them personally on matters that required
a quick decision.

He was not in the least fussy about his food, as is shown by
the following story. When Valerius Leo was entertaining him
to dinner at Milan, he served up asparagus dressed with myrrh
instead of with olive oil. Caesar ate this quite calmly himself
and reprimanded his friends when they objected to the dish. 'If
you didn't like it,' he said, 'there was no need to have eaten it.
But if one reflects on one's host's lack of breeding it merely
shows that one is ill-bred oneself.' There was also an occasion
when he was forced to take refuge from a storm in a poor man's
hut. When he found that this consisted of only one room, and
even this room was scarcely big enough to accommodate one
person, he said to his friends that honours should go to the
strongest, but necessities should go to the weakest, and so he
told Oppius to lie down there, while he himself and the others
slept under the projecting roof of the doorway.

18. His first war in Gaul was against the Helvetii and Tigurini.[50]
These tribes had set fire to their 12 cities and 400 villages and
were pushing forward into the Roman part of Gaul, just as
the Cimbri and Teutones had done in the past.[51] They were
considered to be just as brave as those former invaders and just
as numerous. There were 300,000 of them in all, of whom
190,000 were fighting men. The Tigurini were crushed at the
River Arar, not by Caesar himself, but by Labienus,[52] acting
under Caesar's instructions. Then the Helvetii unexpectedly
attacked Caesar on the march, while he was leading his army
towards a friendly city. He succeeded, however, in falling back
on to a strong position where he brought his men together and
drew them up in order of battle. When a horse was brought to
him he said: 'After I have won the battle, this horse will come
in useful for the pursuit. But now, let us get at the enemy.' And
so he led the charge on foot. There was a long and hard struggle
before he pushed back the enemy's line, but the hardest work
of all was at their rampart of wagons. Here not only did the men
themselves stand firm and fight, but their wives and children too
joined in the resistance and, fighting to the death, were cut

down with the men. It was midnight before the battle was over.
Caesar crowned this great victory by an act more noble still.
This was his settlement of the natives, more than 100,000 of
them, who had survived the battle, and whom he compelled to
go back again to the land which they had left and to the cities
which they had destroyed. His reason for doing this was because
he feared that, if the land were left unoccupied, the Germans
would cross the Rhine and take it for themselves.

19. His second war was fought directly in the interests of the
Gauls.[53] It was against the Germans, although previously, in
Rome, Caesar had made the German King Ariovistus an ally.[54]
However, the Germans were quite intolerable neighbours to
the tribes under Caesar's control. It appeared certain that, once
they got the chance, they would not remain content with what
they had, but would spread over the frontiers and occupy Gaul.
Caesar saw that his officers were frightened of the Germans –
particularly those young men of good families who had come
out with him under the impression that a campaign under his
leadership would mean easy living and easy money.[55] So he
called them to a meeting and told them to go back to Rome;
they must not run any undue risks, he suggested, in their present
cowardly and soft state of mind; he himself proposed to take
just the tenth legion with him and to march against the barbarians; he did not expect to find the enemy any stronger than
the Cimbri had been, and he would not be found a worse
general than Marius. As a result of this the tenth legion sent a
deputation to him to thank him for his words, and the men of
the other legions were furious with their own commanders. The
whole army was now willing and eager for action and they
followed Caesar on a march lasting for many days. Finally they
camped within twenty miles or so of the enemy.

The very fact that they had approached so near had had a
damaging effect on the morale of Ariovistus. He had never
imagined that Romans would attack Germans; in fact he
thought it unlikely that they would put up a resistance when
the Germans attacked. So he was now amazed at Caesar's
daring, and at the same time he noticed a lack of confidence in

his own men. The German spirit was still more discouraged by the prophecies made by their holy women, who used to foretell the future by observing the eddies in the rivers, and by finding signs in the whirling and in the noise of the water. These women warned them not to fight a battle until the appearance of the new moon.

Caesar learned of these prophecies and saw that the Germans were making no move against him. He decided that it would be a good thing to engage them while they were in this disheartened state rather than to sit still and wait until the time suited them. So, by making attacks on their entrenchments and on the hills where they were encamped, he stung them into action and induced them to come down from the hills in a fury to fight the matter out. The result was a brilliant victory for Caesar. He pursued the enemy for forty miles, as far as the Rhine, and filled the whole of the plain with the bodies of the dead and their spoils. Ariovistus, with a few followers, succeeded in getting across the Rhine. The number of killed is said to have been 80,000.

20. After this action Caesar left his army among the Sequani to spend the winter.[56] He himself wished to attend to affairs in Rome and so came south to the part of Gaul along the Po which was part of his province. (The river called the Rubicon is the boundary between Cisalpine Gaul and the rest of Italy.) Here he fixed his quarters and employed his time in political intrigues. Many people came to see him and he gave each one what he wanted; everyone left him with something in hand for the present and with hopes for more in the future. So, during all the rest of the time of his campaigns in Gaul, he was, quite unobserved by Pompey, doing first one, then the other of two things – conquering the enemy by the force of Roman arms, and subduing the Romans and making them his own by means of the money which he had got from the enemy.

But when he heard that the Belgae (who were the most powerful of the Gauls, occupying a third of the whole country) had revolted and got together enormous numbers of armed men, he turned back at once and marched as quickly as possible

to the scene of action.[57] He fell upon the enemy as they were
engaged in plundering the Gauls who were in alliance with him
and, meeting with only a feeble resistance, routed the largest
and most closely organized of their armies. The destruction was
such that lakes and deep rivers were filled up with dead bodies
and became passable to the Romans. Of the tribes who had
revolted, all those who lived by the Ocean submitted without
any fighting at all. Caesar then marched against the Nervii,[58]
the most savage and the most warlike people in these parts.
They lived in thickly wooded country and, after they had put
their families and possessions in some place out of the way in
the depths of the forest, they suddenly fell upon Caesar with a
force of 60,000 men at a time when he was fortifying a camp
and had no idea that the battle was impending. They routed
Caesar's cavalry, surrounded the seventh and twelfth legions,
and killed all their centurions. In all probability the Romans
would have been destroyed to the last man if Caesar himself
had not snatched up a shield, forced his way through to the
front of the fighting, and hurled himself on the natives; and if
the tenth legion, seeing his danger, had not charged down from
the high ground and cut their way through the enemy's ranks.
As it was, Caesar's personal daring had its effect; in the fighting
his men went, as the saying is, beyond themselves – though
even then they never made the Nervii turn and run, but cut
them down fighting on to the end. Out of 60,000 only 500 are
said to have survived the battle, and out of their governing
body of 400 only 3 remained alive.

21. At the news of these victories the senate in Rome decreed
sacrifices to the gods and public holidays and festivals to last
for fifteen days – a longer period than had ever before been
devoted to the celebrations of any victory.[59] The state had been,
it was felt, in great danger, with so many nations breaking out
into revolt at once, and the affection felt for Caesar by the
Roman people made the victory all the more glorious because
it was his.

Caesar himself, once he had settled matters in Gaul, again
spent the winter[60] by the Po and occupied himself with looking

after his interests in Rome. Candidates for office came to get his backing and after bribing the people with the money which he gave them, won their elections and went on to do everything likely to increase his power. Not only this, but there came to meet him at Luca most of the men of highest rank and greatest influence in Rome, including Pompey, Crassus, Appius the governor of Sardinia and Nepos the proconsul of Spain.[61] There were actually 120 lictors in the place and more than 200 members of the senate. The conversations which they held here resulted in the following arrangements: Pompey and Crassus were to be made consuls for the next year;[62] Caesar was to have money voted to him and to have his command renewed for another period of five years. To all right-thinking people it seemed a fantastic thing that those who were getting so much from Caesar should be urging the senate to give him money, as though he had none. Though 'urge' is not the right word. It was rather a question of compulsion, and the senate groaned at the decrees for which it voted. Cato was not there. They had purposely got him out of the way by sending him on a mission to Cyprus.[63] Favonius,[64] however, who was a devoted follower of Cato, finding that normal methods of opposition were being quite ineffectual, came running out into the streets and with loud shouts tried to get the people to listen to his objections. No one paid him any attention. Some were overawed by Pompey and Crassus, and nearly everyone wanted to please Caesar. So they did nothing, living in hopes of future kindnesses from him.

22. Caesar then went back again to his forces in Gaul and found the country involved in a serious war.[65] Two great German nations, the Usipes and the Tenteritae, were aiming at taking land for themselves and had just crossed the Rhine. With regard to the battle fought against these tribes Caesar's own account, given in his 'Commentaries', is as follows: the natives had sent ambassadors to negotiate with him and then, during the period of truce, had attacked him on the march, with the result that with their 800 cavalry they routed his own force of 5,000 cavalry, who were taken off their guard; that afterwards

they sent another deputation to him to deceive him for the second time, but he had kept the deputation under arrest and, taking the view that it was sheer simplemindedness to keep faith with people who had shown that they could not be relied upon themselves to keep a treaty, he had led his army against the natives. Tanusius,[66] however, says that, when the senate voted holidays and sacrifices to celebrate this victory, Cato declared that in his opinion Caesar ought to be surrendered to the natives; so, he said, they would clear Rome of the guilt of breaking a truce and would bring the curse which must follow such an action home to the man who was responsible for it.

Of those who had crossed the Rhine into Gaul, 400,000 men were cut to pieces. The few who managed to get back again found refuge with the German tribe called the Sugambri. This gave Caesar a pretext for invading Germany, and he was in any case anxious to win the fame of being the first man in history to cross the Rhine with an army. So he began to bridge the river, wide as it was, and, at this particular point of its course, very swollen and rough and swift-flowing. Trunks of trees and other timber were swept down the stream and kept battering and tearing away at the supports of the bridge; but Caesar intercepted these by driving great piles of wood into the river bed to form a screen across the channel; so he bridled and yoked the rushing river and in ten days the bridge stood there finished – something that had to be seen to be believed.

23. Next he brought his army across the river. No one dared to offer any opposition. Indeed even the Suevi, the leading nation in Germany, took themselves and their belongings out of the way and hid in deep wooded valleys. Caesar burned and ravaged the country that belonged to hostile tribes, encouraged those who had remained constantly on good terms with Rome, and then, after having spent eighteen days in Germany, retired again to Gaul.

But his expedition against Britain[67] was peculiarly remarkable for its daring. He was the first to bring a navy into the Western Ocean and to sail through the Atlantic Sea with an army to make war. The reported size of the island had appeared incredible and it had become a great matter of controversy among writers and scholars, many of whom asserted that the place did not exist at all and that both its name and the reports about it were pure inventions. So, in his attempts to occupy it, Caesar was carrying the Roman empire beyond the limits of the known world. He twice crossed to the island from the coast of Gaul opposite and fought a number of battles in which he did more harm to the enemy than good to his own men; the inhabitants were so poor and wretched that there was nothing worth taking from them. With the final result of the war he was not himself wholly satisfied; nevertheless, before he sailed away from the island, he had taken hostages from the king and had imposed a tribute.

In Gaul he found letters from his friends in Rome which were just going to be sent across to him. They informed him of the death of his daughter; she had died in childbirth at Pompey's house.[68] Both Pompey himself and Caesar were greatly distressed at this, and their friends were disturbed too, since it seemed to them that the bond of relationship was now broken which had preserved peace and concord in a state which was, apart from this bond, falling to pieces. And the baby died too, only surviving its mother for a few days. As for Julia herself, the people took up her body and, in spite of opposition from the tribunes, carried it to the Field of Mars, where the funeral was held and where she lies buried.

24. Caesar's forces were now so large that he was forced to quarter them in many different areas for the winter. He himself, as was his usual plan, went back in the direction of Italy. It was at this moment that once again the whole of Gaul broke out into revolt.[69] Great armies were raised and went about trying to destroy the winter quarters of the Romans and attacking their fortified camps. The largest and strongest rebel army, under Abriorix, wiped out the whole army of Cotta and Titurius,[70] together with its commanders, and then, with a force of 60,000 men, surrounded and besieged the legion commanded by Cicero.[71] Cicero's camp was very nearly taken by storm, and

every man in it was wounded in the course of a most gallant defence against what seemed to be impossible odds.

Caesar was far on his way when he heard the news of what had happened. He turned back at once, got together 7,000 men in all and hurried to the relief of Cicero. The besiegers, however, got to know of his approach and, feeling nothing but contempt for his small force, came out to meet him and to destroy him. Caesar deceived them by constantly avoiding battle and, when he had found a suitable position for one who was fighting with a small force against superior numbers, he began to fortify a camp. He kept his soldiers from making any attacks on the enemy, and made them act as though they were afraid, building up the ramparts and barricading the gates. This strategy had the effect of making the enemy despise him all the more, until the time came when their confidence led them to make a disorderly attack on the camp. Caesar then led his men out, and routed the enemy, killing great numbers of them.

25. This victory led to the collapse of the many revolts that had started in this part of Gaul; and at the same time Caesar himself, during the winter, was going everywhere and taking strict precautions against any kind of revolutionary activity. Three legions had come to him from Italy to replace the men who had been lost. Two of these had been under the command of Pompey, who now lent them to Caesar, and the other one had been recently recruited from the part of Gaul around the Po.

Nevertheless, in the remoter districts there now began to appear the first signs of the greatest and most dangerous of all Caesar's wars in Gaul. The seeds of this war had for a long time been sown in secret and had been tended by the most powerful men among the chief military nations of the country; and now the movement had gained strength; large bodies of young men had assembled in arms from all parts of Gaul; great sums of money had been brought together into one place; there were strong cities involved in the revolt and areas of country which were very difficult to invade. It was also winter, and at this time of the year the rivers were frozen, the forests were covered in

snow, and the plains had been converted into lakes by the
torrents from the hills, so that in some parts the tracks had
been obliterated by the deep snow and in others, because of the
floodwater from streams and marshes, it was impossible to be
sure of whether a march was practicable or not. All these
difficulties made it seem impossible for Caesar to deal with the
rebellion.[72] There were many tribes in revolt, the leading ones
being the Arverni and the Carnuntini. Vergentorix had been
chosen as supreme commander for the war. His father had been
put to death by the Gauls because they thought he was aiming
at making himself an absolute ruler.

26. He had divided his total force into a number of divisions,
appointed commanders for each of them and was winning over
to his side the whole country round about as far as the water-
shed of the Arar. He knew that there was now a party working
against Caesar in Rome and his plan was to seize this opportunity and bring all Gaul into the war. And in fact, if he had done
this a little later, when Caesar was involved in the civil war,
Italy would have been in the same state of panic as it was in
the days of the Cimbri. However, things happened differently.
Caesar, who more than any man was gifted with the power of
making the right use of every factor in warfare and particularly
of seizing the right moment for action, set out immediately he
received the news of the revolt and marched back over the same
roads by which he had come. The very vigour and speed of his
march in such wintry conditions was a sufficient advertisement
to the natives that an unconquered and unconquerable army
was bearing down upon them. It had seemed incredible that for
a long time even one of his messengers or letter-carriers could
have got through; yet here he was himself with his entire army,
ravaging their land, reducing fortresses, subduing cities and
receiving the allegiance of those who came over to his side. This
was the situation until even the nation of the Aedui came into
the war against him. Up to this time the Aedui had called
themselves the brothers of the Romans[73] and had been treated
with particular distinction; the fact that they now joined the
rebels caused the greatest discouragement in Caesar's army.

Because of this Caesar moved into another area. He crossed through the territory of the Lingones with the idea of reaching the Sequani, who were a friendly tribe and stood like a barrier between Italy and the rest of Gaul. It was here the enemy fell upon him, after surrounding him with tens of thousands of men. Caesar was willing enough to engage them and, after a long time and much slaughter, he overpowered the natives and gained what amounted to a complete victory. At the beginning, however, he seems to have suffered a reverse, and the Arverni still show a short sword hanging up in a temple and claim that it was taken from Caesar. Caesar himself saw this sword later, and smiled, and when his friends urged him to have it taken down, he would not allow it, because he considered it as consecrated.

27. Most of those who escaped from the battle took refuge with their king in the city of Alesia. The place was regarded as impregnable because of the size and strength of the walls and the great numbers of its defenders. Caesar besieged it, however, and, while doing so, was threatened from outside by a quite indescribable danger. Three hundred thousand men, the best fighting troops from every nation in Gaul, assembled together and marched to the relief of Alesia. In the city there were not less than 170,000 fighting men. Caesar now found himself caught between two enormous forces; he was himself besieged and was compelled to build two systems of fortification, one facing the city and one facing the relieving army, since he knew well that, if the two forces should combine, everything would be over with him.

There are many reasons why Caesar's peril at Alesia became justly famous. It affords more examples of his daring and skill than any other struggle in which he was engaged. But perhaps the most remarkable thing of all was that, when he joined battle with and defeated the enormous army outside the city, not only the inhabitants of the city itself but even the Romans who were guarding the interior line of fortifications were unaware of what was going on. The first they knew of the victory was when they heard from Alesia the cries of the men and the lamentations of

the women, who could see from there the Romans in the further
lines carrying into their camp great numbers of shields decorated with gold and silver, breastplates stained with blood,
drinking cups and tents made in the Gallic fashion. So quickly
did this huge army melt away and vanish, like a ghost or a
dream, most of them being killed on the spot.

More trouble remained both for Caesar and for the defenders
of Alesia, but in the end they were forced to surrender.
Vergentorix, the supreme leader in the whole war, put on his
most beautiful armour, had his horse carefully groomed and
rode out through the gates. Caesar was sitting down and
Vergentorix, after riding round him in a circle, leaped down
from his horse, stripped off his armour and sat at Caesar's feet
silent and motionless until he was taken away under arrest, a
prisoner reserved for the triumph.

28. Caesar had long ago decided that Pompey must be removed
from his position of power; and Pompey, for that matter, had
come to just the same decision about Caesar. Crassus, who
had been watching their struggle, ready to take on the winner
himself, had been killed in Parthia;[74] so that now the field was
clear. The man who wanted to be on top had to get rid of the
one who at present held that position: the man who was for
the moment on top had, if he wished to stay there, to get rid of
the man he feared before it was too late. It was only recently
that Pompey had come to fear Caesar. Up till this time he had
despised him. It was through his influence, he thought, that
Caesar had grown great, and it would be just as easy to put
him down as it had been to raise him up. But Caesar's plan had
been laid down from the very beginning. Like an athlete he
had, as it were, withdrawn himself from the ring and, in the
Gallic wars, had undergone a course of training. In these wars
he had brought his army into perfect condition and had won
such fame for himself that he had now reached a height where
his own achievements could challenge comparison with the past
successes of Pompey. He made use too of every argument and
circumstance that was to his advantage. Some of these were
given to him by Pompey himself, some by the general state of

affairs and by the collapse of good government in Rome. Here things had gone so far that candidates for office quite shamelessly bribed the electorate, actually counting out the money in public, and the people who had received the bribes went down to the forum not so much to vote for their benefactors as to fight for them with bows and arrows and swords and slings. Often, before an election was over, the place where it had been held was stained with blood and defiled with dead bodies, and the city was left with no government at all, like a ship adrift with no one to steer her. The result was that intelligent people could only be thankful if, after such a mad and stormy period, things ended in nothing worse than a monarchy. In fact there were many people who actually ventured to declare in public that there was now no other possible remedy for the disease of the state except government by one man, that this remedy was available from the gentlest of physicians (meaning Pompey) and ought to be taken. As for Pompey, so far as words went he put on a show of declining the honour, but in fact did more than anyone else to get himself made dictator. Cato was able to grasp the situation and persuaded the senate to appoint Pompey as sole consul, hoping that he would be satisfied with this more legal form of monarchy and not grasp the dictatorship by force.[75] At the same time the senate voted that his period of government over his provinces should be prolonged.[76] He had two provinces – Spain and all Africa. These were governed by officers appointed by him and he maintained armies in both provinces for which he received 1,000 talents a year from the treasury.

29. Caesar now sent to Rome asking to be allowed to stand for a consulship and to have his own provincial commands prolonged also. At first Pompey himself did not declare himself either way; but Marcellus and Lentulus[77] opposed Caesar's requests. They had always hated Caesar and they now used every means, fair or foul, to dishonour and discredit him. For instance, they took away the rights of Roman citizenship from the people of Novum Comum, which was a colony recently established by Caesar in Gaul,[78] and Marcellus, during his

consulship, had a senator from Novum Comum who had come to Rome beaten with rods. 'I am putting these marks on you,' he said, 'to prove that you are not a Roman. Now go away and show them to Caesar.'

However, by the time that the consulship of Marcellus was over Caesar was already in a most lavish way making available to public figures in Rome the wealth which he had won in Gaul. He paid the enormous debts of the tribune Curio; and he gave the consul Paulus[79] 1,500 talents with which he added to the beauty of the forum by building the famous Basilica which was erected in place of the one known as 'the Fulvia'. Pompey now became alarmed at the party which was forming and came into the open. Both he and his friends began to work for having Caesar replaced by a successor in his provincial command, and he sent to him to ask for the return of the troops whom he had lent to him for the war in Gaul.[80] Caesar sent the soldiers back, after giving each man a present of 250 drachmas. The officers who brought these troops back to Pompey publicly spread rumours about Caesar which were in themselves neither likely nor true, but which had the effect of warping Pompey's judgement and filling him with false hopes. It was Pompey, according to these officers, who was really the idol of Caesar's army, and while Pompey, because of the festering disease of envy in Roman politics, was having some difficulty in controlling things in Rome, the army in Gaul was there, ready for him to use, and, if it once crossed over into Italy, would immediately come over to him, so unpopular had Caesar become because of his innumerable campaigns and so greatly was he suspected of planning to seize supreme power for himself. All this fed Pompey's vanity. On the assumption that he had nothing to fear, he took no measures for the raising of troops, and imagined that he was winning the war against Caesar by speeches and by resolutions of the senate, though in fact all these resolutions meant nothing to Caesar at all. It is said that one of Caesar's centurions, who had been sent by him to Rome, was standing outside the senate house and, when he was told that the senate would not give Caesar an extension of his command, he clapped his hand on the hilt of his sword and said: 'This will give it to him all right.'

30. Yet the demands made by Caesar certainly looked fair enough. What he suggested was that he should lay down his arms and that Pompey should do the same thing; they should then both, as ordinary private individuals, see what favour they could find from their fellow citizens. He argued that those who wanted him to be disarmed while Pompey's own forces were strengthened were simply confirming one man in the tyranny which they accused the other one of aiming at.

When Curio, on Caesar's behalf, put these proposals before the people, he was loudly applauded. Indeed some people actually loaded him with garlands of flowers as though he were some victorious athlete. Antony,[81] too, who was a tribune, produced in front of the people a letter which he had received from Caesar on these points and, in spite of the consuls'[82] efforts to suppress it, read it aloud. In the senate, however, Pompey's father-in-law, Scipio,[83] proposed a motion that Caesar should be declared a public enemy if he had not laid down his arms before a certain date. And when the consuls put the question, first, whether Pompey should disband his troops, and then whether Caesar should, only a very few senators voted for the first proposal and nearly everyone voted for the second. But when Antony once more demanded that both should lay down their commands, the senate welcomed this proposal unanimously. Scipio, however, violently protested against it and the consul Lentulus shouted out that in dealing with a robber what was required was arms, not votes. So for the time being the senate broke up and the senators put on mourning because of this failure to come to an agreement.

31. Soon letters came from Caesar which were even more moderate in tone. He agreed to give up everything else, only asking for Cisalpine Gaul and Illyricum with two legions which he should retain till he stood for his second consulship. The orator Cicero, too, who had just come back from Cilicia,[84] was

working for a reconciliation and trying to make Pompey take up a less rigid attitude, and Pompey agreed to the proposals except that he still insisted that Caesar's soldiers should be taken from him. Cicero then approached Caesar's friends and tried to arrange a compromise by which they would agree to accept the provinces already mentioned and a force of only 6,000 soldiers. This was a figure which Pompey, on his side, was inclined to accept, but the consul Lentulus would not hear of it. He went out of his way to insult Antony and Curio and drove them out of the senate in disgrace. So of his own accord he gave Caesar the best possible excuse for taking action and supplied him with excellent material for propaganda among his troops.[85] For Caesar could now show his soldiers these distinguished men of high office in the state who had fled from Rome in hired carts and dressed as slaves, as they had had to do in their fear when they slipped out of the city.

32. Caesar had with him at the time no more than 300 cavalry and 5,000 legionary soldiers. The rest of his army had been left on the other side of the Alps and was to be brought up to him by officers who had been sent back to do so. He saw, however, that the very beginning and the first stages of his enterprise did not require the use of large forces for the time being. Better results could be obtained by surprise, daring and taking the quickest advantage of the moment; it would be easier, he thought, to strike panic into his enemies by acting in a way which they never expected than it would be to force them back after having first made all the preparations for a regular invasion. So he ordered his centurions and other officers to take just their swords, leaving their other arms behind, and to occupy the large Gallic city of Ariminum; they were to avoid all disturbance and bloodshed as far as they possibly could. He put Hortensius[86] in command of this force and himself spent the day in public, watching gladiators at their exercises. In the late afternoon he had a bath, dressed and went into the banqueting hall where he spoke for a little time with the guests who had been invited to dinner. When it was beginning to get dark he rose from the table and, after addressing a few polite words to the

majority of his guests, whom he begged to remain there until he came back, he went away. He had already given instructions to a few of his friends to follow him, not all on the same route, but some on one way and some on another. He himself got into one of the hired carriages and, setting out at first on a different road, finally turned and took the road to Ariminum. When he came to the river (it is called the Rubicon) which forms the frontier between Cisalpine Gaul and the rest of Italy he became full of thought; for now he was drawing nearer and nearer to the dreadful step, and his mind wavered as he considered what a tremendous venture it was upon which he was engaged. He began to go more slowly and then ordered a halt. For a long time he weighed matters up silently in his own mind, irresolute between the two alternatives. In these moments his purpose was constantly changing. For some time too he discussed his perplexities with his friends who were there, among whom was Asinius Pollio.[87] He thought of the sufferings which his crossing of the river would bring upon mankind and he imagined the fame of the story of it which they would leave to posterity. Finally, in a sort of passion, as though he were casting calculation aside and abandoning himself to whatever lay in store for him, making use too of the expression which is frequently used by those who are on the point of committing themselves to desperate and unpredictable chances, 'Let the die be cast,' he said, and with these words hurried to cross the river. From now on he marched at full speed and before dawn had made his way into and occupied Ariminum. It is said too that on the night before he crossed the river he had an unnatural dream. He dreamed that he was committing incest with his own mother.

33. Ariminum was captured and the broad gates of war were opened on every land and sea alike. The boundaries of the province were down and so was all law and order in the state. Men and women had, on other occasions in the past, fled from one part of Italy to another in terror; but now the impression was rather one of whole cities on the move in a panic-stricken course from one site to the next. Rome was, as it were, inundated as people came in from all the surrounding towns,

escaping from their homes. The authority of magistrates and
the eloquence of orators were ineffective to exert control, and
in this great and stormy tempest the city nearly allowed itself
to go under. On every side violently opposed feelings were
expressed in violent action. Those who were pleased with what
had happened did not keep their feelings to themselves; they
were constantly meeting, as was inevitable in a large city, others
who viewed the situation with fear or anger, and their own easy
confidence with regard to the future naturally led to quarrels.
Pompey's own state of mind was already sufficiently disturbed
and it was made all the more confused by what he had to listen
to from other people. Some attacked him for having armed
Caesar against himself and the state, while others blamed him
for having allowed Lentulus to insult Caesar just at the time
when Caesar was prepared to give way and to accept a reasonable settlement. Favonius told him that now was the time for him
to stamp on the ground – a remark prompted by the fact that
Pompey had previously made a boastful kind of speech to the
senate in the course of which he had said that there was no need
for them to waste their time bothering about preparations for
the war, since, when it came, he had only to stamp with his foot
upon the earth in order to fill the whole of Italy with armies.

Even so, Pompey at this time had more troops available to
him than Caesar had. But no one would allow him to use his
own judgement. Inaccurate and panic-stricken reports kept on
coming in to the effect that Caesar was already close at hand
and sweeping everything before him. Under the influence of
these reports Pompey gave way and allowed himself to be
carried along in the general stream. He issued an edict declaring
that the city was in a state of anarchy, and abandoned Rome.
His orders were that the senate should follow him and that no
one should remain behind except those who preferred tyranny
to freedom and to their own country.

34. The consuls fled at once, without even making the sacrifices
usual before leaving. Most of the senators fled too, taking as
much of their own property as they could lay their hands on
and hurrying off with it as quickly as if they had been robbing

their neighbours. Even some of those who previously had been very much on Caesar's side now became so startled that they were unable to think clearly, and, though there was no need for them to do so, joined in the great rush out of the city. And a sad sight it was indeed to see Rome, with this tempest bearing down on her, like a ship abandoned by the crew and allowed to drift into any rocks that lay in her way. Still, sad as it was to leave the city, people were prepared, for Pompey's sake, to think that in exile they were at home, and they left Rome feeling that it had become Caesar's camp. Even Labienus,[88] one of Caesar's greatest friends, who had been a deputy commander to him and had fought for him with the greatest gallantry in all the Gallic wars, now left him and came over to Pompey.

Caesar sent Labienus' money and baggage after him.[89] He then marched against Domitius who was holding Corfinium with a force of thirty cohorts.[90] Caesar pitched his camp near the city and Domitius, despairing of being able to defend the place, asked his doctor, who was a slave of his, to give him poison. He took the dose that was given him and drank it with the intention of putting an end to his life. Soon afterwards he heard that Caesar was behaving with the most remarkable kindness to his prisoners; he then began to bewail his fate and to reproach himself for having been too hasty in coming to his resolution. His doctor, however, cheered him up by informing him that what he had drunk was not poison at all, but only a sleeping draught. Domitius was delighted. He got up and went to Caesar who gave him his right hand to guarantee his pardon. Domitius deserted him, however, and went back to Pompey. When the news of these events reached Rome, people became easier in their minds and some of the fugitives came back to the city.

35. Caesar took over the army of Domitius and also overran and incorporated in his own forces all the contingents of troops which were being raised for Pompey in the various cities. He was now strong and formidable enough and he marched directly against Pompey himself. Pompey, however, did not wait for him. He fled to Brundisium, sent the consuls and the army over

in advance to Dyrrhachium, and soon afterwards, as Caesar drew near, sailed off himself.[91] (All this will be described in detail in my *Life of Pompey*.) Though Caesar would have liked to pursue him at once, he had no ships; so he turned back to Rome. In sixty days and without any bloodshed he had become master of the whole of Italy.

He found the city in a more settled state than he had expected. Many members of the senate were still there, and he addressed them in a courteous and deferential way, inviting them to send a deputation to Pompey to discuss reasonable terms for a peace. No one, however, would act on this proposal – either because they were frightened of Pompey, whom they had abandoned, or because they thought that Caesar's words were only spoken for effect and that he did not really mean what he said.

When Metellus,[92] the tribune, tried to prevent Caesar from taking money from the state reserve and began to cite various laws, Caesar told him that there was a time for laws and a time for arms. 'As for you,' he said, 'if you don't like what is being done, get out of the way for the present. War has no use for free speech. But when I have laid down my arms and come to terms, then you can come back again and make your speeches to the people. And let me point out that in saying this I am giving up my own just rights. In fact you are my prisoner, you and all the rest of the party acting against me whom I have in my hands.' After saying this to Metellus, Caesar went towards the doors of the treasury and, as the keys could not be found, sent for smiths and ordered them to break the doors down. Metellus once again began to object and there were some who applauded him for doing so. Caesar then raised his voice and threatened to kill him if he did not stop interfering. 'And, young man,' he said, 'you know well enough that I dislike saying this more than I would dislike doing it.' These words had their effect. Metellus went off in a fright and for the future all Caesar's demands for material for the war were promptly and readily obeyed.

36. He now marched into Spain.[93] He had decided first of all to drive out of that country Pompey's commanders, Afranius

and Varro,[94] and to gain possession of their armies and provinces. He would then march against Pompey without having to leave any enemy forces behind his back. In this campaign he often took the personal risk of being cut off and captured, and his army was in the greatest danger because of lack of food; yet he went on relentlessly following up the enemy, offering battle and hemming them in with fortifications, until by main force he had made himself the master of their camps and of their forces. The commanders, however, got away and escaped to Pompey.

37. When Caesar returned to Rome, his father-in-law, Piso, urged him to send a deputation to Pompey to discuss terms of peace; but Isauricus, with the idea of pleasing Caesar, spoke against this proposal. The senate then appointed Caesar dictator.[95] In this capacity he recalled exiles, gave back their civil rights to the children of those who had suffered under Sulla, relieved the burdens of debtors by remitting some of the interest on their debts, and, after dealing with a few other public measures of the same kind, within eleven days resigned from his position of supreme power. He had himself declared consul with Servilius Isauricus as his colleague, and then set out for the war.

With 600 picked cavalry and 5 legions he hurried by forced marches past the rest of his army and put to sea at the time of the winter solstice at the beginning of January.[96] This month corresponds nearly enough to the Athenian Poseideon. After crossing the Ionian Gulf, he captured Oricum and Apollonia, and sent back his transports to Brundisium for the soldiers who had been left behind on the march. These soldiers were no longer as young as they had been; they were tired out by the number of campaigns in which they had fought; and they were full of complaints against Caesar so long as they were on the road. 'Where on earth will this man take us in the end? He keeps dragging us around, as though we could never get tired out and never feel anything. Even swords get worn out with striking, and after such a long time of service one takes some care of one's shield and breastplate. Our wounds, if nothing

else, ought to make Caesar realize that the men he commands
are human beings and that we are subject to the same pains
and sufferings as other mortals. Not even the gods can put back
the winter or make the stormy season at sea non-existent. Yet
this man goes on taking risks as though he were running away
from his enemies instead of chasing after them.'

So they talked as they marched on without hurrying towards
Brundisium. But when they got there and found that Caesar
had set sail, they changed their tune. They cursed themselves as
traitors to their commander-in-chief; they cursed their officers
for not having made them march more quickly; and, sitting on
the cliffs, they looked out over the open sea towards Epirus,
watching for the ships which were to take them across to their
commander.

38. Meanwhile at Apollonia Caesar was in difficulties and his
mind was in a most disturbed state. The army he had with him
was not big enough for him to be able to engage the enemy,
and the rest of his army across the sea was taking a long time
to arrive. Finally he decided on a most dangerous plan, which
was to embark without anyone's knowledge in a twelve-oared
boat and to make the crossing to Brundisium, though the enemy
with their large fleets were in complete command of the sea.[97]
So he went aboard at night after disguising himself in the dress
of a slave, and, throwing himself down on the bottom of the
vessel as though he were a person of no importance, stayed
there quietly. The River Aoüs was carrying the boat down to
the sea, and usually there was a morning breeze which drove
back the waves and made the mouth of the river calm; but on
this occasion the breeze had been overpowered by a strong
wind which had got up during the night and was blowing from
the sea. So the river boiled up angrily at the point where it was
confronted with the oncoming breakers of the sea; what with
the roughness of the water, the great din and the violent swell
beating the current back, the master of the boat found it impossible to force his way forward and ordered the crew to come
about with the intention of going back again. Caesar, seeing
what he was doing, came forward and disclosed himself. The

master of the boat was terrified at seeing him there, but Caesar took him by the hand and said: 'Go ahead, my friend. Be bold and fear nothing. You have got Caesar and Caesar's fortune with you in your boat.' The sailors forgot about the storm. They put all the strength they had into their rowing and did their utmost to force their way down the river. However, it proved an impossible task, and, after the ship had taken in a lot of water and Caesar had put himself into great danger at the very mouth of the river, he very reluctantly allowed the captain to put about. When he got to land he was met by his soldiers who came crowding round him, full of complaints at the way he had behaved and indignant at the fact that he seemed to have thought that he could not conquer with their aid and theirs alone; instead of this, they said, he had got worried and risked his life for the sake of the army across the sea, as though he could not trust the army which he had with him.

39. After this Antony[98] sailed in with the forces from Brundisium and this gave Caesar sufficient confidence to challenge Pompey to battle. Pompey was in an excellent position and could get ample supplies both by land and sea, while Caesar from the very beginning was badly off for supplies and later on was in very serious difficulties because of shortage of food.[99] His soldiers, however, dug up some kind of root which, when mixed with milk, they used for food. On one occasion they made the mixture into loaves, ran up to the enemies' outposts, and threw the loaves inside or tossed them from hand to hand, shouting out that as long as the earth produced such roots they would not give up blockading Pompey. However, Pompey tried to prevent both these loaves and the words which had accompanied them from reaching the main body of his troops. For his soldiers were out of heart. They were thoroughly frightened of the ferocity and physical toughness of their enemies, who seemed to them to be like some species of wild beasts.

Desultory fighting was constantly taking place around Pompey's fortifications and in all these engagements Caesar had the better of things, except on one occasion, when his men were so badly defeated that he was in danger of losing his camp.

To this attack of Pompey no sort of resistance was made by Caesar's men. The trenches were filled with their dead bodies and others, driven back in headlong flight, fell in front of the walls and ramparts of their own camp. Though Caesar met them and tried to make them turn back, his efforts were entirely unsuccessful. When he attempted to grasp hold of the standards himself, the standard bearers threw them away, so that the enemy captured thirty-two of them. Indeed Caesar himself was very nearly killed. He had seized hold of the arm of one of the men running past him, a big strong fellow, and was telling him to stop and to turn round and face the enemy, when the man, in his panic-stricken state of mind, raised his sword to cut Caesar down. But before he could strike the blow, Caesar's shield-bearer lopped his arm off at the shoulder. At this time Caesar must have considered his own position quite desperate. For when Pompey, for some reason or other (possibly over-caution), instead of putting the finishing stroke to his great success, retired as soon as he had driven the routed enemy inside their camp, Caesar, who was with his friends, remarked to them as he was leaving them: 'Today the enemy would have won, if they had a commander who was a winner.' He then retired to his tent and lay down. This was the most miserable night that he had ever passed and he spent it in hard and perplexed thinking. He came to the conclusion that his strategy had been all wrong. The fertile country and rich cities of Macedonia and Thessaly were there before him, but instead of carrying the war in that direction, he had settled down here by the sea, over which the enemy had complete command, and the result was that so far from besieging the enemy with his army he was being besieged himself through lack of provisions. So he passed this disturbed night in gloomy reflection on the extreme difficulty of his position, and in the morning he broke camp. He had decided to lead his army into Macedonia against Scipio.[100] He would then either draw Pompey after him into a district where he would fight without his present advantage of being supplied by sea, or else he would overpower Scipio, if Scipio were left without support.

40. This new move of Caesar's filled Pompey's soldiers and the officers by whom he was surrounded with confidence. They assumed that Caesar was defeated and was running away, and were eager to get their hands on him. Pompey himself was more cautious and did not want to risk a battle on which so much would depend. He was excellently supplied with everything necessary for a long war, and he thought that a war of attrition was the best way to deal with Caesar's army, which, in his view, could not retain its zest and vigour for long. Caesar's best troops were certainly experienced and showed a fighting spirit in all engagements that was irresistible; but the years were having their effect on them – years of long marches, of building camps, of blockading cities, of spending whole nights under arms. Further hardships were more than their physical strength could stand, and, as their strength failed, so did their willingness to go into action. At this time, too, it was said that some kind of an infectious disease was raging through Caesar's army, a disease caused by the bad food they had to eat. And – most important consideration of all – since Caesar was both short of money and short of provisions, it seemed likely that before long his army would break up of its own accord.

41. For these reasons Pompey was against fighting a battle. No one, however, agreed with him except Cato, whose motive was to spare the lives of his fellow citizens. Cato, indeed, even at the sight of the enemy dead in the last battle, who came to the number of a thousand, had burst into tears and turned away with his face covered up. But all the rest were indignant with Pompey for avoiding battle. They goaded him on by giving him such nicknames as 'Agamemnon' and 'King of Kings', implying that what he really wanted was to hold on to his supreme command and satisfy his own vanity by having so many other commanders serving under him and constantly coming to his tent. Favonius, who affected Cato's way of speaking his mind freely, was fool enough to go about complaining that this year too they would not be able to enjoy the figs of Tusculum simply because of Pompey's passion for holding on to power. Afranius, too, had just arrived from Spain. His bad generalship there had

made him suspected of having been bribed to betray his army. Now he kept asking why they would not fight with this merchant who was supposed to have bought the provinces from him. So, with all this kind of talk, Pompey was reluctantly driven to follow Caesar and to offer battle.

Meanwhile Caesar's march had been a difficult one. No one would sell him provisions, since, after his recent defeat, no one thought much of his chances. But his capture of the Thessalian city of Gomphi enabled him not only to provide food for his soldiers but also, in a somewhat unusual way, to restore them to health. In this city they came upon a great quantity of wine which they drank extremely freely. After this they went on marching in a merry kind of drunken orgy and, as the result of being intoxicated, changed the whole habit of their constitution, shook off their illness and became quite well again.

42. When both armies had entered the plain of Pharsalus and encamped there, Pompey again began to think along the lines of his previous resolution, which was against fighting. He was also affected by some unlucky apparitions and by a vision which he saw in the night. He dreamed that he saw himself in his theatre being applauded by the Romans ... * But those who were with him were so confident and so certain of a victory that still remained to be won that Domitius and Spinther and Scipio were already quarrelling bitterly among themselves as to who should succeed Caesar as chief pontiff.[101] Many people too were sending to Rome to make arrangements for renting in advance houses that would be suitable for praetors and consuls, on the assumption that as soon as the war was over they would be holding these offices. The cavalry in particular were impatient for battle. What with the shining armour, the well-fed horses and the personal beauty of the riders, this was a splendidly equipped force, and so far as numbers went they had every reason to be confident, since there were 7,000 of them to

* Translator's footnote: Some words or sentences have fallen out of the text. The dream is more fully described in the Life of Pompey.

Caesar's 1,000. The numbers of the infantry too were unequal. Pompey had 45,000 against Caesar's 22,000.

43. Caesar called his soldiers together and told them that Corfinius was bringing him two legions and was close at hand, and that besides these were fifteen cohorts under Calenus[102] stationed at Athens and Megara. He asked them whether they wanted to wait for these reinforcements or whether they would face the decisive battle by themselves unaided. The soldiers all shouted out asking him not to wait for the others, but on the contrary, to use all his skill as a general to bring them to close quarters with the enemy as soon as possible.

When he was holding a service of purification for the army and had just sacrificed the first animal, the professional prophet in attendance at once said that there would be a decisive battle with the enemy within three days. Caesar asked him whether he could see in the animal's entrails anything which suggested a favourable result, and the prophet replied: 'That is a question which you yourself are best fitted to answer. What the gods reveal is that there will be a complete change and a revolution from the present state of affairs to the opposite. Therefore, if you think that you are doing well as things are now, you must expect bad fortune; but if you think that you are doing badly, then your fortune is good.'

And on the night before the battle, as Caesar was making the rounds of his sentries about midnight, a bright flaming light was seen in the sky which seemed to pass over Caesar's camp in a blaze of fire and then to fall into the camp of Pompey. It was observed too during the morning watch that a kind of panic and confusion seemed to have broken out among the enemy.

Nevertheless, Caesar was not expecting to fight at all on that day. He had begun to break camp with the intention of marching to Scotussa,

44. when, just as the tents had been struck, his scouts rode up and told him that the enemy were coming down into the plain to give battle. Caesar was delighted at the news. He made his

prayers and vows to the gods and then drew up his line in three divisions. He put Domitius Calvinus[103] in command of the centre; Antony commanded the left wing and he himself took the right, where he intended to fight with the tenth legion. He saw, however, that the enemy cavalry were being drawn up opposite him and, since he considered both their fine appearance and their numbers formidable, he gave instructions for six cohorts from the rear of the whole army to move round to him out of sight of the enemy. He placed this force behind the right wing and told them what to do when the enemy cavalry charged.

On the other side Pompey himself commanded the right wing and Domitius[104] the left, while Pompey's father-in-law Scipio commanded the centre. All the cavalry were concentrated on the left wing, with the idea of encircling the enemy's right and thoroughly routing the division where Caesar himself was in command. They thought that no formation of infantry, in whatever depth, could resist them, and expected that the enemy must necessarily be broken and shattered by the shock of so many horsemen all charging together.

When both sides were ready to give the signal for battle Pompey ordered his infantry to stand still in close order with their arms at the ready and to wait for the enemy's attack until they were within the range of a javelin's throw. This is another of the points where Caesar criticizes Pompey's generalship, saying that he appears not to have been aware that when the first contact with the enemy is made with an impetus and on the run, it gives extra force to the blows and is a most important element in the general kindling up and firing of the men's spirits.

As Caesar himself was just about to order his line to advance and was already going up towards the front, his eyes fell first on one of his centurions, a man who had proved reliable to him in the past and who had had experience of many campaigns. He was now urging on the men under his command and challenging them to compete with him in showing courage in action. Caesar called out to him[105] by name and said: 'Well, Gaius Crassinius, what are our prospects? How are we feeling about it?' Then Crassinius stretched out his right hand and shouted at the top of his voice: 'We shall win, Caesar, and win gloriously. And as for me, you shall praise me today, whether I am alive or dead at the end of it.' With these words he charged forward at the double and, followed by the 120 soldiers under his command, was the first man to engage the enemy. He hacked his way through the first rank and was still pressing forward, cutting down men on all sides of him, when he was stopped by a blow of a sword which was thrust into his mouth with such force that the point came out at the back of his neck.

45. So the two infantry armies joined battle and fought hand to hand. And now Pompey's cavalry rode up on the flank in a proud array and deployed their squadrons in order to encircle Caesar's right wing. Before they could charge, the cohorts which Caesar had posted behind him ran forward and, instead of hurling their javelins, as they usually did, or even thrusting at the thighs and legs of the enemy, aimed at their eyes and stabbed upwards at their faces. Caesar had instructed them to do this because he believed that these young men, who had not had much experience of battle and the wounds of battle but who particularly plumed themselves on their good looks, would dislike more than anything the idea of being attacked in this way and, fearing both the danger of the moment and the possibility of disfigurement for the future, would not be able to stand up to it. And in fact this was exactly what happened. They could not face the upward thrusts of the javelins or even the sight of the iron points; they turned their heads away and covered them up in their anxiety to keep their faces unscarred. Soon they were in complete disorder, and finally, in a most disgraceful way, they turned and fled, thereby ruining everything, since the cohorts who had defeated the cavalry at once swept round behind the infantry, fell on their rear, and began to cut them to pieces.

When Pompey, from the other wing, saw his cavalry routed and scattered, he was no longer the same person as before, and no longer remembered that he was Pompey the Great. Looking more like a man whom some god has deprived of his wits, he went off, without saying a word, to his tent and there sat down and waited for what was to come, until his whole army was routed and the enemy had begun to attack the fortifications of his camp and were fighting with the detachments who were guarding it. At this point he seemed to come to his senses. The only words he uttered were, so they say, 'What, into the camp too?' and, with these words, he took off his general's clothes and, changing into other clothes more suitable for a fugitive, stole away. I shall describe in my *Life of Pompey* what happened to him later, and how he put himself into the hands of the Egyptians and was murdered.

46. Caesar, when he came up to Pompey's camp and saw the dead bodies already lying on the ground and others still being cut down, groaned aloud and said, 'They made this happen; they drove me to it. If I had dismissed my army, I, Gaius Caesar, after all my great victories, would have been condemned in their law courts.'[106] Asinius Pollio says that these words, which Caesar afterwards wrote down in Greek, were spoken at the time in Latin. He also says that most of the dead were servants who were killed when the camp was taken, and that not more than 6,000 of the regular soldiers lost their lives. Most of those who were taken alive Caesar incorporated in his own legions, and he gave a free pardon to a number of prominent people. Among these was Brutus, who afterwards killed him. It is said that Caesar was very distressed when Brutus was not to be found, and that he was particularly delighted when, in the end, he was brought to him alive and well.

47. There were a number of signs from heaven foreshadowing this victory, and the most remarkable of these appeared at Tralles. Here, in the temple of Victory, there stood a statue of Caesar. The ground all round the statue was naturally hard and was paved with slabs of stone; yet through this, they say, a palm tree shot up at the base of the statue. Then, at Patavium, there was a well-known prophet called Gaius Cornelius, who was a fellow-citizen and an acquaintance of Livy the historian. On the day of the battle this man happened to be sitting at his prophetic work and first, according to Livy, he realized that the

battle was taking place at that very moment and said to those who were present that now was the time when matters were being decided and now the troops were going into action; then he had a second look and, when he had examined the signs, he jumped up in a kind of ecstasy and cried out: 'Caesar, the victory is yours!' Those who were standing by were amazed at him, but he took the garland from his head and solemnly swore that he would not wear it again until facts had proved that his art had revealed the truth to him. Livy, certainly, is most emphatic that this really happened.

48. To commemorate his victory Caesar gave the people of Thessaly their freedom. He then went in pursuit of Pompey.[107] On reaching Asia he gave their freedom to the people of Cnidus – an act of kindness done for the sake of Theopompus, the author of the collection of fables. He also cut down by a third the taxes of all the inhabitants of the province of Asia.

He arrived at Alexandria just after Pompey's death.[108] When Theodotus came to him with Pompey's head, Caesar refused to look at him, but he took Pompey's signet ring and shed tears as he did so. He offered help and his own friendship to all who had been friends and companions of Pompey and who, without anywhere to go to, had been arrested by the King of Egypt. And he wrote to his friends in Rome to say that, of all the results of his victory, what gave him the most pleasure was that he was so often able to save the lives of fellow citizens who had fought against him.

As for the war in Egypt, some say that it need never have taken place, that it was brought on by Caesar's passion for Cleopatra and that it did him little credit while involving him in great danger. Others blame the king's party for it, and particularly the eunuch Pothinus, who was the most influential person at the court. He had recently killed Pompey, had driven out Cleopatra, and was now secretly plotting against Caesar. Because of this, they say, Caesar now began to sit up for whole nights on end at drinking parties, in order to be sure that he was properly guarded. Even openly Pothinus made himself intolerable, belittling and insulting Caesar both in his words and his actions. For instance, the soldiers were given rations of the oldest and worst possible grain, and Pothinus told them that they must put up with it and learn to like it, since they were eating food that did not belong to them; and at official dinners he gave orders that wooden and earthenware dishes should be used, on the pretext that Caesar had taken all the gold and silver in payment of a debt. The father of the present king did in fact owe Caesar 17½ million drachmas, and, though Caesar had previously remitted part of this debt to the king's children, he now demanded 10 million for the support of his army. Pothinus suggested that for the time being he should go away and attend to more important matters, promising that later on they would be delighted to pay the money; but Caesar told him that Egyptians were the last people he would choose for his advisers, and secretly he sent for Cleopatra from the country.

49. Cleopatra, taking only one of her friends with her (Apollodorus the Sicilian), embarked in a small boat and landed at the palace when it was already getting dark. Since there seemed to be no other way of getting in unobserved, she stretched herself out at full length inside a sleeping bag, and Apollodorus, after tying up the bag, carried it indoors to Caesar. This little trick of Cleopatra's, which showed her provocative impudence, is said to have been the first thing about her which captivated Caesar, and, as he grew to know her better, he was overcome by her charm and arranged that she and her brother should be reconciled and should share the throne of Egypt together. Everyone was invited to a banquet to celebrate the reconciliation, and, while the banquet was in progress, a servant of Caesar who acted as his barber and who, because of his unexampled cowardice, was in the habit of looking into everything, listening to every scrap of gossip and generally having something to do with everything that was going on, managed to find out that the general Achillas and the eunuch Pothinus were plotting together against Caesar. Once Caesar had discovered this, he set a guard round the banqueting hall and had Pothinus killed. Achillas, however, escaped to the camp and

involved Caesar in a full-scale war and one that was very difficult to fight, since he had a great city and a large army against
him and only a few troops with which to defend himself. First
of all the enemy dammed up the canals and he was in danger
of being cut off from his water supply. Then they tried to
intercept his communications by sea and he was forced to deal
with this danger by setting fire to the ships in the docks. This
was the fire which, starting from the dockyards, destroyed the
great library. And thirdly, he was hard pressed during the fighting that took place on Pharos. He had sprung down from the
mole into a small boat and was trying to go to the help of his
men who were engaged in battle, but the Egyptians sailed up
against him from all directions, and he was forced to throw
himself into the sea and swim, only just managing to escape.
This was the time when, according to the story, he was holding a number of papers in his hand and would not let them
go, though he was being shot at from all sides and was often
under water. Holding the papers above the surface with one
hand, he swam with the other. (His small boat had been sunk
immediately.)

Finally, however, after the king had gone over to the side of
the enemy, Caesar marched against him and defeated him in
battle. Many fell in this battle and the king himself was one of
the missing. Caesar then set out for Syria. He left Cleopatra as
Queen of Egypt, and a little later she had a son by him, whom
the Alexandrians called Caesarion.[109]

50. From Syria he went to Asia when he heard that Domitius[110]
had been defeated by Pharnaces, the son of Mithridates, and
had fled from Pontus with the few troops that remained. He
heard too that Pharnaces was making the fullest possible use of
his victory: he was in control of Bithynia and Cappadocia, was
aiming at taking over the country called Lesser Armenia and
was encouraging all the princes and tetrarchs there to revolt.
So, with three legions, he marched against him immediately.
He fought him in a great battle near the city of Zela, drove
him out of Pontus and annihilated his army. In describing the
sharpness and rapidity of this battle Caesar wrote to Amantius,

one of his friends in Rome, and used just three words: 'Came, saw, conquered.' In Latin, however, the words have the same inflexional ending, and this gives them a remarkable effect of brevity and concentration.[111]

51. After this he crossed over to Italy and came to Rome. It was now a year since he had been chosen dictator for the second time though previously this office had never been held for a whole year.[112] And for the following year he was proclaimed consul.[113] People spoke badly of him because, after his soldiers had mutinied and killed two men of praetorian rank, Galba and Cosconius,[114] the only reprimand which he gave to them was to address them as 'Citizens' instead of 'Fellow-soldiers'; after which he gave each man 1,000 drachmas and a large allotment of land in Italy. Other things which were held against him were the irresponsible behaviour of Dolabella,[115] the greed of Amantius, the drunkenness of Antony and the conduct of Corfinius, who enlarged and refurnished Pompey's house, as though it was not grand enough for him. All these things caused much ill-feeling at Rome. Caesar was quite aware of what was going on and disapproved of it, but, because of the general political situation, he was forced to make use of those who would do his will.

52. After the battle at Pharsalus, Cato and Scipio had escaped to Africa, where, with the help of King Juba,[116] they got together a considerable force. Caesar decided to make an expedition against them and crossed over to Sicily about the time of the winter solstice.[117] Here he pitched his own tent on the beach, wishing to make it clear immediately to his officers that they need have no hopes of wasting time by staying in the island. And as soon as the wind blew from the right quarter, he embarked and put to sea with 3,000 infantry and a few cavalry. He landed this force without being observed and then put to sea again, since he was anxious about the larger part of his army. He found them, however, already at sea and brought them all into camp.

He discovered that the enemy were deriving much encouragement from an ancient oracle to the effect that the family of the Scipios must always be victorious in Africa. Here it is difficult to say whether Caesar was in a jesting spirit making a mock of the Scipio in command of the enemy, or whether he was quite seriously trying to appropriate the prophecy for himself. What he did was this. He had with him a man who was a completely negligible character except that he belonged to the family of the Africani. (He was called Scipio Sallustio.) This man Caesar put at the head of his troops in battle as though he were the commander. And Caesar was forced to engage the enemy often and to seek battle with them, since there was not enough food for his men or provisions for his horses.[118] In fact they had to feed the horses on seaweed with the salt washed out of it and a little grass mixed with it to make it palatable. The fast-moving Numidians were everywhere in great numbers and controlled the country. There was one occasion when Caesar's cavalry were off duty and were being entertained by an African who was dancing and playing the flute at the same time in a most remarkable manner. The cavalry-men had given their horses to their servants to hold and were sitting on the ground enjoying the performance, when the enemy suddenly swept all round them and attacked, killing some of them on the spot, and chasing the rest of them, who were flying in disorder, right up to their camp. If Caesar himself, with Asinius Pollio, had not come outside the ramparts to their aid and stopped their flight, the war would have been over then and there. There was also an occasion in another battle when the enemy had got the better of things in the fighting and Caesar, so it is said, seized hold of the standard-bearer who was running away and, gripping him by the neck, made him face about saying: 'Look, that's where the enemy are.'

53. Scipio was encouraged by these successes to risk a decisive action. He left Afranius and Juba encamped each a short distance from the other and himself began to fortify a camp beyond a lake near the city of Thapsus, with the idea that this camp should serve the entire army as a base from which to go into action and as a place into which they could retreat. But while

he was engaged on this operation, Caesar, marching with
incredible speed, made his way through thick woods which
disguised his approach, outflanked one division of the enemy,
and attacked another from the front. After routing them, he
made full use of his opportunity and of the fortune which was
going his way. At the first attack he captured the camp of
Afranius, and at the first attack he overran and sacked the camp
of the Numidians, from which Juba ran away. So in a small
part of a single day he made himself master of three camps and
killed 50,000 of the enemy without losing as many as fifty of
his own men.

This is the account given by some authorities of the battle.
Others say that Caesar was not present personally at the action:
he began to suffer from an attack of his usual illness just as he
was drawing up his troops and ordering them to their positions,
and, being aware at once that the illness was coming on, and
finding that he was already losing the use of his faculties, he
was carried, before they entirely left him, to a tower nearby,
where he rested while the battle was going on. Of the men of
consular or praetorian rank who survived the battle, some
killed themselves as they were being rounded up and others,
who were captured, were put to death by Caesar.

54. Cato was in command of the city of Utica and for that
reason had taken no part in the battle.[119] Being extremely anxious to capture him alive, Caesar hurried to Utica, but found
that he had committed suicide. The news clearly had a disturbing effect on Caesar, though it is difficult to say exactly
why. Certainly he exclaimed: 'Cato, I must grudge you your
death, as you grudged me the opportunity of giving you your
life.' But the essay which he wrote later attacking Cato after his
death does not bear the traces of a kindly or forgiving temper.
After such a pitiless outpouring of anger against the man when
he was dead, one can scarcely imagine that he would have
spared him when he was alive. And yet from the kindness which
he showed to Cicero and Brutus and very many others who had
fought against him it may be inferred that even this essay was
written not so much out of his hatred for Cato as from a desire

to justify his own policy. The essay came to be written because Cicero had composed a work in praise of Cato, which he entitled *Cato*. This was widely read, as was natural considering that it was the work of so great a master of oratory writing on such an excellent theme. Caesar, however, was annoyed, since he considered that Cicero's praise of the dead Cato amounted to an attack upon himself; and so he wrote his own essay, called *Anti-Cato*, in which he put down everything that could be said against him. Both essays have many admirers, just as Cicero and Caesar have.

55. On his return to Rome from Africa Caesar's first reaction was to make a speech to the people in order to impress them with the extent of his victory. He claimed that he had conquered a country large enough to supply the public every year with 200,000 Attic bushels of grain and 3 million pounds of olive oil. He then celebrated three triumphs – one for Egypt, one for Pontus, and one for Africa.[120] The last of these was officially for his victory over King Juba and not for his victory over Scipio. On this occasion Juba, the son of the king and a mere infant, was carried in the triumphal procession, and indeed he was the most fortunate of captives, since instead of growing up as a barbarous Numidian he won a place for himself in the end among the most learned historians of Greece.[121] After the triumphs Caesar gave large rewards to his soldiers and entertained the people with banquets and shows. He gave a feast to the whole people at one time, using 20,000 dining couches for the occasion; and he provided gladiatorial shows and naval battles in honour of his daughter Julia, who had died long before this.

After the shows a census of the people was taken. The old lists had contained 320,000 names: now there were only 150,000 – a measure of the disaster caused by the civil wars and of the great loss suffered by the people of Rome. And this is leaving out of the account all the misfortunes which had overtaken the rest of Italy and the provinces.

56. When all this business was over Caesar was declared consul for the fourth time and set out for Spain against the sons of

Pompey.[122] Though they were still young men, they had got together an amazingly large army and showed that they had the daring and courage to command it. In fact they put Caesar into a position of extreme danger. The great battle was fought near the city of Munda. In this battle Caesar, seeing his men being pressed back and making only a feeble resistance, ran through the ranks among the soldiers and shouted out to them: 'Are you not ashamed to take me and hand me over to these boys?' It was only with great difficulty and after exerting himself to the utmost that he broke the enemy's resistance. He killed over 30,000 of them, but he lost 1,000 of the best troops in his own army. As he was leaving the battlefield he said to his friends that he had often before struggled for victory, but this was the first time that he had had to fight for his life. He won this victory on the day of the feast of Bacchus, the day on which, it is said, four years previously Pompey had set out for the war. The younger of Pompey's sons escaped, but after a few days the head of the elder was brought in by Deidius.

This was Caesar's last war. The triumph which he held for it displeased the Romans more than anything else had done.[123] For this was not a case of his having conquered foreign generals or kings of native tribes; on this occasion what he had done was to annihilate the children and the family of one who had been the greatest of the Romans, and who had met with misfortune. It did not seem right for Caesar to celebrate a triumph for the calamities of his country and to pride himself upon actions for which the only possible excuse that could be made in the eyes both of gods and of men was that they had been forced upon him. Previously too he had never sent dispatches or messengers to make an official announcement of victory in the civil wars; instead he had given the impression of being ashamed to take any credit for such actions.

57. Nevertheless, the Romans gave way before his good fortune and accepted the bit. The rule of one man would give them, they thought, a respite from the miseries of the civil wars, and so they appointed him dictator for life. This meant an undisguised tyranny; his power was now not only absolute but

perpetual. Cicero made the first proposals in the senate for conferring honours on him, and, great as they were, it could be maintained that they were not after all too great for a man. But others, in a kind of spirit of competition among themselves, proposed the most extravagant additions with the result that they made Caesar unpopular and hateful to even the least politically minded among the citizens because of the quite extraordinary pretentiousness of the titles decreed for him. His enemies are thought to have joined with his flatterers in getting these measures passed. They wanted to have every possible pretext to act against him and to appear to have good reasons on their side when they came to make an attempt upon his life. And certainly, in other ways, once the civil wars were over, no one could charge him with doing anything amiss. Indeed it is thought perfectly right that the temple of Clemency was dedicated as a thank-offering for his humane conduct after his victory. He not only pardoned many of those who had fought against him, but gave to some of them honours and offices besides – to Brutus, for instance, and to Cassius, both of whom were now praetors.[124] Pompey's statues too, had been thrown down, but Caesar would not tolerate this and had them put up again. It was on this occasion that Cicero said that Caesar, in setting up Pompey's statues, had firmly fixed and established his own. And when Caesar's friends advised him to have a bodyguard, many of them volunteering to serve in it themselves, Caesar refused to have anything to do with it. It was better, he said, to die once than always to be in fear of death. To surround himself with people's goodwill was, he thought, the best and the truest security, and so he again sought the favour of the people by giving them feasts and allowances of grain, and gratified his soldiers by founding new colonies, the most important of which were at Carthage and at Corinth. It so happened that these two cities had, in earlier days, both been captured at the same time,[125] and now they were both restored at the same time.

58. He dealt with the ruling class by promising praetorships and consulships in the future to some of them, and by winning over others with various offices and honours.[126] All were encouraged

to hope for his favour, since his great desire was to rule over subjects who accepted his rule. Thus, when the consul Maximus[127] died, Caesar made Caninius Rebilius consul for the one day that remained of the term of office.[128] Many people, it appears, went to the new consul to congratulate him and to escort him down to the forum, and this was when Cicero remarked: 'We'd better hurry, or he will be out of office before we get there.'

Caesar was born to do great things and to seek constantly for distinction. His many successes, so far from encouraging him to rest and to enjoy the fruits of all his labours, only served to kindle in him fresh confidence for the future, filling his mind with projects of still greater actions and with a passion for new glory, as though he had run through his stock of the old. His feelings can best be described by saying that he was competing with himself, as though he were someone else, and was struggling to make the future excel the past. He had made his plans and preparations for an expedition against the Parthians; after conquering them he proposed to march round the Black Sea by way of Hyrcania, the Caspian Sea and the Caucasus; he would then invade Scythia, would overrun all the countries bordering on Germany and Germany itself, and would then return to Italy by way of Gaul, thus completing the circuit of his empire which would be bounded on all sides by the ocean. While this expedition was going on he proposed to dig a canal through the isthmus of Corinth, and had already put Anienus in charge of this undertaking. He also planned to divert the Tiber just below the city into a deep channel which would bend round towards Circeium and come out into the sea at Terracina, so that there would be a safe and easy passage for merchantmen to Rome. Then too he proposed to drain the marshes by Pomentium and Setia and to create a plain which could be cultivated by many thousands of men. He also intended to build great breakwaters along the coast where the sea is nearest to Rome, to clear away all the obstructions which were a danger to shipping at Ostia, and to construct harbours and roadsteads big enough for the great fleets which would lie at anchor there.

All these were projects for the future.

59. His reform of the calendar, however, and the corrections made in the irregularity of reckoning time were not only studied by him with the greatest scientific skill, but were brought into effect and proved extremely useful.[129] In very ancient times there had been great confusion among the Romans with regard to the relation of the lunar to the solar year, with the result that festivals and days of sacrifice gradually got out of place and finally came to be celebrated at the very opposite seasons to what was originally intended. Nor was the confusion confined to the remote past. Even at this time most people were completely ignorant on these subjects; only the priests knew the proper time, and they, without giving any notice, would suddenly insert in the calendar the intercalary month known as Mercedonius. It is said that this month was first put in by King Numa who thus managed to find an unsatisfactory and short-lived remedy for the error in the adjustment of the sidereal and solar cycles. I have dealt with this subject in my *Life of Numa*. Caesar, however, put the problem before the best scholars and mathematicians of the day and, out of the various methods of correction already in use he formed a new method of his own which was more accurate than any of them. It is the one still used by the Romans, and it seems that they, better than all other people, have avoided the errors arising from the inequality between the lunar and solar years. Yet even this gave offence to those who looked at Caesar with envious eyes and resented his power. Certainly Cicero, the orator, when someone remarked that the constellation Lyra would rise next day, remarked: 'No doubt. By order' – implying that even the risings of the stars were something that people had to accept under compulsion.

60. But what made Caesar most openly and mortally hated was his passion to be made king. It was this which made the common people hate him for the first time, and it served as a most useful pretext for those others who had long hated him but had up to now disguised their feelings. Yet those who were trying to get this honour conferred on Caesar actually spread the story among the people that it was foretold in the Sibylline books

that Parthia could only be conquered by the Romans if the Roman army was led by a king;[130] and as Caesar was coming down from Alba to Rome they ventured to salute him as 'King', which caused a disturbance among the people. Caesar, upset by this himself, said that his name was not King but Caesar.[131] These words were received in total silence, and he went on his way looking far from pleased. Then there was an occasion when a number of extravagant honours had been voted for him in the senate, and Caesar happened to be sitting above the rostra. Here he was approached by the consuls and the praetors with the whole senate following behind; but instead of rising to receive them, he behaved to them as though they were merely private individuals and, after receiving their message, told them that his honours ought to be cut down rather than increased. This conduct of his offended not only the senate but the people as well, who felt that his treatment of the senators was an insult to the whole state. There was a general air of the deepest dejection and everyone who was in a position to do so went away at once. Caesar himself realized what he had done and immediately turned to go home. He drew back his toga and, uncovering his throat, cried out in a loud voice to his friends that he was ready to receive the blow from anyone who liked to give it to him. Later, however, he excused his behaviour on account of his illness, saying that those who suffer from it are apt to lose control of their senses if they address a large crowd while standing; in these circumstances they are very subject to fits of giddiness and may fall into convulsions and insensibility. This excuse, however, was not true. Caesar himself was perfectly willing to rise to receive the senate; but, so they say, one of his friends, or rather his flatterers, Cornelius Balbus,[132] restrained him from doing so. 'Remember,' he said, 'that you are Caesar. You are their superior and ought to let them treat you as such.'

61. Another thing which caused offence was his insulting treatment of the tribunes. The feast of the Lupercalia was being celebrated and at this time many of the magistrates and many young men of noble families run through the city naked, and,

in their jesting and merry-making, strike those whom they meet with shaggy thongs. And many women of high rank purposely stand in their way and hold out their hands to be struck, like children at school. They believe that the effect will be to give an easy delivery to those who are pregnant, and to help the barren to become pregnant. According to many writers this was in ancient times a shepherds' festival, and has also some connection with the Arcadian Lycaea. Caesar, sitting on a golden throne above the rostra and wearing a triumphal robe, was watching this ceremony; and Antony, who was consul at the time,[133] was one of those taking part in the sacred running. When he came running into the forum, the crowd made way for him. He was carrying a diadem with a wreath of laurel tied round it, and he held this out to Caesar. His action was followed by some applause, but it was not much and it was not spontaneous. But when Caesar pushed the diadem away from him, there was a general shout of applause. Antony then offered him the diadem for the second time, and again only a few applauded, though, when Caesar again rejected it, there was applause from everyone. Caesar, finding that the experiment had proved a failure, rose from his seat and ordered the wreath to be carried to the Capitol. It was then discovered that his statues had been decorated with royal diadems, and two of the tribunes, Flavius and Marullus,[134] went round the statues and tore down the decorations. They then found out who had been the first to salute Caesar as king, and led them off to prison. The people followed the tribunes and were loud in their applause, calling them Brutuses – because it was Brutus who first put an end to the line of kings in Rome and gave to the senate and the people the power that had previously been in the hands of one man. This made Caesar angry. He deprived Marullus and Flavius of their tribuneship and in speaking against them he insulted the people at the same time, frequently referring to them as Brutes and Cymaeans.

62. It was in these circumstances that people began to turn their thoughts towards Marcus Brutus. He was thought to be, on his

father's side, a descendant of the Brutus who had abolished the
monarchy; on his mother's side he came from another famous
family, the Servilii; and he was a son-in-law and a nephew of
Cato.[135] But his own zeal for destroying the new monarchy was
blunted by the honours and favours which he had received from
Caesar. It was not only that at Pharsalus after Pompey's flight
his own life had been spared and the lives of many of his friends
at his request; he was also a person in whom Caesar had
particular trust. He had been given the most important of the
praetorships for this very year[136] and was to be consul three
years later. For this post he had been preferred to Cassius, who
had been the rival candidate. Caesar, indeed, is said to have
admitted that Cassius had the better claims of the two for the
office. 'But,' he added, 'I cannot pass over Brutus.' And once,
when the conspiracy was already formed and some people were
actually accusing Brutus to Caesar of being involved in it,
Caesar laid his hand on his body and said to the accusers:
'Brutus will wait for this skin of mine' – implying that Brutus
certainly had the qualities which would entitle him to power,
but that he would not, for the sake of power, behave basely
and ungratefully.

However, those who were eager for the change and who
looked to Brutus as the only, or at least the most likely, man
to bring it about, used, without venturing to approach him
personally, to come by night and leave papers all over the
platform and the chair where he sat to do his work as praetor.
Most of the messages were of this kind: 'You are asleep, Brutus'
or 'You are no real Brutus.' And when Cassius observed that
they were having at least something of an effect on Brutus'
personal pride, he redoubled his own efforts to incite him
further. Cassius, as I have mentioned in my *Life of Brutus*, had
reasons of his own for hating Caesar;[137] moreover, Caesar was
suspicious of him, and once said to his friends: 'What do you
think Cassius is aiming at? Personally I am not too fond of
him; he is much too pale.' And on another occasion it is said
that, when Antony and Dolabella were accused to him of
plotting a revolution, Caesar said: 'I'm not much afraid of
these fat, long-haired people. It's the other type I'm more

frightened of, the pale thin ones' – by which he meant Brutus and Cassius.

63. Fate, however, seems to be not so much unexpected as unavoidable. Certainly, before this event, they say that strange signs were shown and strange apparitions were seen. As for the lights in the sky, the crashing sounds heard in all sorts of directions by night, the solitary specimens of birds coming down into the forum, all these, perhaps, are scarcely worth mentioning in connection with so great an event as this. But the philosopher Strabo says that a great crowd of men all on fire were seen making a charge; also that from the hand of a soldier's slave a great flame sprang out so that the hand seemed to the spectators to be burning away; but when the flame died out, the man was uninjured. He also says that when Caesar himself was making a sacrifice, the heart of the animal being sacrificed was missing – a very bad omen indeed, since in the ordinary course of nature no animal can exist without a heart. There is plenty of authority too for the following story: a soothsayer warned Caesar to be on his guard against a great danger on the day of the month of March which the Romans call the Ides;[138] and when this day had come, Caesar, on his way to the senate-house, met the soothsayer and greeted him jestingly with the words: 'Well, the Ides of March have come,' to which the soothsayer replied in a soft voice: 'Yes, but they have not yet gone.' And on the previous day Marcus Lepidus[139] was entertaining Caesar at supper and Caesar, according to his usual practice, happened to be signing letters as he reclined at table. Meanwhile the conversation turned to the question of what sort of death was the best, and, before anyone else could express a view on the subject, Caesar cried out: 'The kind that comes unexpectedly.' After this, when he was sleeping as usual by the side of his wife, all the doors and windows of the bedroom flew open at once; Caesar, startled by the noise and by the light of the moon shining down on him, noticed that Calpurnia was fast asleep, but she was saying something in her sleep which he could not make out and was groaning in an inarticulate way. In fact she was dreaming at that time that

she was holding his murdered body in her arms and was weeping over it. Though some say that it was a different dream
which she had. They say that she dreamed that she saw the
gable-ornament of the house torn down and for this reason
fancied that she was weeping and lamenting. (This ornament,
according to Livy, was put up by decree of the senate as a mark
of honour and distinction.) In any case, when it was day, she
implored Caesar, if it was possible, not to go out and begged
him to postpone the meeting of the senate; or if, she said, he
had no confidence in her dreams, then he ought to inquire about
the future by sacrifices and other methods of divination. Caesar
himself, it seems, was somewhat suspicious and afraid; for
he had never before noticed any womanish superstition in
Calpurnia and now he could see that she was in very great
distress. And when the prophets, after making many sacrifices,
told him that the omens were unfavourable, he decided to send
for Antony and to dismiss the senate.

64. At this point Decimus Brutus,[140] surnamed Albinus, intervened. Caesar had such confidence in him that he had made
him the second heir in his will, yet he was in the conspiracy
with the other Brutus and Cassius. Now, fearing that if Caesar
escaped this day the whole plot would come to light, he spoke
derisively of the prophets and told Caesar that he ought not to
give the senate such a good opportunity to complain that they
were being treated discourteously; they had met, he said, on
Caesar's instructions, and they were ready to vote unanimously
that Caesar should be declared king of all the provinces outside
Italy with the right of wearing a diadem in any other place
except Italy, whether on sea or land; but if, when they were
already in session, someone were to come and tell them that
they must go away for the time being and come back again
when Calpurnia had better dreams, it would be easy to imagine
what Caesar's enemies would have to say themselves and what
sort of a reception they would give to Caesar's friends when
they tried to prove that Caesar was not a slave-master or a
tyrant. If, however, he had really made up his mind to treat this
day as inauspicious, then, Decimus Brutus said, it would be

better for him to go himself to the senate, speak personally to the senators, and adjourn the meeting.

While he was speaking, Brutus took Caesar by the hand and began to lead him towards the door. And before he had gone far from the door a slave belonging to someone else tried to approach him, but being unable to get near him because of the crowds who pressed round him, forced his way into the house and put himself into the hands of Calpurnia, asking her to keep him safe until Caesar came back, since he had some very important information to give him.

65. Then there was Artemidorus, a Cnidian by birth, and a teacher of Greek philosophy who, for that reason, had become acquainted with Brutus and his friends. He had thus acquired a very full knowledge of the conspiracy and he came to Caesar with a small document in which he had written down the information which he intended to reveal to him. But when he saw that Caesar took each document that was given to him and then handed it to one of his attendants, he came close up to him and said: 'Read this one, Caesar, and read it quickly and by yourself. I assure you that it is important and that it concerns you personally.' Caesar then took the document and was several times on the point of reading it, but was prevented from doing so by the numbers of people who came to speak to him. It was the only document which he did keep with him and he was still holding it in his hand when he went on into the senate. (According to some accounts, it was another person who gave him this document, and Artemidorus was kept back by the crowd all along the route and failed to get near Caesar at all.)

66. It may be said that all these things could have happened as it were by chance. But the place where the senate was meeting that day and which was to be the scene of the final struggle and of the assassination made it perfectly clear that some heavenly power was at work, guiding the action and directing that it should take place just here. For here stood a statue of Pompey, and the building had been erected and dedicated by Pompey as one of the extra amenities attached to his theatre. Indeed it is

said that, just before the attack was made on him, Cassius
turned his eyes towards the statue of Pompey and silently
prayed for its goodwill. This was in spite of the fact that he was
a follower of the doctrines of Epicurus; yet the moment of crisis,
so it would seem, and the very imminence of the dreadful deed
made him forget his former rationalistic views and filled him
with an emotion that was intuitive or divinely inspired.

Now Antony, who was a true friend of Caesar's and also a
strong man physically, was detained outside the senate house
by Brutus Albinus, who deliberately engaged him in a long conversation. Caesar himself went in and the senate rose in his
honour. Some of Brutus' party took their places behind his
chair and others went to meet him as though they wished to
support the petition being made by Tillius Cimber[141] on behalf
of his brother who was in exile. So, all joining in with him in
his entreaties, they accompanied Caesar to his chair. Caesar
took his seat and continued to reject their request; as they
pressed him more and more urgently, he began to grow angry
with them. Tillius then took hold of his toga with both hands
and pulled it down from his neck. This was the signal for the
attack. The first blow was struck by Casca,[142] who wounded
Caesar in the neck with his dagger. The wound was not mortal
and not even a deep one, coming as it did from a man who was
no doubt much disturbed in mind at the beginning of such a
daring venture. Caesar, therefore, was able to turn round and
grasp the knife and hold on to it. At almost the same moment
the striker of the blow and he who was struck cried out together
– Caesar, in Latin, 'Casca, you villain, what are you doing?'
while Casca called to his brother in Greek: 'Help, brother.'

So it began, and those who were not in the conspiracy were
so horror-struck and amazed at what was being done that they
were afraid to run away and afraid to come to Caesar's help;
they were too afraid even to utter a word. But those who
had come prepared for the murder all bared their daggers and
hemmed Caesar in on every side. Whichever way he turned he
met the blows of daggers and saw the cold steel aimed at his
face and at his eyes. So he was driven this way and that, and
like a wild beast in the toils, had to suffer from the hands of

each one of them; for it had been agreed that they must all take part in this sacrifice and all flesh themselves with his blood. Because of this compact even Brutus gave him one wound in the groin. Some say that Caesar fought back against all the rest, darting this way and that to avoid the blows and crying out for help, but when he saw that Brutus had drawn his dagger, he covered his head with his toga and sank down to the ground. Either by chance or because he was pushed there by his murderers, he fell down against the pedestal on which the statue of Pompey stood, and the pedestal was drenched with his blood, so that one might have thought that Pompey himself was presiding over this act of vengeance against his enemy, who lay there at his feet struggling convulsively under so many wounds. He is said to have received twenty-three wounds. And many of his assailants were wounded by each other, as they tried to plant all those blows in one body.

67. So Caesar was done to death and, when it was over, Brutus stepped forward with the intention of making a speech to explain what had been done. The senators, however, would not wait to hear him. They rushed out through the doors of the building and fled to their homes, thus producing a state of confusion, terror and bewilderment amongst the people. Some bolted their doors; others left their counters and shops and could be observed either running to see the place where Caesar had been killed or, once they had seen it, running back again. Antony and Lepidus, who were Caesar's chief friends, stole away and hid in houses belonging to other people. Brutus and his party, on the other hand, just as they were, still hot and eager from the murder, marched all together in one body from the senate house to the Capitol, holding up their naked daggers in front of them and, far from giving the impression that they wanted to escape, looking glad and confident. They summoned the people in the name of liberty, and they invited the more distinguished persons whom they met to join in with them. Some of these did join in the procession and go up with them to the Capitol, pretending that they had taken part in the deed and thus claiming their share in the glory of it. Among these

were Gaius Octavius and Lentulus Spinther who suffered later for their imposture.[143] They were put to death by Antony and young Caesar, and did not even have the satisfaction of enjoying the fame which caused their death, since no one believed that they had taken part in the action. Even those who inflicted the death penalty on them were punishing them not for what they did but for what they would have liked to have done.

Next day Brutus and his party came down from the Capitol and Brutus made a speech.[144] The people listened to what he said without expressing either pleasure or resentment at what had been done. Their complete silence indicated that they both pitied Caesar and respected Brutus. The senate passed a decree of amnesty and tried to reconcile all parties. It was voted that Caesar should be worshipped as a god and that there should be no alteration made, however small, in any of the measures passed by him while he was in power.[145] On the other hand, provinces and appropriate honours were given to Brutus and his friends.[146] Everyone thought, therefore, that things were not only settled but settled in the best possible way.

68. But when Caesar's will was opened and it was discovered that he had left a considerable legacy to each Roman citizen, and when the people saw his body, all disfigured with its wounds, being carried through the forum, they broke through all bounds of discipline and order.[147] They made a great pile of benches, railings and tables from the forum and, placing the body upon this, burned it there. Then, carrying blazing brands, they ran to set fire to the houses of the murderers, while others went up and down through the city trying to find the men themselves to tear them to pieces. They, however, were well barricaded and not one of them came in the way of the mob. But there was a man called Cinna, one of Caesar's friends, who, they say, happened to have had a strange dream during the previous night. He dreamed that Caesar invited him to supper and he declined the invitation; Caesar then led him along by the hand, though he did not want to go and was pulling in the opposite direction. Now when Cinna heard that they were burning Caesar's body in the forum he got up and went there

out of respect for his memory, though he felt a certain amount of misgiving as a result of his dream and was also suffering from a fever. One of the crowd who saw him there asked who he was and, when he had learned the name, told it to another. So the name was passed on and it was quickly accepted by everyone that here was one of the men who had murdered Caesar; since among the conspirators there was in fact a man with this same name of Cinna.[148] The crowd, thinking that this was he, rushed on him and tore him limb from limb on the spot. It was this more than anything else which frightened Brutus and Cassius, and within a few days they withdrew from the city. What they did and what happened to them before they died has been related in my *Life of Brutus*.

69. Caesar was fifty-six years old when he died. He had survived Pompey by not much more than four years. As for the supreme power which he had pursued during the whole course of his life throughout such dangers and which at last and with such difficulty he had achieved, the only fruit he reaped from it was an empty name and a glory which made him envied by his fellow-citizens. But that great divine power or genius, which had watched over him and helped him in his life, even after his death remained active as an avenger of his murder, pursuing and tracking down the murderers over every land and sea until not one of them was left and visiting with retribution all, without exception, who were in any way concerned either with the death itself or with the planning of it.

So far as human coincidences are concerned, the most remarkable was that which concerned Cassius. After his defeat at Philippi he killed himself with the very same dagger which he had used against Caesar.[149] And of supernatural events there was, first, the great comet, which shone very brightly for seven nights after Caesar's murder and then disappeared; and also the dimming of the sun. For the whole of that year the sun's orb rose dull and pale; the heat which came down from it was feeble and ineffective, so that the atmosphere, with insufficient warmth to penetrate it, lay dark and heavy on the earth and fruits and vegetables never properly ripened, withering away and falling off before they were mature because of the coldness of the air.

But, more than anything else, the phantom which appeared to Brutus made it clear that the murder of Caesar was not pleasing to the gods. The story is as follows: Brutus was about to take his army across from Abydos to the mainland on the other side of the straits, and one night was lying down, as usual, in his tent, not asleep, but thinking about the future. (It is said that of all military commanders Brutus was the one who needed least sleep, and had the greatest natural capacity for staying awake for long hours on end.) He fancied that he heard a noise at the entrance to the tent and, looking towards the light of the lamp which was almost out, he saw a terrible figure, like a man, though unnaturally large and with a very severe expression. He was frightened at first, but, finding that this apparition just stood silently by his bed without doing or saying anything, he said: 'Who are you?' Then the phantom replied: 'Brutus, I am your evil genius. You shall see me at Philippi.' On this occasion Brutus answered courageously: 'Then I shall see you,' and the supernatural visitor at once went away. Time passed and he drew up his army against Antony and Caesar near Philippi. In the first battle he conquered the enemy divisions that were opposed to him, and, after routing them, broke through and sacked Caesar's camp. But in the night before the second battle the same phantom visited him again. It spoke no word, but Brutus realized that his fate was upon him and exposed himself to every danger in the battle. He did not die, however, in the fighting. It was after his troops had been routed that he retired to a steep rocky place, put his naked sword to his breast and with the help of a friend, so they say, who assisted him in driving the blow home, killed himself.

6

CICERO

[106–43 BC]

The life of Cicero makes no serious attempt to present the problems that confronted a 'new man' when he tried to make his way in Roman politics or to explain why Cicero, alone in his generation, was successful in surmounting them. Indeed, Cicero's rise to the consulship *suo anno* receives almost no comment, though Plutarch does seem to understand that the orator was elected largely for negative reasons. He says nothing, however, of Cicero's chief difficulty: the fact that his candidature had received support both from Pompey and from Pompey's enemies, so that Cicero was obliged to spend much of 63 uneasily acting on behalf of the *boni* while pretending to defend the interests of Pompey. But Plutarch had Cicero's works on his consulship, as well as various speeches and letters that have not survived, and so his account of the Catilinarian conspiracy contains valuable additional information, clarifying in particular the tergiversation of the consul designate Silanus. He also preserves some useful examples of Cicero's inability to resist the temptation to make smart remarks, no matter what the consequences. But the account of Cicero's fateful quarrel with Clodius and its results is careless and inaccurate, with nothing on the attitudes of Pompey or of Clodius himself. As in the other lives that deal with this period, the political detail of the fifties is ignored, and in the last, most vital stage of Cicero's career, when he tried in vain to exploit the young Octavian and use him to rid the state of Antony before casting him off in his turn (just as the Catonians had tried to use Pompey against Caesar), Plutarch shows no understanding of his policy.

1. Cicero's mother, Helvia, is reported to have come of a good family and to have lived a good life; widely different accounts, however, are given of his father. Some say that he was born and bred in a fuller's shop,[1] while others say that the family goes back originally to Tullus Attius, a famous king of the Volscians, who waged war very effectively against the Romans. It seems, however, that the member of the family who was first given the surname 'Cicero' must have been a person of some distinction, because his descendants, so far from dropping the name, were proud to bear it, though many people thought it ridiculous. For 'cicer' is the Latin word for a chick-pea, and this ancestor of Cicero no doubt got the name because he had a kind of dent or nick at the end of his nose like the cleft in a chick-pea. Certainly Cicero himself, whose life I am now writing, is said to have given a spirited reply when he first entered politics and stood for office, and his friends thought that he ought either to drop or change his name. He said that he was going to do his best to make the name of Cicero more famous than such names as Scaurus or Catulus.[2] And during his quaestorship in Sicily,[3] when he made an offering to the gods of some silver plate, he had his first two names, Marcus and Tullius, inscribed on the plate and then, by way of a joke, told the craftsman to engrave a chick-pea instead of the third name. So much for what we know about his name.

2. They say that his mother gave birth to him easily and without any labour pains on the third day of the new year – the day when, at the present time, the magistrates offer up prayers and sacrifices for the emperor. It appears that his nurse had a vision in which she was told that the child she was rearing would be a great blessing to all the Romans. This was regarded as a mere dream not worthy of serious attention, but Cicero himself when he reached the age to begin his education soon showed that there was truth in the prophecy. His natural abilities made him altogether remarkable and won him such a name and reputation among the other boys that their fathers used often to go to the schools to see Cicero with their own eyes and to observe the quickness and intelligence which he showed at his work and

which they had heard so much about, though some of them, who had less respect for culture, would get angry with their sons when they saw them walking with Cicero in the streets and giving him the place of honour in the middle of them.

He had that quality which Plato considers ought to be present in natures that are fitted for scholarship and the pursuit of wisdom; that is to say, he was the sort of person who takes gladly to every branch of learning and who rejects no aspect of literature or of education. He had, however, a particular enthusiasm for poetry and there is still extant a little poem of his written when he was only a boy. It is called *Pontius Glaucus* and is in tetrameter verse. And as he grew older and gave his attention more fully to the refinements of this art, he got the name of being not only the best orator but also the best poet in Rome. As for his fame as an orator, that remains secure to this day, in spite of the very considerable changes which have taken place in literary style; but in poetry, since a number of most highly gifted poets came after him, his own work is now entirely neglected and unknown.[4]

3. When his school days were over he attended the lectures of Philon the Academic who, of all the pupils of Cleitomachus, was most admired by the Romans for his eloquence and most loved for his character. At the same time he joined the circle of Mucius Scaevola[5] and gained useful knowledge of the law through consorting in this way with statesmen and leading figures in the senate. For a short time also he did military service under Sulla in the war against the Marsians.[6] Then, seeing that the whole state was splitting up into factions and that the result of this would be the unlimited power of one man, he retired into the life of a scholar and a philosopher, going on with his studies and associating with Greek scholars until the time came when Sulla seized power and it looked as though the political situation had become rather more settled.[7]

At this time Chrysogonus, an ex-slave of Sulla's, put up for auction the estate of a man who, so it was said, had been on one of Sulla's lists of the condemned and so had been put to death.[8] Chrysogonus bought the property himself for 2,000 drachmas. At this Roscius, the son and heir of the deceased, was so indignant that he publicized the fact that the real value of the estate was 250 talents. Sulla was furious at having his actions exposed and, after Chrysogonus had trumped up the evidence, he indicted Roscius for the murder of his father. No lawyer could be found to defend Roscius; Sulla's relentless character was enough to make them all fight shy of the case. And it was at this point that the young man, left all alone, appealed to Cicero for help. Cicero's friends urged him to take on the case, pointing out that he would never again get such a brilliant opportunity for starting his career and making a name for himself. So Cicero undertook the defence of Roscius, won the case and was greatly admired for what he had done. He was afraid of Sulla, however, and went abroad to Greece, after giving it out that the journey was being made for the sake of his health.[9] He was in fact very thin and underweight and had such a poor digestion that he could only manage to take a little light food late in the day. He had a good strong voice on the other hand, though it was harsh and untrained, and since in the violence and heat of his oratory he was always raising it very high, there was some reason for feeling anxiety about his health.

4. On arriving in Athens he attended the lectures of Antiochus of Ascalon and was charmed by the fluency and elegance of his diction, though he did not agree with his innovations in philosophical theory. Antiochus had already taken up a different position from that of what was known as the New Academy and had abandoned the school of Carneades, either because he had become convinced by the view that sense perception is reliable, or, according to some accounts, because he was jealous of and had quarrelled with the disciples of Cleitomachus and Philon and for this reason had changed his views and adopted in most respects the position of the Stoics. Cicero, however, loved the doctrines of the New Academy and was more attached to them than to the views of Antiochus. He planned that, if he were finally deprived of the chance of following a public career, he would retire to Athens, away from the law and politics, and would spend his life there in the quiet pursuit of philosophy.

However, by the time he received the news of Sulla's death,[10] his health, as the result of exercise, was thoroughly re-established and his voice had been brought under control and trained so as to be pleasant to the ear and in keeping with the rest of his physical constitution; his friends in Rome kept on writing to him to urge him to take his part in public life, and Antiochus used his influence to the same effect. So he began again, as it were, to go over his equipment, polishing up his oratory and bringing into service his political faculties; he worked hard at practising declamation and took lessons from the best-known rhetoricians. These studies took him to Asia and to Rhodes. In Asia he studied oratory under Xenocles of Adramyttium, Dionysius of Magnesia, and Menippus the Carian; in Rhodes his teacher in oratory was Apollonius, the son of Molon, and in philosophy Poseidonius. It is said that Apollonius, who did not understand Latin, asked Cicero to declaim in Greek. Cicero was very glad to do so, thinking that in this way it would be easier to have his faults corrected. So he made his declamation and, when it was over, the other listeners were amazed at the performance and vied with each other in the warmth of their congratulations; but Apollonius had shown no particular excitement while he was listening, and now that Cicero had stopped speaking he sat for a long time lost in thought. Cicero was distressed at this, but finally Apollonius said: 'Certainly, Cicero, I congratulate you and I am amazed at you. It is Greece and her fate that I am sorry for. The only glories that were left to us were our culture and our eloquence. Now I see that these too are going to be taken over in your person by Rome.'

5. However, though he was now launching himself on a political career with the highest hopes, Cicero's eagerness was somewhat blunted by a reply which he received from an oracle. He had consulted the god at Delphi, asking how he could gain the greatest honour, and the Pythian priestess had told him that his guide in life should be, not popular opinion, but his own nature. So during the first part of his time in Rome he behaved with caution; he did not thrust himself forward as a candidate for

office and so was passed over unnoticed. People called him 'the Greek' and 'the scholar' – names which come readily enough to the tongues of those Romans who are most lacking in culture or refinement. However, he was ambitious by nature and he was much encouraged by his father and by his friends. So, when he took up his work as an advocate, it was by no means slowly or gradually that he came to the top. He blazed out into fame at once and far surpassed all his competitors at the bar.

He is said to have had difficulty with his elocution, just as Demosthenes did, and to have given the most painstaking attention to the performances of both Roscius the comedian[11] and Aesop the tragic actor. This Aesop, so the story goes, was once acting in a theatre the part of Atreus in the scene where he is plotting his revenge on Thyestes, and he got so far outside his normal self in his feeling for the part that when one of the stagehands suddenly ran across the stage he struck him down with his sceptre and killed him.

In the case of Cicero elocution and delivery were an important element in his powers of persuasion. He used to ridicule those who were given to shouting out their speeches and said that, just as lame men rode on horseback because they could not walk, so these orators shouted because they could not speak. This ready wit and jesting habit of his was regarded as a good and attractive quality in a lawyer; but he carried it too far, often caused offence, and so got the reputation of being malicious.

6. He was appointed quaestor at a time when there was a shortage of grain: Sicily was the province allotted to him, and at first he made himself unpopular with the Sicilians by forcing them to send grain to Rome. Later, however, when they had had experience of his careful management of affairs, his justice and his kindly nature, they honoured him more than any governor they had ever had. It happened too that a number of young men from Rome, all from well-known and distinguished families, came up for trial before the praetor in charge of Sicily on charges of indiscipline or cowardice in the war.[12] Cicero undertook their defence and did it brilliantly, securing their

acquittal. Afterwards, when he was on his way to Rome and, as the result of these successes, was feeling particularly proud of himself, he had, as he informs us, an amusing experience.[13] In Campania he happened to meet a well-known man and one whom he considered a friend of his. Imagining that he had filled the whole of Rome with the fame and glory of his achievements, he asked this man: 'What are people in Rome saying about what I've done? What do they think of it?' To which the reply was: 'But, Cicero, you must tell me where you've been all this time.' At the moment, he tells us, he was thoroughly discouraged by this. He saw that all the news about him had been swallowed up in the city like a drop of water in the ocean with no visible effect at all on his reputation. But afterwards he thought things over and saw that this glory for which he was contending was something infinite, that there was no fixed point at which one could say 'now I have arrived'; and so he introduced some moderation into his ambitious thoughts. It remains true, however, that throughout his life he was always far too fond of praise and too concerned about what people thought of him; and this very often had a disturbing effect on policies of his which were in themselves excellent.

7. Now that he was beginning to go in for politics more seriously he came to the conclusion that it was a disgraceful thing that, while a craftsman who uses inanimate tools and inanimate materials still knows what each of these is called, where it can be found and what it can do, the statesman, who uses men as his instruments for public action, should be slack and indifferent where knowledge of his fellow-citizens is concerned. He therefore trained himself not only to memorize names, but also to know in what part of the city every important person lived, where he had his country houses, who were his friends and who his neighbours. And so, whatever road in Italy Cicero happened to be travelling on, it was easy for him to name and to point out the estates and villas of his friends. His fortune was sufficient for his expenses, but was still small, so that people were surprised and admired him when he took no fees or gifts for his services as an advocate – particularly so at the time when

he took on the case for the prosecution against Verres.[14] Verres had been, as praetor,[15] governor of Sicily and was prosecuted by the Sicilians for his numerous misdeeds. Cicero secured his conviction not by the speech he made but, in a sense, by the speech which he did not make. For the praetors in charge of the courts in Rome were doing what they could for Verres and by various methods of postponement had had the case adjourned until the last possible day on which it could be heard.[16] It therefore seemed obvious to them that, since one day wouldn't be long enough for the speeches of the advocates, the trial could not possibly be concluded. But Cicero stood up and said that there was no need of speeches; he merely called his witnesses and examined them and then asked the jury to cast their votes. There are still on record, however, a number of witty sayings of his in connection with this trial. For instance, when an ex-slave called Caecilius,[17] who was suspected of Jewish practices, wanted to push himself forward instead of the Sicilian witnesses and to make a speech against Verres himself Cicero said: 'What has a Jew got to do with a pig?' – 'verres' being the Roman word for a castrated boar. And when Verres attacked Cicero and said that he was effeminate, Cicero replied: 'Surely this is the sort of language you ought to be using to your sons at home'; Verres having a grown-up son who had the reputation of being little better than a male prostitute. Then there was the remark he made to the orator Hortensius.[18] Hortensius had not dared to speak for Verres at the trial proper, but when it came to the assessment of the fine he was induced to appear for him and received in reward a sphinx made of ivory. In the course of his speech Cicero made some oblique reference to him, and Hortensius interjected: 'I am afraid I am not an expert at solving riddles'; to which Cicero replied: 'Really? In spite of having the sphinx in your house?'

8. When Verres was convicted Cicero assessed the fine at 750,000 denarii, and because of this was suspected of having been bribed to make the fine a low one. However, the Sicilians were certainly grateful to him and when he was aedile[19] they sent him all sorts of livestock and farm produce from their

islands. He used this generosity of theirs only in order to lower the prices of food in Rome, making no profit out of it for himself.

He had a fine country estate at Arpinum, a farm near Naples, and another near Pompeii, neither of them very large. The dowry of his wife Terentia came to 100,000 denarii, and he also received a legacy which brought him 90,000. This was enough to enable him to live in easy circumstances, though on a modest scale, with the Greek and Roman men of letters with whom he associated. He rarely, if ever, had a regular meal before sunset, not so much because he was too busy as because he suffered from a weak digestion. He was indeed very particular and even fussy about his health in general and used to have massages at regular intervals and go for a fixed number of walks. By looking after himself in this way he managed to maintain a state of health which was free from illness and strong enough to support much hard work and many calls upon his energy. The house that used to belong to his father he made over to his brother and lived himself near the Palatine hill, so that those who came to visit him in the morning should not have the trouble of a long walk. And the visitors who came to his house every day were no fewer than those who went to call on Crassus because of his wealth or on Pompey because of his power in the army, these two being the greatest and most sought-after men in Rome. Pompey, in fact, used himself to call on Cicero, and owed much of his power and reputation to Cicero's help in politics.

9. A number of men with great names stood for the praetorship at the same time as he did, but Cicero came out at the top of the poll.[20] And it was generally considered that he handled the legal cases that came before him well and fairly. There is a story told of Licinius Macer[21] when he came up for trial before Cicero on a charge of extortion. Macer was a powerful personality in Rome on his own account and had the additional advantage of being supported by Crassus. Feeling confident because of his own influence and the help given to him by his friends, he left the court and went off home while the jury were still engaged

in voting. He had a quick hair-cut and put on a clean toga with a view to celebrating his acquittal. He was just setting out again to go down to the forum when Crassus met him at the door of his house and told him that he had been convicted by a unanimous vote. He then turned back, threw himself on his bed and died. This case gave Cicero the reputation of being one who took the greatest care in presiding over a court. Then there was Vatinius,[22] a man with rough manners who would often behave insolently to the magistrates in court; and he had a neck which was covered with swellings. Once Vatinius came before the court over which Cicero was presiding and made some request of him. Instead of granting it at once, Cicero took some time to think it over and Vatinius said that he, if he had been praetor, would not have made any question of the matter. 'But,' Cicero replied, 'you have the advantage over me in having much more neck.'

Two or three days before the time came for him to lay down his office Manilius was brought before him on a charge of extortion. Manilius[23] had the enthusiastic support of the people. He was a friend of Pompey's and it was thought that the prosecution were only attacking Manilius because of Pompey. When Manilius asked for several days in which to make his defence, Cicero granted him only one, and that, he said, must be the very next day. There was great popular indignation at this, since as a general rule the praetors used to grant at least ten days to the accused. The tribunes then brought Cicero in front of a public meeting and accused him of acting unfairly. Cicero first asked to be heard and then said that as he had always, within the limits of the law, treated defendants kindly and with consideration, he considered that it would be a bad thing for him not to behave in the same way in the case of Manilius. Since he had only one more day at his disposal as praetor, he had deliberately fixed the trial on that day; to put off the trial so that it would come under the supervision of another praetor was certainly not the part of one who wanted to help Manilius. These words of his produced a remarkable change in the feelings of the people. They praised him to the skies and begged him to take on personally the defence of Manilius.

Cicero readily consented to do so, chiefly for the sake of Pompey, who was not in Italy at the time. He then stood up and made another speech in front of the people, vigorously attacking the oligarchical party and all those who were jealous of Pompey.

10. Both parties, however – that of the nobility and that of the people – combined together to raise him to the consulship. This was done in the interests of the city as a whole, and the reasons were as follows. At first there had seemed to be no sense at all in the change which Sulla had made in the constitution; but now time had passed and people had got used to it, so that the majority considered that it did offer some kind of stability. There were some, however, who, for the sake of their own private interests and not at all for the general good, wished to disturb the existing state of affairs and make a change. Pompey at this time was still engaged in war with the kings in Pontus and Armenia, and there was no force in Rome capable of dealing with these revolutionaries. They had as their leader Lucius Catiline,[24] a bold and versatile character and one who was ready for anything. He was guilty of many serious crimes and had once been accused of taking the virginity of his own daughter and of killing his own brother.[25] Fearing that he would be prosecuted for this murder he had induced Sulla to put down his brother's name, as though he were still alive, on the lists of those condemned to death.[26] This, then, was the man whom these scoundrels took as their leader, and they gave pledges of faith to each other which included the sacrificing of a man and the tasting of his flesh. Catiline had also corrupted a great number of the young men in Rome by approaching them individually and supplying them constantly with amusements, drink and women, pouring out money for them to spend on these dissipations. His agitation had extended to the whole of Etruria, which was now ready for revolt, as was the greater part of Cisalpine Gaul. In Rome itself there were most alarming revolutionary tendencies – the result of the unequal distribution of wealth. While men of the highest reputation and the greatest spirit had beggared themselves by their outlay on

shows, entertainments, election expenses and great buildings, money had accumulated in the hands of people whose families were unknown and of no account. So only a spark was needed to set everything on fire and, since the whole state was rotten within itself, it was in the power of any bold man to over-throw it.

11. Catiline wished nevertheless to obtain first a position of strength from which to start his operations, and so he stood for the consulship.[27] He had great hopes that his colleague in this office would be Gaius Antonius, a man with no aptitude for leadership in any direction, good or bad, but one who could be useful in providing additional strength to someone else who did take the lead. Most of the best people in the state realized this and so they put Cicero forward for the consulship; the people accepted him gladly; Catiline was defeated, and Cicero and Gaius Antonius were elected as consuls. And this in spite of the fact that of all the candidates Cicero was the only one whose father was not a senator but a member of the equestrian order.[28]

12. Catiline's designs were to remain hidden for some time from the general mass of the population, but Cicero was faced with considerable preliminary difficulties as soon as he took up his office. In the first place those people who were disqualified by the laws of Sulla from holding office (and they represented a large and powerful section of the population) now began to put themselves forward and to address public meetings, making many attacks on the tyranny of Sulla. What they said was true enough and perfectly justified, but this was neither a necessary nor a proper time for disturbing the government.[29] In the second place the tribunes were proposing laws which had the same end in view.[30] The proposal was that a commission of ten men should be appointed; these ten should have unlimited powers and be given the right to sell the public land anywhere in Italy, in Syria and in the new territories recently conquered by Pompey; they should be allowed to bring to trial whoever they wished, to send people into exile, to found new cities, to draw money from the treasury, to raise and pay for as many troops

as they wanted. Not unnaturally this law was supported by a number of eminent people and particularly by Cicero's colleague Antonius, who counted upon being one of the ten. But what most alarmed the nobility was that Antonius was suspected of knowing all about Catiline's conspiracy and, because of his enormous debts, looking favourably on it.

Cicero's first task was to render these fears groundless. He arranged that the province of Macedonia should be allotted to Antonius, while he himself declined the province of Gaul, which was offered to him.[31] By doing this favour to Antonius he secured his object of making him, like a hired actor, always take the minor part, leaving to Cicero himself the chief role in the defence of their country. And now that Antonius was under control and had become easy to manage, Cicero proceeded with all the more confidence to deal with the other subversive elements. In the senate he made a carefully argued attack on the proposed law which proved so effective that not even the sponsors of the law could find anything to say in reply. Then, when they made a second attempt to get it passed and, after careful preparation, summoned the consuls to appear before the people, Cicero, without showing the slightest fear, led the way, telling the senate to follow him, and not only got the law rejected but so overpowered the tribunes by the force of his eloquence that he made them abandon the rest of the measures which they were contemplating.

13. Indeed Cicero, more than anyone, made the Romans see how great is the charm which eloquence confers on what is good, how invincible justice is if it is well expressed in words, and how the good and efficient statesman should always in his actions prefer what is right to what will win popularity, and in his words should express the public interest in a manner that will please rather than prove offensive. An incident took place in the theatre during his consulship which showed what charm he could exert in his speaking. In earlier times members of the equestrian order used to have the same seats in the theatres as the ordinary people and took whatever place happened to be available; Marcus Otho, when he was praetor, was the first to

give members of this class the honour of being separated from the rest of the citizens.[32] He allotted to them specially reserved seats of their own – an arrangement which still remains in force today. The people regarded this as an insult to themselves, and when Otho appeared in the theatre they hissed him in a most disrespectful way. The equestrian order, on the other hand, greeted him with loud applause. There was then on the one side renewed and increased hissing, and on the other still more applause. The two parties then turned on each other, shouting out insults, and the whole theatre was in a state of confusion. When Cicero heard of this, he came to the theatre and instructed the people to come out to the Temple of Bellona. Here he reprimanded them for their behaviour and gave them his advice as to how to behave in future. The result was that, when they went back again to the theatre, they applauded Otho loudly and vied with the equestrian order in doing him honour and showing him respect.

14. Now Catiline and his fellow conspirators, who had been cowed at first and too frightened to act, began to recover their confidence. They got together and encouraged each other by demanding that more daring should be shown; matters should be taken in hand, they said, before the return of Pompey, who was now said to be on his way back with his army. In particular the old soldiers of Sulla kept urging Catiline to take action.[33] These were to be found in all parts of Italy, but the greatest numbers of them and the most formidable fighters were distributed among the cities of Etruria and were now dreaming once more of robbing and looting the wealth that seemed to be lying at their feet. With their leader Manlius,[34] who was one of those who had served with distinction under Sulla, they joined in with Catiline and came to Rome to take part in the consular elections. Catiline was once again standing for the consulship and had planned to kill Cicero in the middle of the general disturbance of election day.[35] Heaven itself, it seemed, was foretelling these events; there were earthquakes, thunderbolts and apparitions. There was also information available from men, but this information, accurate as it was, was still not

sufficient to convict a man like Catiline, who was well known and had very powerful connections. Cicero therefore postponed the day of the elections, summoned Catiline to appear before the senate, and questioned him closely on the subject of what was being said about him. Catiline, in the belief that there were a number of people in the senate who wanted a revolution and at the same time wishing to show off in front of his fellow-conspirators, was mad enough to answer Cicero as follows: 'I see two bodies,' he said, 'one thin and wasted, but with a head, the other headless, but big and strong. What is there so dreadful about it, if I myself become the head of the body which needs one?' This riddle of his referred to the senate and the people, and Cicero became all the more alarmed. Wearing a breastplate he was escorted down from his house to the Field of Mars by all the nobility and by many of the young men. By loosening the folds of his tunic on his shoulders he purposely allowed people to see that he was wearing a breastplate, thus showing them the danger in which he stood, and the people indignantly rallied round him.[36] Finally, when the votes were taken, they rejected Catiline once again and elected Silanus and Murena consuls.[37]

15. Soon afterwards Catiline's soldiers began to gather together in Etruria and to form themselves into companies. The day fixed for going into action was drawing near, and at this time there came to Cicero's house about midnight some of the most powerful and greatest men in Rome – Marcus Crassus, Marcus Marcellus and Metellus Scipio.[38] They roused the doorkeeper by their knocking and told him to go and tell Cicero that they were there. Their business was as follows: after dinner Crassus' doorkeeper had given him some letters which had been left by an unknown man; they were addressed to various people and one, which had no signature, was addressed to Crassus himself. This was the only one which Crassus had read. It had informed him that there was going to be much bloodshed by Catiline's orders and advised him to slip away secretly from the city. Crassus had therefore left the other letters unopened and had come at once to Cicero, quite overcome by the nature of the

338 FALL OF THE ROMAN REPUBLIC

news and wishing to do something to clear himself from the suspicion he lay under because of his friendship with Catiline.

After thinking the matter over Cicero convened the senate at dawn. He brought the letters with him, handed them to those to whom they were addressed and ordered them to read them aloud. Every single letter was found to contain information of a plot. Quintus Arrius, a man of praetorian rank, also made a report on the formation of regular bands of soldiers in Etruria; it was announced too that Manlius with a large force was hovering about the cities in that area in constant expectation of some news from Rome. Then the senate passed a decree that matters should be put into the hands of the consuls, who should accept the responsibility of arranging as best they could for the security of the city. This is a decree that is only rarely passed by the senate and only at times when great danger is feared.[39]

16. Armed with these powers, Cicero entrusted the conduct of affairs outside Rome to Quintus Metellus.[40] He himself took charge of the city and went out each day with so large a bodyguard that when he entered the forum a great part of the whole area was filled with the men who were escorting him. Catiline now became impatient of any further delay. He decided that he himself would break out of the city and go to join Manlius and his army; but first he instructed Marcius and Cethegus[41] to take their swords and go to Cicero's house at daybreak as though to pay him their respects. They were then to fall on him and make an end of him. This plot was revealed to Cicero by a lady of good family called Fulvia, who came to him by night and told him to be on his guard against Cethegus and those who were with him. At dawn Cethegus and his party arrived and, when they were refused entry, became angry and created a disturbance at the door of the house, thus making themselves more suspect than ever. Cicero then came out and convened a meeting of the senate in the temple of Jupiter Stesius (or Stator, as the Romans say), which was situated at the beginning of the Sacred Way as you go up to the Palatine hill. Catiline also attended this meeting with the other senators, intending to defend himself. No senator, however, would sit

near him; they all moved away from the bench where he was
sitting. When he began to speak he was shouted down, and
finally Cicero rose up and told him to leave the city.[42] He
himself, he said, was a statesman who achieved his results by
words, whereas Catiline's method was armed force; it was only
right, therefore, that they should be separated from each other
by the city wall. And so Catiline, accompanied by 300 armed
men, left the city at once. He assumed the rods and axes of a
magistrate in office, raised military standards and marched to
join Manlius.[43] By now a force of some 20,000 men had been
got together, and with these he marched round to the various
cities and attempted to persuade them to revolt. It was now
open war and Antonius was sent off with instructions to fight
it out to the end.

17. The remains of Catiline's corrupt crew who had been left
behind in Rome were organized and encouraged by Cornelius
Lentulus, surnamed Sura. Lentulus came from a distinguished
family, but had lived a low life and had once been expelled
from the senate for his debauched conduct. He was now serving
as praetor for the second time, the normal procedure for those
who have regained senatorial rank.[44] He is said to have acquired
his surname of Sura for the following reason. In Sulla's time he
held the office of quaestor[45] and got rid of or wasted large sums
of public money. Sulla was angry and demanded that he should
account for his behaviour in front of the senate. Lentulus then
came forward and, speaking in a very offhand and contemptu-
ous way, said that he had no account to render, but that he
would offer them this – with which words he extended his leg,
as boys do when they are playing ball and miss. After this he
was called Sura – 'sura' being the Roman word for 'leg'. On
another occasion he was on trial and, after having bribed some
of the jury, was acquitted by just two votes. He remarked that
the money which he had spent on one of these two was a pure
waste, since if he had got off by one vote it would have been
quite all right.

Such was the character of Lentulus, who was now pushed
forward by Catiline. He was carried still further in the wrong

direction by the empty hopes held out to him by false prophets
and fortune tellers who recited forged oracles in verse, which
were supposed to have come from the Sibylline books and
which declared that three Cornelii were fated to enjoy absolute
power in Rome; that two of these, Cinna and Sulla, had already
fulfilled their destiny; that now the powers above were coming
to him, the third and last Cornelius, and were offering him
absolute power; and that he ought by all means to accept this
offer and not ruin his opportunities, as Catiline had done, by
delay.[46]

18. There was nothing, then, on a small scale or trivial about
Lentulus' plans. In fact he had decided to kill the entire senate
and as many other citizens as possible, to burn down the city
itself and to spare no one except the children of Pompey. These
were to be seized by the conspirators and held as hostages to
secure a peaceful settlement with Pompey; for it was already
generally and confidently reported that Pompey was on his way
back from his great campaigns. A night – one of the nights of
the Saturnalia – had been fixed for the attack, and swords, tow
and brimstone had been carried to the house of Cethegus and
hidden there. They had also a force of a hundred men, each of
whom had been allotted a particular section of Rome, so that
in a short time many people could start fires and the city would
be in a blaze on all sides. Others were to cut the aqueducts and
to kill anyone who tried to bring water.

There happened to be staying in Rome when these plans were
being made two ambassadors of the Allobroges, a nation which
was then going through a particularly bad time and was disaf-
fected towards the Roman government.[47] Lentulus and his party
thought that these men would be useful in stirring up a revolt
in Gaul and so they took them into the conspiracy. They also
gave them letters to their own senate and letters for Catiline
too. To the senate of the Allobroges they promised freedom
from Roman control; and they urged Catiline to set free the
slaves and to march on Rome. To accompany the ambassadors
on their way to Catiline they sent a man called Titus,[48] a citizen
of Croton, who was to carry the letters.

The conspirators, however, were unbalanced characters who seldom met together without wine and women, while Cicero was following their schemes with patient care, with sober judgement and with exceptional intelligence. He had many agents outside the conspiracy who kept a close watch on what was going on and helped him to collect evidence; and he was also in secret communication with people whom he could trust who were supposed to be in the conspiracy themselves. He therefore heard all about the discussions with the foreign ambassadors and, with the secret cooperation of the Allobroges, laid an ambush by night and arrested the man from Croton with the letters on him.[49]

19. At dawn he assembled the senate in the temple of Concord, read the letters aloud and examined the informers.[50] Iunius Silanus[51] also spoke and declared that Cethegus had been heard saying that three consuls and four praetors were going to be killed. Piso too,[52] a man of consular rank, produced more information of much the same kind. Gaius Sulpicius,[53] one of the praetors, was sent to the house of Cethegus, where he found apart from spears and armour an enormous quantity of swords and knives, all newly sharpened. Finally, after the senate had voted immunity for the man from Croton on condition that he gave information, Lentulus was convicted. He resigned his office (he was praetor at the time), laid aside his purple-bordered robe in the senate, and put on other clothes more in keeping with his present circumstances. He and his associates were then handed over to the praetors to be kept under arrest, though without chains.

It was now evening and the people were waiting outside in dense crowds. Cicero came out of the senate, told his fellow-citizens what had been done and was escorted by them to the house of a neighbouring friend of his, since his own house was taken up by the women who were celebrating the secret rites in honour of the goddess who is called by the Romans the Good and by the Greeks the Women's goddess. Sacrifices are offered to her annually in the house of the consul and are supervised by the consul's wife or mother in the presence of the Vestal

Virgins. Cicero therefore went to his friend's house and began
to consider in his own mind (very few people were with him)
what action he should take with regard to the conspirators.
The extreme penalty was the proper one for such crimes, but
he shrank from inflicting it, his reluctance being due partly to
the kindliness of his nature and partly also to the fact that he
did not want to appear to be using his power too high-handedly
in ruthlessly stamping out men who belonged to the greatest
families and who had powerful friends in Rome. Yet he feared
danger from them in the future if he treated them less severely.
He believed that if they suffered any penalty milder than death
they would, so far from accepting the situation, break out again
and stick at nothing; they would remain as wicked as ever
and would merely have fresh reasons for being infuriated. He
himself, too, would be thought weak and unmanly, particularly
as his reputation for courage among the people of Rome was
not in any case a very high one.

20. While Cicero was in this state of perplexity, a sign was
given to the women who were sacrificing. The fire on the altar
was assumed to have already gone out, but from the ashes and
burned bark a great bright flame sprang up. It was a sight which
terrified most of the women, but the sacred virgins told Cicero's
wife Terentia to go at once to her husband and tell him to act
as he had decided to act for the good of his country, since the
goddess was sending him a great light to promise him both
safety and glory. Terentia was never at any time a shrinking
type of woman; she was bold and energetic by nature, ambitious
and, as Cicero says himself, was more inclined to take a part in
his public life than to share with him any of her domestic
responsibilities. So she now delivered the message and urged
him to take action against the conspirators. His brother Quintus
encouraged him in the same direction, as did Publius Nigidius,
one of his philosopher friends, whose advice he often asked and
made the greatest use of in his political life.

Next day there was a debate in the senate on the punishment
of the conspirators.[54] Silanus, who was asked to give his opinion
first, said that they should be taken to prison and there should

suffer the supreme penalty. All following speakers supported this motion until it came to the turn of Gaius Caesar, who afterwards became dictator. At this time he was still a young man and only at the beginning of his rise to power. He had already committed himself, however, both in his political actions and in his hopes for the future, to the path by which in the end he changed the state of Rome into a monarchy. Others were not aware of this, but Cicero had strong grounds for being suspicious of Caesar, though no evidence strong enough to secure his conviction. Nevertheless there were many who said that Caesar had a very narrow escape from Cicero on this occasion and was nearly caught. Some say, however, that Cicero purposely overlooked and suppressed the information laid against him through fear of his friends and of his power, since it was clear to everyone that, if Caesar were charged with the other conspirators, they were more likely to be acquitted with him than he was to be punished with them.

21. When it was Caesar's turn to give his opinion he rose and proposed that the conspirators should not be put to death, but that their property should be confiscated and that they themselves should be taken to whatever cities in Italy Cicero might choose and there be kept in chains under close arrest until final victory over Catiline had been secured in the field. The proposal was a reasonable one, Caesar, who made it, was a singularly able speaker, and Cicero also lent some weight to it; for when he rose to speak himself he dealt with the subject from both points of view, now putting forward the arguments for the first proposal and now for Caesar's. All his friends too preferred the second proposal to the first, thinking that Caesar's proposal was to the advantage of Cicero, who would be less open to attack subsequently if he did not put the conspirators to death. Silanus also now took up a different position. He excused himself by saying that in his original proposal he too had never meant death; the 'supreme penalty' in the case of a Roman senator was, of course, prison.

The first to speak against Caesar's proposal was Lutatius Catulus[55] and he was followed by Cato who in a very violent speech joined him in trying to fix suspicion on Caesar. This speech had the effect of making the senate both thoroughly angry and determined to assert itself, so that the death sentence was passed on the conspirators. As for the confiscation of their property, Caesar opposed this, thinking it unfair that they should retain just the one part of his proposal which was most severe while they rejected his recommendation for mercy. When many of the senators wished to force this through, he appealed to the tribunes, but they would not do anything. Cicero himself, however, yielded the point and remitted that part of the sentence which called for the confiscation of their property.

22. Cicero then went to fetch the conspirators and the members of the senate went with him. The conspirators were not all in the same place; they had been distributed for safe keeping among the praetors. First he called for Lentulus from the Palatine hill and led him down the Sacred Way through the middle of the forum. The most eminent statesmen formed up in ranks and acted as a bodyguard; but the people shuddered at what was being done and passed along in silence – especially the young, who looked as though they were being initiated with fear and trembling into the sacred rites and mysteries of some time-honoured process of aristocratic power. Cicero crossed the forum to the prison and then delivered Lentulus to the public executioner with orders that he should be put to death. Next was the turn of Cethegus, and so he brought down all the rest in order and had them executed. He observed that there were still standing about in bands in the forum many people who were in the conspiracy and who, not knowing what had been done, were waiting for nightfall, with the idea that their leaders were still alive and could be rescued. To these Cicero shouted out in a loud voice: 'They have lived their lives' – this being the Roman way of indicating death without using the ill-omened word.

It was now evening and Cicero went up through the forum to his house. There was no longer the usual silence and regular order in the crowds of citizens who escorted him there. Wherever he passed people shouted aloud and clapped their hands, calling him the saviour and the founder of his country. The streets were brightly lighted, since people had put lamps and torches in their doorways. The women also showed lights from the roofs of the houses in his honour and so that they might see him going up in this splendid procession with the greatest men in Rome escorting him. Most of these had been the victors in famous campaigns, had entered the city in triumph, and had added great areas of land and sea to the Roman dominions; but now as they walked in this procession they acknowledged to each other that the Roman people owed thanks to many commanders and generals of the time for riches and spoils and power, but for the safety and security of the whole their thanks were due to Cicero and to Cicero alone, who had delivered them from this great and terrible danger. What seemed so wonderful was not so much the fact that he had put a stop to the conspiracy and punished the conspirators as that he had succeeded in crushing this greatest of all revolutions by such comparatively painless methods, with no disturbances and no civil strife. For most of those who had flocked to join Catiline deserted him and went off as soon as they heard what had happened to Lentulus and Cethegus; and when Catiline with what was left of his forces joined battle with Antonius, both he and his army were destroyed.[56]

23. There were, nevertheless, some people who were prepared both in speech and action to attack Cicero for what he had done. Their leaders, among those who were to take up office as magistrates next year,[57] were Caesar, who was to be praetor, and Metellus and Bestia, who were to be tribunes.[58] Cicero still had a few days of his consulship left when they came into office[59] and they refused to allow him to address the people. They set down their benches in front of the rostra and gave him no chance or opportunity to speak, merely telling him that he could, if he wished, just pronounce the oath traditionally taken on leaving office and then come down again from the rostra. Cicero accepted their conditions and came forward to take the oath. When he had obtained silence he pronounced instead of the usual form of words a new oath of his own. 'I swear,' he

said, 'in very truth that I have saved my country and maintained her supremacy.' And all the people assented to the oath and confirmed it with him. This made Caesar and the tribunes all the more angry and they tried to put fresh difficulties in Cicero's path. Among these efforts of theirs was a law which they proposed for the recall of Pompey and his army in order, so they said, to put an end to the tyranny of Cicero. Here Cato, who was tribune at the time, was a great help to Cicero, and to the whole state. While his authority was the same as that of the other tribunes, his reputation was a very much better one, and in opposing these measures of theirs he easily put a stop to their further designs. In a speech which he made to the people he so glorified Cicero's consulship that they voted him the greatest honours that had ever been conferred and called him the father of the fatherland. Cicero was the first, it seems, to receive this title. And Cato gave it to him in his speech before the people.

24. At this time, then, Cicero was the most powerful man in Rome. However, he made himself obnoxious to a number of people, not because of anything which he did wrong but because people grew tired of hearing him continually praising himself and magnifying his achievements. One could attend neither the senate nor a public meeting nor a session of the law courts without having to listen to endless repetitions of the story of Catiline and Lentulus. He went on to fill his books and writings with these praises of himself and made his style of speaking, which was in itself so very pleasant and so exceedingly charming, boring and tedious to listen to, since this unpleasing habit of his clung to him like fate. Nevertheless, it must be said that although he was so unreservedly fond of his own glory, he was quite free from envy of other people. He was, as can be seen from his writings, most liberal in his praises both of his predecessors and his contemporaries. Many such sayings of his are still remembered. For instance, he said of Aristotle that he was a river of flowing gold, and of the dialogues of Plato that, if it were in the nature of Jupiter to converse in human words, this would be how he would do it. He used to call Theophrastus his own special luxury. And when he was asked which speech

CICERO

of Demosthenes he considered the best, he replied: 'The longest one.' Yet some of those who try to copy Demosthenes themselves are apt to dwell on a remark which Cicero makes in a letter to one of his friends to the effect that there are parts of the speeches where Demosthenes seems to be falling asleep. They fail to mention the fact that Cicero constantly praises Demosthenes in the most whole-hearted and wonderful way, or that he gave the title of Philippics to those speeches of his own (the ones against Antony) to which he devoted more attention than to any others.

And as for the distinguished speakers and scholars of his own time, they all, without exception, had their fame increased by what Cicero wrote or said in praise of them. When Caesar was in power he obtained from him the Roman citizenship for Cratippus the Peripatetic; and he got the council of the Areopagus to pass a decree requesting him to stay in Athens as a teacher for the young men and as an ornament to the city. There are also letters from Cicero to Herodes, and others to his son, in which he recommends them to study philosophy with Cratippus. On the other hand, he blames Gorgias the rhetorician for leading the young man into luxurious ways and heavy drinking, and therefore forbids his son to keep company with him. This is almost the only one of his Greek letters (there is one other, addressed to Pelops of Byzantium) which seems to have been written in anger. As for Gorgias, the harsh words are fully justified, if he was the worthless and dissolute character that he is supposed to have been; but in the case of Pelops Cicero shows rather a mean spirit, writing querulously to complain that Pelops has not taken enough trouble about getting honorary decrees passed for him by the people of Byzantium.

25. This kind of thing was characteristic of his love for praise, as was the fact that his ability to put things cleverly would often lead him to forget good manners. For instance, he once defended Munatius in court, and Munatius was no sooner acquitted than he prosecuted Sabinus, a friend of Cicero's. It is said that Cicero was so infuriated at this that he exclaimed: 'Did you imagine, Munatius, that you were acquitted on your

merits? Let me tell you that it was I who produced the necessary
darkness in the court to prevent your guilt from being visible
to everyone.' Then he once made a public speech from the
rostra in praise of Marcus Crassus and got much applause for
it. A day or two later he made another speech attacking him
violently, and Crassus said: 'Were you not standing there yourself and praising me only a few days ago?' To which Cicero
replied: 'Yes, I was. It is good practice in oratory to make a
speech on a bad subject.' On another occasion Crassus first
said that no Crassus had ever lived in Rome to be older than
the age of sixty, and then attempted to deny it. 'What can I
have been thinking of,' he exclaimed, 'to have said that?' 'You
knew,' said Cicero, 'that the Romans would be pleased to hear
it and you were trying to make yourself popular.' And when
Crassus expressed approval of the Stoic doctrine 'The good
man is always rich', Cicero said: 'Are you sure that you don't
mean their doctrine "All things belong to the wise"?' – Crassus
having the reputation of being much too fond of money. Then
Crassus had a son who was thought to resemble a man called
Axius (meaning 'worthy') and as a result there was a certain
amount of scandal connecting his mother with this Axius.
Crassus' son once made a speech in the senate which was well
thought of, and when Cicero was asked his opinion of the
speaker he replied: 'Worthy to be the work of Crassus.'

26. When Crassus was about to set out for Syria[60] he wanted
Cicero to be his friend rather than his enemy and said to him
in a friendly way that he would like to dine with him. Cicero
was glad enough to ask him to his house, but a few days later,
when some friends were interceding with him on behalf of
Vatinius and saying that he genuinely desired to be reconciled
with Cicero and to become his friend (he was an enemy of his),
Cicero replied: 'Surely Vatinius doesn't want to have dinner
with me too?'

So much for the way in which he behaved towards Crassus.
Vatinius himself had swellings on his neck and once, when he
was speaking in the courts, Cicero referred to him as a 'tumid'
orator. On another occasion Cicero was informed that Vatinius

was dead and then shortly afterward learned for certain that he was alive. 'Bad luck to the man,' said Cicero, 'who told the lie.'

Then at the time when Caesar had a decree passed for distributing the land in Campania among his soldiers,[61] many of the senators were strongly opposed to it and Lucius Gellius,[62] who was about the oldest of them, declared that so long as he lived it should never be done. 'Let us wait, then,' said Cicero, 'since Gellius does not ask us to postpone things for long.'

There was also a man called Octavius who was suspected of being of African descent. In the course of a lawsuit this man said that he was unable to hear what Cicero was saying, and Cicero replied: 'That's odd, considering that your ears have been pierced.'

And when Metellus Nepos declared that Cicero had ruined more people as a witness than he had ever saved as a counsel for the defence,[63] 'Yes,' said Cicero, 'I admit that you can have more complete confidence in my word than in my eloquence.'

Then there was a young man who was suspected of having given a poisoned cake to his father. This young man put on a very bold air and said that he proposed to give Cicero a bit of his mind. 'I would much prefer it,' said Cicero, 'to a bit of your cake.'

There was Publius Sextius too who in a lawsuit had engaged Cicero and others as well for his defence, but who insisted on doing all the speaking himself without allowing anyone else to say a word. When it was quite clear that the jury were going to acquit him and while the vote was actually being taken Cicero said to him: 'Make the most of your opportunities today, Sextius. Tomorrow you are going to be a nobody.'

Then there was Publius Consta who wanted to be a lawyer, but was lacking both in learning and in ability. He was summoned by Cicero as a witness in a lawsuit and kept on saying that he knew nothing. 'Perhaps,' said Cicero, 'you are under the impression that you are being examined on points of law.'

There was an occasion too when, in a quarrel with Cicero, Metellus Nepos asked him repeatedly, 'Who is your father?' 'I can scarcely ask you the same question,' Cicero replied, 'since your mother has made it rather a difficult one to answer' –

Nepos' mother being a lady whose reputation for chastity was not high. Nepos himself also was of a flighty disposition. He once suddenly deserted his office as tribune and sailed off to Pompey in Syria, and then, with even less reason, came straight back again.[64] He gave his teacher Philagrus a funeral which was more elaborate than necessary and set up on his tomb the figure of a raven in stone. Cicero's comment was: 'How appropriate! Since instead of teaching you to speak, he taught you how to fly from one place to another.'

Then there was Marcus Appius who opened his speech in a lawsuit by saying that his friend had begged him to show care, eloquence and integrity. 'And how can you be so hard-hearted,' said Cicero, 'as not to exhibit a single one of those qualities which your friend demanded of you?'

27. No doubt it is part of the business of a lawyer to employ these rather cruel jokes at the expense of his enemies and his legal opponents. But Cicero's propensity to attack anyone for the sake of raising a laugh aroused a good deal of ill-feeling against him. A few examples of this may be added. He used to allude to Marcus Aquinius, who had two sons-in-law in exile, as 'Adrastus'. And when Lucius Cotta,[65] who was a very heavy drinker, held the office of censor, Cicero, then canvassing for the consulship, felt thirsty and his friends stood round him while he was drinking. 'You are quite right to be alarmed,' said Cicero. 'The censor may easily make things difficult for me if he finds that it is water that I am drinking.'

Once too he met Voconius in the company of his three daughters who were extremely ugly and he quoted the verse:

'Apollo never meant him to beget.'

Then, when Marcus Gellius, who was thought to be the son of a slave, had read some letters aloud to the senate in a clear ringing voice, Cicero remarked: 'There is nothing to be surprised at. He is one of those who have had to speak up to others.'

And when Faustus, the son of the Sulla who had been dictator

in Rome and had published those long lists of people condemned to die, had run through most of his fortune and, having
got into debt, published a list of his household goods which
were for sale, Cicero said: 'I like this sort of advertising. It is
better than his father's.'

28. As a result of this kind of behaviour, Cicero made a number
of enemies. In particular Clodius[66] and his party combined
against him for the following reasons. Clodius was a member
of a noble family, young in years, but bold in spirit and one
who was determined to get his own way. He was in love with
Caesar's wife, Pompeia, and got into his house secretly by
dressing up as a woman lute player. For the women of Rome
were celebrating in Caesar's house that mysterious ceremony
which men are not allowed to see, and there was no man
present.[67] Clodius, however, being still a youth who had not
grown a beard, hoped to slip through with the women and get
to Pompeia without being noticed. But, as he came in at night
and the house was a large one, he lost his way in the passages;
and, while he was wandering about, a maid of Caesar's mother
Aurelia saw him and asked him what his name was. Since he
was forced to speak, he said that he was looking for one of
Pompeia's servants called Abra, and the maid, realizing that his
voice was not that of a woman, shrieked out and called all the
women together. They shut all the doors and carried out a
thorough search until they found Clodius hiding in the room
of the girl with whom he had come into the house. This affair
caused a great scandal and Caesar divorced Pompeia and instituted proceedings against Clodius on the charge of sacrilege.

29. Cicero was a friend of Clodius and at the time of Catiline's
conspiracy had found him most anxious to help and protect
him. However, when Clodius, in reply to the charge made
against him, insisted that he had never even been in Rome at
the time but had been staying at a place a long way away from
the city, Cicero gave evidence against him and stated that he
had come to his house where he had consulted him on various
matters. This was perfectly true, but it was believed that Cicero

gave his evidence not so much because of the truth of it as because he wished to put himself in the right with his own wife Terentia, who was very hostile to Clodius on account of his sister Clodia.[68] Terentia suspected Clodia of wanting to marry Cicero and thought that she was trying to arrange this with the help of a man called Tullus who was on particularly friendly and intimate terms with Cicero. Terentia's suspicions were aroused by the way in which Tullus kept on visiting and paying attentions to Clodia, who lived close by; and since Terentia had a violent will of her own and had gained the ascendancy over Cicero, she urged him on to join in the attack on Clodius and to give evidence against him. Many of the better class of people also gave evidence against Clodius for perjury, fraud, bribing the people and seductions of women. Lucullus[69] actually produced female slaves who testified that Clodius had had sexual relations with his youngest sister at the time when she was living with Lucullus as his wife. It was generally believed also that Clodius had had intercourse with his other two sisters – Tertia, the wife of Marcius Rex, and Clodia, the wife of Metellus Celer. This last one was called Lady Farthing after the name of the smallest copper coin, because one of her lovers had deceived her by putting copper money instead of silver into a purse and sending it in to her. It was with regard to this sister in particular that Clodius got a bad name. However, the people at this time were united in their opposition to those who had combined to attack Clodius and were giving evidence against him. The members of the jury were terrified; they had to be protected by an armed guard, and most of them gave in voting tablets that were undecipherable. Nevertheless, it appeared that the majority had voted for Clodius' acquittal. A certain amount of bribery also was said to have been employed and it was this which prompted Catulus, when he next met the jurymen, to remark: 'You people were quite rightly concerned about your safety when you asked for a guard. Someone might have taken your money from you.' And when Clodius told Cicero that the jury had not believed his evidence, Cicero replied: 'You will find that twenty-five of them trusted in my word since they voted against you, and that the other thirty did not trust yours, since they did not vote for your acquittal until they had actually got your money in their hands.'

Caesar, though called as a witness, gave no evidence against Clodius and said that he had not divorced his wife because he believed her guilty of adultery, but because Caesar's wife should be not only free from guilt but free also from the very suspicion of it.

30. After Clodius had escaped from this danger he was elected tribune[70] and immediately began to attack Cicero, raking up everything he could and inciting every type of person against him. He won over the people by laws passed in their interest;[71] he had large provinces voted to each of the consuls (Macedonia to Piso and Syria to Gabinius);[72] he organized numbers of the poorer classes into political clubs, and he provided himself with a bodyguard of armed slaves.

The three men with the greatest power in Rome at this time were Crassus, Pompey and Caesar. Crassus was an open enemy of Cicero; Pompey had a foot in both camps; and Caesar was about to set out with an army to Gaul. Cicero therefore attempted to secure Caesar's favour, though Caesar, so far from being his friend, had incurred his suspicions in connection with the affair of Catiline. He asked Caesar to give him an appointment on his staff for the forthcoming campaign and Caesar agreed to do so.[73] Clodius, however, seeing that Cicero was escaping from his authority as a tribune, now pretended that he was anxious for a reconciliation. He put most of the blame for the quarrel on Terentia, always referred to Cicero himself with respect and made the most friendly remarks about him, giving the impression that he was without any hatred or ill-will for him, indeed had nothing against him except a few minor complaints which one friend might make of another. In this way he entirely dispelled Cicero's fears, so that he declined Caesar's offer of an appointment abroad and again began to take part in public affairs. Caesar was angry at this and encouraged Clodius to renew his attacks. Caesar also turned Pompey completely against Cicero[74] and then in a speech which he made himself to a meeting of the people declared that in his view it was neither right nor lawful for men to be put to death without a trial, as had happened in the cases of Lentulus, Cethegus and their party. For this was the accusation against Cicero and this was the charge that he was being called upon to meet.

So, finding himself in danger of prosecution, Cicero put on mourning and, with his hair long and unkempt, went about the city approaching the people as a suppliant. However, he could not enter a single street without being accosted by Clodius with a band of insolent ruffians round him, who effectively interfered with his supplications by making all sorts of rude jokes about his change of clothes and his way of carrying himself, and on many occasions pelted him with mud and stones.

31. In spite of this, in the first place, the members of the equestrian order, almost without exception, changed into mourning in sympathy with Cicero, and at least 20,000 young men went with him and, with their hair untrimmed like his, joined in his supplications. Then the senate met to pass a vote that the people should go into mourning as at times of public calamity. When this motion was opposed by the consuls and Clodius had surrounded the senate house with armed men, many of the senators ran out, tearing their clothes and crying out aloud. This sight, however, aroused no feelings either of pity or of due respect. It was evident that Cicero would either have to go into exile or else meet Clodius with armed force.

At this point Cicero appealed to Pompey for help, but Pompey had purposely got out of the way and was staying at his country house in the Alban hills. First Cicero sent his son-in-law Piso[75] to plead for him; then he went up there himself. Pompey, however, when he heard of his arrival, could not face seeing him. He was bitterly ashamed when he remembered how in the past Cicero had fought his battles on many important occasions and had often taken a particular line in politics for his sake; but he was Caesar's son-in-law, and at Caesar's request he proved false to the obligations of the past. He slipped out of the house by another door and so avoided the interview.

Betrayed as he was by Pompey, and left defenceless, Cicero now turned to the consuls for protection. Gabinius was rough with him, as always, but Piso spoke to him more politely. He advised him to stand aside and give way to Clodius' violence, to accept the fact that the times had changed and to become once more the saviour of his country, which was now, because of Clodius, involved in all the evils of internal strife.

After receiving this answer Cicero consulted with his friends. Lucullus advised him to stay, thinking that he was sure to be the winner in the end; but others advised him to go into exile. Their argument was that once the people had had enough of Clodius' mad irresponsibility they would soon feel the need of Cicero again. Cicero decided to follow this advice. First he took the statue of Minerva out of his house, where it had stood for a long time and had been treated by him with great distinction. He carried this statue to the capitol and dedicated it there with the inscription: 'To Minerva, Guardian of Rome.' Then, escorted by his friends, he left the city secretly in the middle of the night and set out on foot through Lucania with the intention of going to Sicily.

32. As soon as it was known for certain that he had fled, Clodius carried through a vote condemning him to exile and issued an edict that he should be refused fire and water and that no man should give him shelter within 500 miles of Italy.[76] Most people paid not the slightest attention to this edict. They respected Cicero himself, and escorted him on his way with every mark of kindness. But at Hipponium, a city in Lucania, now called Vibo, a Sicilian called Vibius, who had gained much from Cicero's friendship – particularly by being made prefect of engineers during his consulship – would not receive him at his house. He sent word instead that he would reserve accommodation for him at his country estate. And Gaius Vergilius,[77] the praetor of Sicily, who had been on the most friendly terms with Cicero, wrote telling him not to land in Sicily.

Disheartened by this, Cicero set out for Brundisium and, with a fair wind, attempted to make the crossing from there to Dyrrhachium. However, the wind turned and blew from the sea, so he came back next day and then set sail again. When he reached the harbour at Dyrrhachium and was about to go ashore, it is said that there was an earthquake and at the same time a great convulsion of the sea. From these events the sooth-sayers conjectured that Cicero's exile would not last long, since they are signs foretelling change.

Numbers of people showed their goodwill to him by coming to visit him and the Greek cities vied with each other in sending deputations to do him honour. Yet he remained for most of the time miserable and disconsolate, keeping his eyes fixed, like a distressed lover, on Italy; his spirit was not great enough to rise above his misfortunes, and he became more dejected than one would have thought it possible for a man to be who had enjoyed such advantages in training and education. This was the man who used often to tell his friends that they should describe him not as an orator but as a philosopher, since it was philosophy that was his real occupation and he only used oratory as an instrument for attaining his objects in public life. Public opinion, however, has the strange power of being able, as it were, to erase from a man's character the lines formed there by reason; and, by the force of habit and association, it can impress the passions and feelings of the mob on those who engage in politics, unless one is very much on one's guard and makes up one's mind that in dealing with what is outside oneself one will be concerned only with the practical problems themselves and not with the passions that arise out of them.

33. Meanwhile, after he had driven Cicero out of Italy, Clodius burned down his villas and burned down his house in Rome.[78] On the site he built a temple to Liberty. The rest of his property he put up to auction and advertised it every day, but no one would buy anything. His conduct terrorized the nobility; he swept the people along with him on an unbridled course of extravagant action and insolent behaviour; and finally he turned on Pompey, violently attacking some of the arrange-ments made by him for the countries conquered by him on his campaigns.[79] The disgrace of this made Pompey bitterly reproach himself for the way in which he had abandoned Cicero. He now changed round again and, with the help of his friends, did everything he possibly could to have Cicero

recalled. Clodius, of course, opposed all such plans, and the senate decided that, unless Cicero was allowed to return, they would refuse in the meantime to ratify any legislation or to transact any public business. During the consulship of Lentulus[80] the disorders increased to such an extent that tribunes were wounded in the forum[81] and Cicero's brother Quintus was left lying unnoticed among the bodies of the dead, presumed to be dead himself.[82] After this there was a change in popular feeling; one of the tribunes, Annius Milo,[83] first showed sufficient courage to come forward and prosecute Clodius for acts of violence; and a large party both from the Roman people and from the nearby cities was formed to support Pompey. With their aid Pompey moved into the city, drove Clodius out of the forum and then summoned the citizens to vote on the question of Cicero's recall. It is said that on no other occasion did the people vote with such unanimity. The senate, too, not to be left behind by the people, wrote letters of thanks to all the cities which had afforded hospitality to Cicero during his exile, and decreed that his house in Rome and his country houses which had been destroyed by Clodius should be rebuilt at the public expense.

So Cicero came home after an exile of sixteen months. There was such joy among the cities and people were so eager to come out and meet him that what Cicero himself said later – namely, that Italy had taken him on her shoulders and carried him back to Rome – is far from being an exaggeration. And at Rome even Crassus, who had been his enemy before his exile, was now ready enough to come out to meet him and to be reconciled. He did this, he said, to please his son Publius, who was a great admirer of Cicero's.

34. After only a short time had passed, Cicero, who had waited until Clodius happened to be out of Rome, went up to the Capitol with a crowd of his supporters and tore down and destroyed the tablets on which were recorded the measures passed by the tribunes. Clodius brought a charge against him for this, and Cicero replied that as Clodius who was of a patrician family had illegally got himself elected tribune,[84] none

of the measures for which he was responsible could be regarded as valid. Cato, however, was indignant at this and spoke against Cicero. Not that he approved of Clodius; in fact he was strongly opposed to his whole policy. He maintained, however, that it would be an irregular and violent course to take if the senate were to vote for the cancellation of so many acts and decrees, among which were those which concerned his own administration of Cyprus and Byzantium.[85] This led to a certain amount of ill-feeling between Cicero and Cato, which, while it was not expressed openly, had the effect of rather impairing their friendship.

35. After this Clodius was killed by Milo,[86] and Milo, being prosecuted for the murder, engaged Cicero as counsel for the defence. Milo was a person of importance, noted for his proud spirit, and the senate, fearing that his trial would be the occasion for disturbances in the city, entrusted the supervision of this and other trials to Pompey, who was to take measures to guarantee the security both of Rome and of the law courts.[87] Pompey, therefore, while it was still night, posted his soldiers on the high ground commanding the forum; and Milo, who was afraid that Cicero would be disturbed by such an unusual sight and so fail to conduct the case as well as he might, persuaded him to be carried down to the forum in a litter and to wait there quietly until the jury had assembled and the courtroom was full. Indeed it appears that Cicero not only lacked courage at the sight of armed men, but was always timid at the beginning of a speech and in many trials scarcely stopped quivering and trembling even when he had really got going and was at the height of his eloquence. There was the occasion, for instance, when he was defending Licinius Murena in a case brought against him by Cato.[88] Hortensius had made a speech which had won much applause and Cicero, in his ambitious anxiety to do still better, passed a completely sleepless night, with the result that his powers were impaired by lack of sleep and overanxiety and his speech was considered to be not up to his usual standard. So on this occasion, when he came out of the litter to speak in Milo's defence and saw Pompey stationed

on the high ground as though in command of a military operation, and arms flashing in every direction round the forum, he
broke down completely; his body shook, his voice faltered and
he could scarcely begin his speech.[89] Milo, on the other hand,
behaved with admirable courage at the trial; he did not deign
to let his hair grow long or to put on mourning, and this seems
to have been one of the chief reasons why he was condemned.
Nevertheless, Cicero's behaviour was considered to show not
so much cowardice as devotion to his friend.

36. He was made one of the priests, whom the Romans call
Augurs, in the place of the younger Crassus, who had died in
the Parthian campaign.[90] Then he was appointed by lot to the
province of Cilicia with an army of 12,000 infantry and 2,600
cavalry.[91] He sailed out to his province with instructions to
keep Cappadocia friendly and obedient to King Ariobarzanes.
He succeeded in carrying out this mission satisfactorily, making
the necessary arrangements without going to war. He observed
that, after the Roman disaster in Parthia and the revolt in Syria,
the Cilicians were in an unsettled state, and he brought them
to a more reasonable frame of mind by the considerate way in
which he acted as governor.[92] He would accept no presents, not
even when they were offered by the kings, and, while he relieved
the provincials from having to spend money on entertainments,
he would daily receive at his own house people whom he found
agreeable and entertain them to meals that were generous without being extravagant. His house had no doorkeeper to keep
people out, nor was he ever seen by anyone lying abed. As soon
as it was light he would be standing or walking in front of his
room, ready to receive those who came to pay him their
respects. It is said too that he never ordered anyone to be beaten
with rods or to be stripped of his clothing, that he never used
insulting language in a fit of temper or inflicted punishments
designed to wound a person's self-respect. He found that there
had been a lot of embezzlement of public funds and he saw to
it that the cities regained their financial stability, while at the
same time he inflicted no further punishment on those who
repaid what they had embezzled, but allowed them to retain

their rights as citizens. He engaged in a military campaign also, and routed the robbers who lived on Mount Amanus. For this he was actually saluted by his soldiers as 'Imperator'. When Caelius,[93] the orator, asked him to send some panthers from Cilicia for some show which he was giving at Rome, Cicero, in a mood of self-glorification at what he had achieved, wrote to say that there were no panthers in Cilicia; they had all run off to Caria in indignation at the fact that they were the only creatures that were being attacked while everyone else was enjoying peace.

On his voyage back from his province he first put in at Rhodes, and then was most happy to stay a while in Athens, since he had the fondest memories of the times he had spent there in the past. He met the most distinguished men in all branches of culture, greeted those who had been his friends and companions in the old days, and after receiving from Greece the honours that were due to him, returned to Rome which he found, as it were, in the preliminary stages of that fever which was to lead to the civil war.

37. In the senate, when his fellow-members were voting him a triumph,[94] he said that he would rather follow in Caesar's triumphal procession, if only matters could be settled satisfactorily. And in private he wrote many letters to Caesar, giving him his advice, and had many personal interviews in which he interceded with Pompey – trying to calm the feelings of each of them and to bring them to reason. Soon, however, things had gone too far for any remedy. Caesar was advancing on Rome and Pompey did not stay to meet him. With many other good men he abandoned the city. In this exodus Cicero took no part and he was believed to be throwing in his lot with Caesar. It is certainly evident that, with his judgement pulling him in both directions, he was in great distress of mind. He writes in his letters that he does not know which way he ought to turn.[95] 'Pompey,' he says, 'has fair and honourable reasons for going to war: but Caesar has managed his affairs better and is more competent to look after himself and his friends. I know, therefore, whom I should fly from, but not whom I should fly to.'

But when Trebatius,[96] one of Caesar's close friends, wrote to him to say that in Caesar's view much the best thing would be for Cicero to range himself on his side and share his hopes, but that, if he felt himself to be too old for this, then he ought to go to Greece and live there quietly without committing himself to either side, Cicero expressed surprise that Caesar had not written to him personally and angrily replied that he would do nothing unworthy of his past career in politics. So much for the evidence of the letters.

38. When Caesar set out for Spain, Cicero sailed immediately to join Pompey. His appearance was generally welcomed, but when Cato saw him, he spoke to him in private and told him that, in coming over to Pompey's side, he had made a mistake. As for himself, Cato said, he was bound by honour not to forsake the general line in politics which he had taken up from the beginning; but Cicero would be more useful to his country and to his friends if he stayed at home without taking sides and adapted himself to events when he knew what the result would be; now, however, unnecessarily and for no good reason, he had made himself an enemy of Caesar and had come out there and involved himself in the great dangers which threatened them all.

Those words had a most disturbing effect on Cicero's mind, and he was also upset by the fact that Pompey made no great use of him. For this, however, he was himself to blame. He made no secret of the fact that he was sorry he had come; he belittled Pompey's military resources and was always criticizing his plans behind his back; he could not refrain from making sarcastic remarks and jokes about his comrades in arms;[97] in fact, though he always went about the camp himself with a severe look on his face and without a smile, he made others laugh in spite of themselves. It is worth giving some examples of this. There was, for instance, an occasion when Domitius[98] had put a man of no military experience into a post of responsibility and excused himself by saying that the man had a most agreeable personality and was a sound character. 'Why, then,' said Cicero, 'don't you give him a job as a schoolmaster?' Then there was Theophanes the Lesbian,[99] who was chief of engineers

in the army. Some people were praising him for the wonderful
way in which he had consoled the Rhodians for the loss of their
fleet,[100] and Cicero remarked: 'It is indeed a mercy to have a
Greek in command.' Then, when things were going very well
for Caesar and he was indeed practically besieging them,
Lentulus[101] said that he had heard that Caesar's friends were
out of heart; to which Cicero replied: 'It must be that they don't
want him to win.' And when a man called Marcius, who had
recently arrived from Italy, mentioned that in Rome there
was strong rumour that Pompey was being blockaded, Cicero
said: 'And then, no doubt, you sailed out here to see it with
your own eyes.' And after the defeat, when Nonnius[102] said that
they ought still to have hope since there were seven eagles left
in Pompey's camp, Cicero replied: 'Excellent advice, if only
we were fighting against jackdaws.' Labienus,[103] too, kept on
stressing the importance of certain prophecies and saying that
Pompey was bound to win. 'Exactly the sort of strategy,' com-
mented Cicero, 'which has just led to the loss of our camp.'

39. Cicero took no part in the battle of Pharsalus because of
ill health. But when the battle was over and Pompey was in
flight, Cato, who had a considerable army and a large fleet at
Dyrrhachium, called upon Cicero, in accordance with custom
and his superior rank as an ex-consul, to take over the command. Cicero, however, rejected the offer of the command and
indeed refused to have anything whatever to do with further
operations. Because of this he very nearly lost his life. Young
Pompey and his friends called him a traitor and drew their
swords on him; but Cato interposed and, not without considerable difficulty, succeeded in rescuing him and sending him away
from the camp.

He then put in to Brundisium and stayed there waiting for
Caesar who was delayed by his activities in Asia and Egypt.
Finally the news came that Caesar had landed at Tarentum[104]
and was coming round by land from there to Brundisium.
Cicero hurried out to meet him. He was not altogether without
hope of the result, but he felt ashamed at having to test, as it
were, the reactions of an enemy and a conqueror in front of so

many witnesses. As it happened there was no need at all for him to do or say anything unworthy of himself. He was some way ahead of the rest when Caesar saw him coming, and he immediately got down and embraced him and then took him along with him for a considerable distance, talking to him privately. Afterwards, too, Caesar always honoured him and showed him kindness, and in his reply to the encomium on Cato which Cicero published, he wrote in the warmest terms of Cicero who, he said, both in his eloquence and in his life, strongly resembled Pericles and Theramenes. (Cicero's essay was called 'Cato' and Caesar's 'Anti-Cato'.) It is said too that when Quintus Ligarius[105] was being prosecuted as one of Caesar's enemies and Cicero was defending him, Caesar said to his friends: 'Why should we not hear a speech from Cicero after all this time? As for Ligarius we have long known him to be guilty and an enemy.' But when Cicero began to speak his words were incredibly moving; and as his speech proceeded, ranging in the most wonderfully charming language from one emotion to another, the colour came and went on Caesar's face and it was evident that every passion of his soul was being stirred. And finally, when the orator touched on the battle at Pharsalus, Caesar was so deeply affected that his whole body shook and some of the papers that he was holding dropped from his hand. So he was, as it were, overpowered and acquitted Ligarius.

40. After this, when the government had been changed to a monarchy, Cicero retired from public life and gave up his time to those of the young men who wanted to study philosophy.[106] It was chiefly because of his association with these young men, who came from the best and most powerful families, that he once again exercised a great influence in the state. He occupied himself also in writing and translating philosophical dialogues[107] and in rendering into Latin the various terms used in logic and in natural science. It was he, they say, who first, or principally, provided Latin names for 'phantasia', 'synkatathesis', 'epoche', and 'katalepsis', and also for 'atomon', 'ameres,' 'kenon', and other such technical words, which he

managed to make intelligible and familiar either by using meta-
phors or by finding new and appropriate terms for them. He
found much pleasure too in exercising his facility for writing
poetry. It is said, indeed, that when he set his mind to it, he
would compose 500 lines of verse in a night.

At this period of his life he spent most of his time at his
country estate in Tusculum. He used to write to his friends that
he was living the life of a Laertes – this remark being either one
of his usual jokes or else prompted by his ambition and his
desire to take part in public affairs which made him dissatisfied
with the state of things as they were. He went down to Rome
rarely and only to pay his respects to Caesar, and he took the
leading part among those who used to propose honours for
him and were always trying to find new terms of praise for
Caesar himself or for his achievements. For example, there is
the remark he made about Pompey's statues. These had been
thrown down and removed, but Caesar had ordered them to
be set up again. When this had been done, Cicero said that by
his generous action Caesar had not only set up Pompey's statues
but had firmly fixed and established his own.

41. He had planned, it is said, to write a comprehensive history
of his own country, combining with it much of the history of
Greece and incorporating in it all the stories and legends of the
past which he had collected. But he was prevented from doing
this by the pressure of much public business which he had no
wish to do and by various private troubles which, for the most
part, he seems to have brought upon himself. In the first place
he divorced his wife Terentia.[108] He considered that she had
neglected him during the war; she had allowed him to set out
without sufficient means for his journey; and even when he got
back to Italy he did not find her any kinder to him. Though he
waited for a long time at Brundisium, she did not come there
herself; and when his daughter, a young girl, made the long
journey, she failed to provide her with a proper escort or sufficient money for her expenses. In fact, she had actually stripped
Cicero's house of everything it possessed and had incurred a
number of large debts besides. These, certainly, are the most

plausible reasons given for the divorce. Terentia, however, denied them all, and Cicero himself, by marrying a virgin soon afterwards,[109] made what she said in her defence look very credible. Terentia charged him with having made this marriage because he had been swept off his feet by the girl's youth and charm; but according to Tiro, Cicero's freedman, it was to get money to pay his debts; for the girl was extremely rich and Cicero had been left her trustee and was in charge of her property. Since he owed great sums of money, he was persuaded by his friends and relations to marry the girl in spite of the disparity between their ages and to use her money for satisfying his creditors. Antony, in his replies to Cicero's Philippics, refers to this marriage and says that he put out of doors the wife with whom he had grown old; and he goes on to make some witty remarks about Cicero's domesticity and his inactive, unsoldierlike ways.

Not long after the marriage Cicero's daughter died in childbirth at the house of Lentulus, to whom she had been married after the death of her former husband, Piso.[110] Cicero's friends came together from all sides to comfort him; but his grief at the misfortune was so excessive that he actually divorced his newly married wife because she seemed to be pleased at Tullia's death.

42. So much, then, for Cicero's domestic affairs. In the plot that was taking shape against Caesar he took no part, although he was a particular friend of Brutus, and it was considered that he, more than anyone, was dissatisfied with the present state of affairs and longed for the past. The conspirators, however, were apprehensive about him: he was not very daring by nature, and he had reached an age when even the boldest spirits are apt to lose something of their resolution.

When the deed had been done by Brutus, Cassius and the rest, the friends of Caesar combined together against them and it was feared that Rome would again be plunged into civil war. At this point Antony, as consul, called a meeting of the senate and said a few words on the subject of preserving peace and concord.[111] Cicero followed with a long speech well suited to the occasion and persuaded the senate to imitate the Athenians and to vote an amnesty for those who had taken part in the killing of Caesar and to assign provinces to Brutus and Cassius. These proposals, however, came to nothing. The people's sympathies were in any case with Caesar, and when they saw his dead body being carried through the forum, and when Antony showed them the garments all drenched with blood and pierced through in every place with swords, they went mad with rage, searched all over the forum for the murderers and, with torches in their hands, ran to burn down their houses. The conspirators were prepared for this danger beforehand and so escaped it; but, fearing more and greater dangers in the future, they left Rome.

43. Antony's mood was now one of exultation. Everyone was afraid that he would seek supreme power for himself, and Cicero was more afraid of this than anyone. Antony, realizing that Cicero was once again becoming a power in the state and that he was a friend to Brutus and his party, disliked the idea of his presence in Rome. And even before this time they had been rather suspicious of each other because of the very wide difference in their ways of living. Cicero therefore feared Antony and at first was inclined to take an appointment on Dolabella's staff and sail out with him to Syria,[112] But the consuls elected to succeed Antony were Hirtius and Pansa,[113] both good men and admirers of Cicero. They begged him not to desert them and said that, if Cicero would stay in Rome, they would guarantee to deal with Antony. Cicero, without being entirely confident in these assurances, believed them up to a point and let Dolabella go without him. He agreed with Hirtius and Pansa to spend the summer in Athens and to return again to Rome when they had taken up office. So he set out by himself.[114] His voyage, however, was delayed in some way or other, and, as often happens, the news from Rome suddenly seemed to change. It was now said that there had been an astonishing alteration in Antony's behaviour; all his actions and policies were now directed to please the senate,[115] and it only needed Cicero's presence for everything to be settled in the most satisfactory manner possible. Cicero therefore reproached

himself for having been overcautious. He turned back again to Rome and in his first expectations was not disappointed. People rejoiced to see him and longed for his presence. Such great crowds poured out to meet him that the greetings and speeches of welcome at the city gates and during his entry into the city took up nearly a whole day.

Next day Antony called a meeting of the senate and invited Cicero to attend. Cicero, however, did not come. He stayed in bed, pretending that he was ill after the fatigues of his journey. But the truth seemed to be that, as the result of some suspicion or other and of some information which had suddenly reached him on the road, he was afraid of a plot against him. Antony was extremely angry at the implication and was for sending soldiers with orders either to bring Cicero or to burn down his house. Many people, however, protested against this and begged him not to do anything of the sort; and so he contented himself merely with receiving sureties for Cicero's good behaviour. After this they made no sign of recognition when they met, and they kept up this attitude, each being on his guard against the other, until the time when young Caesar came from Apollonia to receive the inheritance left to him by the elder Caesar and engaged in a dispute with Antony, who was holding back 25 million drachmas from the estate.[116]

44. As the result of this Philippus and Marcellus,[117] the husbands respectively of young Caesar's mother and sister, came with the young man to Cicero and made an arrangement by which Cicero was to use his powers of oratory and political influence on Caesar's behalf in the senate and before the people, and Caesar with his wealth and armed forces was to guarantee Cicero's security. The young man had already attached to him many of the soldiers who had served under the elder Caesar. It was thought that there was another and stronger reason, too, which induced Cicero to accept Caesar's friendship so readily. It seems that, while Pompey and Caesar were still alive, Cicero had a dream in which someone invited the sons of the senators to the Capitol because Jupiter was going to appoint one of them to be the ruler of Rome. The citizens came running up eagerly

and posted themselves round the temple, and the boys in their purple-bordered togas took their places in silence. Suddenly the doors opened and one by one the boys rose up and walked round past the god, who inspected each of them in turn. All, to their sorrow, were dismissed until this young Caesar came into the god's presence. Then the god stretched out his hand and said: 'Romans, you shall have an end of civil wars, when this boy becomes your ruler.' This, they say, was the sort of dream which Cicero had, and from it he received a very vivid impression of the boy's appearance, and retained this impression clearly, though he did not know the boy personally. Next day, however, he was going down to the Field of Mars at the time when the boys had just finished their exercise and were coming away. Among them Cicero saw for the first time the boy who had appeared in his dream. He was amazed and inquired who his parents were. His father was Octavius, who was not a person of great importance, but his mother was Attia, a daughter of Caesar's sister.[118] For this reason Caesar, who had no children of his own, left him in his will his property and his family name. After this, they say, Cicero was always careful to take some notice of the young man whenever they met, and he on his side welcomed these kind attentions; it happened too that he was born in the year of Cicero's consulship.

45. Though these were the reasons spoken of, what really attached Cicero to young Caesar was, firstly, his hatred of Antony, and secondly, his natural passion for distinction. He imagined that he was adding Caesar's power to his own political influence. And the young man played up to him, going so far as actually to call him 'father'. This made Brutus extremely angry. In his letters to Atticus he wrote sharply of Cicero, saying that in courting Caesar because he feared Antony, Cicero was making it plain that, instead of working for the liberty of his country, he was wooing a tyrant who would be kind to him personally.[119] In spite of this Brutus took up Cicero's son,[120] who was studying philosophy in Athens, gave him a command and used his services in a number of successful undertakings.

It was at this time that Cicero's power in Rome reached its

greatest height. In fact, he was strong enough to do exactly as he pleased. He raised a party against Antony and drove him out of the city; then he sent out the two consuls, Hirtius and Pansa, to make war on him. As for Caesar, he persuaded the senate to vote him the lictors and insignia of a praetor, on the ground that he was fighting in defence of his country.[121] But when Antony was defeated and both consuls had died after the battle,[122] their forces joined up with those of Caesar and the senate became alarmed at the thought of this young man who was enjoying such extraordinary good fortune. By gifts and honours they attempted to draw his army away from him and to limit his power, giving it out that, now that Antony had taken to flight, there was no longer any need for a defence force. This attitude of theirs made Caesar apprehensive. He secretly sent to Cicero agents of his to do all they could to persuade him to obtain the consulship for them both; they were to say that, once he was in office, Cicero should arrange matters just as he thought best and should direct in everything the conduct of his young colleague, whose one desire was glory and a good name. And Caesar himself admitted afterwards that it was because he was afraid of having his troops disbanded and of finding himself isolated that he made use, in the emergency, of Cicero's passion for power and, promising him his own help and cooperation in the canvassing, persuaded him to stand for the consulship.

46. Here, certainly Cicero in his old age allowed himself to be carried away by the words of a youth and was utterly taken in by him. He helped Caesar in the canvassing and procured for him the goodwill of the senate. For this he was blamed by his friends at the time, and soon afterwards he too realized that he had ruined himself and betrayed the liberty of his country. Once the young man had established himself and secured the consulship,[123] he paid no further attention to Cicero. Instead he made friends with Antony and Lepidus, joined forces with them and divided the government with them as though it were a piece of property.[124] A list was drawn up of the names of more than 200 men who were to be put to death. But what

caused most trouble at their discussions was the question of including Cicero's name in this list. Antony refused to come to terms unless Cicero was marked down first for death; Lepidus sided with Antony, and Caesar held out against them both. They met secretly by themselves near the city of Bononia, and these meetings lasted for three days. They came together at a place surrounded by a river and at some distance from their camps. It is said that for the first two days Caesar kept up the struggle to save Cicero, but gave in on the third day and abandoned him. The terms of their mutual concessions were as follows: Caesar was to desert Cicero, Lepidus, his brother Paulus[125] and Antony, Lucius Caesar,[126] who was his uncle on his mother's side. So all considerations of humanity were swept aside by their rage and fury; or was this, rather, a demonstration that no wild beast is more savage than man when his passions are armed with power?

47. While this was going on, Cicero was at his country estate in Tusculum. He had his brother there with him. When they heard of the proscriptions they decided to move on to Astura, a place belonging to Cicero on the coast, and from there to sail to Brutus in Macedonia.[127] (There was already news of his being there in some strength.) So they were carried on their way in litters. They were quite overwhelmed with grief and on the journey would often stop and, with the litters placed side by side, would condole with each other. Quintus was the more disheartened of the two. He began to think of his destitute condition. He had taken nothing, he said, from home; and Cicero too had insufficient money for the journey; it was better, therefore, he said, for Cicero to carry on with his flight, and he would hurry after him once he had got from home what he needed. This was the course they decided upon, and so, after they had embraced each other, they parted with many tears.

Only a few days later Quintus was betrayed by his servants to those who were looking for him and was put to death, together with his son. Cicero, however, was carried to Astura, where he found a boat and immediately went on board. He sailed down the coast as far as Circaeum with a following wind.

From here the pilots wanted to sail on at once, but Cicero, either because he feared the sea or because he had not yet entirely lost his faith in Caesar, went ashore and travelled on foot about twelve miles in the direction of Rome. Again he lost his resolution and changed his mind, going back to the sea at Astura. Here he passed a night with his mind full of terrible thoughts and desperate plans. He actually decided to go secretly to Caesar's home and to kill himself there on the hearthstone, so as to bring a curse from Heaven upon him; but fear, the fear of torture, turned him from this course also. So, after turning over in his mind all sorts of confused schemes and contradictory projects, he put himself in the hands of his servants to be taken by sea to Caieta. Here he had an estate which was a most agreeable place to go to in the summer, when the Etesian winds are so pleasant.

In this place also there is a temple of Apollo, a little above the sea, and from the temple a flight of crows rose up into the air with a great noise and came flying towards Cicero's ship as it was being rowed to land. They perched on either side of the yard, some croaking and some pecking at the ends of the ropes, and everyone regarded this as a bad omen. Cicero, however, disembarked, went to his villa and lay down to rest. Then, while most of the crows perched round the window, making a tremendous noise with their cawing, one of them flew down on to the bed where Cicero was lying with his head all covered up, and little by little began to drag away with its bill the garment from his face. When the servants saw this they reproached themselves for standing by as spectators waiting for their master to be murdered, and doing nothing to defend him, while these wild brute creatures were helping him and caring for him in his undeserved ill fortune. So, partly by entreaty and partly by force, they took him up and carried him in his litter towards the sea.

48. Meanwhile, however, the murderers had arrived. These were the centurion Herennius and Popillius,[128] an officer in the army, who had in the past been defended by Cicero when he was prosecuted for having murdered his father. They had their

helpers with them. They found the doors shut and broke them down; but Cicero was not to be seen and the people in the house said that they did not know where he was. Then, we are told, a young man who had been educated by Cicero in literature and philosophy, an ex-slave of Cicero's brother Quintus, Philologus by name, told the officer that the litter was being carried down to the sea by a path that was under the cover of the trees. The officer took a few men with him and hurried round to the place where the path came out of the woods, and Herennius went running down the path. Cicero heard him coming and ordered his servants to set the litter down where they were. He himself, in that characteristic posture of his, with his chin resting on his left hand, looked steadfastly at his murderers. He was all covered in dust; his hair was long and disordered, and his face was pinched and wasted with his anxieties – so that most of those who stood by covered their faces while Herennius was killing him. His throat was cut as he stretched his neck out from the litter. He was in his sixty-fourth year. By Antony's orders Herennius cut off his head and his hands – the hands with which he had written the Philippics. (It was Cicero himself who called these speeches against Antony 'the Philippics'; and they have retained the title to the present day.)

49. When these severed extremities of Cicero's person were brought to Rome Antony happened to be organizing an election. Hearing the news and seeing the sight, he cried out: 'Now let there be an end of our proscriptions.' Then he ordered the head and the hands to be fastened up over the ships' rams on the public platform in the forum. It was a sight to make the Romans shudder. They seemed to see there, not so much the face of Cicero, as the image of the soul of Antony. However, in all this Antony did show one sign of decent feeling. He handed over Philologus to Pomponia,[129] the wife of Quintus. And she, when she had got the man in her power, inflicted all sorts of terrible punishments on him and finally made him cut off his own flesh bit by bit, roast the pieces and then eat them. This, at least, is the account given by some historians; though

Cicero's own ex-slave, Tiro, makes no reference at all to the treachery of Philologus.

A long time afterwards, so I have been told, Caesar was visiting one of his daughter's sons. The boy had a book of Cicero's in his hands and, terrified of his grandfather, tried to hide it under his cloak. Caesar noticed this and, after taking the book from him, stood there and read a great part of it. He then handed it back to the young man with the words: 'A learned man, my child, a learned man and a lover of his country.'

And directly after the final defeat of Antony, when Caesar was consul himself, he chose Cicero's son to be his colleague.[130] It was thus in his consulship that the senate took down all the statues of Antony, cancelled all the other honours that had been given to him, and decreed that in the future no member of the family should bear the name of Marcus. In this way Heaven entrusted to the family of Cicero the final acts in the punishment of Antony.

COMPARISON OF
DEMOSTHENES AND CICERO

1. These, then, are the memorable incidents in the recorded careers of Demosthenes and Cicero that have come to our knowledge. And though I have refrained from a comparison of their oratorical styles, I should not, I think, leave this unsaid. Demosthenes devoted to the rhetorical art all the powers of speech that he possessed by nature or acquired by practice, surpassing in force and ingenuity his rivals in forensic pleading, in pomp and majesty of utterance the professional declaimers, and in precision and skill the sophists. Cicero, on the other hand, became widely learned and had a variety of interests in the pursuit of letters, and left behind him not a few philosophical treatises of his own, conforming to the tenets of the Academy. Indeed, even in the speeches he wrote for the courts he clearly wants to display in passing a considerable acquaintance with letters.

It is possible also to get a glimpse of the character of each in his style of speaking. For that of Demosthenes, which had no prettiness or pleasantry, but was condensed with a view to power and seriousness, did not smell of lampwicks, as Pytheas mockingly said, but of water-drinking and anxious thought and what men called the bitterness and sullenness of his disposition. But Cicero was often carried away by his love of mockery into scurrility, and when he treated serious matters with ironical wit and facetiousness to gain his ends in his cases, he became careless of propriety. Thus in his defence of Caelius he said that his client, surrounded as he was by great luxury and extravagance, was doing nothing out of the way by indulging in pleasures, for not to enjoy what one has is madness, particularly when the most eminent philosophers assert that true happiness consists in pleasure.[1] And we are told that when Cato prosecuted Murena, Cicero, who was then consul, defended him, and because of Cato's beliefs made much fun of the Stoic school, on account of the absurdities of their so-called paradoxes.[2] When loud laughter spread from the audience to the jurors, Cato, with a quiet smile, said to those sitting close by: 'What a witty consul we have, my friends!' And it would seem that Cicero was naturally inclined to laughter and mockery; his face too was smiling and peaceful. But in that of Demosthenes there was always a certain seriousness, and this look of thoughtfulness and anxiety he did not easily lay aside. For this reason his enemies, as he himself says, called him morose and ill-mannered.

2. Furthermore, in their writings it is possible to see that Demosthenes touches on his own praises in a cautious and inoffensive manner, when it was necessary for some more important purpose, while on other occasions he is careful and moderate. But Cicero's immoderate self-praise in his speeches proves that he had an unmitigated desire for fame, declaring that arms must give precedence to the toga and the triumphal laurel to the tongue. In the end he praises not only his deeds and actions, but also his speeches, both those he actually delivered and those he published as pamphlets, as if he were childishly competing with Isocrates and Anaximenes the sophists, not claiming the right to lead and instruct the Roman people,

'steadfast, clad in heavy armour, destructive of enemies'.

It is necessary indeed that a political leader should prevail by reason of his eloquence, but ignoble for him to admire and crave the fame that springs from it. So in this respect Demosthenes is more stately and magnificent, since he declares that his ability in speaking was a mere matter of experience, depending greatly on the goodwill of his audience, and considers those who are puffed up by such success to be sordid and vulgar, as they are.

3. It is true that in public speaking and politics both had equal power, so that even those who controlled armies and camps had need of their services: Chares, Diopeithes and Leosthenes needed Demosthenes, while Pompey and the young Caesar[3] needed Cicero, as Caesar himself admits in his memoirs addressed to Agrippa and Maecenas. But what is believed and said most of all to reveal and test the character of a man, namely power and authority, which stimulate every passion and uncover every vice, Demosthenes did not have, nor did he give any such proof of himself, since he held no significant office; he did not even command the force that he raised against Philip. Cicero on the other hand was sent out as quaestor to Sicily and proconsul to Cilicia and Cappadocia, at a time when the lust for wealth was at its greatest height and when those who were sent out as governors and generals, feeling that theft was an ignoble thing, turned to plunder. For the taking of property was not considered wrong, but acceptable provided it was done in moderation. Yet Cicero gave many proofs of his contempt for wealth and of his humanity and goodness. And when in Rome itself he was appointed consul in name but really received the absolute power of a dictator against Catiline and his conspirators; he bore witness to the truth of Plato's prophecy that states would enjoy a respite from evil when by some happy chance great power and wisdom were found together with justice in one and the same individual.

Moreover, it is said against Demosthenes that he made money by his eloquence, since he secretly wrote speeches for Phormio and Apollodorus who were adversaries in the same case, was accused in the matter of the Persian king's money and condemned for taking that of Harpalus. And even if we were to say that those who write these things (and they are not few) are lying, it is still pointless to deny that Demosthenes could not bring himself to look with indifference on gifts offered by kings as marks of honour and favour, and that this could not be expected of a man who made bottomry loans. But in the case of Cicero it has been said that the Sicilians when he was quaestor, the King of Cappadocia when he was proconsul and his friends in Rome when he was going into exile all offered him large sums of money and begged him to accept, but he refused.

4. And surely for the one at least his banishment was disgraceful, since he had been convicted of peculation, but for the other it was most honourable, since he had rid his country of dangerous men. Therefore no attention was paid to Demosthenes when he went into exile, but for Cicero the senate changed its clothing and put on mourning and refused to discuss any business until his recall had been decreed. However, Cicero spent his exile in idleness, remaining quietly in Macedonia, but even the exile of Demosthenes proved to be a major element in his service to the state. For he took part in the struggles of the Greeks, as has been said, and drove out the Macedonian envoys from the cities he visited, and so showed himself to be a far better citizen than Themistocles or Alcibiades when they were in the same position. Moreover, when he returned from exile, he again devoted himself to this same public cause and continued to wage war on Antipater and the Macedonians. Cicero, on the other hand, was criticized in the senate by Laelius for sitting silent when Caesar asked leave to stand for the consulship, illegally, since he was still a beardless youth. Brutus too, in one of his letters, accused him of fostering a tyranny greater and more severe than the one Brutus himself had overthrown.

5. And when all is said and done the one is to be pitied for the manner of his death – an old man ignobly carried up and down by servants, trying to escape death, hiding from his pursuers, who were not far in advance of nature, and then beheaded. But in the case of the other, even though it inclined a little towards supplication, we must admire the preparation of the poison and its safekeeping, must admire, too, the use he made of it: since the god would not grant him asylum, he took refuge at a greater altar, as it were, made his escape from the mercenaries and their weapons, and laughed to scorn the cruelty of Antipater.

Abbreviations

Badian, *FC* = E. Badian, *Foreign Clientelae (264–70 B.C.)*, Oxford, 1958.

Badian, *Studies* = E. Badian, *Studies in Greek and Roman History*, Oxford (Blackwell), 1964.

CAH = *The Cambridge Ancient History.*

Carney = T. F. Carney, *A Biography of C. Marius*, 1961.

CR = *Classical Review.*

FGH = F. Jacoby, *Die Fragmente der griechischen Historiker.*

GC = A. H. J. Greenidge & A. M. Clay, *Sources for Roman History 133–70 B.C.*, ²revised E. W. Gray, Oxford, 1960.

Gelzer, *Caesar* = M. Gelzer, *Caesar, Politician and Statesman*, Oxford (Blackwell), 1968.

Gelzer, *RN* = M. Gelzer, *The Roman Nobility*, Oxford (Blackwell), 1969.

JRS = *Journal of Roman Studies.*

MRR = T. R. S. Broughton, *The Magistrates of the Roman Republic*, New York, I 1951, II 1952, Supplement 1960.

Peter, *HRR* = H. Peter, *Historicorum Romanorum Reliquiae*, Leipzig, I² 1914, II 1906.

Syme, *RR* = R. Syme, *The Roman Revolution*, Oxford, 1939.

TAPA = *Transactions of the American Philological Association.*

A Note on Roman Names

Every male Roman citizen had at least two names, a personal first name (*praenomen*) and a family or gentile name (*nomen*). Many members of the ruling class also had one or more surnames (*cognomina*) and one or more additional names (*agnomina*). These additional names served to distinguish members of different branches of a family or to signal personal characteristics or achievements of the original holder. Thus they often referred to physical features or traits of character and were frequently uncomplimentary, e.g. Brutus ('stupid'), Calvus ('bald'), Strabo ('squinteyed'), Verrucosus ('warty'). More flattering were those derived from regions in which or peoples against whom the original recipient of the name had fought, e.g. Africanus, Allobrogicus, Macedonicus, Numidicus.

Praenomina normally appear as an initial or abbreviation: A. = Aulus, Ap. = Appius, C. = Gaius, Cn. = Gnaeus, D. = Decimus, K. = Kaeso, L. = Lucius, M. = Marcus, M'. = Manius, Mam. = Mamercus, N. = Numerius, P. = Publius, Q. = Quintus, Ser. = Servius, Sex. = Sextus, T. = Titus, Ti. = Tiberius.

If a man was adopted he took the name of his adoptive father but showed his original family either by taking as a *cognomen* a version of his original *nomen* ending in -ianus or by keeping his original *cognomen*. Thus Scipio Aemilianus was born L. Aemilius Paullus and adopted by a P. Cornelius Scipio. So he became P. Cornelius Scipio Aemilianus. His final nomenclature, after his victories over Carthage and Numantia, was P. Cornelius Scipio Aemilianus Africanus Minor Numantinus (Minor to distinguish him from P. Cornelius Scipio Africanus the conqueror of Hannibal). Metellus Scipio, Pompey's father-in-law, was born P. Cornelius Scipio Nasica and adopted by Q. Caecilius Metellus Pius. He thus became Q. Caecilius Metellus Pius Scipio Nasica (keeping two *cognomina* to show which branch of the Scipiones he came from).

Glossary of Roman Technical Terms

aedile (*aed.*). The aedileship was a junior annual magistracy, the functions of which included supervision of streets, public places and markets and the giving of lavish games.

censor (*cens.*). Two censors were appointed from among ex-consuls every five years. Their duties included the revision of the lists of citizens, senators and the equestrian order, the letting of public contracts and the performance of various rites of purification.

consul (*cos.*). The consulship was the highest of the annual magistracies. In the early and middle republic the two consuls had regularly commanded armies, but in the late republic they did so only in emergencies and usually did little more than preside in the senate and at legislative and electoral assemblies. A consul was designate (*cos. des.*) between his election and the time he assumed office. A suffect consul (*cos. suff.*) or other magistrate was one appointed on the death, resignation or disqualification of the man originally elected.

dictator (*dict.*). A magistrate appointed to deal with a specific crisis, with no colleague of equal power and not subject to tribunician veto. The appointment may have been for a maximum of six months, but in any case the dictator was expected to abdicate as soon as the problem was solved.

imperium. The power held by dictators, consuls, praetors and provincial governors. In theory it gave the right to bind, beat and execute, as symbolized by the cords, rods and axes which made up the *fasces* carried by the attendants (lictors) of those who held *imperium*. But within the city limits it was restricted by the tribunician veto and the right of appeal to the people on capital charges.

legate (*leg.*). (1) A subordinate officer whose *imperium* derived from that of the consul, governor or commander who appointed him. (2) An envoy.

praetor (*pr.*). The number of praetors elected each year gradually increased from one to eight. They held *imperium* inferior to that of a consul and could command troops. But in the late republic their functions were primarily judicial: they heard civil cases and presided in the various standing criminal courts.

quaestor (*q.*). The quaestors were the most junior of the annual magistrates. They performed various administrative duties and acted as adjutants to consuls and provincial governors.

tribune, military (*tr. mil.*). Junior officers, usually young men; some were elected by the people, others directly appointed by their commander.

tribune of the plebs (*tr. pl.*). Originally created to protect the common people against aristocratic oppression, the tribunes (ten each year in the late republic) could veto the actions of all magistrates (except a dictator) and each other and also introduce legislation in the plebeian assembly. But their power extended only a mile outside the city.

Notes

GAIUS MARIUS

1. *Quintus Sertorius*: Q. Sertorius, whose biography by Plutarch is extant (translated in *Makers of Rome*, Penguin Classics), retired after his praetorship to his province of Hispania Citerior when Sulla invaded Italy in 83, and maintained himself there until his murder in 73.

2. *Lucius Mummius . . . Corinth*: L. Mummius, *cos.* 146, sacked and destroyed Corinth in that year.

3. *He was by nature . . . civilian life*: On Marius' background cf. Carney, 8 ff.; Evans, 146 ff.

4. *after his second triumph*: The triumph of 101, for the victories over Cimbri and Teutones.

5. *His parents . . . their own hands*: On Marius' family cf. Carney, 8 f; Evans, 146 ff.

6. *His first military service . . . Numantia*: 134–3.

7. *Caecilius Metellus*: Probably Q. Caecilius Metellus Baliaricus, *cos.* 123.

8. *While tribune . . . courts of justice*: 119; cf. Cicero, *De Legibus* 3.38. The consul was L. Aurelius Cotta.

9. *higher aedileship*: That is, the curule aedileship, probably in 118 for 117.

10. *stood for the praetorship and very nearly failed again*: In 116 for 115.

11. *When he returned . . . and eloquence*: On their importance cf. Gelzer, *RN*, 23 ff., 80 ff., 110 ff.

12. *modelled himself on Marius*: Cf. Plutarch, *Caesar* 6, Suetonius, *Iulius* 11, Velleius, 2.43.4.

13. *Metellus . . . as a legate*: Q. Caecilius Metellus, named Numidicus

after his exploits in the Jugurthine War (for which see Sallust's *Bellum Iugurthinum*), *cos.* 109.

14. *condemn the man to death*: Cf. Sallust, *BJ* 69.

15. *triumphantly elected ... raise troops*: In 108 for 107. On the enrolment of the *capite censi* cf. Sallust, *BJ* 86, Valerius Maximus 2.3.1, Gellius 16.10.10.

16. *violent speeches ... offended the aristocracy*: Cf. Sallust, *BJ* 85.

17. *Bestia ... Albinus*: L. Calpurnius Bestia, *cos.* 111, cf. *MRR* I, 540; Sp. Postumius Albinus, *cos.* 110 cf. *MRR* I, 543.

18. *Rutilius*: P. Rutilius Rufus, *cos.* 105.

19. *Privately ... course of the campaign*: For sources and chronology cf. *MRR* I, 551, 554, 556.

20. *proclaimed consul*: For 104.

21. *Cimbri*: The Cimbric War had actually begun in 113.

22. *their generals ... destroyed*: Cn. Papirius Carbo, *cos.* 113, near Noreia; M. Iunius Silanus, *cos.* 109; L. Cassius Longinus, *cos.* 107; Q. Servilius Caepio, *cos.* 106, and Cn. Manlius Maximus, *cos.* 105, at Arausio (Orange) in 105.

23. *made Scipio consul*: In 147.

24. *third consulship*: 103.

25. *colleague ... had died*: L. Aurelius Orestes.

26. *Manius Aquillius*: Cos. 101.

27. *Lucius Saturninus*: L. Appuleius Saturninus, *tr pl.* 103, 100, 99.

28. *Lutatius Catulus*: Q. Lutatius Catulus, *cos.* 102.

29. *Carbo and Caepio*: Cf. n. 22.

30. *The senate ... from the platform*: In 102.

31. *Aquae Sextiae*: Aix-en-Provence.

32. *Manlius and Caepio*: Cf. n. 22.

33. *Claudius Marcellus*: M. Claudius Marcellus, cf. *MRR* I, 569.

34. *consul for the fifth time*: For 101.

35. *They say ... twist in the point*: Cf. Parker, *Roman Legions*, 43 f.

36. *two javelins ... heavy swords*: On German weapons cf. Thompson, *The Early Germans*, 111 ff.

37. *he is said ... voice of the law*: In 101: cf. Valerius Maximus, 5.2.8, Cicero, *Pro Balbo* 46.

38. *Marius therefore schemed to have Metellus exiled*: Cf. Appian, *Bella Civilia* 1.29 ff. C. Servilius Glaucia, *pr.* 100; for Saturninus cf. n. 27.

39. *Rutilius ... quarrel with Marius*: The consul of 105. For his history cf. Peter, *HRR* I², CCLIV ff., 187 ff.

40. *this sixth consulship ... fellow consul*: For 100; his colleague, L. Valerius Flaccus, was censor in 97, interrex when Sulla became dictator in 82.

41. *Corvinus Valerius*: Plutarch means M. Valerius Maximus Corvus, *cos.* 348, 346, 343, 335, 300, 299.

42. *election to the tribuneship*: In fact at the elections of 101 for 100. The victim's name is variously given as Nunnius, Ninnius and Nunnus.

43. *Saturninus ... not oppose it in any way*: Cf. Appian, *BC* 1.29 ff.; *MRR* I, 575; *GC*, 106.

44. *'Life' of him*: Either lost or never written.

45. *he did bring ... lack of water*: Probably about October 100; cf. Badian, *Chiron* 14, 1984, 106.

46. *they surrendered ... 'the public faith'*: Cf. Cicero, *Pro Rabirio perduellionis* 28.

47. *When it was officially proposed ... being carried*: Cf. Orosius 5.17, Dio fr. 95.2, Appian, *BC* 1.33.147 ff., Cicero, *Post reditum ad Quirites* 11, *Post reditum in senatu* 37.

48. *Marius ... Galatia*: 98.

49. *outbreak of war ... Italian allies*: The Social War broke out in 91; cf. Brunt, *JRS* 55, 1965, 90 ff.

50. *Publius Silo*: Rather Q. Poppaedius Silo.

51. *war against Mithridates*: 88.

52. *Sulpicius ... pro-consul*: On P. Sulpicius and his legislation cf. *GC*, 160 ff. On his name, cf. Mattingly, *Athenaeum* 53, 1975, 264 f.

53. *his son seized and killed*: Q. Pompeius Rufus.

54. *led them against Rome*: Cf. *GC*, 163 f.

55. *In the course of the proceedings ... mark of disgrace*: Cf. Valerius Maximus 8.2.3; Watson, *Law of Persons in the Later Roman Republic*, 68 f.

56. *Cethegus ... ask his help*: P. Cornelius Cethegus; cf. Appian, *BC* 1.60.271, 62.280.

57. *Sextilius*: P. Sextilius, cf. *MRR* II, 41.

58. *the ruins of Carthage*: Carthage had been destroyed by Scipio Aemilianus in 146.

59. *the two consuls had ended in open violence*: Cn. Octavius and L. Cornelius Cinna, the consuls of 87. Cf. *GC*, 171 ff.; Badian, *Studies*, 206 ff.; Bulst, *Historia* 13, 1964, 307 ff.

60. *Cornelius Merula consul in his place*: L. Cornelius Merula, the *flamen Dialis*.

61. *And when Metellus ... intrigues of Marius*: Q. Caecilius Metellus

Pius, *cos.* 80, still in arms after his command in the Social War as praetor in 88.

62. *Ancharius*: Q. Ancharius, *pr.* ?88, cf. *MRR* II, 40.

63. *Marcus Antonius*: M. Antonius, *cos.* 99, grandfather of Mark Antony.

64. *Annius*: P. Annius, a military tribune, cf. *MRR* II, 49.

65. *Sertorius*: On Sertorius cf. n. 1.

66. *Marius was elected consul for the seventh time*: For 86.

67. *Gaius Piso ... different account*: Perhaps C. Calpurnius Piso, *cos.* 67; cf. Peter, *HRR* I², CCCLXXX.

68. *For Marius ... men in Rome*: The executions were carried out in 82 by the praetor L. Iunius Brutus Damasippus, on Marius' orders. The victims were P. Antistius, who according to Plutarch, *Pompey* 4, was praetor when he presided at Pompey's trial for embezzlement in 86, but is called *aedilicius* by Velleius 2.26.2 at the time of his death; C. Papirius Carbo Arvina, *tr. pl.* 90; L. Domitius Ahenobarbus, *cos.* 94; Q. Mucius Scaevola, *cos.* 95. Cf. Appian, *BC* 1.88.403 f.; *GC*, 197 f.

69. *he killed himself*: In 82, cf. *GC*, 207 f.

SULLA

1. *Rufinus*: P. Cornelius Rufinus, *cos.* 290, 277.

2. *African campaign*: 107–105.

3. *make war on Jugurtha*: Cf. Plutarch's *Life of Marius* and Sallust's *Bellum Jugurthinum*.

4. *staff officer ... colonel in his third*: That is, as a legate in 104 and a military tribune in 103.

5. *aedileship*: On the importance of aedilician games cf. Gelzer, *RN*, 57, 111, 115.

6. *following year ... also by bribery*: For 93, according to the usual view, but cf. Badian, cited in the next note. The Caesar of the anecdote is C. Iulius Caesar Strabo, *aed.* 90.

7. *After his praetorship ... he controlled already*: Cf. Badian, *Studies*, 157 ff.; *MRR* Supplement, 20 f.

8. *Censorinus*: C. Marcius Censorinus, cf. *MRR* II, 49, 71.

9. *The quarrel between Sulla and Marius ... for the time being*: Cf. *Marius*, n. 49.

10. *Metellus*: Q. Caecilius Metellus Pius, consul with Sulla in 80, cousin to Sulla's wife Metella.

11. *Lucullus*: L. Licinius Lucullus, *cos.* 74, who served under Sulla

against Mithridates and was appointed as guardian to Sulla's son in Sulla's will.

12. *Albinus by name*: A. Postumius Albinus, *cos.* 99; cf. *MRR* II, 37.

13. *elected consul with Quintus Pompeius*: For 88.

14. *Metellus the chief pontiff*: L. Caecilius Metellus Delmaticus, *cos.* 119.

15. *Ilia . . . Aelia . . . Cloelia*: Ilia must be either an error, perhaps for Iulia, or a doublet of Aelia; Aelia and Cloelia are otherwise unknown.

16. *Marius . . . on account of his age*: Cf. *GC*, 161 ff.

17. *Sulpicius*: On Sulpicius cf. *Marius*, n. 52.

18. *He also sent . . . over to Marius*: According to Appian, *BC* 1.56.248, Sulla's army was at Capua.

19. *Brutus and Servilius*: M. Iunius Brutus (cf. *MRR* II, 40); Servilius is otherwise unknown.

20. *Lucius Basillus and Gaius Mummius*: They were presumably legates. L. Minucius Basilus distinguished himself at the battle of Orchomenus as military tribune in 86.

21. *Nonius*: Nonius is perhaps Sex. Nonius Sufenas, *pr.* 81.

22. *Lucius Cinna*: L. Cornelius Cinna, *cos.* 87–84. On his period of power cf. Badian, *Studies*, 206 ff.; Bulst, *Historia* 13, 1964, 307 ff.

23. *Virginius*: Rather M. Vergilius, cf. Cicero, *Brutus* 179.

24. *Sentius the governor of Macedonia*: C. Sentius, *pr.* 94. He had been in Macedonia since 93. His legate Q. Bruttius Sura had also probably been in the province since that date.

25. *Lucius Lucullus*: On Lucullus cf. n. 11. At this point he was Sulla's quaestor; he may have been the only one of Sulla's officers who did not refuse to join him in the march on Rome, cf. Badian, *Studies*, 220.

26. *Flamininus . . . Macedonia*: T. Quinctius Flamininus, *cos.* 198, served in Greece and Macedonia 198–194, bringing to a conclusion the war against Philip V of Macedon and proclaiming the freedom of the Greeks at the Isthmian Games of 196. M'. Acilius Glabrio, *cos.* 191, drove Antiochus the Great of Syria out of Greece in that year. L. Aemilius Paullus, *cos.* 182, 168, defeated Perseus of Macedon at Pydna in his second consulship. Cf. Plutarch's lives of Flamininus and Paullus; Walbank, *Philip V of Macedon*; Badian, *FC*, 55–115, *Studies*, 112 ff.; Balsdon, *Phoenix* 21, 1967, 177 ff.

27. *Cinna's party ... Flaccus*: Cn. Octavius, *cos.* 87, was killed in
    office when his colleague Cinna and Marius marched on Rome
    (cf. *MRR* II, 46). L. Valerius Flaccus replaced Marius as consul
    in 86 and assumed the command against Mithridates on behalf
    of Cinna's government. He was murdered by his legate C. Flavius
    Fimbria, who took over command of the army (cf. *MRR* II,
    53, 56).

28. *Curio*: C. Scribonius Curio, *cos.* 76, one of Sulla's legates (cf.
    MRR II, 56).

29. *Hortensius*: L. Hortensius, another legate.

30. *Gabinius*: A. Gabinius, a military tribune (cf. *MRR* II, 55); not
    the famous *tr. pl.* 67, *cos.* 58.

31. *Juba*: King Juba of Mauretania (c. 50 BC – AD 23) was a prolific
    writer; for the surviving fragments of his works cf. Jacoby, *FGH*
    IIIA, 127 ff. (no. 275). Nothing more is known of Ericius.

32. *Murena*: L. Licinius Murena, a legate; father of the consul of 62.

33. *Galba*: Ser. Sulpicius Galba, another legate.

34. *Flaccus ... used against himself*: On Flaccus and Fimbria cf.
    n. 27. Against this partisan interpretation of their mission cf.
    Memnon 434F24; Sulla was asked to cooperate or at least to
    fight Mithridates first. Cf. Badian, *Studies*, 224.

35. *Meanwhile in Rome ... amounted to a senate*: Cf. Badian,
    Studies, 215 ff.

36. *Sulla granted his request ... ally of Rome*: On the Peace of
    Dardanus in 85 and the preliminary negotiations cf. *GC*, 187 f.

37. *The main reason for this ... against the king himself*: On
    Fimbria's military successes cf. *GC*, 185 f.

38. *committed suicide in his camp*: On Fimbria's suicide cf. *GC*, 188 f.

39. *It was in this very place ... Norbanus*: In 83, in which C.
    Norbanus was consul; the presence of C. Marius the younger,
    cos. 82, is not otherwise attested.

40. *brother of the Lucullus ... Tigranes*: M. Terentius Varro Luc-
    ullus, *cos.* 73. On his position and his victory at Fidentia (82) cf.
    MRR II, 70.

41. *Scipio*: L. Cornelius Scipio Asiaticus, *cos.* 83; on his abandon-
    ment by his army cf. *MRR* II, 62.

42. *Dolabella*: Cn. Cornelius Dolabella, *cos.* 81. The battle is more
    usually known as Sacriportus.

43. *Pompey, Crassus, Metellus and Servilius*: Pompey had at first
    been a member of Cinna's army, but withdrew to his estates in
    Picenum shortly before Cinna's death in 84 at the hands of his
    mutinous troops. Crassus had escaped to Spain after the murder

of his father at Marius' instigation in 87. Metellus Pius had fled to Africa. All three joined Sulla when he invaded Italy. Cf. *GC*, 175 ff., 190 f., 194 f.; *MRR* II, 63 ff., 68, 70; Badian, *FC*, 266 ff. Servilius is probably P. Servilius Vatia Isauricus, *cos.* 79, cf. *MRR* II, 72.

44. *Carbo*: Cn. Papirius Carbo, *cos.* 85, 84, 82, the leading figure in the government after Cinna's murder. From Africa he moved to Sicily, where he was captured and put to death while still in office by Pompey, cf. *GC*, 208, especially Valerius Maximus 9.13.2; *MRR* II, 73 n. 1.

45. *In the final struggle . . . gates of Rome*: On Sulla and the Samnites cf. Seager, *CAH* IX^2, 191.

46. *Appius Claudius . . . a good man himself*: Elder son of C. Claudius Pulcher, *cos.* 92.

47. *Balbus*: Cf. *MRR* II, 72.

48. *Torquatus*: L. Manlius Torquatus, *cos.* 65, proquaestor under Sulla since 84 (cf. *MRR* II, 70).

49. *Gaius Metellus*: C. Caecilius Metellus, cf. *MRR* II, 475.

50. *Fufidius*: L. (?) Fufidius, *pr.* 81 (called L. Fursidius, *primipilaris*, by Orosius 5.21, who interprets the incident to make him responsible for the introduction of the proscriptions).

51. *Sulla published a list of eighty men to be condemned*: On the proscriptions cf. *GC*, 198 ff.

52. *he took away all civil rights . . . property of all of them*: An attempt to restore their rights to the descendants of the proscribed was made in 63, but successfully opposed by Cicero; the injustice was eventually righted by Antony as tribune under Caesar's auspices in 49, cf. *MRR* II, 258.

53. *Lucius Catiline*: L. Sergius Catilina, *pr.* 68, on whose armed rebellion in 63 cf. the Catilinarian speeches of Cicero and Sallust's *Bellum Catilinae*. For his part in the proscriptions cf. *GC*, 200; Asconius 84. The 'brother' is probably Catiline's brother-in-law Q. Caecilius. M. Marius Gratidianus, nephew by birth and adoption of the great Marius, had been praetor twice, probably in 85 and 84.

54. *Apart altogether from the massacres . . . at his pleasure*: Sources for Sulla's powers as dictator: *MRR* II, 66 f. He was elected by the centuriate assembly under the presidency of the interrex L. Valerius Flaccus (*cos.* 100), whom he appointed as his master of horse.

55. *Then there was the case . . . a family connection*: Cf. Badian, *FC*, 268.

56. *Scaurus . . . Manius Glabrio*: M. Aemilius Scaurus, *cos.* 115; M'.
     Acilius Glabrio, *cos.* 67.
57. *Lucretius Ofella . . . siege of Marius*: Cf. Appian, *BC* 1.101.471
     ff. His name was probably Q. Lucretius Afella; cf. Badian, *JRS*
     57, 1967, 227 f.
58. *His triumph . . . greater still*: 27 and 28 January 81.
59. *Felix*: Cf. Balsdon, *JRS* 41, 1951, 1 ff.
60. *he laid down his dictatorship . . . electing consuls*: Probably
     shortly before the end of 81; cf. Seager, *CAH* IX², 205.
61. *In these elections . . . elected consul*: For 78.
62. *Catulus*: Q. Lutatius Catulus, son of Marius' colleague and
     enemy, was in fact also elected for 78.
63. *Lepidus . . . Pompey's party*: On the revolt of Lepidus cf. *GC*,
     232 ff.
64. *he spared no expense at her funeral . . . such expenditure*: Cf.
     GC, 222.
65. *Valeria*: Her brother was M. Valerius Messalla Rufus, *cos.* 53;
     the identity of her previous husband is unknown. The marriage
     took place in 80.
66. *Roscius the comedian*: Q. Roscius, defended by Cicero; on his
     relations with Sulla cf. also Macrobius 3.14.13.
67. *Mucius the jurist*: Q. Mucius Scaevola the Augur, *cos.* 117.
68. *Sicilian slave war*: 134–132.
69. *died on the next day . . . took part in his funeral*: For Sulla's
     death and funeral (78) cf. *GC*, 231 f.

COMPARISON OF LYSANDER
AND SULLA

1.   *Dolabella . . . Lucretius Ofella*: Cn. Cornelius Dolabella, *cos.* 81.
     Nothing more is known of his naval command (as a legate in the
     Mithridatic war) or his brush with Sulla, which are not men-
     tioned in the Life or in any other source. On Q. Lucretius Afella
     and his name, cf. the Life, n. 57.

CRASSUS

1.   *Marcus Crassus' father . . . in a small house*: P. Licinius Crassus,
     cos. 97, *cens.* 89. He served in Hispania Ulterior 97–93 and tri-
     umphed over the Lusitani. He committed suicide in 87, cf. *GC*,
     175 f. Of his other sons, Publius was killed by Fimbria in 87.

2.   *Licinia . . . Plotius*: Perhaps in 73, cf. *MRR* II, 114.
3.   *during his consulship*: 70.
4.   *expedition to Parthia*: 55.
5.   *Sulla, after his occupation of Rome . . . put to death*: On Sulla's proscriptions cf. *Sulla*, n. 51.
6.   *frequent and everyday occurrences . . . close proximity to each other*: On living conditions at Rome cf. Yavetz, *Latomus* 17, 1958, 500 ff.
7.   *At the time when Cinna and Marius seized power*: In 87.
8.   *They killed . . . Crassus' father and brother among them*: Cf. *GC*, 175 f.
9.   *He had been in Spain before . . . friends in the country*: Cf. Badian, *RC*, 266 f., 316, and on Vibius Paciaecus ibid. 308; the date of the elder Crassus' praetorship is unknown, nor is it certain that he served in Spain then as well as in his consulship.
10. *Fenestella*: On the historian Fenestella, who wrote under Augustus, cf. Peter, *HRR* II, cviii ff., and for the fragments ibid. 79 ff.
11. *Cinna was dead*: 84.
12. *Metellus Pius, a well-known man who had raised a considerable army*: Q. Caecilius Metellus Pius, *cos.* 80. Cf. Badian, *FC*, 266 f.
13. *his father . . . disliked by his fellow citizens*: Cn. Pompeius Strabo, *cos.* 89.
14. *Pompey stood out . . . saluted him by the title of 'Imperator'*: On relations between Sulla and Pompey cf. Badian, *FC*, 267 ff.
15. *Pompey's successes . . . received from his fellow citizens*: Pompey entered the senate as consul in 70, without having held any of the requisite lower magistracies. By this time he had already defeated Cn. Domitius in Africa, M. Lepidus, Sertorius in Spain and the remnants of Spartacus' forces, and had triumphed twice, in 81 (probably) and 71.
16. *It is true . . . '. . . I have been captured!'*: In 75.
17. *the time when . . . had no money*: In 62. He had expended large sums in the previous year to secure his election as both praetor and pontifex maximus.
18. *Sicinius*: Cn. (or L.) Sicinius, *tr. pl.* 76, who began the campaign to restore to the tribunes the powers of which Sulla had deprived them. Cf. *GC*, 242; *MRR* II, 93.
19. *The rising of the gladiators . . . began as follows*: In 73. Cf. *GC*, 261, 263, 268 f.
20. *Clodius*: C. Claudius Glaber, *pr.* 73, cf. *MRR* II, 109.
21. *Publius Varinus . . . Cossinius*: P. Varinius, also *pr.* 73, cf. *MRR*

II, 110; L. (?) Furius, *pr.* 75, cf. *MRR* II, 112; L. Cossinius, perhaps *pr.* 73, cf. *MRR* II, 110.

22. *both consuls*: L. Gellius Publicola and Cn. Cornelius Lentulus Clodianus, *coss.* 72.

23. *Cassius*: C. Cassius Longinus, *cos.* 73.

24. *Crassus was appointed to the supreme command of the war*: He was probably praetor in 73 and appointed to the command as proconsul in 72, cf. *MRR* II, 118, 121 n. 2.

25. *Mummius*: Otherwise unknown.

26. *Quintus ... Scrofa followed closely in his tracks*: Perhaps Q. Marcius Rufus, recorded as a legate in the preceding battle (Frontinus, *Stratagems* 2.4.7); Cn. Tremellius Scrofa, *q.* 71, who rose to the praetorship at an unknown date.

27. *Pompey then celebrated ... war in Spain*: Cf. *GC*, 266 f.

28. *Pompey ... consulship*: He was already in fact consul designate when he triumphed.

29. *member of the senate*: Cf. n. 15.

30. *censor ... nothing at all*: In 65.

31. *Catulus*: Q. Lutatius Catulus, *cos.* 78. Cf. *MRR* II, 157.

32. *conspirators*: On the Catilinarian conspiracy cf. Cicero's speeches *In Catilinam, Pro Murena* and *Pro Sulla*, and Sallust's *Bellum Catilinae*. Cicero's other works on his consulate are lost. Crassus was accused by L. Tarquinius, cf. Sallust, *BC* 48.3 ff.

33. *his speeches ... were implicated*: On this work cf. Cicero, *Ad Atticum* 2.6.2, 14.17.6; Dio 39.10.13; Brunt, *CR* 71, 1957, 193 ff.; Seager, *Historia* 13, 1964, 346 f.

34. *Cicero says ... conspiracy really existed*: Cf. Plutarch, *Cicero* 15, Dio 37.31.

35. *Publius ... attached to Cicero*: He served under Caesar in Gaul and under his father in Syria, where he was killed in battle in 53.

36. *his trial*: In 58. Cicero was not of course actually put on trial.

37. *Caesar ... the consulship*: In 60 for 59. He had governed Hispania Ulterior after his praetorship of 62.

38. *He therefore set out to reconcile them*: Cf. Cicero, *Att* 2.3.3; Suetonius, *Iul.* 19.2; Dio 37.54.3.

39. *put Gaul into his hands*: The *lex Vatinia* gave Caesar Cisalpine Gaul and Illyricum for 5 years; Transalpine Gaul was added by a decree of the senate sponsored by Pompey.

40. *When Caesar came south ... to meet him*: Spring 56. Cf. Cicero, *Ad Familiares* 1.9.9; *MRR* II, 211.

41. *second consulship*: For 55.

42. *Marcellinus and Domitius*: Cn. Cornelius Lentulus Marcellinus,

consul at the time; L. Domitius Ahenobarbus, eventually *cos.* 54.

43. *Cato encouraged Domitius ... fight the election*: Domitius was married to Cato's sister; cf. Syme, *RR*, table II.

44. *Caesar's command ... Spanish provinces to Pompey*: Caesar's command was prorogued by a *lex Licinia Pompeia*; Pompey and Crassus received their provinces by a tribunician *lex Trebonia*. Cf. *MRR* II, 215, 217.

45. *in love with his wife*: Caesar's daughter Julia, whom he had married in 59.

46. *Lucullus against Tigranes and those of Pompey against Mithridates*: L. Licinius Lucullus, *cos.* 74, went out to the war against Mithridates of Pontus in his consulship. It was not until 69 that he invaded Armenia, defeated Tigranes and captured Tigranocerta (cf. *MRR* II, 133). He was superseded in 67 (cf. *MRR* II, 146). Pompey was given the command against Mithridates by the *lex Manilia* of 66. On his achievements cf. *MRR* II, 155, 159, 163 f., 169 f., 176.

47. *Ateius by name*: C. Ateius Capito, cf. *MRR* II, 216.

48. *by treaties of friendship*: On Rome and Parthia cf. *CAH* IX², 262 ff.

49. *King Deiotarus*: On Deiotarus of Galatia cf. Cicero's speech in his defence; Gelzer, *RN*, 91 f.

50. *The young man ... first-class cavalry*: On young Crassus' service with Caesar cf. Caesar, *Bellum Gallicum* 1.52.7, 2.34, 3.7–9, 11, 20–27.

51. *Cassius the quaestor*: C. Cassius Longinus, *q.* 53, *pr.* 44, the assassin of Caesar. On his service in Syria cf. *MRR* II, 229, 237, 242. He remained in the province until 51 and successfully defended it against the Parthians.

52. *Censorinus ... Megabacchus*: Both otherwise unknown.

53. *Lucullus ... Antiochus*: On Lucullus and Tigranes cf. n. 46; L. Cornelius Scipio Asiaticus, *cos.* 190, defeated Antiochus the Great of Syria at Magnesia in that year, cf. *MRR* I, 356.

54. *Octavius ... Egnatius ... Coponius ... Vargunteius*: Octavius, Egnatius, Coponius and Vargunteius are otherwise unknown.

55. *Petronius ... two brothers Roscii*: Otherwise unknown.

56. *Pacorus who was defeated in battle by the Romans*: In 38 by the proconsul P. Ventidius Bassus, *cos. suff.* 43, cf. *MRR* II, 393.

57. *His son Phraates ... strangled him*: Stricken with grief at the death of Pacorus, Orodes II abdicated in favour of Phraates IV, who began to execute his numerous brothers as potential rivals.

It was when Orodes protested against this that he too was put to death. Cf. Justin 42.4 f.

POMPEY

1. *Strabo*: Cn. Pompeius Strabo, *cos*. 89, who took Asculum in the Social War. On his political significance cf. Gelzer, *RN*, 93 ff.; Badian, *FC*, index s.v. Pompeius.
2. *loving Pompey . . . dealing with people*: Contrast Cicero, *Att*. 1.13.4.
3. *Lucius Philippus*: L. Marcius Philippus, *cos*. 91, who defended Pompey when he was prosecuted for *peculatus* in 86. He later backed Pompey's claim to command against Sertorius in Spain.
4. *Geminius*: He was responsible in 77, on Pompey's orders, for the death of Lepidus' legate, M. Iunius Brutus.
5. *Caecilius Metellus*: Which Metellus is not known.
6. *Demetrius*: He came from Gadara, which was reconstituted by Pompey in his reorganization of the East after the defeat of Mithridates. Cf. Josephus, *Bellum Judaicum* 1.155, *Antiquitates Judaicae* 14.75.
7. *campaign against Cinna*: In 87. Strabo's attitude in the struggle between Cinna and Octavius was ambiguous, cf. *GC*, 172 ff.
8. *after Strabo's death*: In 86. Cf. Cicero, *Brut*. 230.
9. *Asculum*: On the siege and capture of Asculum in 89 cf. *GC*, 154 ff.
10. *Antistius who, as praetor*: According to Velleius 2.26.2, P. Antistius had risen no higher than the aedileship when he was killed on the orders of the younger Marius in 82. Cf. *MRR* II, 57 n. 3.
11. *he killed him*: In 84. Cf. *GC*, 189 f.
12. *Carbo . . . supreme power*: On Carbo cf. *Sulla*, n. 44.
13. *three whole legions*: One legion according to Appian, *BC* 1.80.366; three also in Livy, *Perioche* 85.
14. *Carrinas, Cloelius and Brutus*: C. Carrinas, *pr*. 82, T. Cluilius (cf. *MRR* II, 65), and L. Iunius Brutus Damasippus, *pr*. 82.
15. *Scipio*: On Scipio cf. *Sulla*, n. 41.
16. *Marius*: The younger C. Marius, *cos*. 82.
17. *Metellus*: Q. Caecilius Metellus Pius, *cos*. 80.
18. *Aemilia already had a husband*: Aemilia's husband was M'. Acilius Glabrio, *cos*. 67. Cf. *Sulla*, n. 56; Badian, *FC*, 268.
19. *Antistius, who had been murdered*: On the murder of Antistius cf. *Marius*, n. 68.

20. *Perpenna*: M. Perperna Veiento, probably praetor in this year (82). On being driven out of Sicily he is said to have fled to Sertorius in Spain (cf. *MRR* II, 67 f.), but cf. n. 39 and, on the problem, Badian, *FC*, 270 n. 3.

21. *Carbo ... Domitius*: On Carbo cf. *Sulla*, n. 44; Cn. Domitius Ahenobarbus, cf. *MRR* II, 69.

22. *proscriptions*: For the proscriptions cf. *Sulla*, n. 51.

23. *Mamertines in Messana*: On the Mamertines cf. Badian, *FC*, 31, 34 f.

24. *ordered him to be taken away and put to death*: *Sulla*, n. 44.

25. *Gaius Oppius*: On him, cf. Gelzer, *Caesar*, Index s.v.

26. *Sthenius*: On Pompey's later dealings with Sthenius and Sthenius' other Roman connections cf. Cicero, *Second Verrine* 2.83 f., 96, 100, 110 f., 117; Badian, *FC*, 155, 282 f.

27. *not so long ago*: In 87.

28. *left his sister's husband, Memmius*: Cf. *MRR* II, 78.

29. *On his return ... supersede him*: Cf. Badian, *FC*, 273 ff.

30. *Marius*: The younger C. Marius, *cos.* 82.

31. *sent to Spain ... Sertorius*: In 77, cf. *MRR* II, 90.

32. *Valerius ... Fabius Rullus*: M'. Valerius Maximus, *dict.* 494, who at the time of the first secession of the plebs persuaded the plebeians not to refuse military service; cf. *MRR* I, 14; Q. Fabius Maximus Rullianus, *cos.* 322, 310, 308, 297, 295, as censor in 304.

33. *Scipios ... consul nor a praetor*: P. Cornelius Scipio Africanus the elder, proconsul in Spain 216–210; he appears never to have been praetor and was not consul till 205 (and again in 194).

34. *Servilius ... his triumph*: P. Servilius Vatia Isauricus, *cos.* 79; the probable date of the triumph is 81, cf. Badian, *Hermes* 83, 1955, 107 ff.; *MRR* Supplement, 47.

35. *Lepidus*: M. Aemilius Lepidus, *cos.* 78; on his attempted coup d'état cf. *MRR* II, 85, 89; Badian, *FC*, 275 ff.

36. *his son*: Faustus Cornelius Sulla, *q.* 54.

37. *In fact ... mark of honour*: Cf. *GC*, 232.

38. *Brutus ... Cisalpine Gaul*: M. Iunius Brutus, probably a legate. Cf. *MRR* II, 90 f.

39. *Lepidus ... Sardinia*: Many of his supporters, led by M. Perperna Veiento (cf. n. 20). escaped to Spain and joined Sertorius.

40. *his wife*: An Appuleia, probably a relative of Saturninus; cf. Badian, *FC*, 200.

41. *Metellus Pius*: Q. Caecilius Metellus Pius, *cos.* 80.

42. *Lucius Philippus*: L. Marcius Philippus, *cos.* 91; for his remark

cf. Cicero, *Philippic* 11.18; *GC*, 238. As the Cicero passage makes clear, the consuls were unwilling to go; cf. Badian, *FC*, 277 n. 6.

43. *Herennius and Perpenna*: C. Herennius, *tr. pl.* 88 (or possibly 80, but cf. Badian, *Hermes* 83, 1955, 107 ff.); he was killed in this battle. On Perperna cf. n. 41.

44. *request was not granted. Lucullus was consul at this time*: Sallust, *Histories* 2.98 (*GC*, 248), cf. Badian, *FC*, 279 f. L. Licinius Lucullus, *cos.* 74.

45. *About this time*: In 73, cf. *GC*, 259 ff.

46. *Slave War*: The rising of Spartacus broke out in 73 (cf. *GC*, 261, 263); Pompey returned to Italy in 71 (cf. *GC*, 268 f.).

47. *Sulla had taken away from them*: Sulla had deprived the tribunes of their legislative powers and had also debarred them from higher office. The latter disability had been removed in 75 by a law of the consul C. Aurelius Cotta (cf. *GC*, 245). On the campaign for the restoration of legislative powers 76–71 cf. *GC*, 242, 250, 256, 266; on Pompey cf. Cicero, *First Verrine* 45.

48. *declared consul*: For 70; on the triumph (29 December 71) cf. *GC*, 267.

49. *In the senate ... in the law courts*: The courts had been restored to senatorial control by Sulla; the law of L. Aurelius Cotta, *pr.* 70, divided them between senators, *equites* and *tribuni aerarii*. For the law cf. *GC*, 272 f.; for earlier agitation cf. *GC*, 250, 266.

50. *Gellius and Lentulus*: L. Gellius Publicola and Cn. Cornelius Lentulus Clodianus, *coss.* 72; they had already shown themselves favourable to Pompey in their consulship, cf. *MRR* II, 116.

51. *Sextilius and Bellienus*: On these men and the date (perhaps 68) cf. *MRR* II, 138, 141 n. 3.

52. *Antonius ... a triumph*: M. Antonius, *cos.* 99, who was sent against the pirates as praetor in 102 and triumphed in 100 (cf. *GC*, 110).

53. *Gabinius*: A. Gabinius, *cos.* 58. He passed the law as tribune in 67. On its terms cf. *MRR* II, 144.

54. *one of the consuls*: C. Calpurnius Piso.

55. *Catulus*: Q. Lutatius Catulus, *cos.* 78.

56. *Roscius*: L. Roscius Otho, another tribune, cf. *MRR* II, 145.

57. *commander with a fixed number of ships*: For the names of Pompey's legates cf. *MRR* II, 145.

58. *consul Piso ... before their time*: On Piso's activities cf. *MRR* II, 142 f.

59. *Metellus in Crete*: Q. Caecilius Metellus Creticus, *cos.* 69; for the stemma cf. Syme, *RR*, Table I.

60. *He also wrote ... Lucius Octavius*: Cf. *MRR* II, 147.

61. *When it was announced ... Mithridates and Tigranes*: C. Manilius, *tr. pl.* 66. For the law cf. *MRR* II, 153. Lucullus had been in command against Mithridates since his consulship of 74. He lost Cilicia to Q. Marcius Rex in 68, Bithynia and Pontus to M'. Acilius Glabrio by a law of Gabinius in 67.

62. *two triumphs*: In 81 and 71, cf. nn. 34, 48.

63. *Upon this ... Pompey's triumph*: His escape was engineered in 58 by Clodius, cf. ch. 48; Dio 38.30.2.

64. *Afranius*: L. Afranius, *cos.* 60.

65. *Pompey ... was met by Servilius*: Cf. *MRR* II, 160.

66. *Theophanes ... Romans in Asia*: A member of one of the leading families of Mytilene, who was enfranchised by Pompey and became his confidential adviser. Cf. Anderson, *Pompey, his Friends, and the Literature of the First Century BC*, 34 ff., and for the fragments of Theophanes' work Jacoby, *FGH* IIB, 919 ff. P. Rutilius Rufus, *cos.* 105, cf. *Marius*, n. 39.

67. *Triarius*: C. Valerius Triarius, *pr.* 78, a legate of Lucullus 73–66. He obtained numerous successes before suffering a heavy defeat in 67 (*MRR* II, 148).

68. *Cato the philosopher*: M. Porcius Cato, *pr.* 54, Rome's leading exponent of Stoicism. On Demetrius cf. Anderson, 54.

69. *third triumph*: 28–29 September 61.

70. *death of Mithridates*: In 63.

71. *in Cicero's letters*: Not in the only surviving reference, *Att.* 1.12.3. Suetonius, *Iul. 50*, names Caesar among her lovers. The divorce provoked the violent opposition to Pompey's designs of Mucia's half-brother, Q. Caecilius Metellus Celer, as consul in 60.

72. *Piso*: M. Pupius Piso, *cos.* 61.

73. *Cato had two nieces ... married to his son*: The two Iuniae, daughters of D. Iunius Silanus, *cos.* 62, and Cato's half-sister Servilia (cf. Syme, *RR*, Table II).

74. *Afranius elected consul*: For 60. On the bribery cf. Cicero, *Att.* 1.16.12.

75. *two separate days were devoted to it*: Cf. n. 69; *MRR* II, 181.

76. *Lucullus had been treated ... for his own views*: On the rescinding of Lucullus' arrangements cf. *MRR* II, 154; on the opposition to Pompey's wishes in 60 cf. Cicero, *Att.* 1.18–20; Dio 37.49 f.; Plutarch, *Cato* 31.

77. *Clodius*: P. Clodius Pulcher, *aed.* 56.

78. *fled from Rome*: In 58, the year of Clodius' tribunate. Cf. Seager, *Latomus* 24, 1965, 519 ff.

79. *his province*: Hispania Ulterior, which he governed after his praetorship of 62.

80. *Caesar, then, was elected consul . . . distribution of land*: For 59. Cf. *MRR* II, 187 f.

81. *Bibulus*: M. Calpurnius Bibulus, Cato's son-in-law.

82. *Caepio*: Perhaps M. Brutus, the future assassin of Caesar; more probably his adoptive father, Q. Servilius Caepio. On the problems involved cf. Gelzer, *Caesar*, 80 n. 1; *MRR* II, 149.

83. *Piso*: L. Calpurnius Piso Caesoninus, *cos.* 58.

84. *Gauls and Illyricum . . . at full strength*: Cisalpine Gaul and Illyricum were granted him by a law of the tribune P. Vatinius; Transalpine Gaul was added by the senate on Pompey's proposal.

85. *Gabinius*: The tribune of 67, author of the law giving Pompey command against the pirates.

86. *tribune of the people*: For 58.

87. *military commission*: Cf. *MRR* II, 196.

88. *Tigranes . . . own company*: Cf. n. 66.

89. *was discovered . . . towards Pompey*: On 11 August 58.

90. *Culleo*: Q. Terentius Culleo, *tr. pl.* 58, cf. *MRR* II, 197.

91. *Cicero's brother*: Q. Tullius Cicero, *pr.* 62.

92. *Cicero's recall*: Summer 57, by the consuls P. Cornelius Lentulus Spinther and Q. Caecilius Metellus Nepos (*MRR* II, 200); for earlier attempts cf. *MRR* II, 196 f., 202.

93. *he made Pompey . . . sea and land*: Cf. *MRR* II, 200, 202.

94. *King Ptolemy . . . Canidius*: On the various proposals for the restoration of Ptolemy Auletes to the Egyptian throne cf. *MRR* II, 207 ff. L. Caninius Gallus, *tr. pl.* 56, cf. *MRR* II, 209.

95. *with Crassus and Pompey he came to the following understanding . . . Caesar's doors*: The meeting of Pompey, Caesar and Crassus took place in April 56. Cf. in particular Cicero, *Fam.* 1.9; other sources: *MRR* II, 211.

96. *Marcellinus*: Cn. Cornelius Lentulus Marcellinus, *cos.* 56.

97. *Lucius Domitius*: L. Domitius Ahenobarbus, eventually *cos.* 54, Cato's brother-in-law.

98. *Vatinius . . . Trebonius*: P. Vatinius, *cos.* 47, the Caesarian tribune of 59. C. Trebonius, *cos. suff.* 45, cf. *MRR* II, 217. The statement that Pompey received Africa as well as the Spains is incorrect; Caesar's command was perhaps renewed, not by Trebonius, but by a consular law of Pompey and Crassus (*MRR* II, 215).

99. *but she died . . . a few days*: August 54.
100. *Crassus had lost his life in Parthia*: 9 June 53; cf. *MRR* II, 224, 230.
101. *Lucilius . . . Pompey as dictator*: C. Lucilius Hirrus, *tr. pl.* 53, a cousin of Pompey. He was joined in his unsuccessful proposal by another tribune, M. Coelius Vinicianus, cf. *MRR* II, 228.
102. *Domitius and Messalla were made consuls*: For 53: Cn. Domitius Calvinus and M. Valerius Messalla Rufus; they did not enter office till July 53 and were themselves unable to hold elections for 52.
103. *proposed . . . as sole consul*: In the intercalary month between February and March 52; cf. *MRR* II, 234.
104. *Sulpicius the interrex*: Ser. Sulpicius Rufus, *cos.* 51, the great jurist; cf. *MRR* II, 236.
105. *Metellus Scipio*: Q. Caecilius Metellus Pius Scipio, who became consul in August 52.
106. *his conduct . . . at the trials*: For Pompey's legislation of 52 cf. *MRR* II, 234.
107. *Plancus*: T. Munatius Plancus Byrsa, *tr. pl.* 52, cf. *MRR* II, 235 and the comment of Tacitus, *Annals* 3.28 on Pompey's attitude to his own laws.
108. *Hypsaeus, a man of consular rank*: P. Plautius Hypsaeus, who had served under Pompey; he had never reached the consulship, for which he was an unsuccessful candidate in 53. Cf. Asconius 30 ff.
109. *period of four years*: More probably 5 years, cf. *MRR* II, 238.
110. *Appius*: Perhaps Ap. Claudius Pulcher, *cos.* 38, cf. *MRR* Supplement, 16.
111. *Paulus . . . Curio*: L. Aemilius Paullus, *cos.* 50. C. Scribonius Curio, *tr. pl. suff.* 50.
112. *claims and demands . . . fair enough*: Cf. *MRR* II, 249.
113. *Marcellus*: C. Claudius Marcellus, *cos.* 50.
114. *Piso*: The consul of 58, Caesar's father-in-law, censor in 50.
115. *Lentulus*: L. Cornelius Lentulus Crus, *cos.* 49.
116. *But when Pompey . . . without any enthusiasm*: On Pompey's difficulties with the levy cf. Cicero, *Att.* 7.13, 14, 21, 23; 8.12d.
117. *boundary of his own legal province*: Between Cisalpine Gaul and Italy in the restricted sense then current.
118. *Tullus . . . Favonius*: L. Volcacius Tullus, *cos.* 66. M. Favonius, *pr.* 49.
119. *respective districts*: List: *MRR* II, 259 ff.
120. *Metellus*: L. Caecilius Metellus, cf. *MRR* II, 259.

121. *Numerius*: N. Magius.
122. *no transports available*: Cf. Caesar, *Bellum Civile*, 1.29.1.
123. *Labienus ... Brutus*: T. Labienus, *tr. pl.* 63; on him cf. Syme, *JRS* 28, 1938, 113 ff. M. Iunius Brutus (Q. Servilius Caepio Brutus), *pr.* 44, the assassin of Caesar; his father, legate of the rebel proconsul M. Lepidus in 77, had been captured and killed by Pompey at Mutina.
124. *Caesar also showed himself merciful as a conqueror*: On Caesar's clemency cf. e.g. Cicero, *Att.* 8.9.4, 8.11.5; 9.7c.1; Caesar, *BC* 1.13.5, 1.18.4, 1.23.3.
125. *Vibullius*: L. Vibullius Rufus, cf. *MRR* II, 271.
126. *found himself ... seek a battle*: Cf. Caesar, *BC* 3.42, 44.
127. *Afranius*: L. Afranius, *cos.* 60.
128. *Scipio*: Metellus Scipio, Pompey's father-in-law.
129. *Domitius Ahenobarbus*: The consul of 54.
130. *lost his forces in Spain*: Cf. *MRR* II, 266.
131. *Spinther, Domitius and Scipio ... chief pontiff*: Caesar, *BC* 3.82 f.
132. *Lucius Calvinus*: Actually Cn. Calvinus, *cos.* 53, 40.
133. *Crassianus ... 120 men*: Cf. Caesar, *BC* 3.91, 99, who gives the name as Crastinus.
134. *Asinius Pollio*: C. Asinius Pollio, *cos.* 40, the historian of the civil wars.
135. *Lentuli*: The consuls of 57 and 49.
136. *his father*: Ptolemy Auletes, whose claim to the throne had been ratified by Caesar with Pompey's approval in 59 (*MRR* II, 188) and who had been restored by Pompey's friend Gabinius in 55 (*MRR* II, 218).
137. *his sister*: Cleopatra.
138. *Different opinions were expressed*: Cf. Caesar, *BC* 3.104.1.
139. *Septimius*: L. Septimius, who had served as a centurion in the pirate war.
140. *Lucius Lentulus*: Lentulus Crus, the consul of 49.
141. *But after Marcus Brutus had killed Caesar and come into power*: In 43 or 42.

COMPARISON OF AGESILAUS
AND POMPEY

1. *funeral obsequies ... Sulla's son Faustus*: Pompey's role at Sulla's funeral is not mentioned in the Life, but is treated at *Sulla* 38.

The marriage of Pompeia and Faustus Sulla does not appear in the Lives of either Pompey or Sulla.

CAESAR

1. *[100–44 BC]*: Cf. Gelzer, *Caesar*, 1 n. 1; Badian, *Studies*, 140 ff.
2. *confiscated her dowry*: The marriage took place in 84 and was dissolved in 82. Cf. Gelzer, *Caesar*, 20 f.
3. *Caesar's cousin*: See the stemma in Gelzer's *Caesar*.
4. *so many people were being killed*: On the Sullan proscriptions cf. *Sulla*, n. 51.
5. *priesthood*: The office of *flamen Dialis*.
6. *on his voyage back ... smaller craft*: In 75; Plutarch's account is confused, cf. Gelzer, *Caesar*, 21 ff.
7. *Junius*: M. Iuncus, *pr.* 76, cf. *MRR* II, 98.
8. *Sulla's power was declining*: Sulla had been dead for three years.
9. *Dolabella ... with evidence*: Cn. Cornelius Dolabella, *cos.* 81. The province was Macedonia; the trial took place in 77.
10. *Marcus Lucullus, the praetor of Macedonia*: Rather C. Antonius, *cos.* 63. His misdeeds in Greece dated to *c.*84 when he served there under Sulla. M. Terentius Varro Lucullus (brother of Lucius), *cos.* 73, was not governor of Macedonia but peregrine praetor in 76.
11. *The first proof ... on the list*: For 71. C. Popillius, *tr. pl.* probably 68 (cf. *MRR* II, 130 n. 4, 141 n. 8).
12. *brilliant public speech ... Marius himself*: In the year of his quaestorship, 69.
13. *his own wife died*: In the same year.
14. *Vetus ... praetor*: C. Antistius Vetus, *pr.* 70, who governed Further Spain in 69. Antistius Vetus, *q.* 61, *tr. pl.* 56. (His quaestorship is omitted from *MRR* II, 180 and Index, 530, though see 214 n. 2.)
15. *married Pompeia as his third wife*: Probably in 68. Daughter of Q. Pompeius Rufus, *cos.* 88, whose wife was a daughter of Sulla.
16. *By Cornelia ... Pompey the Great*: In 59.
17. *when he was aedile*: In 65.
18. *provided a show ... holders of the office*: On the importance of lavish expenditure in the aedileship cf. Gelzer, *RN*, 57, 111, 115.
19. *There were two parties ... show their heads*: There was a number of prominent senators devoted to maintaining the relics of Sulla's constitutional settlement and therewith their own supremacy, but

to speak of Sullan and especially of Marian 'parties' is completely misleading.

20. *Marius' victories over the Cimbri*: Cf. Plutarch's life of Marius.

21. *Lutatius Catulus*: Q. Lutatius Catulus, *cos.* 78, son of Marius' colleague of 102.

22. *Metellus*: Q. Caecilius Metellus Pius, *cos.* 80; he died in 63.

23. *Isauricus*: P. Servilius Vatia Isauricus, *cos.* 79.

24. *Piso*: C. Calpurnius Piso, *cos.* 67, prosecuted by Caesar in 63.

25. *Catiline*: On the alleged conspiracy of L. Sergius Catilina, *pr.* 68, see Cicero's speeches *In Catilinam*, *Pro Murena* and *Pro Sulla*, and Sallust's monograph.

26. *Whether or not Caesar ... death penalty*: Cf. Sallust, *Bellum Catilinae* 51 and Cicero's *Fourth Catilinarian*.

27. *Cato*: Cf. Sallust, *BC* 52.

28. *Curio*: C. Scribonius Curio, who later served Caesar well as *tr. pl.* 50.

29. *7½ million drachmas a year*: As tribune in 62, cf. *MRR* II, 175.

30. *elected praetor for the next year*: 62.

31. *during his praetorship*: On the contrary the disturbances were sufficient to provoke the passing of the *senatus consultum ultimum* and Caesar's temporary suspension from office; cf. *MRR* II, 173.

32. *Caesar's mother, Aurelia*: See the stemma in Gelzer's *Caesar*.

33. *One of the tribunes*: The court which tried Clodius was constituted by a law of Q. Fufius Calenus (*tr. pl.* 61, *cos.* 47), cf. *MRR* II, 180.

34. *wife of Lucullus*: Clodius had three sisters (cf. Syme, *RR*, table I) who married Q. Metellus Celer (*cos.* 60), L. Lucullus (*cos.* 74) and Q. Marcius Rex (*cos.* 68).

35. *Caesar received Spain as his province*: Hispania Ulterior.

36. *at the time of the consular elections*: Summer 60.

37. *Caesar, who arrived at Rome ... outside the city*: Cf. *MRR* II, 185.

38. *Calpurnius Bibulus*: M. Calpurnius Bibulus, Cato's son-in-law.

39. *So Caesar ... from a consul*: On Caesar's legislation cf. *MRR* II, 187 f. On the authorship of the laws cf. Pocock, *A Commentary on Cicero In Vatinium*, 161 ff.

40. *Julia ... Servilius Caepio*: Cf. *Pompey*, n. 82.

41. *Piso*: L. Calpurnius Piso Caesoninus, *cos.* 58.

42. *Pompey, directly after his marriage ... army of four legions*: Cf. *Pompey*, n. 84.

43. *But the most disgraceful ... out of Italy*: Cf. Seager, *Latomus* 24, 1965, 519 ff.

44. *Fabius and Scipio and Metellus*: Q. Fabius Maximus Verrucosus, *cos*. 233, 228, 215, 214, 209, whose strategy contributed much to the defeat of Hannibal (cf. *MRR* I, 243); either P. Cornelius Scipio Africanus, *cos*. 205, 194, who won the final victory over Hannibal at Zama in 202 (cf. *MRR* I, 317), or P. Cornelius Scipio Africanus Aemilianus, *cos*. 147, 134, who destroyed Carthage in 146 and Numantia in 133 (cf. *MRR* I, 467, 494); probably Q. Caecilius Metellus Numidicus, *cos*. 109, who fought Jugurtha (cf. the life of Marius and Sallust's *Bellum Jugurthinum*).

45. *Acilius*: Not recorded in Caesar, *BC* 2.4–7.

46. *Cassius Scaeva*: Cf. Caesar, *BC* 3.53.

47. *Scipio*: Q. Caecilius Metellus Pius Scipio, *cos*. 52, commander of the Pompeian forces in Africa after Pompey's death; cf. *MRR* II, 275, 288, 297.

48. *Granius Petro*: Cf. *MRR* II, 296.

49. *Oppius*: On C. Oppius cf. Gelzer, *Caesar*, Index, s.v.

50. *His first war ... Tigurini*: In 58. Cf. Caesar, *BG* 1.1–30.

51. *These tribes ... in the past*: Cf. *Marius*, nn. 21, 22.

52. *The Tigurini ... Labienus*: Contra Caesar, *BG* 1.12. On Labienus cf. *Pompey*, n. 123.

53. *His second war ... the Gauls*: So Caesar said, cf. *BG* 1.31–33. On the campaign, also in 58, cf. *BG* 1.34–54.

54. *Caesar had made the German King Ariovistus an ally*: In 59.

55. *Caesar saw that his officers ... easy money*: Cf. Caesar, *BG* 1.39.2. Cicero's friend C. Trebatius Testa is a good example, cf. Gelzer, *RN*, 117, *Caesar*, 138.

56. *spent the winter*: Of 58/7.

57. *scene of the action*: On the campaign cf. Caesar, *BG* 2.1 ff.

58. *Caesar then marched against the Nervii*: Cf. *Caesar*, *BG* 2.15–19, 28–32.

59. *At the news of these victories ... any victory*: Cf. Caesar, *BG*, 2.35.4.

60. *spend the winter*: Of 57/6.

61. *to meet him at Luca ... proconsul of Spain*: Cf. *Pompey*, n. 95.

62. *the next year*: 55.

63. *sending him on a mission to Cyprus*: In 58, by a law of Clodius. Cf. *MRR* II, 198.

64. *Favonius*: M. Favonius, *pr*. 49.

65. *involved in a serious war*: On the campaign of 55 against the Usipetes and Tencteri cf. Caesar, *BG* 4.1–19.

66. *Tanusius*: On Tanusius Geminus, a historian hostile to Caesar, cf. Peter, *HRR* II, LXV f. and the fragments ibid. 49 ff.

67. *his expedition against Britain*: On the British expeditions of 55
     and 54 cf. Caesar, *BG* 4.20–38; 5.8–23.
68. *died in childbirth at Pompey's house*: August 54.
69. *Gaul broke out into revolt*: Winter 54/3. Cf. Caesar, *BG* 5.25–
     52.
70. *Abriorix ... Titurius*: Ambiorix, chief of the Eburones; L. Aurun-
     culeius Cotta and M. Titurius Sabinus, cf. *MRR* II, 225 f.
71. *Cicero*: Q. Tullius Cicero, *pr.* 62, the orator's younger brother;
     cf. *MRR* II, 226.
72. *rebellion*: On the rebellion of Vercingetorix which broke out in
     52 cf. Caesar, *BG* 7. Plutarch omits the campaign of 53.
73. *the Aedui ... the Romans*: On the relationship between Rome
     and the Aedui, which Caesar exploited as a pretext for inter-
     vention in Gaul, cf. Caesar, *BG* 1.14, 33, 43, 45; 2.15; 5.7; 6.12.
74. *Crassus ... killed in Parthia*: 9 June 53, cf. *MRR* II, 230.
75. *Cato was able ... by force*: In 52, cf. *MRR* II, 234.
76. *should be prolonged*: For 5 years, cf. *MRR* II, 238. The statement
     that he controlled Africa is false.
77. *Marcellus and Lentulus*: M. Claudius Marcellus, *cos.* 51. L.
     Cornelius Lentulus Crus, *cos.* 49.
78. *they took away the rights ... established by Caesar in Gaul*: By
     a law of Vatinius in 59, cf. *MRR* II, 190.
79. *Curio; and he gave the consul Paulus*: C. Scribonius Curio, *tr.
     pl. suff.* 50, cf. *MRR* II, 249. L. Aemilius Paullus, *cos.* 50, cf.
     MRR II, 247.
80. *to ask for the return ... war in Gaul*: Each commander was to
     give up one legion for the defence of Syria; Pompey gave a legion
     loaned to Caesar in 53, so that in fact Caesar lost two legions,
     Pompey none.
81. *Antony*: The future triumvir, *tr. pl.* 49, cf. *MRR* II, 258.
82. *in spite of the consuls'*: C. Claudius Marcellus, L. Cornelius
     Lentulus Crus.
83. *In the senate ... Scipio*: Cf. Caesar, *BC* 1.2.6.
84. *Cilicia*: Which he had governed in 51.
85. *he gave Caesar ... among his troops*: Cf. Caesar, *BC* 1.7, 22.
86. *Hortensius*: Q. Hortensius, *pr.* 45, cf. *MRR* II, 267.
87. *Asinius Pollio*: C. Asinius Pollio, *cos.* 40, the historian of the
     civil wars.
88. *Labienus*: Cf. *Pompey*, n. 123.
89. *Caesar sent Labienus' money and baggage after him*: Cf. *MRR*
     II, 268.
90. *marched against Domitius ... force of thirty cohorts*: L. Domit-

ius Ahenobarbus, *cos.* 54. Cf. Caesar, *BC* 1.15–20, 23–25; *MRR* II, 261 f.

91. *He fled ... sailed off himself*: Cf. Caesar, *BC* 1.29.1.

92. *When Metellus*: Cf. *Pompey*, n. 120.

93. *marched into Spain*: On the Spanish campaign cf. Caesar, *BC* 1.30–2.22.

94. *Afranius and Varro*: L. Afranius, *cos.* 60, legate of Nearer Spain, and M. Terentius Varro, legate of Hispania Ulterior; cf. *MRR* II, 266, 269.

95. *Piso ... Isauricus ... appointed Caesar dictator*: L. Calpurnius Piso Caesoninus, *cos.* 58; cf. Gelzer, *Caesar*, 222. P. Servilius Vatia Isauricus, *cos.* 48, 41, son of the consul of 79. Caesar was named dictator before his return to Rome, while he was still at Massilia, by the praetor M. Aemilius Lepidus (the future triumvir). Cf. Caesar, *BC* 3.1 f.; *MRR* II 256 f.

96. *January*: In 48. Cf. Caesar, *BC* 3.3–9.

97. *Finally he decided ... command of the sea*: Cf. Caesar, *BC* 3.5.2.

98. *After this Antony*: Cf. *MRR* II, 280.

99. *shortage of food*: Cf. Caesar, *BC* 3.17, 42.

100. *Scipio*: Pompey's father-in-law, who was bringing forces from Asia to Greece; cf. *MRR* II, 275.

101. *succeed Caesar as chief pontiff*: Cf. Caesar, *BC* 3.83.

102. *Corfinius ... Calenus*: Probably Q. Cornificius, *quaestor pro praetore* in Illyricum, cf. *MRR* II, 276. Q. Fufius Calenus, *cos.* 47, a legate; cf. *MRR* II, 281.

103. *Domitius Calvinus*: The consul of 53 and 40.

104. *Domitius*: The consul of 54. He was killed in the battle (Caesar, *BC* 3.99.5).

105. *Caesar called out to him*: On C. Crastinus cf. Caesar, *BC* 3.91, 99.

106. *They made this happen ... their law courts*: Cf. Suetonius, *Iul.* 30.4.

107. *He then went in pursuit of Pompey*: Cf. Caesar, *BC* 3.102.1.

108. *He arrived at Alexandria just after Pompey's death*: Cf. Caesar, *BC* 3.106.

109. *she had a son ... Caesarion*: Caesar's paternity is very doubtful, though cf. Gelzer, *Caesar*, 257 n. 1.

110. *Domitius*: Domitius Calvinus.

111. *So, with three legions ... brevity and concentration*: On the campaign cf. *Bellum Alexandrinum* 34 ff.

112. *for a whole year*: The traditional period, when one was specified, was 6 months; none had been laid down for Sulla (*dict.* 82–81).

113. *proclaimed consul*: For 46.

114. *Cosconius*: C. Cosconius, *pr.* ?54 (*MRR* II, 273); Galba cannot be identified.

115. *Dolabella*: P. Cornelius Dolabella, *tr. pl.* 47, *cos. suff.* 44, Cicero's son-in-law; cf. *MRR* II, 287.

116. *King Juba*: Father of the historian (*Sulla*, n. 31); cf. Gelzer, *Caesar*, Index s.v.

117. *winter solstice*: Of 47. On the campaign cf. the *Bellum Africum*.

118. *Caesar was forced . . . for his horses*: Cf. BAfr. 8, 9, 20, 24.

119. *Cato was in command . . . no part in the battle*: Cf. *MRR* II, 298.

120. *He then celebrated . . . Africa*: 20 September–1 October 47, cf. *MRR* II, 293. Plutarch omits the triumph for the conquest of Gaul.

121. *Juba, the son of the king . . . historians of Greece*: On him cf. *Sulla*, n. 31.

122. *set out for Spain against the sons of Pompey*: For 45, without a colleague (*MRR* II, 304). On the campaign cf. the *Bellum Hispaniense*. On Cn. Pompeius Magnus, killed at Munda, cf. *MRR* II, 298, 309. The younger son was Sex. Pompeius Magnus Pius, *cos. des.* 35, the opponent of Octavian.

123. *The triumph . . . anything else had done*: Early October 45.

124. *Brutus, for instance, and to Cassius, both of whom were now praetors*: M. Iunius Brutus and C. Cassius Longinus, the assassins, urban and peregrine praetors respectively in 44. Cf. *MRR* II, 320 f.

125. *at the same time*: In 146, by Scipio Aemilianus and L. Mummius respectively.

126. *He dealt with . . . offices and honours*: Cf. Syme, *RR*, 61 ff.

127. *consul Maximus*: Q. Fabius Maximus, *cos.* 45.

128. *Caninius Rebilius . . . term of office*: C. Caninius Rebilus, *cos.* 31 December 45. Cf. Cicero, *Fam.* 7.30.1 f.

129. *His reform of the calendar . . . proved extremely useful*: On Caesar and the calendar cf. Gelzer, *Caesar*, 289.

130. *Yet those who . . . led by a king*: Cf. Cicero, *De divinatione* 2.110.

131. *said that his name was not King but Caesar*: 'Non Rex sum sed Caesar': like Caesar, Rex was a Roman cognomen, used by one branch of the Marcii.

132. *Cornelius Balbus*: L. Cornelius Balbus of Gades, *cos. suff.* 40, defended by Cicero in 56 (cf. the *Pro Balbo*); cf. Gelzer, *Caesar*, Index s.v.

133. *Antony, who was consul at the time*: In 44. The Lupercalia took
place on 15 February.
134. *Flavius and Marullus*: L. Caesetius Flavus and C. Epidius
Marullus, cf. *MRR* II, 323.
135. *son-in-law and a nephew of Cato*: Cf. Syme, *RR*, table II.
136. *most important of the praetorships for this very year*: The urban
praetorship of 44.
137. *Cassius ... hating Caesar*: Cf. Plutarch, *Brut.* 8.
138. *the Ides*: 15 March.
139. *Marcus Lepidus*: M. Aemilius Lepidus, *cos.* 46, 42, Caesar's
master of horse and the future triumvir.
140. *Decimus Brutus*: D. Iunius Brutus Albinus, *cos. des.* 42.
141. *Tillius Cimber*: L. Tillius Cimber, *pr.* ?45.
142. *Casca*: C. Servilius Casca, *tr. pl.* 44.
143. *Gaius Octavius ... for their imposture*: C. Octavius Balbus, cf.
Valerius Maximus, 5.7.3; Appian, *BC* 4.85.
144. *Brutus made a speech*: Cf. Syme, *RR*, 97 ff.
145. *It was voted ... while he was in power*: 17 March; cf. Cicero,
Phil. 1.2, 31.
146. *provinces ... given to Brutus and his friends*: Brutus and Cassius
were first offered posts in connection with the corn supply in
Sicily and Asia, though not till 5 June, then, about 1 August, the
minor provinces of Crete and Cyrene. Cf. *MRR* II, 320 f.
147. *when the people saw his body ... discipline and order*: Cf. Syme,
RR, 98 f.
148. *Cinna*: C. Helvius Cinna, *tr. pl.* 44, poet and friend of Catullus,
was murdered by mistake for the praetor L. Cornelius Cinna,
brother of Caesar's first wife and son of the consul of 87. Cf.
MRR II, 320 f., 324.
149. *After his defeat at Philippi ... against Caesar*: The second battle
of Philippi was on 23 October 42, cf. *MRR* II, 360 f.; the first,
after which Cassius killed himself, shortly before.

CICERO

1. *born and bred in a fuller's shop*: Cf. Gelzer, *RN*, 15.
2. *Scaurus or Catulus*: M. Aemilius Scaurus, *cos.* 115; Q. Lutatius
Catulus, *cos.* 102, and his homonymous son, *cos.* 78.
3. *his quaestorship in Sicily*: In 75.
4. *but in poetry ... neglected and unknown*: For the fragments of
Cicero's poetry cf. Morel, *Frag. Poet. Lat.*, 66 ff.
5. *Mucius Scaevola*: Q. Mucius Scaevola the augur, *cos.* 117; after

his death *c.*87 Cicero joined Q. Mucius Scaevola the pontifex, *cos.* 95.

6. *he did military service . . . against the Marsians*: In 89 (Cicero, *div.* 1.72, 2.65); he also served in 90/89 under Cn. Pompeius Strabo (Cicero, *Phil.* 12.27).

7. *Sulla seized power . . . more settled*: In 82.

8. *estate of a man . . . been put to death*: Sex. Roscius of Ameria, in 80; cf. the extant speech and Badian, *FC*, 249 ff.

9. *went abroad . . . sake of his health*: From 79 to 77; the motives, despite Plutarch, health and study.

10. *Sulla's death*: In 78.

11. *Roscius the comedian*: Whom he defended *c.*76 in the partially extant speech.

12. *in the war*: What war Plutarch means is entirely obscure; the governor was Sex. Peducaeus, *pr.* 77.

13. *an amusing experience*: Cicero, *Pro Plancio* 64 ff., cf. Gelzer, *RN*, 61.

14. *prosecution against Verres*: In 70. Cf. the Verrine speeches; Gelzer, *RN*, 73 f., 77 f.; Badian, *FC*, 282 ff.

15. *praetor*: He had been urban praetor in 74 and subsequently propraetor in Sicily till 71.

16. *For the praetors in charge . . . could be heard*: This is garbled. Verres' friends wanted to postpone the trial till 69, when the president of the court would be friendly; the praetor presiding in 70, M'. Acilius Glabrio, *cos.* 67, was, according to Cicero, honest.

17. *Caecilius*: Q. Caecilius Niger, who competed with Cicero for the right to prosecute Verres with the intention of assisting the defendant by collusion; cf. the *Divinatio in Caecilium*.

18. *Hortensius*: Q. Hortensius, *cos.* 69.

19. *he was aedile*: In 69.

20. *Cicero came out at the top of the poll*: For 66.

21. *Licinius Macer*: C. Licinius Macer, *pr.* ?68, the historian. Cf. *MRR* II, 152.

22. *Vatinius*: P. Vatinius, *cos.* 47, the Caesarian tribune of 59.

23. *Manilius*: C. Manilius, *tr. pl.* 66, author of the law giving Pompey the command against Mithridates. The charge was *repetundae*, not *peculatus*. Cf. *MRR* II, 153.

24. *Lucius Catiline*: On L. Sergius Catilina, *pr.* 68, cf. the Catilinarian speeches, the *Pro Murena* and *Pro Sulla*, and Sallust's *Bellum Catilinae*.

25. *had once been accused . . . killing his own brother*: A more

detailed version of Catiline's alleged incest in Asconius 91 f.; an alternative story in Sallust, *BC* 15.2. On the 'brother' cf. *Sulla*, n. 53.

26. *lists of those condemned to death*: On the Sullan proscriptions cf. *GC*, 198 ff.

27. *the consulship*: For 63.

28. *all the candidates Cicero . . . equestrian order*: The other candidates are listed in Asconius 82. Cf. in general the *Commentariolum Petitionis* attributed to Q. Cicero; Gelzer, *RN*, 54 ff.

29. *What they said . . . disturbing the government*: Cicero's speech *De proscriptorum liberis* is lost; cf. *Sulla*, n. 52.

30. *the tribunes were proposing . . . same end in view*: The chief proposer was P. Servilius Rullus. Cf. Cicero's speeches *De lege agraria* and for a more rational interpretation Summer, *TAPA* 97, 1966, 569 ff.

31. *He arranged . . . province of Gaul, which was offered to him*: Cf. *MRR* II, 166.

32. *Marcus Otho . . . rest of the citizens*: Rather L. Roscius Otho, probably praetor in 63 when supported by Cicero; he had passed the law as tribune in 67. Cf. *MRR* II, 167.

33. *soldiers of Sulla kept urging Catiline to take action*: Cf. Cicero, *Cat.* 2.17 f.

34. *With their leader Manlius*: Cf. Cicero, *Cat.* 1.5, 7, 10, 23 f.; 2.14; *Mur.* 49.

35. *Catiline was once again . . . disturbance of election day*: Cf. Cicero, *Cat.* 1.11; the elections for 62.

36. *By loosening . . . rallied round him*: Cf. Cicero, *Mur.* 52.

37. *Silanus and Murena consuls*: D. Iunius Silanus, L. Licinius Murena.

38. *Marcus Marcellus and Metellus Scipio*: M. Claudius Marcellus, *cos.* 51, Q. Caecilius Metellus Pius Scipio, *cos.* 52.

39. *Then the senate . . . great danger is feared*: The so-called *senatus consultum ultimum*, first employed in 121 by L. Opimius against C. Gracchus.

40. *Quintus Metellus*: Q. Caecilius Metellus Celer, *cos.* 60, praetor in this year.

41. *He decided . . . Marcius and Cethegus*: Cf. Cicero, *Cat.* 1.9, *Sull.* 18, 52; Sallust, *BC* 28.1: the volunteers were C. Cornelius (not Cethegus) and L. Vargunteius.

42. *When he began . . . to leave the city*: In the first Catilinarian, 7 or 8 November 63.

43. *He assumed . . . to join Manlius*: Cf. Sallust, *BC* 36.

44. *Cornelius Lentulus ... senatorial rank*: P. Cornelius Lentulus
    Sura, *cos.* 71, expelled from the senate in 70 by the censors; men
    in this position could regain senatorial status by securing election
    to the praetorship.
45. *held the office of quaestor*: In 81.
46. *Such was the character ... as Catiline had done, by delay*: Cf.
    Cicero, *Cat.* 3.9 f.
47. *There happened to be staying ... Roman government*: Cf. Cicero,
    Cat. 3.4 ff., Sallust, *BC* 40 ff.
48. *Titus*: T. Volturcius.
49. *secret cooperation of the Allobroges ... with the letters on him*:
    Cf. Cicero, *Cat.* 3.4 ff., Sallust, *BC* 46.
50. *At dawn ... examined the informers*: Cf. Cicero, *Cat.* 3.8 ff.,
    Sallust, *BC* 47.
51. *Iunius Silanus*: The consul designate for 62.
52. *Piso too*: C. Calpurnius Piso, *cos.* 67.
53. *Gaius Sulpicius*: Cf. Cicero, *Cat.* 3.8
54. *Next day ... punishment of the conspirators*: 5 December 63,
    the occasion of the fourth Catilinarian; cf. Sallust, *BC* 50 ff.
55. *Lutatius Catulus*: Q. Lutatius Catulus, *cos.* 78, defeated by
    Caesar in this year in the election for the office of pontifex
    maximus.
56. *he and his army were destroyed*: Early in 62, cf. *MRR* II, 175.
57. *next year*: 62.
58. *Metellus and Bestia, who were to be tribunes*: Q. Caecilius
    Metellus Nepos, *cos.* 57, L. Calpurnius Bestia (*MRR* II, 174).
59. *came into office*: On 10 December 63.
60. *set out for Syria*: November 55.
61. *Then at the time ... among his soldiers*: In 59, cf. *MRR* II, 188.
62. *Lucius Gellius*: Presumably the consul of 72.
63. *And when Metellus Nepos ... counsel for the defence*: Cf. the
    remarks of L. Manlius Torquatus quoted in Cicero, *Sull.* 40, 48.
64. *He once suddenly ... came straight back again*: Cf. *MRR* II,
    174.
65. *Lucius Cotta*: L. Aurelius Cotta, *cos.* 65, *cens.* 64.
66. *Clodius*: P. Clodius Pulcher, *tr. pl.* 58, *aed.* 56.
67. *there was no man present*: November 62.
68. *Clodia*: The eldest of the three sisters, wife of Q. Metellus Celer,
    cos. 60, and probably the Lesbia of Catullus. Cf. Cicero's *Pro
    Caelio*.
69. *Lucullus*: L. Licinius Lucullus, *cos.* 74, with whose army Clodius
    had tampered in 68/7 (cf. *MRR* II, 140); husband of the middle

sister, not of the youngest, who was married to Q. Marcius Rex, *cos.* 68.

70. *elected tribune*: For 58, cf. *MRR* II, 195.

71. *He won over the people by laws passed in their interest*: Cf. *MRR* II, 195 f.

72. *Macedonia to Piso and Syria to Gabinius*: L. Calpurnius Piso Caesoninus and A. Gabinius, *coss.* 58.

73. *He asked Caesar . . . Caesar agreed to do so*: In fact Caesar offered such a post but Cicero refused, cf. Cicero, *Att.* 2.18.3.

74. *turned Pompey completely against Cicero*: On Pompey's attitude cf. Seager, *Latomus* 24, 1965, 519 ff.

75. *Piso*: C. Calpurnius Piso Frugi, *q.* 58.

76. *Clodius carried through a vote . . . 500 miles of Italy*: Cf. *MRR* II, 195.

77. *Gaius Vergilius*: C. Vergilius, *pr.* 62, governor of Sicily since 61; cf. Cicero, *Planc.* 95 f.

78. *Meanwhile . . . his house in Rome*: Cf. Cicero's speech of 57, *De domo sua*.

79. *he turned on Pompey . . . on his campaigns*: The annexation of Cyprus and the appointment of Brogitarus as high priest of Cybele at Pessinus both interfered with Pompey's arrangements. Cf. *MRR* II, 196.

80. *Lentulus*: P. Cornelius Lentulus Spinther, consul with Q. Caecilius Metellus Nepos in 57.

81. *tribunes were wounded in the forum*: P. Sestius, cf. Cicero, *Pro Sestio* 85 and in general *MRR* II, 202.

82. *Cicero's brother Quintus . . . presumed to be dead himself*: Cf. Cicero, *Sest.* 76 ff.

83. *Annius Milo*: T. Annius Milo, *pr.* 55, cf. *MRR* II, 201 and Cicero's *Pro Milone*.

84. *Cicero replied . . . elected tribune*: Clodius had been adopted into a plebeian family to enable him to stand for the tribunate in 59, but his enemies regarded this adoption as invalid because of unfavourable omens.

85. *He maintained . . . Cyprus and Byzantium*: This was the chief reason why Clodius devised Cato's mission to Cyprus.

86. *Clodius was killed by Milo*: 18 January 52, cf. Asconius 30 ff. and the *Pro Milone*.

87. *Milo was a person of importance . . . the law courts*: Cf. *MRR* II, 234.

88. *Licinius Murena . . . by Cato*: L. Licinius Murena, *cos.* 62, prosecuted for bribery in autumn 63 by Ser. Sulpicius Rufus, son of

an unsuccessful competitor, with the support of Cato. Cf. Cicero's *Pro Murena*.

89. *scarcely begin his speech*: The *Pro Milone* as we have it is an exercise written when Cicero had recovered his composure.

90. *Parthian campaign*: In 53; he was nominated by Pompey and Hortensius.

91. *Then he was appointed ... 2,600 cavalry*: For 51.

92. *He observed that ... acted as governor*: Cf. Cicero's letters from Cilicia.

93. *Caelius*: M. Caelius Rufus, *pr.* 48; cf. his letters in Cicero, *Fam.* 8.2.2, 8.4.5, 8.9.3, 8.8.10, 8.6.5 and for Cicero's reply *Fam.* 2.11.2.

94. *voting him a triumph*: Despite Cicero's eagerness for a triumph (cf. especially *Fam.* 15.4) he was in fact decreed only a *supplicatio* (cf. *MRR* II, 251).

95. *He writes ... which way he ought to turn*: Cf. Cicero, *Att.* 7.1, 7.5, 7.9.4, etc.

96. *Trebatius*: C. Trebatius Testa, originally recommended to Caesar by Cicero; cf. *Caesar*, n. 55.

97. *He made no secret ... his comrades in arms*: Cf. Cicero, *Att.* 7.12, 13, 20, 21, 8.2, 9, 11, 16; *Fam.* 4.7, 9, 14, 6.6, 7.3, 9.6, 13.29; *Pro Ligario* 28; *Phil.* 2.38 f.

98. *Domitius*: L. Domitius Ahenobarbus, *cos.* 54.

99. *Theophanes the Lesbian*: Cf. *Pompey*, n. 66.

100. *Some people were praising ... loss of their fleet*: Cf. Caesar, *BC* 3.26 f.

101. *Lentulus*: L. Cornelius Lentulus Crus, *cos.* 49.

102. *Nonnius*: Perhaps M. Nonius Sufenas, *pr.* ?52.

103. *Labienus*: Cf. *Pompey*, n. 123.

104. *landed at Tarentum*: 24 September 47.

105. *when Quintus Ligarius*: Autumn 45, cf. Cicero's *Pro Ligario*.

106. *Cicero retired ... study philosophy*: Cf. Cicero, *Fam.* 7.33, 9.16, 18.

107. *philosophical dialogues*: Hortensius, Academica, De Finibus (45); Timaeus, Tusculan Disputations, De Natura Deorum, De Divinatione, De Fato, Cato Maior, Laelius, De Gloria, De Officiis (44).

108. *divorced his wife Terentia*: In 46, cf. Cicero, *Fam.* 4.14.3.

109. *by marrying a virgin soon afterwards*: Publilia, in December 46.

110. *Piso*: Piso died probably early in 57; Tullia married, not a Lentulus, but P. Cornelius Dolabella, *cos. suff.* 44, in summer 50. She died in February 45.

111. *Antony, as consul ... peace and concord*: 17 March 44; cf. Cicero, *Phil.* 1.2,31. On this period cf. Syme, *RR*, 97–201.

112. *Cicero therefore feared ... Syria*: Cf. *MRR* II, 317.

113. *Hirtius and Pansa*: For 43: A. Hirtius, Caesar's secretary and author of the eighth book of the *Bellum Gallicum*, and C. Vibius Pansa Caetronianus; cf. *MRR* II, 334 f.

114. *set out by himself*: 17 July 44.

115. *all his actions and policies were now directed to please the senate*: Provoked by the arrival and growing popularity of Octavian; cf. Cicero, *Phil.* 1.8, *Att.* 16.7.1.

116. *when young Caesar ... from the estate*: Octavian arrived in Italy in April 44; cf. Cicero, *Att.* 14.10.3; Syme, *RR*, 112 f.

117. *Philippus and Marcellus*: L. Marcius Philippus, *cos.* 56, husband of Atia, and C. Claudius Marcellus, *cos.* 50, husband of Octavia; cf. Syme, *RR*, table III.

118. *Attia, a daughter of Caesar's sister*: Julia had married M. Atius (not Attius) Balbus; cf. Syme, *RR*, table III.

119. *saying that in courting Caesar ... who would be kind to him personally*: In fact Cicero merely wished to use Octavian to get rid of Antony.

120. *Cicero's son*: M. Tullius Cicero, *cos. suff.* 30.

121. *he persuaded the senate ... in defence of his country*: 1 January 43; cf. Syme, *RR*, 167.

122. *the battle*: The battle of Mutina, 21 April 43; Hirtius was killed in it, while Pansa died on 23 April of wounds received at the previous battle of Forum Gallorum. Cf. *MRR* II, 334 f.

123. *secured the consulship*: As suffect consul on 19 August 43; cf. *MRR* II, 336.

124. *Instead he made friends ... a piece of property*: On the establishment of the triumvirate cf. *MRR* II, 337 f.

125. *Paulus*: L. Aemilius Paullus, *cos.* 50.

126. *Lucius Caesar*: The consul of 64, whose sister married M. Antonius, *pr.* 74.

127. *Macedonia*: Which Brutus had occupied towards the end of 44, cf. *MRR* II, 321 f., 346.

128. *Popillius*: C. Popillius Laenas, probably a military tribune; nothing is known of the defence.

129. *Pomponia*: Sister of Cicero's friend and correspondent, T. Pomponius Atticus.

130. *chose Cicero's son to be his colleague*: In 30.

COMPARISON OF DEMOSTHENES
AND CICERO

1. *defence of Caelius ... in pleasure*: Cicero defended M. Caelius
    Rufus in 56. For the views to which Plutarch alludes, cf. *Pro
    Caelio*. 28 ff. and esp 39. ff.
2. *Cato prosecuted Murena ... so-called paradoxes*: L. Licinius
    Murena was prosecuted by Ser. Sulpicius Rufus, the homony-
    mous son of one of his fellow-candidates for the consulship, the
    great jurist Servius, eventually *cos.* 51. Cato was one of the
    supporting prosecutors. For Cicero's remarks about his Stoic
    beliefs, cf. *Mur.* 58 ff.
3. *young Caesar*: That is, Octavian.